Crime and Justice

Crime and Justice

An Annual Review of Research

Edited by Norval Morris and Michael Tonry

VOLUME I

The University of Chicago Press, Chicago and London

The University of Chicago Press, Chicago 60637
The University of Chicago Press, Ltd., London

ISSN: 0192-3234
ISBN: 0-226-53955-5

This volume was prepared under Contract Number J-LEAA-023-77
awarded to Aspen Systems Corporation by the National Institute
of Law Enforcement and Criminal Justice, Law Enforcement
Assistance Administration, U.S. Department of Justice, under the
Omnibus Crime Control and Safe Streets Act of 1968 as amended.
Points of view or opinions expressed in this volume are those of
the editors or authors and do not necessarily represent the official
position or policies of the U.S. Department of Justice. The editors
are grateful for the valuable assistance provided by the National
Criminal Justice Reference Service.

Contents

Introduction

This is the first in a series of annual volumes of commissioned essays on research in crime and justice, designed to survey the contours of knowledge of crime and of society's methods to understand and deal with it.

Knowledge in criminology, as in other fields of research, grows by artificial isolation of a segment of a topic for close analysis and by the deliberate juxtaposition of insights gained from the study of other segments. We must both specialize and look across the borders of our own specialties. No one can see all the problems whole. No one can keep abreast of the major literature, for it far exceeds time and energy; but some effort at a broad overview is essential if only to lend direction to one's own specialty. Such an overview of research and knowledge in crime and justice is the ambitious purpose of this series.

The series is necessarily interdisciplinary. At this early stage of criminological knowledge, what we have is a variety of scholars in the social and biological sciences turning their attention to problems of crime, justice, and juvenile delinquency. Around a core concern for measuring, understanding, and influencing our efforts to contain and control crime, there revolves a wide diversity of professional and scholarly interests.

The idea for the series was born in the bureaucracy—a setting not always regarded as congenial to the production of obviously useful plans. Blair Ewing, the acting director of the National Institute of Law Enforcement and Criminal Justice, suggested it to several academics active in research. The series was swiftly launched, an editorial board convened, editors selected, authors invited, a publisher induced, essays written and rewritten or rejected—and thus the first volume.

Essays will be of several types. The staple will be a summary by a leading scholar of the state of the art on a defined topic, together with his views on the policy and research implications of that knowledge. Others will be more speculative and idiosyncratic, and will report on analytical, conceptual or empirical developments, or consider promising but novel lines of inquiry.

We are in no doubt of the need for a series like this; whether this enterprise will help build bridges between the islands of parochialism that characterize research in and knowledge of crime and criminal justice is, of course, more speculative.

Research in crime and justice remains scattered, dependent on a variety of disparate disciplines, and plagued by the difficulty of measuring, from generally inadequate data bases, the consequences of governmental policy and practice. As things stand, the academic criminal lawyer and the sociologist specializing in criminology are barely cognizant of each other's concerns; the psychologist and the systems engineer interested in criminal justice tend to be unacquainted with research outside their own disciplines; and those few political scientists, philosophers, physiologists, psychiatrists, economists, anthropologists, demographers and historians who concern themselves with criminal behavior are rump groups talking to themselves.

The need for a sharing of knowledge is great; but that does not mean that the need is easy to meet. Certainly no "School," no single theoretical viewpoint, will suffice. As many readers will appreciate, the editorial board represents a diversity of viewpoints. Here is the membership of the board:

Professor Alfred Blumstein, Director, Urban Systems Institute, School of Urban and Public Affairs, Carnegie-Mellon University;

Professor Daniel Glaser, Department of Sociology, University of Southern California;

Professor Ted Robert Gurr, Chairman, Political Science Department, Northwestern University;

The Honorable Wade McCree, Solicitor General of the
United States;

Professor Sheldon Messinger, Center for the Study of Law
and Society, University of California Law School;

Professor Norval Morris, Professor of Law and Criminology,
University of Chicago Law School;

Patrick V. Murphy, President, The Police Foundation;

Professor Albert J. Reiss, Jr., Professor of Law and Sociology,
Yale Law School;

Professor Michael Tonry, University of Maryland Law School;

Professor Nigel Walker, Director, Institute of Criminology,
Cambridge University.

Unlike most advisory boards, this board bears a heavy burden of
responsibility; it did not advise, it designed. In our discussions
we did not struggle for the easy middle ground of harmonious
concurrence on issues that remain in conflict—and we do not
expect that of our authors. What we hope for are precise statements of our present knowledge, to help form links of understanding between the various disciplines on which criminological
research depends and will continue to depend.

The need for such a series as this comes also from the character
of the field of study. Ranging as it does from the complexities
of social organization to the behavior of man, from the Constitution to the gene, there is no more difficult area of research, of
scholarship, or of administration than that of criminal justice.
No one can be an adequately trained researcher of criminal
justice. We all need the props of summaries of the best work of
neighboring scholars.

It would be unfair to judge the coverage of the series from the
topics treated in the first volume. After four or five years such
an assessment could fairly be made, but the first collection cannot
be comprehensive or even adequately representative of the many
fields of scholarship contributing to an understanding of adult and
youth crime and of diverse governmental and institutional responses to it.

By one measure judgment can fairly be made: the quality of the essays. And on this some housekeeping details are appropriate. Here is how responsibilities were shared. The editorial board selected the topics to be addressed and directed the editors whom to approach as potential authors. The editors did their best to convey the board's sometimes elliptic outlines of the topic to the author and to assist the author, subject to appropriate freedom of development of the lines of his interest, to shape the essay. The charge to each author was not to write for the small group who are already acquainted with the literature and whom he sees as his peer critics; rather he was to address those scholars of crime and justice who likely did not share his specialized focus and also that mythical intelligent layman who is willing to read at a level deeper than that of the encapsulated weeklies. Tell him what is known; how it is known; and what are the policy and research implications of that knowledge.

Every essay commissioned was read by at least two members of the editorial board and by the editors. Several were rejected or held over for rewriting for later volumes. Of those accepted, extensive redrafting was pursued in every case in response to the comments of the readers and editors. When appropriate, as it often was, we also solicited critical evaluations by scholars not on the editorial board. In other words, we have taken on the serious task of trying to produce a series characterized by high standards of scholarship, which means, with proper counsel, being prepared to reject the work of leading scholars and to criticize closely the work of all. One author added a vigorous postscript to his essay to reply to the lines of criticism it had received. Another, whose essay also appears in this first volume, thanked the editors for their praise but reacted to nine single-spaced pages of criticism with wonderment as to what would have been said about an essay we did not characterize as "splendid."

So much for the plan of the series. A book should speak for itself; no lengthy prefatory lure should be necessary. Each essay is preceded by an abstract and each author has included early in his essay a road-map of the line of argument to be followed. Hence, a brief comment on this volume should suffice.

Important problems are addressed, important alike to emerging theory and to professional practice. There are two essays on the police, two on etiology, two on correctional practice, one on youth violence, and one on longitudinal research, an essential research method in which this country is comparatively weak. It is a catholic collection but obviously not comprehensive. Of necessity, a great deal that is important has been neglected and only the flow of volumes in this series will tell if we and our successors can make of it an instrument of general use to theory and practice in relation to the diminution and better treatment of crime.

Norval Morris

Michael Tonry

James B. Jacobs

Race Relations and the Prisoner Subculture

ABSTRACT

The extensive scholarly literature on prisoner subculture has, until quite recently, virtually ignored race relations. The oversight is significant; prisons have a long history of segregation and racial discrimination. Descriptions and theories of prisoner subculture which do not take racial cleavages into account are incomplete and need to be reconsidered. Since the late 1950s race relations have precipitated enormous changes in prisoner subcultures and in prison organization. The Black Muslims challenged the hegemony of white officials and prisoners and their legal activism led to the intervention of the federal courts in prison administration. Present-day prisoner subcultures are characterized by racial polarization and conflict, and by the dominance of blacks and other minorities who now constitute the majority of the national prisoner population. The next generation of research should link the prison society, including its patterns of race relations, to both the unique characteristics of prisons and the culture and social structure of the larger society.

Blacks, Mexicans, Puerto Ricans and members of other racial minorities now constitute the majority of American prisoners. Behind the walls, white, black and Spanish-speaking inmates exist in separate conflict-ridden social worlds. While the racial composition of American prisons is often reported by the media[1] and is obvious to prison employees, inmates, and visitors, most soci-

James B. Jacobs is Associate Professor of Law and Sociology, Cornell University.

[1] The *New York Times*, for example, printed 120 articles on race relations in prison between 1968 and 1977. Taken together they illuminate a situation of tension, strain, and conflict among prisoners and between prisoners and staff.

I

ologists who have studied prisons have ignored race relations entirely. When, in preparing this essay, I began reviewing the enormous corpus of prisoner subculture research, I was astonished to find a consistent failure to attend to race relations dating back to the original sociological prison studies of the 1930s (e.g., Reimer 1937; Hayner and Ash 1940).

The core prisoner subculture tradition in sociology can be traced to Donald Clemmer's *The Prison Community* (1940). Clemmer's classic study of the prisoner subculture at the Illinois southern maximum security prison at Menard did not mention prevailing racial etiquette and norms, despite his intent to describe the prisoners' social organization and culture. The oversight is curious in light of Clemmer's decision to report the percentage of blacks in the prison population (22–28 percent) and to dichotomize several tables (e.g., intelligence, family background, recidivism) by race. Clemmer did point out that two of fourteen prisoner leaders were Negroes, but he did not say whether leadership bridged racial lines,[2] nor are we told whether blacks were proportionately represented in the prisoners' class system or whether primary groups were racially heterogeneous.

The generation of prison scholars which followed Clemmer did not build on his investigation of prisoners' social backgrounds. For the most part, this generation pursued Clemmer's analysis of "the inmate code" (prisoners' special norms), "argot roles" (prisoners' unique social roles related to "the primary axes of prison life"), and the process of "prisonization" (the socialization of new inmates). The work of Gresham Sykes marked the pinnacle of this body of research. In *Society of Captives* (1958) he presented an elaborate description of inmate argot roles[3] and argued that they were functionally adapted to conditions of maximum security confinement and that they could be accounted for by the unique economic, social, and psychological deprivations

[2] Another study of prisoner leadership in the mid-1950s (Schrag 1954, p. 41) did state that "whites choose whites with rare exceptions, while Negroes tend to choose Negroes."

[3] The argot roles identified by Sykes (1958) were: rats, center men, gorillas, merchants, wolves, punks, fags, ball busters, real men, toughs, and hipsters.

imposed by imprisonment. Sykes and a co-author (Sykes and Messinger 1960) extended this descriptive and theoretical analysis of prisoner subculture, identifying and explaining the tenets of the inmate code by use of structural/functional analysis.[4] The tradition which Sykes enriched and stimulated came to be known as the "indigenous origin" model of prisoner subculture. Those who followed Sykes continued to discover new argot roles and to test commitment to the inmate code, but no important new conceptualizations were made. Some policy-oriented scholars attempted to explain recidivism in terms of prisoners' commitment to the code and argot role playing. None of these studies, however, considered the importance of race for the society of prisoners. Even though 50 percent of New Jersey's prisoners were black when Sykes studied Rahway Prison, his work contained no explicit reference to race relations. He did mention in passing that "the inmate population is shot through with a variety of ethnic and social cleavages which sharply reduce the possibility of continued mass action" (Sykes 1958, p. 81). Other scholars during this period continued the color-blind approach.

In 1962, John Irwin and Donald Cressey published their influential article "Thieves, Convicts and the Inmate Culture" directly attacking the dominant structural/functional model of the prisoner subculture. While their article did not mention race, their argument (now known as the "importation hypothesis") that prisoner subculture is rooted in criminal and conventional subcultures outside the prison encouraged later researchers, including Irwin himself (1970), to focus on racial groupings. Since 1970 a small number of important studies on prisons have dealt explicitly with prisoners' race relations. This essay attempts to develop the race relations perspective suggested by these studies, thereby pointing to new directions for prisoner subculture research. Section I sketches the history of race relations in American prisons. Section II explores the implications of this social his-

---

[4] Sykes and Messinger (1960, pp. 6–9) classified the tenets of the inmate code into five major groups: (1) Don't interfere with inmate interests; be loyal to your class—the cons. (2) Don't lose your head; play it cool and do your own time. (3) Don't exploit inmates; be right. (4) Don't weaken; be a man. (5) Don't be a sucker; be sharp.

tory for the core tradition of prisoner subculture research. Section III suggests how the race relations perspective could enrich future research on the prisoner subculture.

I. A Capsule History of Prison Race Relations

Prisons in every section of the United States have long been characterized by racial segregation and discrimination.[5] In their seminal criminology text, Barnes and Teeters (1959, p. 466) state:

> Negroes have been segregated from whites in most prisons where they appear in appreciable numbers. Negroes make up the bulk of the population of southern prison camps. Few northern prisons exercise the courage and social insight to break with outmoded customs of racial segregation.

(See also Sutherland and Cressey 1974, p. 499.)

State laws in the south often required that prisoners, especially juveniles, be incarcerated in racially homogeneous facilities. In some states, particularly those where prison officials controlled vast plantations, black and white adult offenders were assigned to separate camps. In Arkansas, for example, Tucker Prison Farm housed white inmates and Cummins mostly blacks. In states with only a single penitentiary, or where racially heterogeneous prisons were maintained, segregation was enforced by cell and work assignments, and in all "extracurricular" activities. Consider the following description of prison race relations in Oklahoma in the early 1970s (Battle v. Anderson, 376 F. Supp. 402 at 410 [E.D. Okla. 1974]):

> Prior to the July [1973] riot, the policy and practice at the Oklahoma State Penitentiary was to maintain a prison system segregated by race and by means of which black inmates were subjected to discriminatory and unequal treatment.

---

[5] It is a mistake to speak of prisons and prisoner subcultures as if only a single type existed throughout the United States. The distinctive features of each region's social structure and culture are found in prisons as well as in other political institutions. A comprehensive history of prison race relations would examine each region (and subregion). No such history has yet been written, and my reading of the record is likely to blur important regional and state variations.

> Except for the maximum security unit, . . . all inmates were routinely assigned to housing units on the basis of race. The reception center, the mess hall, the recreation yard and barber facilities were racially segregated. Black inmates were discriminated against in job assignments and were subjected to more frequent and disparate punishment than white inmates.

The situation in Oklahoma was not unique; between 1963 and 1974 various courts declared racially segregated penal facilities to be unconstitutional in Alabama, Arkansas, the District of Columbia, Georgia, Louisiana, Maryland, Mississippi, and Nebraska.[6]

Racial segregation, or a racial caste system based upon pervasive discrimination against blacks, also characterized northern prisons. The New York State Special Commission on Attica (1972, p. 80) reported that Attica had been administered on a segregated basis until the mid-1960s. "There were black and white sports teams, different barbers for blacks and whites, and separate ice buckets for black and white inmates on July 4." Likewise, in the wake of serious racial protests at Pendleton Reformatory, the Indiana State Committee to the U.S. Commission on Civil Rights (1971) found that state to have had "a very segregated prison system" and extensive racial discrimination.

Prisoners' race relations cannot be divorced from prison race relations, the racial context in which all the actors in the prison organization relate to one another. Until recently, and in all regions of the country, there were few, if any, members of racial

---

[6] Cases declaring prison segregation unconstitutional are: Alabama—Washington v. Lee, 263 F. Supp. 327 (M.D. Ala. 1966), aff'd *per curiam*, 390 U.S. 333 (1968); Arkansas—Board of Managers of the Arkansas Training School for Boys at Wrightsville et al. v. George, 377 F.2d 228 (8th Cir. 1967); District of Columbia—Dixon v. Duncan, 218 F. Supp. 157 (E.D. Va. 1963); Georgia—Wilson v. Kelley, 294 F. Supp. 1005 (N.D. Ga. 1968); Louisiana—Major v. Sowers, 298 F. Supp. 1039 (E.D. La. 1969); Maryland—State Board of Public Welfare v. Meyers, 224 Md. 246, 167 A.2d 765 (1961); Mississippi—Gates v. Collier, 349 F. Supp. 881 (N.D. Miss. 1972); Nebraska—McClelland v. Sigler, 327 F. Supp. 829 (D. Neb. 1971); Oklahoma—Battle v. Anderson, 376 F. Supp. 402 (E.D. Okla. 1974). See also Singleton v. Board of Commissioners of State Institutions et al., 356 F.2d 771 (5th Cir. 1966) (remanding challenge to Florida statute requiring racial segregation of male juveniles).

minorities on the staffs of prisons.[7] To the extent that race mattered at all, the preferences, biases, and values of individual whites predominated. An account of the prisoner subculture, past or present, which did not consider the influence of the racially dominant group among the staff in structuring the patterns of interaction and opportunities (licit and illicit) among the prisoners would be hopelessly incomplete.

Unfortunately, little research has been done on the social backgrounds and values of white prison officials and, more particularly, on their attitudes toward blacks and other racial minorities. A working assumption could reasonably be made that most wardens shared the biases of the rural white populations of the areas where prisons were located and from which prison guards and other officials were drawn. In these areas, as in American society generally, at least until recently, blacks were viewed as a lower racial caste. This assumption is supported at Stateville Penitentiary in Illinois, where I have conducted research (Jacobs 1977). The warden who served from 1936 to 1961, and the guards whom he recruited to serve with him, came from rural southern Illinois. While the regime was not vulgarly racist, it simply expected black prisoners to accept their lower caste status.

In the late 1950s, blacks began to protest segregation and discrimination in prisons as in other sectors of the society. Their vehicle of protest was the Black Muslim movement, and in this sense the prison situation is unique. The Black Muslims actively proselytized black prisoners, preaching a doctrine of black superiority. They imported the spirit of "black nationalism" into the prisons, catalyzed the frustration and bitterness of black prisoners, and provided organizational and ideological tools for challenging the authority of white prison officials. Prison officials saw in the Muslims not only a threat to prison authority but also a broader revolutionary challenge to American society (see Jacobs

[7] Until 1963 only thirty blacks had ever been appointed to guard positions in Stateville and Joliet prisons in Illinois (Jacobs 1977, p. 184). "In September 1971, there were over 500 people who were free to leave Attica every day: the Superintendent, two Deputy Superintendents, a uniformed correctional staff of 398 (supervisors and officers), and 145 civilians. There was one black civilian teacher, no black correction officers, and one Puerto Rican correction officer" (New York State Special Commission on Attica 1972, p. 24).

1977, chap. 3). Until the mid-1960s, and sometimes later, they did everything in their power to crush the Muslims. Paradoxically, this may have contributed to the vigor and success of the Muslims' efforts. In any case, the modern "crisis in corrections" is attributable to the changing pattern of race relations which began with the Muslim protests.

At the 1960 convention of the American Correctional Association, Donald Clemmer, head of the District of Columbia Department of Correction (and author of *The Prison Community*), reported that the Black Muslims in D.C. prisons were a seriously disruptive force. "The disturbing phenomena of the Muslims in prison are their nonconformance and their bitter racial attitudes" (Clemmer and Wilson 1960, p. 153). Clemmer explained that the Black Muslims preached racial hatred and defied authority by actively proselytizing other black prisoners and by congregating in the prison yard for meetings and prayer. He responded by locking the "cult" in punitive segregation, not to punish them for their religious beliefs, but for "direct violation of standard rules" (p. 154).[8] The American Correctional Association subsequently passed a resolution denouncing the Black Muslims, and rejecting their claim to be a bona fide religion.[9]

At Stateville Penitentiary in Illinois an internal memorandum of 23 March 1960 reported that 58 Negro prisoners were affiliated with the Muslims (Jacobs 1977, chap. 3). In July 1960 the first collective disturbance at Stateville in more than a decade occurred when the Muslims demonstrated in the segregation unit where they had been placed as punishment for congregating in the yard. Four years later, the Muslims became the first prisoners in Stateville's history to present written demands to the administration. They called for an end to interference with Muslim religious

[8] Two years after Clemmer's talk at the American Correctional Association convention, a federal court ordered him to stop treating the Muslims differently from other religious groups. Fulwood v. Clemmer, 206 F. Supp. 370 (D. D.C. 1962). A series of lawsuits against District of Columbia penal facilities soon ended segregationist practices such as separate barbers for blacks and whites. See Bolden v. Pegelow, 329 F.2d 95 (4th Cir. 1964).

[9] John Irwin (1977, p. 25) reports that "In 1964 at a meeting of the Southern Conference on Corrections all five of the papers on 'The Guts of Riot and Disturbance' dealt specifically with Black Muslims."

practices and to racial discrimination. Illinois officials resisted every demand, including opportunities for group prayer, reading of the Koran, contact with ministers, and access to *Muhammad Speaks*, the official Black Muslim newspaper.

When C. Eric Lincoln published his history of the Black Muslims in 1961, there were already three Muslim temples behind the walls. Claude Brown (1965), Malcolm X [Little] (1965), Eldridge Cleaver (1968), and George Jackson (1970, 1972) all pointed in their writings to the significance of the Black Muslims in the prisons during the late 1950s and early 1960s. These authors, except Claude Brown, were themselves politicized through their contacts with the Black Muslims in prison.[10]

The ideology of black superiority, preached by Elijah Muhammad and his followers, appealed to many black inmates. It provided a vehicle for venting frustration and hostility against the prison officials who had assigned blacks to second-class status in an institution which already denied its inhabitants the rights of citizenship. The Muslims claimed that American blacks had been repressed and degraded by white society and blamed white prison officials for continuing that repression.

As the numbers of Muslims increased and their influence grew, the social organization of the prison underwent profound changes. Through the Muslims black nationalism penetrated the prison and politicized the minority prisoners. First, the Muslims directly and successfully challenged the caste system which assigned blacks to a subservient position. Second, the Muslims challenged a basic tenet of penal administration—that every prisoner "must do his own time." Like the Jehovah's Witnesses who had been incarcerated en masse in the federal prisons for draft resistance during World War II (Sibley and Wardlaw 1945), the Muslims wanted to be recognized, not as individuals, but as a group with its own authority structure and communal interests. Thus, the Muslims contributed to the balkanization of prisoner society, a salient

[10] In a "random sample" of seventy-one wardens and superintendents of federal and state prisons, Caldwell (1968) found that 31 percent claimed "substantial Muslim activity." Another 21 percent reported "some or limited Muslim activity." According to the author, "those who reported no Muslim activity came from states with relatively small Negro populations and small percentages of Negroes in prison."

characteristic of prisoner subculture ever since. Third, the Muslims initiated litigation which resulted in federal court intervention in prison administration. In hundreds of lawsuits the Muslims protested censorship, disciplinary practices, and, of course, religious discrimination.[11] The Muslims won most of the opportunities for religious worship enjoyed by members of conventional religions, although full equality has yet to be achieved.[12] They were responsible for a new era of federal court involvement in prison administration. David Rothman points out (1973, pp. 14–15):

> When Black Muslims in 1961 pressed the cause of religious
> freedom in prison, judges found the right too traditional, the
> request too reasonable, and the implications of intervention
> ostensibly so limited that they had to act. They ruled that
> inmates should be allowed to attend services and to talk with
> ministers without fear of penalty. "Whatever may be the view
> with regard to ordinary problems of prison discipline,"
> declared the court in *Pierce v. LaVallee* (1961), "we think
> that a charge of religious persecution falls into quite a
> different category." That the litigants were black, at a time
> when courts were growing accustomed to protecting blacks
> from discrimination, made the intervention all the more
> logical.

No studies were made of the impact of the Black Muslims on the prisoners' informal network of social relations. The Muslims appear to have heightened tensions between black and white prisoners. While the Muslims were more antagonistic to white officials than to white prisoners, white prisoners often complained of racist talk and behavior by blacks (Jacobs 1977, chap. 3). Undoubtedly members of the dominant white caste were made uncomfortable by the Muslims. By achieving such a high degree of solidarity the Muslims probably strengthened the positions of

---

[11] Between 1961 and 1978 there were sixty-six reported federal court decisions pertaining to the Muslims.

[12] Few prisons, for example, hire Muslim ministers on the same basis as Catholic and Protestant chaplains. Pork-free diets, Arabic Korans, religious medallions, and opportunities for daily prayer continue to be litigated.

individual members in the prisoner subculture and perhaps increased their opportunities for economic gain within the prisoner economy. Ironically, after their religious grievances were redressed, the Muslims became a quiescent and stabilizing force in many prisons, which began to be rocked by new cohorts of violent and disorganized ghetto youth (see, e.g., Glaser 1964, pp. 152–54; New York State Special Commission on Attica 1972, p. 112).

By 1970 racial avoidance and conflict had become the most salient aspect of the prisoner subculture. John Irwin (1970, p. 80) now supplemented the earlier Irwin-Cressey (1962) "importation hypothesis" with explicit attention to the subject of race:

> For quite some time in California prisons, hostility and
> distance between three segments of the populations—white,
> Negroes and Mexicans—have increased. For several years
> the Negroes have assumed a more militant and ethnocentric
> posture, and recently the Mexicans—already ethnocentric and
> aggressive—have followed with a more organized, militant
> stance. Correspondingly, there is a growing trend among
> these two segments to establish, reestablish or enhance
> racial-ethnic pride and identity. Many "Blacks" and
> "Chicanos" are supplanting their criminal identity with a
> racial-ethnic one.

The prisons were an especially ripe arena for protest and conflict because of their long history of segregation and discrimination. Once again, the findings of the New York State Special Commission on Attica (1972, p. 4) are illuminating:

> Above all, for both inmates and officers, "correction" meant
> an atmosphere charged with racism. Racism was manifested
> in job assignments, discipline, self-segregation in the inmate
> mess halls, and in the daily interaction of inmate and officer
> and among the inmates themselves. There was no escape
> within the walls from the growing mistrust between white
> middle America and the residents of urban ghettos. Indeed,
> at Attica, racial polarity and mistrust were magnified by

the constant reminder that the keepers were white and the kept were largely black and Spanish-speaking. The young black inmate tended to see the white officer as the symbol of a racist, oppressive system which put him behind bars.

By 1974, a nationwide census of penal facilities revealed that 47 percent of all prisoners were black (Gottfredson, Hindelang, and Parisi 1978). In many state prisons blacks were in the majority.[13] The numbers of Puerto Ricans and Mexicans also increased, but nationwide figures are unavailable since statistics in most states still make no distinction between Spanish-speaking and "white" prisoners.[14] In a few north central states, native Americans in the prisons emerged as an increasingly militant group.[15] Race relations are characterized by avoidance, strain, tension, and conflict.[16] The most publicized racial polarization has occurred in California, where Chicanos, blacks, and whites compete for power and dominance (Minton 1971; Irwin 1970; Pell 1972; Yee 1973; Wright 1973; Davidson 1974; Irwin 1977). Each racial bloc promotes its own culture and values, and attains what supremacy can be achieved at the expense of the others. A disaffected San Quentin staff member describes the prisoner subculture in the early 1970s in the following terms:

[13] In 1973 the states with a majority or near majority of black prisoners were Alabama (62 percent), Arkansas (48 percent), Delaware (60 percent), Florida (49 percent), Georgia (64 percent), Illinois (58 percent), Louisiana (71 percent), Maryland (74 percent), Michigan (58 percent), Mississippi (63 percent), New Jersey (50 percent), New York (58 percent), North Carolina (54 percent), Ohio (46 percent), Pennsylvania (57 percent), South Carolina (59 percent), and Virginia (59 percent) (U.S. Department of Justice 1976).

[14] In 1973 Arizona reported 25 percent Mexicans. Theodore Davidson (1974) reports that 18 percent of the prisoners at San Quentin were Mexican at the time of his study, 1966–68.

[15] North Dakota and Minnesota are two states with a visible native American presence in prison. One Minnesota official told me that one cell house wing at the Stillwater maximum security unit is known as "the reservation." Minnesota listed 10 percent of its prisoner population as "other" in 1973 and North Dakota 15 percent (see U.S. Department of Justice 1976).

[16] Fox (1972, p. 14) points out that the first prison race riot in American history occurred in Virginia in 1962. In a survey using the *New York Times* Index, the South Carolina Department of Corrections (1973) identified race as at least one of the causes of eleven different riots between 1969 and 1971. A survey of the *New York Times* Index for 1972–78 reveals scores of conflicts in which race is named as a contributing factor. Of course many other collective disturbances may not have come to the attention of the *Times*, or may not have been reported.

The dining hall continued to be segregated, and any man sitting out of his racially determined place was risking his life. The television viewing room in each living unit was segregated, proximity to the TV set being determined by which racial group possessed the greatest power at any particular time. Within the living units, any man who became too friendly with a man of another race would be visited by representatives of his own racial group and pressured into maintaining segregation. If he did not, he would be ostracized from his group and would run the risk of physical attack or even death at the hands of his own race. (Rundle 1973, pp. 167–68)

A Soledad prisoner writes:

CTF Central at Soledad, California, is a prison under the control of the California Department of Corrections. . . . However, by the 1960s the prison had earned the label of "Gladiator School"; this was primarily because of the never-ending race wars and general personal violence which destroyed any illusions about CTF Central being an institution of rehabilitation. . . . Two of the wings—O and X—are operated under maximum custody under the care of armed guards. There is no conflict between policy, reality and intent here: These are the specially segregated areas where murder, insanity and the destruction of men is accepted as a daily way of life. It is within these wings that the race wars become the most irrational; where the atmosphere of paranoia and loneliness congeal to create day-to-day existence composed of terror. (Minton 1971, p. 84)[17]

[17] In an interesting and thoughtful account of racial violence in Soledad and San Quentin, journalist Minn Yee (1973) traces a macabre series of events which began when three black prisoners were fatally shot by a white guard in a Soledad exercise yard in early 1970. A white guard was reputedly murdered in retaliation. George Jackson and two other "Soledad Brothers" were charged with the crime. Jonathan Jackson's attempt to free the Soledad Brothers in a guerrilla-style attack on the Marin County Court House led to his own death, that of a judge and several others. A few months later, six prisoners and guards, and George Jackson himself, were killed in a bizarre "escape attempt" at San Quentin.

Racial polarization was reinforced by the proliferation of formal organizations built around racial symbolism and ideology. The Black Guerrilla Family emerged as an umbrella organization for blacks and the Aryan Brotherhood, a neo-Nazi organization, served to organize whites, particularly rural "okies" and "bikers" (motorcycle gang members). Race relations deteriorated to such an extent that California officials felt compelled to segregate their maximum security "adjustment centers" to avoid bloodshed.

California's Chicano prisoners have also attracted a great deal of attention, probably because of the murderous feud which has for several years raged between two factions, La Familia and Mexican Mafia (Park 1976). Theodore Davidson (1974), an anthropologist, studied the organization of La Familia at San Quentin before the internal feuding began. He pointed out that La Familia emerged in response to staff racism and the Chicanos' own feeling of cultural isolation. La Familia's organization and code of secrecy are rooted in the barrio culture and the creed of *machismo*.

Numerous killings and knifings (58 deaths and 268 stabbings in 1971–73), largely attributable to the feud between the two Chicano groups, have led to official attempts to separate La Familia and Mafia in different prisons. Since it has not been possible to identify all members accurately, the violence continues. The real and imaginary structure and activities of the two organizations have captured the imagination of many California prison officials and prisoners (Park 1976, pp. 93–94).

Racial polarization is also evident in California's juvenile institutions. Dishotsky and Pfefferbaum (1978, p. 4) report that

> the ordinary events of everyday life at Northern California
> Youth Center, like those at the maximum security
> penitentiaries, were dictated by a code of ethnic separation.
> Afro-American, Caucasian-American and Mexican-American
> inmates lived side by side but maintained three distinct
> adolescent ethnic cultures by selected ingroup relatedness
> and outgroup avoidance. Inmates did not eat at the same
> table, share food, drinks, cigarettes or bathroom facilities

, with individuals of other ethnic groups. They would not sit in the same row while viewing television or even talk for more than brief interchanges with members of a different ethnic group. These customs were enforced by the power faction within each ethnic group.

Members of "white power," "black power," and "Mexican power" factions are hard core racists (Dishotsky and Pfefferbaum 1978, p. 6):

> Symbols of ethnic group and power subgroup identification were a prominent feature of adolescent inmate culture. Body tattoos were indelible symbols of group identification. Among Mexican-American youths, the tattoos were ethnic group symbols—such as "La Raza," and the hometown barrio. Among Caucasians the tattoos were subgroup symbols such as "White Power," the swastika and NSWPP, the initials of the National Socialist White Peoples Party—a derivative of the American Nazi Party.

Leo Carroll (1974) found the same pattern of racial separatism, albeit with less violence, at Rhode Island's maximum security prison in 1970–71. He found that, despite efforts by the administration to integrate the facility, the prisoners voluntarily segregated themselves in all facets of the daily round. Black and white prisoners lived and worked next to each other, but their interaction was limited. Each group organized its own social and economic systems. Despite their shared status as prisoners, the gap between blacks and whites was unbridgeable. The cultural world of black prisoners revolved around "soul" and "black nationalism." Blacks defined whites as weak and exploitable; they related to each other as "brothers" and "partners." To the extent that divisions existed among the black prisoners, it was on the basis of politicization; Carroll distinguished "revolutionaries," "halfsteppers," and "toms."

Ianni's (1974, p. 162) research on New York State prisons led him to conclude that ethnic segregation is the first rule of inmate social organization. A study of an Ohio juvenile facility with equal numbers of blacks and whites further supports the claim that today's prisoner subculture is dominated by racial polarization and conflict (Bartollas, Miller, and Dinitz 1976). Lower-class blacks are the dominant group, followed by middle-class blacks, lower-class whites, and middle-class whites. Inmate norms for blacks are: exploit whites, do not force sex on blacks, and defend your brother. In contrast whites' norms include: do not trust anyone, and each man for himself.

My own study of Stateville Penitentiary (Jacobs 1977) also reveals a prisoner subculture divided along racial lines. The blacks are the dominant group, although divided into three warring "super gangs" which have been transported from Chicago's streets. The "Latinos" define themselves as separate from blacks and whites. They voluntarily interact only with other Spanish-speaking inmates and have achieved some solidarity through the Latin Kings, a Chicago street gang. The whites constitute a weak minority (except for an Italian clique associated with the Mafia), lacking any organization or cohesion; white prisoners are highly vulnerable to exploitation.

The prisoner subculture at Stateville is an extension of gang life in the ghetto. Inside the prison interracial hostilities intensify because intraracial peer groups completely dominate the lives of the prisoners. Few, if any, other activities or interests compete for a prisoner's energies. Inmates live as if in fish tanks where behavior is continuously scrutinized. Under such circumstances "hardline" racist norms are easy for leaders to enforce and difficult for individual prisoners to ignore.

By the mid-1970s the dominance of racial cleavages in American prisons was evident to growing numbers of observers, including scholars. In every region of the country race is the most important determinant of an individual's prison experience. Explicit discrimination by staff members may have decreased over the past decade, but racial polarization and conflict between prisoners have intensified. And staff members have been charged with exacerbating and manipulating interprisoner racial hostilities as a means of maintaining control (see, e.g., Ianni 1974, p. 171; Yee 1973).

The status and opportunity structures of prisoners and of their culture are now, in many prisons, dominated by blacks and Spanish-speaking inmates. The prison, like the urban school, has undergone a massive demographic transition. As in the case of the school, the influx of urban blacks and other minorities has had enormous effect on the "client culture" and the formal organization.

One of the most striking facts about contemporary prison race relations is the dominance of the black prisoners. Francis Ianni (1974, p. 178) contrasts the positions of a typical black and a typical white prisoner in one of New York State's penal facilities:

> Hicks is typical of the young, black inmate from the urban ghetto whose posture toward the authorities has become offensive rather than smiling-at-the-man-while-picking-his-pocket. He operates on an awareness that, in terms of sheer presence, the black inmates are the largest, and because of their numbers the most influential group in prison. McChesney [a white prisoner] is more typical of traditional inmate attitudes of "doing your own time" which include attitudes of guilt and submissiveness toward the authorities. His cloak-and-dagger schemes are the result of his sense of isolation and his fearful outlook.

Even in prisons where blacks constitute less than a majority, they exercise dominion.[18] At the Rhode Island Adult Correctional Institution, where blacks were only 25 percent of the prisoner population, Leo Carroll found that 75 percent of the homosexual rapes involved black aggressors and white victims (1974, p. 182). There were no cases of white aggressors and black victims (see also Davis 1968; Scacco 1975, chap. 4). As one black prisoner told Carroll (p. 184):

> Every can I been in that's the way it is. . . . It's gettin' even I guess. . . . You guys been cuttin' our b——s off ever since we been in this country. Now we're just gettin' even.

The black prisoners completely dominated whites in an Ohio juvenile institution studied by Bartollas, Miller, and Dinitz (1976).

---

[18] In McClelland v. Sigler, 327 F. Supp. 829 at 830 (D. Neb. 1971), the District Court referred to Warden Sigler's testimony that "a small percentage of black men in prisons have a tendency to prey on young, weak, white men."

The inmate leaders, except one, were black, even though almost 50 percent of the inmates were white. The white prisoners were unable to organize. Consequently, they were highly vulnerable to exploitation.

> The exploitation matrix typically consists of four groups, and the form of exploitation found in each is fairly clear cut. At the top normally is a black leader called a "heavy." He is followed closely by three or four black lieutenants. The third group, a mixture of eight to sixteen black and white youths, do the bidding of those at the top. This group is divided into a top half of mostly blacks, known as "alright guys," with the bottom half comprised mostly of whites, designated as "chumps." One or two white scapegoats make up the fourth group in each cottage. These scapegoats become the sexual victims of the first three groups. (Bartollas, Miller, and Dinitz 1976, p. 72)

The black prisoners not only wielded physical power, but "through their prevailing position, blacks control[led] the music played, the television programs watched, the kinds of food eaten, the style of clothing worn, and the language employed" (Bartollas, Miller, and Dinitz 1976, p. 61). White youths seeking to improve their status adopt black language, mannerisms, and clothing styles.

Numbers will not fully explain the hegemony of black and other minority prisoners, even when the dominant group is also a majority. The key to black dominance is their greater solidarity and ability to intimidate whites. As the distinct minority in the larger society, blacks have long experienced racial discrimination. They have necessarily defined themselves in terms of their racial identity and have linked their opportunities in the larger society to the fate of their race. Whites, especially outside the south, have had almost no experience in grouping together on the basis of being white. Ethnicity has been a more important basis for social interaction, although even ethnicity has been a weaker basis of collective action for whites than race for blacks. "Whiteness" simply possesses no ideological or cultural significance in American society, except for racist fringe groups. Consequently, whites face imprisonment alone or in small cliques based on outside friendships, neighborhood, or ethnic background.

Aside from Italian cliques clothed in the Mafia mystique (see Carroll 1974, pp. 67–68; Jacobs 1977, p. 159), white cliques are too weak to offer individuals any protection in the predatory prisoner subculture. Only in California does it appear that white prisoners have been able to achieve a strong enough organization to protect themselves. It is significant that such organization has been achieved by groups which already had some sense of group consciousness ("okies" and "bikers"), and only then by an extreme emphasis upon white racism. Neo-Nazi prisoner movements have also appeared in Illinois, especially at Menard, and may in the long run be the basis on which white prisoners achieve solidarity.

This picture of intense racial polarization, perhaps leading toward extreme racism on all sides, poses tremendous challenges to prison officials. Unfortunately, the challenge comes at a time when prison officials have lost confidence in themselves owing to the repudiation of both punishment and rehabilitation as justifications for imprisonment. Authority has also been lost to the courts and to outside agencies, including centralized correctional bureaucracies. In addition, the legitimacy of prison regimes has been sharply questioned on racial grounds. Several national commissions, academic critics, and numerous prisoner petitions have attacked the hegemony of whites in elite as well as staff positions in the prisons (see Jacobs and Kraft 1978). Affirmative action efforts have slowly increased the number of minorities (see American Bar Association 1973), but it is questionable whether this has increased the legitimacy of prison regimes in the eyes of the prisoners. Furthermore, the politics of race have created intrastaff tensions, with some white guards doubting the loyalty of black employees (Jacobs 1977, p. 186). Lawsuits have been brought by both black and white guards charging discrimination, and patterns of racial self-segregation are now evident among prison staff as well as among the prisoners.

II. Prison Race Relations and the Core Tradition
of Sociological Prison Research

Despite the importance of race relations for staff-prisoner, prisoner-prisoner, and staff-staff relations, and for stimulating the intervention of the courts into prison administration, few studies of prison race relations were carried out prior to 1970. It is beyond the scope of this essay to explain why prison scholars of the 1950s and 1960s failed to include race in their descriptions and analyses of prisoner subcultures. One might ask why researchers in many disciplines for so long ignored the roles of women and blacks. Perhaps an intellectual history of research on prisoner subcultures will reveal that white sociologists simply were not sensitive to the pains and affronts of the prison's racial caste system. We should not forget that many studies were carried out at a time when race relations throughout American society were characterized by segregation and discrimination. It may even be that race relations in some prisons were more "progressive" than in other social contexts.[19] At least in prisons like Stateville, blacks and whites lived and worked in close physical proximity.

Another possible explanation lies in the intellectual history of sociology itself. As John Irwin (1977) has noted, prison sociology historically has followed the discipline's dominant concepts and theories. Sociologists like Donald Clemmer sought to apply concepts like "primary group" and "culture." Sociologists in the 1950s and 1960s strove to fit prison research into the structural/functional paradigm. Later, as conflict theory became popular, some sociologists (e.g., Wright 1973) began to view the prison in a more political light, especially emphasizing the fact that blacks and other minorities were overrepresented in prisoner populations by five times and more.

A theory, or even an intellectual tradition, can be criticized for internal inconsistencies or for failing to account for observable phenomena which the theory purports to explain. However, a theory cannot fairly be criticized for failing to explain what it

---

[19] Professor Daniel Glaser has made this observation in personal correspondence drawing on his own experience at Stateville from 1950 to 1954.

does not purport to explain. The core tradition of prisoner sub-culture research has been subjected to extensive criticism on grounds of internal consistency, methodology, and inability to find confirmation in empirical studies. Indeed, "reviews of the literature" themselves are increasing so rapidly that a "review of the reviews" will soon be in order (see, e.g., Hawkins 1976; Thomas and Petersen 1977; Bowker 1977). These internal criti-cisms will not be repeated here. Instead, we may inquire whether data about prison race relations invalidate the model of prisoner subculture based upon an inclusive inmate code and a functionally interlocking system of argot roles.

One may ask whether there ever existed an inmate code which was known by all prisoners and which commanded their lip service. If such a code did exist, in what sense did it provide standards by which members of prisoner society evaluated their own actions and those of fellow prisoners? In light of what is known about prison race relations through the mid-1960s and assuming the existence of an inmate code, it seems implausible that black and white prisoners were equally committed to each of its tenets or that members of each racial group applied the code uniformly to themselves and to members of the other group. The tenet requiring class solidarity among prisoners seems par-ticularly vulnerable in light of the systematic discrimination against black prisoners by white officials and white prisoners. Likewise, members of the Black Muslims explicitly rejected the notion that all prisoners should be treated the same and that all prisoners should do their own time.

The second strand of the core tradition's description of the prisoner community was a system of functionally interlocking argot roles, unique to prison life—e.g., rats, ball busters, dings, politicians, punks, square johns, and real men. The number and types of argot roles and their definitions varied from study to study. The race relations perspective does not deny the existence of such roles; it does suggest that argot roles, like other roles, are differentially available to different segments of a population ac-cording to salient background characteristics, particularly race. Sykes's research, and that of other prison scholars, would have been enriched by an analysis of the racial distribution of the various argot roles. Where whites were established as the dominant caste it seems unlikely that the argot roles organized around illicit economic transactions (e.g., merchants) would have been equally available to blacks and whites. If so, it surely undermines the validity of the conceptualization of the prisoner social system as a system of functionally interlocking roles.

Whether one focuses on the normative (inmate code) or action (argot role) components of prisoner subculture as depicted in the core tradition, integration and consensus appear to have been overemphasized at the expense of factionalism and conflict. However, this does not mean that the prisoner subculture would more adequately have been described as two cultures—one black and one white—any more than American society as a whole would be best described in such dualistic terms. It is possible both to speak of prisoners as a class or group and, at the same time, to recognize this class to be internally fragmented.

The only social science journal article on race relations covering the period of officially sanctioned racial segregation in prison supports this view. Nathan Kantrowitz, a staff sociologist at Stateville, studied prisoner vocabulary during the late 1950s and early 1960s (Kantrowitz 1969). He concluded that black and white prisoners lived in two separate linguistic worlds. Of 114 words used by prisoners to connote race, only 8 were used by both blacks and whites; Negro prisoners had 56 words referring to race, which they alone used; whites had 50 unique words. With respect to other aspects of prison life (e.g., drugs, sex, religion, etc.) common vocabulary far exceeded separate vocabularies. Thus, Kantrowitz concluded (p. 32), "Among convicts, the worlds of black men and white men are separate and in conflict. But each of their—ironically, separate but equal—worlds contains an 'inmate culture' almost identical with the other."

The prisoner subculture can be analyzed in abstract holistic terms or it can be studied more concretely with stress on its strains and divisions. At different times, in different regions, and in different prisons either the inclusive or divisive aspects of the prisoner subculture may appear more salient. Beginning in the late 1950s racial divisions in prison came closer to the surface. Racial protests and even race riots were soon reported by the press.[20] Since that time the core tradition has seemed less useful in explaining what is happening in American prisons. Although Lee Bowker (1977) devotes only two pages to race and ethnic group relations in his book-length review of prisoner subculture research, he offers this curious conclusion (1977, p. 126): "In surveying the literature on prisoner subcultures, we find that the more contemporary the study, the less likely the unitary subculture model is to be consistent with the data collected. Wherever minority groups begin to gain numbers, multiple subcultures arise." His view reflects the gropings of many contemporary prison scholars, and perhaps of those criminologists who commissioned this essay. The old prisoner subculture research seems to be exhausted; there is a pressing need for new descriptions and conceptualization.

III. Race Relations and Future Prisoner Subculture Research

Future research should focus on the racial composition of various prisoner subcultures. Do prisoner populations with a black majority, or large minority, behave differently than do prisoner populations where blacks comprise a smaller percentage of the total? To what extent are prisoner subcultures consisting of three or more racial groups different from prisoner subcultures where there are only two racial groups? And in the multiracial group prisons do the same interracial group alliances always form? Studies along these lines must correct the long-standing tendency to ignore regional differences. It should make a difference whether prisons are located in the southwest, with its large Mexican-American population, in the north central states, where native American movements are becoming significant, or in the south, with its distinctive history of paternalistic race relations. Few, if any, of the prisoner subculture studies reported in the literature have been conducted in these regions.

The prison is but one setting, albeit with very special charac-

[20] See n. 16.

teristics, in which relationships between the races in American society are undergoing change. How race relations in prison differ from race relations in other societal contexts should be a prime issue for research, the answer to which will reveal much about the nature of prison and the functioning of the contemporary prisoner subculture.

Unfortunately, no systematic study of race relations in prisons has yet appeared. However, the studies discussed in the first part of this essay suggest a situation of avoidance, self-segregation and interracial conflict. It is crucial to compare the *degree* of avoidance, self-segregation, and conflict in the prisoner subculture with other settings such as housing projects, schools, and the military where members of different racial groups are involuntarily thrown together.[21]

It is hard to imagine a setting which would be less conducive to accommodative race relations than the prison. Its inmate population is recruited from the least successful and most unstable elements of both majority and minority racial groups. Prisoners are disproportionately representative of the more violence-prone members of society. As a result of crowding, idleness, boredom, sexual deprivation, and constant surveillance prisons produce enormous inter-personal tension.

Future prisoner subculture research needs to consider what factors serve to stabilize prisoners' race relations. Carroll (1974) points out that a group of white Mafia in the Rhode Island prison exerted their influence to prevent prison race relations from further deterioration. In California, despite an extraordinary amount of violence, an uneasy power balance exists between three racial blocs, with groups of Chicanos allied with both blacks and whites. At Stateville, prison officials provided some protection

[21] Charles Moskos (1973, p. 98), the foremost student of the enlisted ranks of the American armed forces, writes: "The too brief era of harmonious race relations in the military ended with the end of the 1960s. The present period is characterized by polarization between the races within the context of formal integration. Engendered by real and perceived discrimination, near mutinous actions of groups of black servicemen in the early 1970s reached such proportions as to undermine the very fighting capability of America's armed forces. Less dramatic than race riots aboard ships or 'fraggings' of officers and noncoms in Vietnam, but ultimately more significant, has been the emergence of race consciousness throughout the rank and file of black servicemen."

for the vulnerable white minority.[22] Latinos protected themselves through a high degree of solidarity and the strength of the Latin Kings, a well-organized street gang which posed a credible threat of retaliation for assaults on Latino prisoners. How prevalent and effective each of these social control mechanisms is for preventing racial conflict in the prisoner subculture are questions which can only be answered by extensive empirical research.

Do prisoner race relations differ according to levels of security? My own observations at Vienna, a model minimum security unit in Illinois (Jacobs 1976), indicated a prisoner subculture highly polarized along racial lines, although the level of violence was very low. The two studies of male juvenile institutions discussed earlier in this essay (Dishotsky and Pfefferbaum 1978; Bartollas, Miller, and Dinitz 1976) suggest that prisoner race relations in juvenile institutions are quite similar to adult male prisons. Perhaps the race relations perspective will lead to integration of prisoner subculture research on adult, juvenile, and women's institutions.

IV. Conclusion

The view of the prison as a primitive society, governed by its own norms and inhabited by its own distinctive social types, was always somewhat exaggerated. Racial divisions are not the only cleavages that exist within the prisoner subculture, but in many contemporary prisons racial politics set the background against which all prisoner activities are played out. Taking race relations into account will help correct the overemphasis on the uniqueness of prisons and will lead to a fuller understanding of the prison's role as an institution of social control. No prison study of any kind can afford to overlook the fact that minorities are overrepresented in the prisoner population by a factor of five, and that prison, ironically, may be the one institution in American society which blacks "control."

[22] Scores of whites sought protection by having themselves assigned to "protective custody"—twenty-four-hour-a-day confinement in special tiers. Ongoing research by John Conrad and his associates at the Center for Studies in Contemporary Problems indicates that it is a nationwide trend for white prisoners to seek protective custody (Conrad and Dinitz 1977).

REFERENCES

American Bar Association, Commission on Correctional Facilities and Services. 1973. *Minority Recruitment in Corrections*. Washington, D.C.

Barnes, Harry Elmer, and Negley K. Teeters. 1959. *New Horizons in Criminology*. Englewood Cliffs, N.J.: Prentice-Hall.

Bartollas, Clemens, Stuart Miller, and Simon Dinitz. 1976. *Juvenile Victimization: The Institutional Paradox*. New York: Wiley.

Bowker, Lee. 1977. *Prisoner Subcultures*. Lexington, Mass.: Lexington Books.

Brown, Claude. 1965. *Manchild in the Promised Land*. New York: Macmillan.

Caldwell, Wallace. 1968. "A Survey of Attitudes toward Black Muslims in Prison," *Journal of Human Relations* 16:220–38.

Carroll, Leo. 1974. *Hacks, Blacks and Cons: Race Relations in a Maximum Security Prison*. Lexington, Mass.: Lexington Books.

Cleaver, Eldridge. 1968. *Soul on Ice*. New York: McGraw-Hill.

Clemmer, Donald. 1940. *The Prison Community*. New York: Holt, Rinehart & Winston.

Clemmer, Donald, and John Wilson. 1960. "The Black Muslims in Prison," *Proceedings of the American Correctional Association*.

Conrad, John, and Simon Dinitz. 1977. "Position Paper for the Seminar on the Isolated Offender." Columbus, Ohio: Academy for Contemporary Problems. Unpublished.

Davidson, Theodore. 1974. *Chicano Prisoners, the Key to San Quentin*. New York: Holt, Rinehart & Winston.

Davis, Alan. 1968. "Sexual Assaults in the Philadelphia Prison System and Sheriff's Vans," *Transaction* 6:8–16.

Dishotsky, Norman, and Adolph Pfefferbaum. 1978. "Ethnic Polarization in a Correction System." Unpublished manuscript.

Fox, Vernon. 1972. "Racial Issues in Corrections," *American Journal of Corrections* 34(no. 6):12–17.

Glaser, Daniel. 1964. *The Effectiveness of a Prison and Parole System*. Indianapolis: Bobbs-Merrill.

Goffman, Erving. 1961. *Asylums*. Garden City, N.Y.: Doubleday.

Gottfredson, Michael, Michael Hindelang, and Nicolette Parisi. 1978. *Sourcebook of Criminal Justice Statistics—1977*. Washington, D.C.: U.S. Government Printing Office.

Hawkins, Gordon. 1976. *The Prison—Policy and Practice*. Chicago: University of Chicago Press.

Hayner, Norman, and Ellis Ash. 1940. "The Prison as a Community," *American Sociological Review* 5:577–83.

Ianni, Francis. 1974. *Black Mafia: Ethnic Succession in Organized Crime*. New York: Simon & Schuster.

Irwin, John. 1970. *The Felon.* Englewood Cliffs, N.J.: Prentice-Hall.

———. 1977. "The Changing Social Structure of the Men's Prison." In *Corrections and Punishment,* ed. David Greenberg. Beverley Hills, Calif.: Sage Publications.

Irwin, John, and Donald Cressey. 1962. "Thieves, Convicts and the Inmate Culture," *Social Problems* 10:142–55.

Jackson, George. 1970. *Soledad Brother: The Prison Letters of George Jackson.* New York: Coward-McCann.

———. 1972. *Blood in My Eye.* New York: Random House.

Jacobs, James. 1976. "The Politics of Corrections: Town/Prison Relations as a Determinant of Reform," *Social Service Review* 50: 623–31.

———. 1977. *Stateville: The Penitentiary in Mass Society.* Chicago: University of Chicago Press.

Jacobs, James, and Lawrence Kraft. 1978. "Integrating the Keepers: A Comparison of Black and White Prison Guards in Illinois," *Social Problems* 25:304–18.

Kantrowitz, Nathan. 1969. "The Vocabulary of Race Relations in a Prison," *Publication of the American Dialect Society* 51:23–34.

Lincoln, C. Eric. 1961. *The Black Muslims in America.* Boston: Beacon Press.

Little, Malcolm. 1965. *The Autobiography of Malcolm X.* New York: Grove Press.

Minton, Robert, ed. 1971. *Inside Prison American Style.* New York: Random House.

Moskos, Charles. 1973. "The American Dilemma in Uniform: Race in the Armed Forces," *Annals of the American Academy of Political and Social Science* 406:94–106.

New York State Special Commission on Attica. 1972. *Official Report.* New York: Bantam Books.

Park, George. 1976. "The Organization of Prison Violence." In *Prison Violence,* ed. Albert K. Cohen, George F. Cole, and Robert G. Bayley. Lexington, Mass.: Lexington Books.

Pell, Eve, ed. 1972. *Maximum Security: Letters from California's Prisons.* New York: Dutton.

Reimer, Hans. 1937. "Socialization in the Prison Community," *Proceedings of the American Prison Association.*

Rothman, David. 1973. "Decarcerating Prisoners and Patients," *Civil Liberties Review* 1:9–30.

Rundle, Frank. 1973. "The Roots of Violence at Soledad." In *The Politics of Punishment: A Critical Analysis of Prisons in America,* ed. Erik Olin Wright. New York: Harper & Row.

Scacco, Anthony. 1975. *Rape in Prison*. Springfield, Ill.: C. C. Thomas.

Schrag, Clarence. 1954. "Leadership among Prison Inmates," *American Sociological Review* 19:37–42.

Sibley, Mulford, and Ada Wardlaw. 1945. *Conscientious Objectors in Prison, 1940–1945*. Philadelphia: Pacifist Research Bureau.

South Carolina Department of Corrections. 1973. *Collective Violence in Correctional Institutions: A Search for Causes*. Columbia: South Carolina Department of Corrections.

Sutherland, Edwin, and Donald Cressey. 1974. *Criminology*. 9th ed. Philadelphia: Lippincott.

Sykes, Gresham. 1958. *The Society of Captives*. Princeton, N.J.: Princeton University Press.

Sykes, Gresham, and Sheldon Messinger. 1960. "The Inmate Social System." In *Theoretical Studies in the Social Organization of the Prison*, ed. Richard Cloward. New York: Social Science Research Council.

Thomas, Charles W., and David M. Peterson. 1977. *Prison Organization and Inmate Subcultures*. Indianapolis: Bobbs-Merrill.

U.S. Commission on Civil Rights. 1971. *Racial Conditions in Indiana Penal Institutions: A Report of the Indiana State Committee*. Washington, D.C.: U.S. Government Printing Office.

U.S. Department of Justice. 1976. *National Prisoner Statistics Special Report, Census of Prisoners in State Correctional Facilities*. Washington, D.C.: U.S. Government Printing Office.

Wright, Erik, ed. 1973. *The Politics of Punishment: A Critical Analysis of Prisons in America*. New York: Harper & Row.

Yee, Minn S. 1973. *The Melancholy History of Soledad Prison*. New York: Harper's Magazine Press.

John Baldwin

Ecological and Areal Studies in Great Britain and the United States

ABSTRACT

Despite a growing body of criticism of the ecological approach to the study of delinquency, the number of criminological studies based upon it, both in Great Britain and in the United States, has shown no signs of decreasing. Given the sheer numbers of such studies that have been conducted in postwar years and their increasing statistical complexity, it is important to make some critical assessment of their contribution to our understanding of delinquency. In much of this work, the objectives of the research have become blurred, conceptual difficulties and ambiguities have been overlooked, and conclusions have been presented as if the use of a technically sophisticated methodology obviated the need for careful explanation.

There are some promising directions for further research. Particular attention should be paid to the research that has been stimulated in recent years by the publication of Oscar Newman's *Defensible Space* (1972). New sources of crime data—particularly victimization studies and self-reported delinquency studies—may enrich areal research. Future research must be sensitive to the politics of delinquency definitions and should investigate the social processes that create and reinforce the unfavorable reputations of delinquency areas.

The roots of academic criminology lie in ecological studies of crime. In France, Guerry (1833) and Quételet (1835) were mapping the distribution of criminal behavior even before the birth of Lombroso, who is often regarded, somewhat erroneously, as the founding father of criminology. Vast numbers of social

John Baldwin is Lecturer in Judicial Administration, Faculty of Law, University of Birmingham.

researchers have since attempted to identify, from a great variety of viewpoints, the factors that give crime its distinctive areal distribution. Approaches and methods have changed over the decades, as have theoretical concerns, but the basic question has changed little—how to explain the uneven distribution of criminal behavior in different areas of large cities.

The ecological approach has generated an immense and complex literature and, in this essay, an attempt is made to examine those aspects which have attracted most interest and to evaluate the contribution that the ecological approach has made to our understanding of crime and delinquency. Section I describes the ecological approach to delinquency studies developed at the University of Chicago during the 1920s and 1930s and summarizes their basic findings and the major criticisms to which they have been subjected. Section II discusses the major ecological research traditions which have emerged since World War II, notably social area analysis and various forms of multivariate statistical analysis. The argument developed in this section is that neither research tradition has been very productive; nor does it seem to me that either should play more than a subsidiary role in further research. Much of this review is critical; in recent years many researchers have carelessly used inappropriate techniques. Though such techniques have produced impressive arrays of statistical relationships between many variables, there has often been a signal lack of careful explanation of what these complex interrelationships mean. Such technically sophisticated manipulations of elaborate bodies of data have scarcely advanced our knowledge of the nature of criminal areas. Section III discusses evolving approaches to ecological research, including those influenced by Oscar Newman's concept of "defensible space," and seeks to identify promising lines of future inquiry.

I. The Chicago School of Sociology and Its Critics

The interest of criminologists in the ecological approach can be traced to the early nineteenth century[1] and to a more general

---

[1] Excellent descriptions of these early pioneers of quantitative methods are to be found in Chevalier (1958); Morris (1957); and Radzinowicz (1966).

concern with the so-called dangerous classes.[2] But the main up-surge in interest was provided by the monumental research that was conducted by sociologists at the University of Chicago in the 1920s and 1930s, and in particular by Clifford Shaw and Henry McKay.[3] Shaw and McKay set out to examine the nature of the relationship between levels of juvenile delinquency and the physical and social characteristics of the neighborhoods in which high rates were typically located. Their examination, though it may now appear somewhat crude and simplistic, was a landmark in criminological discovery. Their patient mapping of delinquency data, drawn from a large number of American cities, provided many new insights into the patterning of delinquency and its relationship to the social and cultural context in which it occurred.

The main conclusions of Shaw and McKay may be briefly summarized as follows.[4] First, they found that rates of delinquency in over twenty large American cities followed a remarkably uniform pattern, being highest in the areas adjacent to the central business district (in the "interstitial" slum areas and in the heavy industrial areas) and varying inversely with the distance from the city center. This pattern was maintained regardless of whether delinquency rates were measured according to census tracts, zones, or radials.[5] Secondly, high rates of delinquency were consistently found in the same areas over long periods of time despite the fact that one characteristic of such areas was a rate of population turnover such that its composition might well change within a generation. The persistence of high delinquency rates was explained by reference to underlying criminogenic influences, delinquency being seen as "culturally transmitted" from genera-

[2] On this question, see particularly Chevalier (1958) and Monkkonen (1975).

[3] Their most influential publications include Shaw (1929, 1930) and Shaw and McKay (1931, 1942). A comprehensive bibliography of their work is given in Snodgrass (1976b).

[4] Good summaries of their work are included in many criminological texts: see particularly Morris (1957).

[5] Zones and radials were different methods used by Shaw and McKay to demonstrate how levels of delinquency varied from innercity areas to outlying areas of the city. These devices demonstrated, more vividly than did the census tract rates, that there was a remarkably uniform decline in areal delinquency rates from the central city area to suburban areas.

tion to generation. Thirdly, and central to an understanding of the social processes which operated in such areas, the concept of "social disorganization" (implying a confusion of moral standards in which the family and local community became ineffective as socializing agents) was used to explain the high rates of delinquency. Finally, the similar distribution of juvenile delinquency, adult crime, truancy, infant mortality, mental illness, and other disorders was interpreted in terms of the social conditions existing in certain communities, the solution to which lay in the physical renewal of the slum neighborhoods and in programs which drew on the institutional and human resources of the local community.[6]

The quality, originality, and importance of Shaw and McKay's work is indicated by its influence, almost half a century later, as a source of ideas for the development of sociological theory. Criminological theories, embodying concepts such as anomie and subculture, and the more recent writings of the symbolic interactionist school, owe a profound debt to the work of the Chicago sociologists.[7] Their perseverance in mapping the distribution of crime, juvenile delinquency, gangs, mental illness, vice, and a host of other forms of social malaise continues to stimulate research to this day. Yet the theoretical background to their work was, to say the least, problematic. The theoretical framework they employed was that provided by Burgess (1925), whose essay on the growth and social organization of the city has provided a natural starting point for almost all theoretical developments within the field of urban sociology. Burgess argued that, in the process of growth, cities in the United States tended to follow a uniform pattern. Employing concepts which had been widely used in plant ecology, he emphasized the organic nature of the city, illustrating the process of growth as representing a series of concentric circles with the city center as the hub. These circles broadly defined and delineated distinct types of area, each with its own social characteristics. Central to the theory were

[6] This policy implication led to the Chicago Area Project, on which see Kobrin (1959) and Snodgrass (1976a).

[7] See, generally, Morris (1957) and Faris (1967). On the symbolic interactionist perspective, see particularly Becker (1963, 1964); the distinguishing characteristic of this approach has been its emphasis upon the social reaction to lawbreaking, viz., that deviance cannot be understood independently of the response it provokes.

the ecological processes of invasion and succession which Burgess borrowed from biology to describe the process by which inner zones encroached upon outer zones. The zone closest to the city center, which was of great social and criminological importance, he saw as constantly being invaded by commercial and industrial undertakings and, in an impressive range of subsequent studies, it was seen as housing "a residuum of the defeated, leaderless and helpless." This zone was characterized by various indices of social and physical deterioration, and Burgess argued that, as people were able, they retreated outwards toward the more prosperous areas.

There was of course nothing new in the observation that crime (and other social ills) clustered in distinctive types of social area. Mayhew (1861) in particular had identified such areas in London in the mid-nineteenth century, and his graphic descriptions of life in these areas have yet to be surpassed.[8] What was new in the work of Shaw and McKay was the wealth of statistical material they amassed, their painstaking mapping of this material, and their distinctive theoretical orientation. Yet they were at once blessed and cursed by their reliance on the Burgess framework for, although it contributed to the significance of their results, it rendered them at the same time subject to the many criticisms that had been made of it.[9] However, as Alihan (1938) noted, Shaw and his colleagues had attempted in only a half-hearted way to interpret their findings, as it were, "ecologically" and in this sense had managed to sidestep some of the more serious criticisms made of Burgess's presentation. Commenting on Shaw's *Delinquency Areas* (1929), Alihan writes:

> [Shaw] neither investigates symbiotic and competitive relations, nor does he probe into the organic, natural reactions of the delinquents. In fact, there is little in Shaw's study to suggest Park's and other ecologists' interpretation

[8] See further Levin and Lindesmith (1937) and Morris (1957).

[9] The 1930s and 1940s saw an increasing disenchantment with the Burgess theoretical structure. Alihan (1938), for example, had been extremely critical of its overdrawn biological analogy. Other researchers had found that the zonal model simply did not fit the cities that they examined, and other approaches were subsequently developed by urban sociologists. A good summary of these developments and the criticisms of classical ecological theory is given by Robson (1969, pp. 8–38).

of the biotic sub-structure. Instead, Shaw confined himself
to the finding of correlations between the frequency of a
social phenomenon, delinquency, in various areas and the
relative distance of these areas from the center of the city,
following the ideal zonal pattern into which every city
supposedly tends to fall. This done, he interprets delinquency
primarily in terms of social, cultural, and economic factors.
He does not submit any evidence to show that the different
frequencies of delinquency in different areas are ecological
adaptations to the particular areas. (p. 83)

This raises a terminological point of some importance. To describe
the work of the Chicago sociologists as "ecological" is clearly
misleading since the biological analogy cannot be said to have
been seriously pursued. Yet the term is still used to characterize
subsequent research even when the researchers in question
would vehemently eschew the Burgess framework. Though it is
often difficult to avoid this imprecise usage, the term is certainly
confusing and it is more appropriate to refer to "areal" studies
of crime than to "ecological" studies.

Despite the debt that contemporary criminology undoubtedly
owes to Shaw and McKay, their work has attracted its fair share
of criticism. It is worth discussing these criticisms at some
length since they are as relevant to research carried out on
criminal areas today as they were in the 1930s in the heyday of
Chicago sociology. Perhaps the most serious weakness that has
been noted is that virtually all area studies have been based on
officially recorded rates of criminality, whether from police,
court, or institutional sources. Criminologists are often accused
of acknowledging the crippling weaknesses of such statistics but
continuing nevertheless to base research upon them. A great
variety of studies might serve to inform our judgment as to, say,
the extent of police biases (e.g., Piliavin and Briar 1964; Black
and Reiss 1970) or the weaknesses of the official crime statistics
(e.g., Ennis 1967; Gold 1970; Sparks, Genn, and Dodd 1977) or
the influence of "rate-producing agencies" (e.g., Kitsuse and
Cicourel 1963; Cicourel 1968). Despite the consistencies that

have emerged from such sources, one can still find evidence to support almost any of one's prejudices. Certainly the two main alternative sources of data—victimization studies and self-reported delinquency studies—while casting considerable doubts on the validity of official measures, are themselves subject to as many limitations as are the official statistics.[10]

Secondly, "ecological" research is, almost by definition, based upon areal units (such as census tracts, wards, enumeration districts)[11] and, as such, is subject to the telling critique of Robinson (1950) concerning the "ecological fallacy." Robinson argued that it is a mistake to assume that there is a simple correspondence between properties of areas and the properties of the individuals who live in the areas. As he pointed out, researchers are not primarily interested in the areal units per se but in the behavior of the people who live in these areas, and it is mainly because information on these people is not available, or is too difficult to obtain, that areal data are employed. This means that, at the very least, the greatest care is needed in interpreting areal data. Although this may now seem an obvious point, a remarkable number of researchers have fallen foul of the "ecological fallacy" when interpreting their results.[12]

Thirdly, and again relevant to the question of interpretation, is

[10] Christie (cited in Hood and Sparks 1970, p. 23), for example, observes that: "present studies of self-reported crime have the same principal weaknesses as the official crime statistics. We have exchanged the official system of registration for some social scientists' system of registration." Booth, Johnson, and Choldin (1977) make a similar observation about the use of rates derived from victimization surveys. They argue that official crime measures and victimization measures are "sufficiently incongruous to make it problematic to examine the characteristics of cities in order to understand why their crime rates differ. . . . Lacking evidence showing one measure as the more valid indicator of crime, we conclude that neither is a satisfactory index of crime" (p. 196).

[11] This raises the question of the social homogeneity of the areal units used. Can they be regarded as distinct social areas (or "natural areas") as the Chicago sociologists claimed? Subsequent research has cast serious doubts on this claim and it appears that even quite small units, such as census tracts or enumeration districts, commonly include within their boundaries extremely diverse populations: see Robison (1936); Myers (1954); Mabry (1958); and Brantingham, Dyreson, and Brantingham (1976). Careless use of census data has frequently led to misinterpretation and confusion since intra-area variations may be more important in some cases than inter-area variations.

[12] This point is pursued further in the second part of this paper. The studies of Polk (1957) and Willie (1967), which are there discussed, seem to provide striking examples of the "ecological fallacy."

the difficulty in determining to what extent slums produce delinquents (an inference favored by Shaw and McKay and to some extent supported by some early English studies)[13] and to what extent the gravitation or drift to the slums by social deviants explains the distribution (a conclusion supported by Taft's limited study [1933], and by research in England concerned with the areal distribution of the mentally ill).[14] The simple truth is that this question—so fundamental to "ecological" interpretation—is no nearer resolution now than it was almost half a century ago and remains a subject of controversy.

The final criticism that has been made of Shaw and McKay's work (though it applies much more generally) concerns the broader theoretical and ideological assumptions that they made. The stance they adopt, albeit implicitly, is at root politically conservative. They are said to have seen delinquency areas as deteriorated and degraded because of social disorganization and lack of community control. An alternative explanation—that the degradation and squalor of such neighborhoods may reflect the indifference of landowners and industrialists in those areas—is at least as viable. Snodgrass (1976a) tendentiously describes the view sometimes attributed to Shaw and McKay as follows:

> It was not the decisions, actions and policies of business executives, landowners and political officials which created these miserable sections of Chicago; it was the laws of nature. . . . The "plant-like" metaphor had the benevolent hand of nature regulating the process. The laws of nature created a cheap labour market, human degradation and exploitation, and pre-ordained that one would have slums and delinquency . . . one would hardly attempt to organise politically to overcome or overthrow the laws of nature. (pp. 11–12)

Identifying "delinquency" or "problem" areas is a delicate business and, as will be seen later, such labels may well be vehemently rejected by the residents of the areas concerned. It is now clear that the social processes which operate to give

[13] See especially Spinley (1953); Mays (1954); and Kerr (1958).
[14] See Goldberg and Morrison (1963) and Parkin, Kenning, and Wilder (1971).

certain areas in cities distinctive reputations is much more complex and subtle than the mapping of convicted offenders might suggest.[15]

II. Areal Studies since World War II

In postwar years, the "ecological" approach to the study of social problems is commonly assumed to have experienced a steady decline in importance,[16] yet, paradoxically, the number of such studies has not decreased either in the United States or in Great Britain. Somewhat different research traditions have been pursued in the two countries: in the United States, new methods of classifying urban subareas have been borrowed by criminologists from geographers and urban sociologists and used in studies of delinquency areas, whereas in England these kinds of technical and statistical exercises only became possible when small area data (in the form of census enumeration districts) were made available for the first time in the 1960s.[17] But this factor alone does not explain why the research conducted in the two countries has followed different directions. The main reason is that, in Great Britain, publicly owned housing (council housing) and extensive slum clearance by public authorities have had a profound effect on the distribution of delinquency. As much as half of the housing in large English cities is nowadays owned and built by public bodies—a situation which certainly did not apply in North American cities at the time the Chicago sociologists were formulating their theories of city growth and which applies to only a limited extent today.[18] Because of land prices, most

[15] See further Armstrong and Wilson (1973); Taylor, Walton, and Young (1973, pp. 123–27); Damer (1974); and Baldwin (1974a).

[16] Mannheim (1965) writes, for example, "ecological theory . . . after arousing a great deal of interest already in the middle of the nineteenth century, reached the peak of its popularity in the period between the two world wars, but has gradually retreated into the background in the decades after 1945" (p. 532).

[17] Census data in Britain had been available for many years only for wards (large local government units) covering populations of many thousands. Since the 1961 census, however, information has become available for census enumeration districts—areas within which about seven hundred people are resident. Wards have generally been considered too large for sophisticated statistical analyses of crime, though they have been used for other purposes by social geographers.

[18] Though several writers in England have argued that the concentric zone model is of some relevance in understanding city growth, Robson (1969) is much nearer the mark when he writes: "The appearance of such large areas of local authority

council housing is to be found at a considerable distance from city centers. The spatial distribution of indices of criminal behavior is thus critically affected by public rehousing programs, and this has increasingly shifted the focus of interest of researchers away from the slum areas toward the problems generated by the "difficult" housing estate. A good deal of research has, over the years, been conducted to examine the effect on delinquency rates of rehousing families from slum areas to newer council properties[19] and, more recently, to investigate the nature of the factors that operate to produce "problem" estates.[20] The studies concerned with the effects of rehousing programs on levels of delinquency have demonstrated that new council estates, though structurally superior to slum residences, have had no profound effect on overall levels of officially recorded delinquency, except sometimes a slightly adverse effect.[21]

Criminologists in Great Britain have, therefore, been forced to move away from explanations of crime based on some form of environmental determinism toward explanations which take account of independent social processes operating to produce high delinquency council estates. In a study that a colleague and I undertook in Sheffield (Baldwin and Bottoms 1976), an attempt was made to examine various hypotheses put forward to explain how council estates, with populations of comparable socio-economic composition, nevertheless showed vastly different rates of apprehended delinquents. It rapidly became apparent that an adequate explanation had to take account of public housing policy, the desire of residents to move to other estates and, most important of all, the way that the adverse reputations of some estates were created and maintained over time. There seemed to be a serious danger that, once such a reputation had developed,

housing has made nonsense of the rings or sectors of the classical ecological theory. Indeed the game of hunt-the-Chicago-model seems to be exhausted so far as the analysis of modern developments in British urban areas is concerned" (p. 132).

[19] See, for instance, Bagot (1941); Ferguson (1952); Maule and Martin (1956); and Jones (1958).

[20] On this, see particularly Morris (1957); Jones (1958); Wilson (1963); Bagley (1965); Armstrong and Wilson (1973); Damer (1974); Herbert (1975); and Baldwin and Bottoms (1976).

[21] See, for example, Maule and Martin (1956). These questions are discussed in Baldwin and Bottoms (1976, pp. 146–49).

the responses of the local community and of the housing authority toward the estate in question could produce a self-fulfilling prophecy.[22] Other writers in Great Britain, who had examined the same phenomenon, emphasized more the reaction of law enforcement agencies and the political power exercised by the local housing corporation,[23] but the common objective of researchers in England has been to explain how certain areas acquire unfavorable reputations in the first place, how such reputations persist over time (despite being in some cases grossly at variance with the "facts"), and how the reputation may have an "amplifying" effect on levels of delinquency in the locality.

The emphasis on "problem" council estates has thus created a peculiarly British research tradition. In at least two other aspects, however, the somewhat divergent paths followed by researchers in the two countries have tended in recent years to converge. There has been, first, a growing interest in Great Britain in more sophisticated statistical analyses of data, along the lines of those undertaken in the United States by Lander (1954) and Schmid (1960). Secondly, in both countries something of a minor revolution in areal research has taken place since the publication of Oscar Newman's *Defensible Space* (1972), with its emphasis on architectural design in crime prevention. Since enormous effort and expense have already been devoted to each of these approaches, it is clearly important to attempt some evaluation of the progress that has been made so far.

The search for new methods of classifying urban areas continues among urban sociologists and social geographers and, in consequence, there have been many attempts in the past twenty years to use these alternative methods in the study of delinquency areas. Two methods particularly have stimulated much research in criminology, though both have raised formidable difficulties when applied to crime data. The first method—that of social area analysis as developed by Eshref Shevky and his colleagues[24]—

[22] See further Baldwin (1974a, 1975a).

[23] See, particularly, Armstrong and Wilson (1973); Damer (1974); and Byrne (1974).

[24] Their most important publications are Shevky and Williams (1949) and Shevky and Bell (1955).

has been used as the starting point for a number of criminological studies concerned with the social patterning of crime within the American city. In the second, areal description is based on more technical statistical methods, such as factor analysis and component analysis, and these methods have been used quite widely, both in the United States and in Great Britain.

A. Social Area Analysis

Shevky and Bell (1955) attempted to relate the internal structure of cities to changes taking place in the wider society. They developed three postulates, derived from Wirth's classic essay, "Urbanism as a Way of Life" (1938), which they argued were indicative of aspects of the increasing scale of industrial society. In a well-known (and much criticized) passage, Shevky and Bell outlined the construction of their three basic dimensions of urban social structure:

> . . . from certain broad postulates concerning modern society and from the analysis of temporal trends, we have selected three structural reflections of change which can be used as factors for the study of social differentiation and stratification at a particular time in modern society. These factors are social rank, urbanization and segregation. (pp. 3–5)

These two sentences are at once important and troubling. Almost by sleight of hand, Shevky and Bell move from a theoretical discussion of societal scale to the narrower question of how areas within cities (not within societies) become socially differentiated. Indeed, it is still far from clear how this theoretical "hiatus" can be bridged. As their theory stands it must be concluded that Shevky and Bell failed adequately to relate their elaborate theoretical discourse to the empirical problems with which they were dealing.[25]

Shevky and Bell use a number of census variables to measure the three social area constructs. Social rank is measured by

[25] Further discussion of the theoretical limitations of the Shevky-Bell framework, together with a critique of the criminological applications, is given in Baldwin (1974b).

combinations of census variables relating to occupation, education, and rent; urbanization by variables relating to fertility,
women at work, and single-family dwelling units; and segregation
by the proportions of racial and national groups living in relative
isolation. Each census tract is identified in terms of its score on
each dimension and tracts which have similar scores are grouped
together in "social space." A good deal of discussion has focused
on the definitions of the three constructs. The urbanization construct in particular has generated a great deal of confusion,[26] a
situation not helped by conflicting opinions about the meaning
of the construct expressed by both Shevky and Bell in an appendix
to their book.[27]

Social area analysis has provoked fierce controversy since its
introduction, caused in no small part by the exaggerated claims
that Shevky and Bell made for it.[28] As will be apparent in due
course, many criminologists who have used their framework
appear to have accepted these claims without question. Of
particular relevance here is their claim that:

> The concepts of "natural area" and "subculture" are not
> unrelated to our concept "social area" for we view a social
> area as containing persons with similar social positions in
> the larger society. The social area, however, is not bounded
> by the geographical frame of reference as is the natural
> area, nor by implications concerning the degree of interaction
> between persons in the local community as is the subculture.

[26] Duncan (1955), for instance, has pointed out that even in Shevky and Bell's
original application of this construct, two of the three census variables which make
up the construct change in the hypothesized direction of greater urbanization, whereas
the other variable moves in the opposite direction. As Duncan puts it, it is "a uni-
dimensional construct with a two-way split."

[27] Shevky favors the term "urbanization" mainly on the grounds that the census
variables used for this construct are "indicants of structural functional changes at a
level transcending the immediate family interaction." Bell, on the other hand, prefers
the description "family status" because this "limits the conception of urbanization,
but more precisely directs attention to that aspect of urbanization being measured
with the index as presently constructed." For further details of the authors' differing
interpretations of the other constructs, see Shevky and Bell (1955, p. 68).

[28] Their claim, for example, that their model was "a logically demonstrable reflection of those major changes which have produced modern, urban society" is so strong
that one observer noted that it was "almost unique in the social science literature"
(Timms 1971, p. 134).

> We do claim, however, that the social area generally contains
> persons having the same level of living, the same way of
> life, and the same ethnic background. (p. 20)

This last claim is, to put it bluntly, absurd, since census data,
while useful in illuminating broad socioeconomic differences
between areas, cannot be legitimately used to indicate "ways of
life," "levels of living," and the like.[29]

Even this brief discussion of the framework of social area
analysis gives some idea of its many serious theoretical, methodological, and empirical shortcomings. These difficulties are of
the greatest importance in any application of the model, yet in
much research the constructs are accepted uncritically; their
conceptual weaknesses and definitional ambiguities are left
largely unexplored. This often leads to faulty or exaggerated
interpretation of results. Although such studies have been viewed
as significant advances and refinements of the "ecological"
approach, taken together, they have contributed little to an understanding of the areal distribution of delinquency. It is not possible
here to review in detail the individual studies;[30] rather, an indication of the main pitfalls is offered. The broad approach adopted
by criminological researchers using this framework has been to
correlate the three constructs with various crime indices in an
attempt to discover how the "social structure" (as measured and
defined by the constructs) is related to crime patterns. But this
ignores the ambiguity that surrounds the meaning of the constructs themselves, and the literature contains several examples
of the thoroughly misleading interpretation of the constructs.
Boggs (1965), for instance, spuriously attributes the meaning of
"anomie" to the urbanization construct and several other writers
(in particular Polk 1957, 1967; Quinney 1964) claim much
greater theoretical import for the constructs than they warrant.[31]
Some researchers, confronted by statistical correlations which

[29] As already indicated, even the smallest areal units are likely to encompass quite
disparate populations (see above, n. 11).

[30] A detailed review of this kind is given in Baldwin (1974b, pp. 157–66).

[31] See further Gordon's excellent critique (1967) in which he raises doubts about
Polk's surprising finding that delinquency levels in San Diego were not highly correlated with the economic status construct. Gordon suggests that the construct is defined in an inappropriate way since it fails to encompass the full range of workers

appear to mean very little, are content, as it were, to leave it to the reader to draw his own conclusions. While this approach avoids the dangers in exaggerated interpretation, it nonetheless makes for sterile analysis. Schmid (1960), in one of the most often quoted studies, provides a striking example of this kind of timidity. In his massive study of crime areas in Seattle, he employs the gamut of "ecological" techniques (zones, gradients, isopleth maps, social area analysis, and various other urban typologies) in analyzing a series of crime variables. Each analysis is conducted with an impressive degree of statistical sophistication, yet Schmid can apparently make little sense of it. His analysis ends with a discussion of the relevance to his results of six criminological hypotheses,[32] but he concludes limply that "each . . . presumably accounts for the characteristic patterning of crime in the large American city" (p. 675). In other words, it appears that the study cannot help in the assessment of the relevance of the hypotheses; indeed, it would seem from his discussion that the results fit any or all of them.[33]

It might be thought that the interpretative lapses so common within this body of literature would be sufficient in themselves to render the Shevky-Bell framework of questionable utility in delinquency research. Yet it is even more remarkable to note the number of occasions on which these researchers have fallen into the trap of the "ecological fallacy" discussed above. This is perhaps indicative of the spurious interpretation and strained attribution of meaning to results which probably mean very little. The two following examples are good illustrations:

> . . . we were not able to accept the hypothesis that areas
> with greater amounts of family life have lower rates of

---

of lower socioeconomic status and excludes the unemployed. Gordon concludes that "it does seem likely, in view of the breadth of his categories, that Polk's ethnic status index, which correlated more highly with delinquency than his SES index, was actually the more valid indicator of extremely low socioeconomic status" (p. 942).

[32] These are concerned with differences in opportunities for committing crimes; the "drift" hypothesis; differential association and cultural transmission; the social alienation hypothesis; anomie; and Cloward's variant based on "illegitimate opportunity."

[33] Schmid's methodology and interpretation of his results are discussed in n. 36 and in text preceding n. 43.

delinquency. These findings did not support the theory that juvenile delinquency may be an indication of a breakdown in the normal function of family life. (Polk 1957, p. 215)

. . . some juvenile delinquency is associated with unstable family life which is unstable because of impoverished economic circumstances; and some juvenile delinquency is associated with families which are economically impoverished and . . . these families are impoverished because they are unstable. . . . The preventive potential of two-parent households against juvenile delinquency tends to be impaired by circumstances of poverty. The preventive potential of affluent economic status against juvenile delinquency tends to be impaired by family instability. (Willie 1967, p. 334)

These quotations contain extraordinary examples of the "ecological fallacy." Both writers are guilty of assuming that what is true on an areal level holds on a family or individual level. For the conclusions to be valid, some information concerning individual families is necessary (i.e., not areal data). None of the authors in question attempts to adduce such information.

What, then, is the contribution of social area analysis to the ecological study of delinquency? The simple answer is, in the view of the present writer, that it has provided a suspect theoretical framework which has produced much ambiguity and confusion. None of the studies makes explicit the acute conceptual and methodological problems to which use of the three constructs gives rise. These problems are fundamental to any application of the Shevky-Bell framework, and this omission inevitably reduces one's confidence in the results presented. Furthermore, many of the studies make excessive claims for the framework and impute too much sociological significance to the constructs, which are after all no more than configurations of census variables. It is far from clear in any event that the social areas, formed from census tracts, are in any real sense socially homogeneous. Finally, this group of researchers rarely shows an appreciation of the objectives to be achieved by employing social area analysis and often attempts to test hypotheses for which an areal framework is at best inefficient and at worst wholly inappropriate and misleading. In many cases, the hypotheses could be more simply and more satisfactorily tested on an individual basis.

B. The Use of Multivariate Statistical Methods

The most damaging criticisms leveled against the Shevky-Bell approach concern the procedure by which the three constructs were derived, i.e., a priori theorization. Several writers have argued that this limits the scope of the analysis to a handful of variables, and in consequence fails to do justice to the complexity of city structure.[34] Researchers have increasingly been directing their attention to multivariate techniques (such as factor analysis and the closely related technique of principal component analysis) which can take into account a much greater number of variables. By so doing, it is argued, such techniques produce a more complete and objective description of city structure. Robson (1969) sums up the advantages as follows:

> Whereas the Shevky technique selects its constructs, and
> the variables which compose them, on the basis of possibly
> suspect theory, multivariate analysis selects its discriminating
> factors solely on the basis of the intercorrelations of the
> data itself—and a large body of data at that. (p. 58)

Multivariate techniques seek, then, to reduce a large number of variables into a small number of factors or categories according to the intercorrelations of the variables. The main objective is "scientific parsimony or economy of description" (Holzinger and Harman 1941). Factor analysis and related methods have often been viewed as sensible ways of reducing to manageable proportions the vast quantity of information now available from population censuses and, therefore, as useful methods in the delineation of urban social areas. The main advantage of factor analysis over simpler approaches has been seen as its ability to absorb large quantities of complex information without the need for

---

[34] See, for instance, Robson (1969, pp. 47–67) and Baldwin and Bottoms (1976, pp. 18–21, 197–201).

prior formulation of theory. Several writers, mindful of the latter
consideration, have been tempted to refer to it as an "objective"
method.[35] This is, however, to ignore two crucial elements in
the procedure which are anything but objective. First, the selection of appropriate variables to be included in the analysis involves
a highly subjective element and, secondly, interpretation of the
resulting factors often involves tortuous intellectual gymnastics
in the process of which the researcher's own presuppositions and
prejudices can be given full rein. There is no guarantee that
other researchers would interpret the factors in the same way.
Indeed, sometimes the interpretation of factors is all but impossible
and it is the rule rather than the exception that researchers are
less than convincing in their interpretation.[36] Blalock (1960)
states the problem succinctly:

> It is very possible . . . to end up with a set of factors which
> have very little theoretical meaning. We then have merely
> replaced a large number of clear-cut operational indices by a
> smaller number of theoretically meaningless factors. Factor
> analysis will, therefore, be of relatively little value unless
> the factors obtained can be identified. (p. 384)

These difficulties of multivariate analysis, though well recognized by Blalock and other statisticians, have been largely
ignored by criminologists, who have used it in two fairly distinct,
though not unrelated, ways. Some researchers, by far the most
prominent of whom is Bernard Lander (1954), have analyzed a
small number of census variables which seemed a priori of
relevance to delinquency data; others have been much less
selective and have included many more variables so as to allow,
as it were, the analysis itself to sift out those that are most
relevant. It is often unclear how either group of researchers made
their choice of "relevant" variables in the first place.[37] The short

[35] On this see, for instance, Robson (1969, pp. 58, 72) and Herbert (1968, p. 280).
[36] To give just one example of this, Schmid (1960) uses factor analysis in his
examination of social and crime variables. One of the factors extracted shows fairly
high correlations for three of his crime categories—those of nonresidential burglary,
indecent exposure, and bicycle theft. Schmid, presumably in desperation, interprets
this as "an atypical crime pattern."
[37] Lander, for instance, states that he picked the census variables he used not because "theoretically, they are . . . necessarily the best measures of the socio-economic

point is that one can get out of factor analysis no more than one puts in, and the nature of the factors extracted is likely to be heavily determined by the initial selection of variables.

So much for the limitations of the method; how has it been used by criminologists to make sense of delinquency areas? Lander's famous application of factor analysis in his study of juvenile delinquency in Baltimore has proved to be both the most important and the most controversial use of the technique in criminological research. Lander sought to ascertain the extent to which seven social variables (relating to housing, population, and socioeconomic characteristics of census tracts)[38] influenced the rate of delinquency and, by factor analysis, to extract "underlying" factors which accounted for the intercorrelations among the variables. His factor analysis was carried out on the seven census variables together with the delinquency rate, and he extracted two factors which were in some measure related to each other. He argued that the more important of them could appropriately be called an "anomic" factor and the other a socioeconomic factor. His conclusion that "The factor analysis clearly demonstrates that delinquency in Baltimore is fundamentally related to the stability or anomie of an area and is not a function of nor is it basically associated with the economic characteristics of an area" (p. 59) is a surprising one for criminologists, who have traditionally regarded the correlation between delinquency and social class as one of the few criminological regularities. But Lander goes further:

> The correlation between the anomic and socio-economic factors is . . . high (.684). It provides an explanation of the fact that delinquency is so highly correlated with the socio-economic properties of a tract. The association between the factors however is statistical. The factor analysis indicates that, in Baltimore, areas characterized by

---

factors or the best predictors of the incidence of juvenile delinquency, but they appeared to be the best of those available" (1954, pp. 11–12).

[38] The seven variables used by Lander were median school years completed, median monthly rent, percentage of homes overcrowded, percentage of nonwhites, percentage of homes owner-occupied, percentage of substandard housing, and percentage of foreign-born.

instability and anomie are frequently the same districts
which are also characterized by bad housing, low rentals and
over-crowding. But the delinquency is fundamentally
related only to the anomie and not to the poor
socio-economic conditions of the tract. (p. 59)

Several writers have noted the circularity of this conclusion:[39]
delinquency is "fundamentally related" to the anomie factor
precisely because the delinquency rate is a variable which actually
constitutes it. In other words, Lander makes the mistake of
including the dependent variable (the delinquency rate—the
variable to be explained) together with the independent variables
(the variables to be used in the explanation).[40] Furthermore,
Hirschi and Selvin (1967) draw attention to the problem of
"causal order" (i.e., unless one knows which variables precede
other variables, one cannot draw causal inferences)[41] and ask
whether the variables making up the anomie factor precede or
follow those constituting the socioeconomic factor. Without
consideration of this problem, factor analysis proves inappropriate
since it treats all variables alike. One other point, which tends to
be overlooked in technical discussions of factor analysis, is the
inappropriateness of attaching the label "anomie" (which Lander
concedes is arbitrary) to the factor, since it is likely that, had
more variables been included, no such factor could have been
identified.[42]

[39] See particularly, Bordua (1958); Gordon (1967); and Hirschi and Selvin (1967).

[40] See further here, Hirschi and Selvin (1967), who argue that factor analysis
"should be used only with collections of variables on the same conceptual level—
measures of personality, indicators of socio-economic status, or forms of delinquent
behavior. Putting independent and dependent variables into the same factor analysis
can only generate confusion" (pp. 153–54).

[41] As Hirschi and Selvin (1967) put it, by way of example, "variables like age
often have such strong relations with later independent variables and with delinquency as to make the relations between these independent variables and delinquency
spurious" (p. 154).

[42] Lander's variables do not in any meaningful way reflect "anomie"; see further
Chilton (1964) and Gordon (1967). Gordon also criticizes Lander's conclusion that
delinquency is fundamentally related to the anomie of an area but not to its socioeconomic characteristics. He draws particular attention to Lander's misuse of the
technique of partial correlation, by which he artificially eliminates the influence of
some census variables by holding other related variables constant. This "partialling
fallacy" is also relevant to studies employing the Shevky-Bell framework in which
attempts have been made to hold constant the influence of individual, but related,

Despite the serious difficulties involved with the use of factor analysis in general and Lander's study in particular, researchers have not been discouraged from replicating his study. There have been two main attempts at replication and reevaluation of his findings—one by Bordua (1958) in Detroit, the other by Chilton (1964) in Indianapolis. Bordua used Lander's original seven variables and introduced two others which he considered reflected Lander's "socioeconomic" and "anomie" factors. He extracted three independent factors which he identified as "deteriorated areas of high non-white settlement," "socio-economic status," and "a poverty or social disorganization factor." The delinquency rate was fairly closely related to the first and the third, but not to the second, which suggested some support for Lander's claim that socioeconomic factors were not "fundamentally" associated with delinquency. Bordua, however, recognizing the tautological nature of Lander's anomie factor, aptly states that "anomie cannot cause delinquency. Delinquency is a species of anomie" (p. 237). Chilton attempted not only to replicate the studies of Lander and of Bordua but also to re-analyze parts of their data. Though he notes that similar factors are associated with delinquency in each of the three cities, he strongly disputes Lander's contention that socioeconomic factors are relatively unimportant in the distribution of delinquency and, as to anomie, he wryly observes that "a number of variables might be interpreted as indicators of anomie but so classifying these variables does not increase our understanding of delinquency or anomie" (p. 82).

Though much criticized, Lander's pioneering study nevertheless remains a seminal work which has provoked others to modify and refine his approach. Contemporary researchers are increasingly using multivariate techniques in the analysis of much larger numbers of crime and social variables than Lander had contemplated. Many of these studies, though conducted with considerable technical skill, betray a lack of clarity in their objectives as well as ambiguity in the interpretation of results unearthed. Since a

---

constructs. On the "partialling fallacy" generally, see Chilton (1964); Hirschi and Selvin (1967); and Gordon (1967).

growing number of researchers, both in the United States and in Great Britain, are turning to this method of urban analysis in relation to area studies of delinquency, it seems important to make some critical evaluation of research undertaken so far.

The most serious difficulty encountered by researchers has been the identification and interpretation of the factors the analysis produces. The literature is filled with examples of researchers vainly attempting to attribute sociological meaning to factors which they have succeeded without difficulty in extracting and which constitute statistical unities. In some cases, it is quite evident that the factors consist of nothing more than miscellaneous assortments of diverse variables which lack meaning. Schmid (1960), for example, included thirty-eight variables in his factor analysis but had very great difficulty in making much sense of the eight factors he extracted. His objective was to use factor analysis as a step in "determining the underlying social and demographic dimensions of crime as well as in identifying and describing crime areas" (p. 535), but it is difficult to see in what way his analysis illuminated these questions.

Two British studies similar to Schmid's have been conducted in recent years—one by Giggs (1970) in the town of Barry in Wales, the other by Brown, McCulloch, and Hiscox (1972) in a northern English town. Giggs analyzed an even greater number of variables than Schmid had used—no fewer than fifty-six in his main analysis—relating to social defects (crime, juvenile delinquency, etc.) and to "intra-urban characteristics." His aim was to "determine the basic factors in the distribution of social defects, and to describe more precisely the specific attributes of disorganised areas" (pp. 105–6). Giggs's attempts at identification of the factors is thoroughly unsatisfactory, and he becomes involved in a convoluted and circular exercise.[43] In his main analysis, no fewer than ten factors emerge, many of them highly ambiguous. More crucial than this, Giggs makes the same error as Lander (and Schmid) by including in the same analysis the dependent variables (relating to social defects) and the inde-

---

[43] Further details of my criticisms of Giggs's interpretation of his factors are given in Baldwin (1975b, pp. 217–19).

pendent variables intended to describe the attributes of "disorganised areas." The result is inevitably tautological. "The sociological concept of anomie," Giggs suggests, "seems to provide a . . . plausible explanation of the existence of disorganisation in the town's social structure" (pp. 132–33). He is arguing that "anomie," used as a synonym for "social disorganization," explains the existence of social defects, yet the indices of disorganization he uses include some of these very defects.

"Social disorganization" (criminality, divorce, etc.) explains the existence of social defects (including criminality and divorce). This circularity of argument serves to reemphasize the point that multivariate techniques should be used only after careful consideration of the objectives to be achieved.

The other main study in this group, carried out by Brown, McCulloch, and Hiscox (1972), is similarly flawed by a lack of clarity as to objectives and by results that are confused and ambiguous. Their approach is to examine the intercorrelations of thirty-five social variables (including ten relating to crime), organized according to electoral wards in a northern industrial town. As with the analyses by Schmid and Giggs, the authors fail to treat the dependent and independent variables separately and, in consequence, seem able to make little sense of the resulting correlations. Indeed, it appears that their results offer support for almost any of the main criminological theories. Citing their conclusions perhaps illustrates best the confusion in which the study is steeped:

> To demonstrate the complexity of criminological thought and the lack of a comprehensive causal theory of deviance, we can look at the correlations between types of offence and social variables from several angles.
>
> (1) "The main features associated with offences against the person appear to be rented council houses, unemployment and poverty." This could be explained in terms of anomie, working-class culture, subculture, or differential association.
>
> (2) The offences involved with drinking, which are

associated with "areas of highest unemployment and persons on social security benefit" seem to support Merton's (1957) retreatism or Cloward and Ohlin's (1960) "double failure" hypotheses.

(3) The negative correlation between owner-occupied houses and conflict with the law, as well as being the obverse side of the theories expressed in (1) above, cannot be looked at in isolation from the role of the police, white-collar crime, and interactionist theories in general. (pp. 264–65)

In other words, their study sheds no light on the theoretical issues involved. Indeed, their results, as presented, appear to support a great number of mutually incompatible theoretical stances.

This review of statistical models used in areal analysis indicates that, as a general tendency, the more technically complex the analysis becomes, the easier it is for the original objectives to become blurred or lost. If the researcher's objective is descriptive (as appears usually to be the case), much confusion and ambiguity is created by concocting concepts such as "anomie" or by introducing theoretical notions which are inappropriately examined within an areal framework.[44] Researchers using statistical methods in areal research ought not to be tempted to assume that the need for careful thought and plausible explanation has been obviated by a technically sophisticated methodology.

Since we have reached this assessment of statistical methods, it may seem surprising that colleagues and I used a similar approach in a study of crime areas in Sheffield (Baldwin and Bottoms 1976). In that study, we made use of regression analysis which we believed avoided some of the more serious pitfalls associated with techniques such as factor analysis.[45] It seemed to

[44] Some researchers have in recent years attempted to correct the theoretical aridity in the use of factor analysis, and "confirmatory" factor analysis has been used in an effort specifically to test theory. Factor analysis has been used, in other words, to study the "fit" between theoretical expectations and the data available. I am indebted to Professor James F. Short of Washington State University for drawing my attention to this point.

[45] A similar view is taken by Hirschi and Selvin (1967, pp. 156–59); Gordon (1967, 1968); and Herbert (1977).

us that there was little to be gained by including in the analysis vast numbers of variables, since earlier researchers in Britain (e.g., Robson 1969; Herbert 1970) had already found with considerable consistency that a small number of variables adequately differentiated urban subareas. The aim of urban analysis, as we saw it, was to provide categorizations of areas which are homogeneous. In pursuing this aim, the use of relatively few simple concepts which can "explain" much of the other statistical variation in the census data is a great advantage. Thus, it seemed sensible to include variables relating to three basic concepts— social class, type of housing tenure, and density of living—the sociological meanings of which were perfectly clear.[46] The ensuing regression analysis suggested marked differences in offender rates according to areas of different tenure types (rented from the council, private ownership, or privately rented) even when the basic concepts were held constant. We drew attention to the relevance of sociological concepts such as "housing class" and "socio-ecological system" and the need to relate ecological analyses of crime to a more general conflict framework.[47] Though this approach did not satisfy all our critics,[48] we took the view that the use of clearly defined concepts (derived from a small number of variables) represented something of an improvement on earlier ventures. At least we could legitimately claim to have simplified the complex and tortuous process of interpretation that other researchers had undergone.

To return to the discussion of the criminological applications of social area analysis and factorial analysis, we must, it seems, stress the fundamental sterility of each approach. Neither has yielded many new insights and, despite the immense effort expended, our knowledge of delinquency areas has been scarcely advanced. The preoccupation of most of the researchers in question appears to have been the manipulation of complex bodies

[46] After further analysis of the residual correlation matrix, a fourth concept emerged composed of variables which we argued represented an index of social disorganization; see further Baldwin and Bottoms (1976, pp. 100–103).

[47] See further Rex (1968) and Pahl (1970a, 1970b) whose work is discussed by Bottoms (1976a, pp. 21–25).

[48] See, for instance, the review by S. Damer of *The Urban Criminal* in the *British Journal of Criminology* 17 (1977): 75–77.

of statistical material, with explanation, let alone theory, almost totally neglected. Though much remains to be discovered about the nature of delinquency areas, it is unlikely, in the view of the present writer, that the continued application of such approaches will add significantly to our knowledge.

III. Promising Directions in Theory and Research

No book published in the past thirty years has stimulated, and changed the direction of, areal research as much as Oscar Newman's *Defensible Space* (1972). Newman posits a direct link between architectural design and levels of crime and vandalism. Other writers, most notably Jacobs in 1961 and Jeffery in 1971, had earlier argued along similar lines[49] and the approach harks back to some of the older and cruder forms of "architectural determinism." Newman has been criticized for somewhat grudgingly acknowledging his indebtedness to earlier writers, but he must be credited with succeeding, where others failed, in firing the public imagination and in bringing about an unusual dialogue between criminologists and members of the architectural and planning professions. His ideas, expressed in a readable if polemical style,[50] have fascinated researchers and newspaper reporters alike, and a substantial body of published research testifies to this fascination.

Newman argues that crime can be reduced by modifying physical features of the environment (and, specifically, by the maximization of "defensible space").[51] "Defensible space," says Newman, is

> a model for residential environments which inhibits crime by
> creating the physical expression of a social fabric that
> defends itself. . . . "Defensible space" is a surrogate term
> for the range of mechanisms—real and symbolic barriers,
> strongly defined areas of influence, and improved

[49] Similar statements had also been put forward by Duhl (1966); Sagalyn (1966); Angel (1968); and Luedtke (1970); see generally Harries (1974).

[50] Mawby (1977a) argues, for instance, that "Newman's writing style is predisposed towards political oratory rather than serious scientific endeavour" (p. 169).

[51] See also Newman (1973, 1976) and U.S. Department of Justice, Law Enforcement Assistance Administration (1975a).

opportunities for surveillance—that combine to bring an environment under the control of its residents. (p. 3)

This statement has been attacked by many critics. Some have noted that the empirical support which Newman adduces is much less secure than he appears to realize;[52] others have drawn attention to his disregard of criminological theory and research.[53] Though the main thrust of Newman's book is a pragmatic concern with the control of crime rather than its etiology, it seems likely that his emphasis upon physical features of housing areas will exert a growing influence on thinking about the social patterning of crime and delinquency.

Newman's ideas have proved difficult to test empirically, principally because of a lack of clarity in his concepts and the more general difficulty of setting them satisfactorily within the context of research. Nevertheless, numerous researchers in Great Britain and in the United States have produced in a matter of five or six years a considerable body of illuminating research material. Though many of the writers concerned have claimed a theoretical interest, most demonstrate a greater concern with narrow questions of policy.[54] It is not possible to discuss here in much detail the research that Newman's concept "defensible space" has provoked, but illustration may indicate its broad compass.

In England, some efforts to examine Newman's thesis have been made by researchers in Sheffield (Baldwin 1975a; Bottoms 1976b; and Mawby 1977a, 1977b) and in London by members of the Home Office Research Unit (Marshall 1976; Wilson and Sturman 1976; and Wilson 1977). Both attempts at validation are admittedly partial and tentative, yet both suggest that the defensible space concept has some limited relevance to levels of delinquency (particularly vandalism) in English housing areas.

[52] See, for instance, Bottoms (1974, 1976b); Reppetto (1976); and Mawby (1977a, 1977b).

[53] Jeffery (1977), for example, writes: "Unfortunately, most of Newman's discussion involves hardware: floor materials, fire doors, window materials, window bars and grills . . . and other hardening of the target techniques. This is not a very imaginative approach to environment-behavior interaction, though it represents the thinking of today on crime prevention" (p. 224).

[54] Clear examples of this tendency are to be found in Duffala (1976); Molumby (1976); Pyle (1976); and Wilson and Sturman (1976).

Marshall (1976), for example, argues in the following passage that the sheer number of children living in an area and their tendency to commit acts of vandalism close to their homes seem to be more important determinants of the geographical patterning of vandalism than the defensible space concept, though this is not entirely irrelevant. He writes:

> The influence of overall design . . . was not straightforward as all types of block suffered from a problem of some kind. . . . Where there were large numbers of children, all estates tended to have a vandalism problem, only moderately affected by the design of the buildings. But if the number of children is kept within a certain limit, only those buildings which are "indefensible" in Newman's terms had more vandalism, and this tended to be restricted to specific areas which are especially vulnerable. Children tend not to move far from their "home territory" to commit crime, so that their immediate environment is likely to suffer, whether design and layout factors are inducive to vandalism or not. (pp. 626–27)

Perhaps the most careful test was carried out by Mawby (1977b) in a study of telephone box vandalism. There was again some support, if weak, for Newman's thesis, in the sense that there was a relationship between levels of vandalism of particular telephone boxes and defensible space measures, but other factors (particularly the extent to which the public used the boxes) were much more closely related to vandalism. More generally, and more crudely, no relationship has been found in Sheffield between high-rise housing (where good defensible space is more difficult to attain) and levels of vandalism or delinquency.[55]

The research conducted in the United States has been more varied, but no less equivocal, than that carried out in England. Much of it has also been concerned with narrow policy implica-

[55] The high-rise estates are for the most part relatively new and their rates of vandalism and juvenile delinquency are very similar to those of other kinds of estate, built to quite different designs in the same era. The research in Sheffield suggests that, as far as delinquency is concerned, the problem remains in the older housing estates: see further, Baldwin (1975a) and Mawby (1977a).

tions—blocking off roads, erecting gate posts, improving street lighting, and the like—rather than with testing or clarifying theoretical concepts. Perhaps the strongest support for Newman comes from Brantingham and Brantingham (1975a, 1975b), whose analysis of burglary rates on a city block basis is one of the most detailed and careful in the literature. They draw on some of the results of interviews with convicted burglars conducted by Reppetto (1974) and combine them with the insights that detailed analysis at this level of refinement[56] can offer. Their general conclusion that the border blocks in city housing areas are much more vulnerable to burglary offenses than the interior blocks offers quite strong support for Newman's thesis.

Several authors have drawn attention to the problem of "displacement" of criminal activity through adoption of architectural design techniques, viz., that criminal activity may simply be diverted to other places or into different channels, from, say, residential burglary into street crimes.[57] The displacement problem raises serious difficulties for research. If such diversion occurs, it is hard to see how even the most careful researcher could measure it. Even the narrow question of the effectiveness of control strategies can, then, only be empirically tested in a limited and artificial way. Physical design is merely one factor (and probably a relatively minor one) in crime prevention. A recognition of this would encourage the incorporation of other aspects of general criminological theory into Newman's presentation.[58] It is clear nonetheless that Newman has provided a welcome stimulus to areal research. Downes (1976) succinctly summarizes Newman's contribution:

> Vandalism is the supreme expression of disregard for the
> cheap facilities, the poor layouts, the lack of scope for play,
> the isolation and anonymity of so many new developments.

[56] The populations of the city blocks in their sample are a mere 2 percent of the populations of census tracts, which are the most commonly used areal units.

[57] As Nieberg (1974) puts it, "Creating ramparts, battlements, parapets and walls in high-crime areas may deter criminal attacks in a specific area, but it leaves untouched the real social causes of criminal behaviour and may . . . disperse bad actors into secret nooks and crannies elsewhere" (p. 42).

[58] A much more elaborate theoretical statement is given by Jeffery (1977).

Whether or not Oscar Newman is right to lay such stress on the "defensible space" aspect of design, he has coined a vivid metaphor for the pitting of environment against social forms. (p. 53)

If Newman has brought about something of a revolution in areal research, we should be aware that the new sources of information about levels of crime, derived from victimization and self-reported delinquency studies, raise the serious possibility that our understanding of the nature of delinquency areas may be no more than rudimentary. The national studies of criminal victimization, funded by the Law Enforcement Assistance Administration of the U.S. Department of Justice[59] and conducted throughout the United States over the past decade, suggest that the continued use of official measures of delinquency in areal research is at least questionable. The only English study of this kind (Sparks, Genn, and Dodd 1977) strongly supports the same conclusion. When one introduces the more complex and disparate information from the great number of studies of self-reported delinquency,[60] one begins to wonder whether entirely new definitions of delinquency areas are now required. Though, to my knowledge, no systematic attempt has so far been made to use this new information on an areal basis,[61] the implications for areal research are apparent. It is misleading to try to define delinquency areas in any rigid manner since the differences between these and other areas of the city are, it appears, exaggerated by official measures of crime. We now know that only a small and unrepresentative fraction of criminal violations comes to the notice of the police. Though this is less true of serious criminal offenses than of minor ones, it would be mistaken, in my view, to regard offenses which are reported to the police as more

[59] See particularly, Ennis (1967); U.S. Department of Justice, Law Enforcement Assistance Administration (1974, 1975b, 1977a, 1977b); and Skogan (1976).

[60] Conducting such studies has been one of the major preoccupations of postwar criminology though, as was noted earlier in this essay, the results taken as a whole present a somewhat ambivalent picture. Excellent reviews of this literature are given in Hood and Sparks (1970) and by Empey (1978).

[61] This is now being attempted in Sheffield: see Bottoms (1976b) and Mawby (1977b).

than an extremely crude index of all offenses committed in the community. Indeed, understanding the process by which certain offenses are excluded at the reporting and recording stages may ultimately prove a more sociologically rewarding exercise than analyzing the minority of offenses that are included among the official crime statistics.

There is, however, one fundamental point which is often overlooked when alternative sources of data are discussed. Whatever doubts might be raised about the appropriateness of using official measures of crime in areal research, it is important to bear in mind that the official measures create the reality of delinquency areas; in other words, to live in an area that has been labeled a problem area has consequences of its own, whether the label is justifiably attached or not. For those who have to live there, it *is* a problem area if only because it has been so defined and is being treated as such. This is a good reason for studying such areas, whatever conclusion one draws about the validity of official crime measures. Even if official crime measures are valueless, we need to know more about how adverse reputations develop and change, and how they are reinforced or resisted by those subject to them. There are few detailed observational studies of the kind so sensitively conducted in the heyday of Chicago sociology and latterly resurrected in Chicago by Gerald Suttles (1968). Studies in Great Britain suggest ways in which the stereotypical responses to delinquency areas on the part of the socially powerful can reinforce, or even create, familiar delinquency spirals.[62] Such descriptions of the "natural history" of delinquency areas, particularly when informed by an appreciation of the residents' own construction of the reality of life in the area, can reveal important new insights which more traditional "ecological" approaches cannot possibly provide.

With the dawn of the new criminology, it is timely to argue in favor of a greater awareness of the politics of delinquency definitions and to call for research which will illuminate the

[62] See particularly Armstrong and Wilson (1973); Damer (1974); and Gill (1976, 1977).

complex and subtle social processes which operate to create delinquency areas. There is no doubt in my view that efforts expended in that direction will ultimately produce more real knowledge about such areas than will the continued amassing of complex statistical correlations.

REFERENCES

Alihan, M. A. 1938. *Social Ecology: A Critical Analysis*. New York: Columbia University Press.
Angel, S. 1968. *Discouraging Crime through City Planning*. Working Paper No. 75. Berkeley, Calif.: University of California.
Armstrong, D., and M. Wilson. 1973. "City Politics and Deviancy Amplification." In *Politics and Deviance*, ed. I. Taylor and L. Taylor. Harmondsworth: Penguin.
Bagley, C. 1965. "Juvenile Delinquency in Exeter: An Ecological and Comparative Study," *Urban Studies* 2:33–50.
Bagot, J. H. 1941. *Juvenile Delinquency*. London: Cape.
Baldwin, John. 1974a. "Problem Housing Estates—Perceptions of Tenants, City Officials and Criminologists," *Social and Economic Administration* 8:116–35.
————. 1974b. "Social Area Analysis and Studies of Delinquency," *Social Science Research* 3:151–68.
————. 1975a. "Urban Criminality and the 'Problem' Estate," *Local Government Studies* 1:12–20.
————. 1975b. "British Areal Studies of Crime: An Assessment," *British Journal of Criminology* 15:211–27.
Baldwin, John, and A. E. Bottoms. 1976. *The Urban Criminal*. London: Tavistock.
Becker, Howard S. 1963. *Outsiders: Studies in the Sociology of Deviance*. New York: Free Press.
————. 1964. *The Other Side*. New York: Free Press.
Black, Donald J., and A. J. Reiss. 1970. "Police Control of Juveniles," *American Sociological Review* 35:63–77.
Blalock, H. M. 1960. *Social Statistics*. New York: McGraw-Hill.
Boggs, S. L. 1965. "Urban Crime Patterns," *American Sociological Review* 30:899–908.
Booth, A., D. R. Johnson, and H. M. Choldin. 1977. "Correlates of City Crime Rates: Victimization Surveys versus Official Statistics," *Social Problems* 25:187–97.

Bordua, David J. 1958. "Juvenile Delinquency and 'Anomie': An Attempt at Replication," *Social Problems* 6:230–38.

Bottoms, Anthony E. 1974. Review of *Defensible Space, British Journal of Criminology* 14:203–6.

———. 1976a. "Criminology and Urban Sociology: Introductory Essay." In *The Urban Criminal*, by J. Baldwin and A. E. Bottoms. London: Tavistock.

———. 1976b. "Crime in a City," *New Society* 8 Apr.: 64–66.

Brantingham, P. J., and P. L. Brantingham. 1975a. "The Spatial Patterning of Burglary," *Howard Journal* 14:11–23.

———. 1975b. "Residential Burglary and Urban Form," *Urban Studies* 12:273–84.

Brantingham, P. J., D. A. Dyreson, and P. L. Brantingham. 1976. "Crime Seen through a Cone of Resolution," *American Behavioral Scientist* 20:261–73.

Brown, M. J., J. W. McCulloch, and J. Hiscox. 1972. "Criminal Offenses in an Urban Area and Their Associated Social Variables," *British Journal of Criminology* 12:250–68.

Burgess, Ernst W. 1925. "The Growth of the City: An Introduction to a Research Project." In *The City*, by R. E. Park, E. W. Burgess, and R. D. McKenzie. Chicago: University of Chicago Press.

Byrne, D. S. 1974. *Problem Families: A Housing Lumpenproletariat.* Working Paper in Sociology, No. 5. Durham, England: University of Durham.

Chevalier, L. 1958. *Classes laborieuses et classes dangéreuses à Paris pendant la première moitié du XIXᵉ siècle.* Paris: Librairie Plon.

Chilton, R. J. 1964. "Continuity in Delinquency Area Research: A Comparison of Studies for Baltimore, Detroit and Indianapolis," *American Sociological Review* 29:71–83.

Cicourel, Aaron V. 1968. *The Social Organization of Juvenile Justice.* New York: Wiley.

Cloward, Richard A., and L. E. Ohlin. 1960. *Delinquency and Opportunity.* Chicago: Free Press.

Damer, S. 1974. "Wine Alley: The Sociology of a Dreadful Enclosure," *Sociological Review* 22:221–48.

Downes, D. 1976. "Interpreting Delinquency." In *Signs of Trouble: Aspects of Delinquency*, by L. Taylor, A. Morris, and D. Downes. London: B.B.C. Publications.

Duffala, D. C. 1976. "Convenience Stores, Armed Robbery and Physical Environmental Features," *American Behavioral Scientist* 20:227–46.

Duhl, L. J. 1966. "The Possibilities of Minimizing Crime-Inducing Factors by the Design and Construction of City Areas." President's Commission on Law Enforcement and Administration of Justice, *Na-*

tional Symposium on Science and the Administration of Justice. Washington, D.C.: U.S. Government Printing Office.

Duncan, O. D. 1955. Review of *Social Area Analysis, American Journal of Sociology* 61:84–85.

Empey, LaMar. 1978. *American Delinquency.* Homewood, Ill.: Dorsey Press.

Ennis, P. H. 1967. "Criminal Victimization in the United States: A Report of a National Survey." President's Commission on Law Enforcement and the Administration of Justice, *Field Surveys II.* Washington, D.C.: U.S. Government Printing Office.

Faris, R. E. L. 1967. *Chicago Sociology, 1920–1932.* Chicago: University of Chicago Press.

Ferguson, T. 1952. *The Young Delinquent in His Social Setting.* London: Oxford University Press.

Giggs, J. A. 1970. "The Socially Disorganised Areas of Barry: A Multivariate Analysis." In *Urban Essays,* ed. H. Carter and W. K. D. Davies. London: Longmans.

Gill, O. 1976. "Urban Stereotypes and Delinquent Incidents." *British Journal of Criminology* 16:321–36.

———. 1977. *Luke Street: Housing Policy, Conflict and the Creation of the Delinquency Area.* London: Macmillan.

Gold, M. 1970. *Delinquent Behavior in an American City.* Belmont, Calif.: Brooks Cole.

Goldberg, E. M., and S. L. Morrison. 1963. "Schizophrenia and Social Class," *British Journal of Psychiatry* 109:785–802.

Gordon, R. A. 1967. "Issues in the Ecological Study of Delinquency," *American Sociological Review* 32:927–44.

———. 1968. "Issues in Multiple Regression," *American Journal of Sociology* 73:592–616.

Guerry, A. M. 1833. *Essai sur la statistique morale de la France.* Paris: Crochard.

Harries, K. D. 1974. *The Geography of Crime and Justice.* New York: McGraw-Hill.

Herbert, D. T. 1968. "Principal Components Analysis and British Studies of Urban-Social Structure," *Professional Geographer* 20:280–83.

———. 1970. "Principal Components Analysis and Urban Social Structure: A Study of Cardiff and Swansea." In *Urban Essays,* ed. H. Carter and W. K. D. Davies. London: Longmans.

———. 1975. "Urban Deprivation: Definition, Measurement and Spatial Qualities," *Geographical Journal* 141:362–72.

———. 1977. "Crime, Delinquency and the Urban Environment," *Progress in Human Geography* 1:208–39.

Hirschi, Travis, and H. C. Selvin. 1967. *Delinquency Research.* New York: Free Press.

Holzinger, K. J., and H. H. Harman. 1941. *Factor Analysis: A Synthesis of Factorial Methods.* Chicago: University of Chicago Press.

Hood, Roger, and R. Sparks. 1970. *Key Issues in Criminology.* London: Weidenfeld & Nicolson.

Jacobs, Jane. 1961. *The Death and Life of Great American Cities.* New York: Random House.

Jeffery, C. R. 1977. *Crime Prevention through Environmental Design.* Rev. ed. Beverly Hills, Calif.: Sage. (Original ed. pub. 1971.)

Jones, H. 1958. "Approaches to an Ecological Study," *British Journal of Delinquency* 8:277–93.

Kerr, M. 1958. *The People of Ship Street.* London: Routledge & Kegan Paul.

Kitsuse, J. I., and A. K. Cicourel. 1963. "A Note on the Use of Official Statistics," *Social Problems* 11:131–39.

Kobrin, Solomon. 1959. "The Chicago Area Project: A 25-year Assessment," *Annals of American Academy of Political and Social Science* 322: 20–29.

Lander, B. 1954. *Towards an Understanding of Juvenile Delinquency.* New York: Columbia University Press.

Levin, Y., and A. Lindesmith. 1937. "English Ecology and Criminology of the Past Century," *Journal of Criminal Law, Criminology and Police Science* 27:801–16.

Luedtke, G. 1970. *Crime and the Physical City: Neighborhood Design Techniques for Crime Prevention.* Springfield, Va.: National Technical Information Service.

Mabry, J. H. 1958. "Census Tract Variation in Urban Research," *American Sociological Review* 23:193–96.

Mannheim, Hermann. 1965. *Comparative Criminology.* London: Routledge & Kegan Paul.

Marshall, A. 1976. "Vandalism: The Seeds of Destruction," *New Society* 17 June:625–27.

Maule, H. G., and F. M. Martin. 1956. "Social and Psychological Aspects of Rehousing," *Advancement of Science* 12:443–53.

Mawby, R. I. 1977a. "Defensible Space: A Theoretical and Empirical Appraisal," *Urban Studies* 14:169–79.

———. 1977b. "Kiosk Vandalism: A Sheffield Study," *British Journal of Criminology* 17:30–46.

Mayhew, H. 1861. *London Labour and the London Poor.* London: Griffin, Bohn.

Mays, J. B. 1954. *Growing Up in the City.* Liverpool: Liverpool University Press.

Merton, Robert K. 1957. *Social Theory and Social Structure.* Rev. ed. New York: Free Press.

Molumby, T. 1976. "Patterns of Crime in a University Housing Project," *American Behavioral Scientist* 20:247–59.

Monkkonen, Eric H. 1975. *The Dangerous Class: Crime and Poverty in Columbus, Ohio, 1860–1885.* Cambridge, Mass.: Harvard University Press.

Morris, Terence P. 1957. *The Criminal Area: A Study in Social Ecology.* London: Routledge & Kegan Paul.

Myers, J. K. 1954. "Note on the Homogeneity of Census Tracts," *Social Forces* 32:364–66.

Newman, Oscar. 1972. *Defensible Space.* London: Architectural Press.

———. 1973. *Architectural Design for Crime Prevention.* Washington, D.C.: U.S. Government Printing Office.

———. 1976. *Design Guidelines for Creating Defensible Space.* Washington, D.C.: U.S. Government Printing Office.

Nieburg, H. L. 1974. "Crime Prevention by Urban Design," *Society* 12:41–47.

Pahl, R. E. 1970a. *Patterns of Urban Life.* London: Longmans.

———. 1970b. *Whose City?* London: Longmans.

Parkin, D., P. Kenning, and J. Wilder. 1971. *Mental Illness in a Northern City.* London: Psychiatric Rehabilitation Association.

Piliavin, I., and S. Briar. 1964. "Police Encounters with Juveniles," *American Journal of Sociology* 70:206–14.

Polk, K. 1957. "Juvenile Delinquency and Social Areas," *Social Problems* 5:214–17.

———. 1967. "Urban Social Areas and Delinquency," *Social Problems* 14:320–25.

Pyle, G. F. 1976. "Spatial and Temporal Aspects of Crime in Cleveland, Ohio," *American Behavioral Scientist* 20:175–98.

Quételet, A. L. J. 1835. *Essai de physique sociale.* Paris.

Quinney, Richard. 1964. "Crime, Delinquency and Social Areas," *Journal of Research in Crime and Delinquency* 1:149–54.

Radzinowicz, Leon. 1966. *Ideology and Crime.* London: Heinemann.

Reppetto, T. A. 1974. *Residential Crime.* Cambridge, Mass.: Ballinger.

———. 1976. "Crime Prevention through Environmental Policy: A Critique," *American Behavioral Scientist* 20:275–88.

Rex, J. 1968. "The Sociology of a Zone in Transition." In *Readings in Urban Sociology,* ed. R. E. Pahl, Oxford: Pergamon.

Robinson, W. S. 1950. "Ecological Correlations and the Behavior of Individuals," *American Sociological Review* 15:351–57.

Robison, S. M. 1936. *Can Delinquency Be Measured?* New York: Columbia University Press.

Robson, B. T. 1969. *Urban Analysis: A Study of City Structure*. Cambridge: Cambridge University Press.

Sagalyn, A. 1966. "Take the Opportunity Out of Crime." President's Commission on Law Enforcement and the Administration of Justice, *National Symposium on Science and Administration of Justice*. Washington, D.C.: U.S. Government Printing Office.

Schmid, C. F. 1960. "Urban Crime Areas," *American Sociological Review* 25:527–54, 655–78.

Shaw, Clifford R. 1929. *Delinquency Areas*. Chicago: University of Chicago Press.

————. 1930. *The Jack Roller*. Chicago: University of Chicago Press.

Shaw, C. R., and H. D. McKay. 1931. *Social Factors in Juvenile Delinquency*. Washington, D.C.: U.S. Government Printing Office.

————. 1942. *Juvenile Delinquency and Urban Areas*. Chicago: University of Chicago Press.

Shevky, E., and W. Bell. 1955. *Social Area Analysis: Theory, Illustrative Application and Computational Procedures*. Stanford: Stanford University Press.

Shevky, E., and M. Williams. 1949. *The Social Areas of Los Angeles: Analysis and Typology*. Berkeley, Calif.: University of California Press.

Skogan, Wesley G. 1976. *Sample Surveys of the Victims of Crime*. Cambridge, Mass.: Ballinger.

Snodgrass, J. 1976a. "Clifford R. Shaw and Henry D. McKay: Chicago Criminologists," *British Journal of Criminology* 16:1–19.

————. 1976b. "Bibliography of and on Shaw and McKay," *British Journal of Criminology* 16:289–93.

Sparks, Richard F., H. G. Genn, and D. J. Dodd. 1977. *Surveying Victims: A Study of the Measurement of Criminal Victimization*. New York: Wiley.

Spinley, B. M. 1953. *The Deprived and the Privileged*. London: Routledge & Kegan Paul.

Suttles, Gerald D. 1968. *The Social Order of the Slum*. Chicago: University of Chicago Press.

Taft, D. R. 1933. "Testing the Selective Influence of Areas of Delinquency," *American Journal of Sociology* 38:699–712.

Taylor, Ian, P. Walton, and J. Young. 1973. *The New Criminology*. London: Routledge & Kegan Paul.

Timms, D. W. G. 1971. *The Urban Mosaic: Towards a Theory of Residential Differentiation*. Cambridge: Cambridge University Press.

U.S. Department of Justice, Law Enforcement Assistance Administration. 1974. *Crimes and Victims*. Washington, D.C.: U.S. Government Printing Office.

———. 1975a. *Policy Development Seminar on Architecture, Design and Criminal Justice.* Washington, D.C.: U.S. Government Printing Office.

———. 1975b. *Criminal Victimization Surveys in 13 American Cities.* Washington, D.C.: U.S. Government Printing Office.

———. 1977a. *Criminal Victimization in the United States: A Comparison of 1975 and 1976 Findings.* Washington, D.C.: U.S. Government Printing Office.

———. 1977b. *Criminal Victimization in the United States 1975.* Washington, D.C.· U.S. Government Printing Office.

Willie, C. V. 1967. "The Relative Contribution of Family Status and Economic Status to Juvenile Delinquency," *Social Problems* 14:326–35.

Wilson, R., 1963. *Difficult Housing Estates.* London: Tavistock.

Wilson, S. 1977. "Vandalism and Design," *Architects Journal* 26 Oct.: 795–98.

Wilson, S., and A. Sturman. 1976. "Vandalism Research Aimed at Specific Remedies," *Municipal Engineering* 7 May:705–13.

Wirth, L. 1938. "Urbanism as a Way of Life," *American Journal of Sociology* 44:1–24.

Franklin E. Zimring

American Youth Violence: Issues and Trends

ABSTRACT

Census and arrest data suggest that all forms of violent youth crime
increased more than the youth population during the 1960s. Since
1970, however, per capita rates of youth homicide and rape have
been stable as measured by arrest trends. Robbery by young
offenders in 1977 was close to the per capita rate in 1970. Only
the heterogeneous crime of aggravated assault has increased
significantly through the 1970s, and this increase may be a result
of different patterns of police classification and reporting. Recent
studies of youth crime have produced insufficient information on
the concentration, predictability, and responsiveness to sanctions
of youth violence. The data collected to date are far more ambiguous
than has been acknowledged in the current debates about "cracking
down" on youth violence or identifying and isolating "hard core"
or career adolescent offenders.

In recent years, violent crimes committed by young offenders
have become a focal point for public and political debate about
crime and criminal justice policy. Of course, the problem is not
in any sense novel or recent in origin. Presidential commissions
and daily tabloids have long viewed serious crime by the young
as a problem requiring attention and control (President's Commission on Law Enforcement and Administration of Justice 1967).
But since the early 1970s, the violent young offender has moved

Franklin E. Zimring is Professor of Law and Director, Center for Studies in
Criminal Justice, University of Chicago Law School.

Fred Ackerson, a second-year student at the University of Chicago Law School,
provided able and energetic research assistance in the preparation of this essay.
Albert Reiss, Michael Tonry, Ted Gurr, Sheldon Messinger, and Norval Morris were
kind enough to comment on an earlier draft.

steadily up the list of public concerns about crime until it is fair to characterize youth violence as a central theme of the politics of crime control in 1979.

Evidence for this last assertion comes from the multiplicity of books (Boland and Wilson 1978; Strasburg 1978; Zimring 1978), media coverage,[1] and legislative proposals[2] that have emerged since the mid-seventies. The new notoriety of youth violence has already shifted discussions of juvenile justice reform from single-minded efforts to reduce overintervention in the lives of status offenders to acrimonious debate about appropriate responses to serious youth crime. The juvenile court's announced tradition of solicitous concern for its clientele is being tempered by the felt public need to deal with the predatory young. Thus, since 1976, New York's Family Court has had within its jurisdiction a category of "designated felons" for which extended terms of custodial confinement may be imposed upon adjudication of delinquency.[3] The dissonant ring of the conjunction of such terms as "Family Court" and "designated felon" is neither superficial nor solely linguistic. Serious violence by young

---

[1] See, e.g., "The Youth Crime Plague," *Time*, 11 July 1977, pp. 18–30; "Beyond the Teen-Age Gun," *New York Times*, editorial, 28 June 1978, p. 30; American Broadcasting Company, "Youth Terror: The View from behind the Gun," television documentary presented 28 June 1978.

[2] A New York state law which took effect in September 1978 lowers the age of criminal responsibility to 13 years for first degree murder, kidnapping, arson, assault, manslaughter, rape, sodomy, and robbery; second degree murder, kidnapping, and arson; attempted murder, kidnapping, and arson. The age of criminal responsibility is 14 years for second degree robbery and assault when the juvenile has previously committed one of the enumerated felonies. When a juvenile has committed two prior felonies, he becomes criminally responsible for any felony committed after age 7. The criminal responsibility accorded these "designated felony acts" is the penalty of "restrictive placement" of the juvenile, initially in a secure facility. The court may order restrictive placement after considering the background and best interests of the juvenile, the circumstances of the offense (including injuries inflicted), the need for community protection, and the age and physical condition of the victim. More severe penalties are provided for murder, kidnapping, arson, and repeated offenses; restrictive placement is mandatory for a designated felony offense in which the victim is 62 or more years of age and sustains "serious physical injury." N.Y. Jud. Law §§712, 753(a)(1978). Pennsylvania provides that juvenile felons 14 years and older may be transferred from the juvenile to the criminal courts if "the child is not amenable to treatment" through juvenile facilities and "the interests of the community require that the child be placed under legal restraint or discipline or that the offense is one which would carry a sentence of more than three years if committed by an adult." 11 Pa. Cons. Stat. Ann. §50-325 (1972)(Purdon).

[3] N.Y.S.L. 1976, c. 878, §3 (1976).

offenders represents a substantial threat to the institutional credibility and to the mission of the contemporary Juvenile Court (Zimring 1978, chap. 5). Acts of violence committed by the young produce the worst conflicts between protecting young offenders and defending society that the legal system is likely to confront. Thus, the incidence and control of youth violence are important topics in their own right. Equally significant, the changing perceived importance of youth violence may have a broader impact on the treatment of young offenders in the legal system.

This essay reviews recent trends in youth violence as reported in police statistics and criminological studies of various youth populations. Section I discusses the uses and limits of official statistics on the four standard violent offenses collected by the Uniform Crime Reporting Program, and the utility of the violent offense index that is derived from adding these four offenses together. My reading of these official statistics suggests that the dramatic increase in youth violence during the 1960s has been followed in the 1970s by a period of relative stability in the rate of three of the four violent offenses. The single exception to this moderating pattern—aggravated assault—shows large increases in the 1970s, but deaths from youth assault are stable. For that reason, it can be argued that changes in reporting practices may have influenced the statistics on assault and the entire violence index.

Section II discusses the supplementary methods used to measure youth violence. While much of this supplementary work is promising, police statistics are, and will remain, the primary source of information on the incidence and distribution of serious youth violence. Refinement and reform of official reporting is thus a necessity.

Section III addresses the uses that are made of currently available data in relation to policy issues relating to social control of the violent young offender. Gaps in current knowledge are identified, and some suggestions for further research are put forward.

This essay is by no means a comprehensive treatment of youth violence. The following pages do not address current debate about the etiology of violent criminality or trends in the equally important and volatile area of youth corrections. In thus truncating what might be considered the "front" and "back" ends of a complex area of human behavior I yield important topics to other volumes and to other authors.

Two further preliminary considerations merit mention. This essay was solicited as a review of juvenile violence. In a survey of national patterns, the term "juvenile violence" may not be meaningless, but it certainly may be misleading. The maximum age for juvenile court jurisdiction varies among American states from an offender's sixteenth birthday in New York and Vermont to the nineteenth birthday in recent Wyoming legislation.[4] More serious violent crimes are committed by individuals *between* these ages than by the total population under age sixteen.[5] The variance and the arbitrariness of the legal boundary for juvenile court jurisdiction makes the concept of juvenile violence a singularly unhelpful criminological tool. To use an extreme example, reduction of the maximum age of juvenile court delinquency jurisdiction to the tenth birthday would abolish the problem of "juvenile violence" without any noticeable contribution to either criminological theory or social welfare. For that reason, this essay discusses the incidence of violent crime between ages 13 and 20, a period that encompasses the beginnings of violent careers in all but the most unusual cases and continues through to well beyond the typical maximum age of juvenile court involvement.

A second preliminary caution is necessary in relation to the types of violent acts that are the focus here. As Paul Strasburg has pointed out, dictionary definitions of violence are quite broad, typically including "rough or injurious physical force, action or treatment" (1978, p. 3). My focus is narrower, encompassing the four index offense categories thought by police and public to constitute violent crime—homicide, rape, aggravated assault, and

[4] Wyoming Statutes §14-155, 411 (1976). For a national survey of jurisdictional age see Zimring 1978, pp. 45–46.

[5] In 1975 there were 68,928 arrests for violent crimes (murder, forcible rape, robbery, aggravated assault) of offenders aged 16–18 compared to 40,946 arrests of offenders under 16 (U.S. Dept. of Justice, FBI 1975, table 36).

robbery. Within these offense categories, special emphasis will be accorded to acts of violence which generate substantial risks of death or serious bodily injury. The offenses surveyed do not exhaust the potential definition of violence. Vandalism, an offense which is almost the exclusive province of the young, often contains elements of threat or intimidation and is excluded from this discussion, just as it is excluded from most of the literature on youth violence under scrutiny.[6] Traffic offenses, perhaps the single most lethal form of adolescent crime, are also excluded from the data upon which this review is based.[7] The absence of youthful traffic "violence" from the public discussion of youth crime reflects a general tendency in American society to regard dangerous driving as normal and the risks associated with traffic as essentially noncriminal. Whether this omission reflects a public perception of the lack of intention to injure or American equanimity about the risks of driving, or both, is beyond the scope of this discussion.

But it is important to note that, in narrowing the emphasis of this essay to those offenses publicly perceived as most serious, the biases reflected in public perception will influence not only the behaviors selected for analysis but also some of the apparent conclusions one might draw about violent youth criminality. Crimes of prey, such as robbery, are concentrated in urban areas, and the offender population is disproportionately composed of minority males. Lethal (and criminal) traffic "violence" is more widely distributed across the youth population.[8] An analysis which focuses on the former will show much more substantial urban, race, and class concentration than would result from a broader definition of violent criminality. As is true in the debate

[6] In 1975, 65 percent of the 175,865 reported vandalism arrests were of youths under 18; 38 percent were of youths under 15 (U.S. Dept. of Justice, FBI 1975, table 36).

[7] Of 55,511 motor vehicle accident deaths in 1973, 9,309 (17 percent) were fatalities in the 15–19-year age group (U.S. Dept. of Health, Education, and Welfare 1975, table 4-2).

[8] Measuring "traffic violence" by resulting fatalities, we find a race and geographic distribution similar to that of the national population. In 1973, 86 percent of auto accident fatalities were white and 58 percent occurred in non-urban areas (U.S. Dept. of Health, Education, and Welfare 1975, tables 4-2 and 7-9).

between those who wish to focus on "street crime" and those who point out the harm and more substantial distribution of some white-collar crimes, there is no single focus of inquiry that is obviously preferable in analyzing behavior as heterogeneous as violations of the criminal law.

I. Patterns and Trends in Youth Violence: Official Statistics

However one chooses to measure, crime in the United States is predominantly the province of the young. Males between the ages of 13 and 20 comprise about 9 percent of the population but account for more than half of all property crime arrests and more than a third of all arrests for offenses typically regarded as involving violence. While such arrest statistics may be a biased sample of offenses, they are an important data set and deserve detailed consideration. Figure 1, using 1975 statistics, contrasts the age concentration of arrests for index property offenses

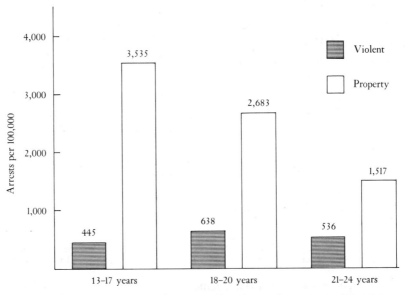

Fig. 1. Arrest rates by age for violent and property offenses, 1975. The violent offenses included are homicide, forcible rape, robbery, and aggravated assault. The property offenses are burglary, larceny-theft, and motor vehicle theft. Sources: U.S. Department of Justice, Federal Bureau of Investigation, *Uniform Crime Reports, 1975;* U.S. Department of Commerce, Bureau of the Census, *Current Population Reports,* Series P-25, No. 643 (January 1977).

(burglary, larceny, auto theft) with arrests for violent crime. Property crimes are concentrated earlier in the adolescent years, while the aggregate category of crimes of violence peaks during ages 18–20. But this is too rough a comparison: a single category, "violent crime," is too heterogeneous for informed analysis. Public and legislative concern about violent crimes committed by young people tends to crystallize around well-publicized and unrepresentative episodes of violent crime committed by young offenders.

Any case that makes the front page of the *New York Times* is almost certainly unrepresentative of the typical violent crime or violent offender. Homicide and rape are candidates for front-page treatment and public alarm, particularly where the offender is young and the victim is aged, vulnerable, or well known.[9] Yet, 90 percent of all youth arrests for crimes classified by the FBI as violent are for robbery and aggravated assault. Robberies range from unarmed schoolyard extortions through armed, life-threatening, predatory confrontations. Most robberies by young adolescent offenders tend to fall toward the less serious end of the scale, although precise statistics are not available. Similarly, aggravated assault as defined by the police varies from fistfights through shootings, carrying vastly different death risks and policy implications.

Figure 2 attempts to carry the analysis one step forward by separately considering the inevitably serious offenses of homicide and forcible rape and the more heterogeneous high-volume offenses of violence, using arrest statistics to reflect age-specific patterns of violent criminality. Arrests for homicide and rape are more frequent among 18-, 19-, and 20-year-olds than among the entire under-18 population, even though youths aged 13–17 constitute a substantially higher population at risk. The 18–20-year age group also experiences higher *rates* of arrests for the "heterogeneous" offenses of robbery and aggravated assault, but the *number* of under-18 arrests for these offenses exceeds the

[9] See, e.g., "Boy, 15, Who Killed 2 and Tried to Kill a Third, is Given 5 Years," *New York Times*, 29 June 1978, p. 1; "Carey, in Shift, Backs Trial in Adult Court for Some Juveniles," *New York Times*, 30 June 1978, p. 1.

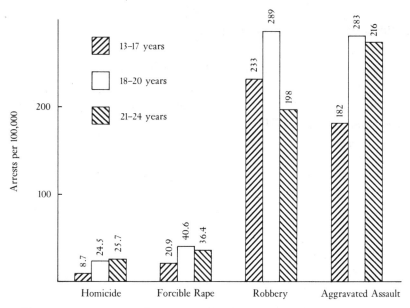

Fig. 2. Arrest rates by age for homicide, forcible rape, robbery, aggravated assault, 1975. Sources: U.S. Department of Justice, Federal Bureau of Investigation, *Uniform Crime Reports, 1975;* U.S. Department of Commerce, Bureau of the Census, *Current Population Reports*, Series P-25, No. 643 (January 1977).

absolute number of 18–20-year-old arrests; and the youth share of total arrests is thus more substantial.[10]

Two important conclusions can be drawn from these data. First, where the offense category is extremely serious, the number of under-18 arrests is small, at least in relative terms. Second, the bulk of adolescent arrests for crimes of violence, particularly in the under-18 category, are in the two classes of police-defined violence where the label of the arrest tells us relatively little about the degree of seriousness of the offense. For this reason, our ability to draw confident conclusions about the seriousness of youth violence over time or in comparing different areas on the basis of official statistics is quite limited as long as we deal with aggregated totals dominated by heterogeneous offenses (Strasburg 1978, pp. 4–5).

[10] While 18–20-year-olds had a higher arrest rate, the under-18 population had more total arrests for robbery and aggravated assault in 1975. See Appendix, table A.

A. Homicide and Rape

Table 1 examines arrest patterns for the two "homogeneous" serious offenses of violence over time for the period 1960 through 1977. While these official arrest statistics are hardly an ideal method of measuring youth violence, age-specific arrest statistics can serve as limited indicators in homogeneously serious offenses with relatively high clearance rates. With respect to homicide, youth arrest rates increased dramatically during the 1960s, leveled off from 1970 through 1975, and have since declined. If arrest rates are a reliable guide, persons under 21 were responsible for 18 percent of intentional homicide in 1960 and 25 percent of criminal homicide reported by the police in 1975. This is, however, an overestimate, because younger offenders are far more frequently arrested in groups and thus tend to have a higher arrest-to-crime ratio than other age categories. In Philadelphia, for example, we found that more than *two* offenders under 18 were

TABLE 1

Trends in Homicide and Forcible Rape Arrests for Offenders Aged 13–20, 1960–77

| | Estimated Arrests per 100,000 | |
	Homicide*	Forcible Rape
1960	7.6	24.0
1970	14.0	28.0
Change (1960–70)	84%	17%
1975	14.6	28.3
Change (1970–75)	4%	1%
1977	13.4	28.3
Change (1975–77)	−8%	. . .

* Homicide here includes murder and non-negligent manslaughter.

Sources: U.S. Department of Justice, Federal Bureau of Investigation, *Uniform Crime Reports, 1960, 1970, 1975, 1977;* U.S. Department of Commerce, Bureau of the Census, *Characteristics of the Population: United States Summary* (1960, 1970); U.S. Department of Commerce, Bureau of the Census, *Current Population Reports*, Series P-25, No. 643 (January 1977) and No. 541 (February 1975).

arrested for every *one* homicide attributed to this group.[11] In 1975, age-specific rates of homicide as measured by arrest increase sharply from very low levels in the earlier teens—a total of 142 arrests for 13- and 14-year-olds nationwide in 1975—to rates typical of young adults in the age categories of 18, 19, and 20.[12]

The statistics on rape arrests suggest concentration of offenses in the older teen years, with 17-, 18-, and 19-year-olds arrested at rates that are approximately three times those of the age group 13–15.[13] The arrest rate per 100,000 at risk for rape rose modestly during the 1960s and has been stable through the 1970s. For these two serious offenses of violence, the offense rate under 18 is modest when compared with any other form of youth criminality, and while the 1960–70 growth rate in homicide is substantial, it was growth from a low base. The homicide arrest rate for young adults (ages 21–24) was twice the youth rate in 1975, and this probably understates the difference in offenses.[14] Forcible rape, with a higher base rate, experienced more modest relative growth during the period.

The specific rates of homicide and rape arrests reported in table 1 are important only as rough indicators of trends: there is no magic significance to the fact that the number of arrested young people within the FBI's sample of reporting agencies works out to a 14.1 per 100,000 rate in 1975 when compared with the presumed population aged 13–20 during the same year in those areas. In any discussion of "juvenile" or "youth" violence, the specific rate estimate for 1975 would almost double if the arrest rate per 100,000 males were separately reported,[15] and could be increased even more substantially if an estimated

[11] Unpublished data collected by Joel Eigen (1977). Earlier published data can be found in Zimring, Eigen, and O'Malley 1976.

[12] In 1975 there were 2,576 homicide arrests in the 18–20-year age group and 2,423 arrests in the 21–23-year group (U.S. Dept. of Justice, FBI 1975, table 36).

[13] The 17–19 age group showed an arrest rate of 38.8 per 100,000 compared to 13.4 per 100,000 for the 13–15-year group for forcible rape in 1975 (U.S. Dept. of Justice, FBI 1975, table 36).

[14] Multiple arrests for a single offense are more likely to occur in the younger age group (Eigen 1977).

[15] In 1975 female arrests accounted for 15.6 percent of criminal homicide, 1 percent of forcible rape, 7 percent of robbery and 13.1 percent of aggravated assault arrests (U.S. Dept. of Justice, FBI 1975, table 38).

crime rate were derived from arrest statistics by estimating the number of offenders not apprehended.[16] Factoring in the decline in clearance rates would also magnify apparent increases in arrests over time.[17] Finally, the growth in homogeneous youth violence could be made to appear still more substantial if the number of arrests rather than the rate of arrests per 100,000 population were used as the measure, because the youth population expanded dramatically during the period under study.[18] On the other hand, those seeking to minimize the involvement of young persons in homicide and rape could dramatically lower the estimate by reducing the impact of multiple arrests for the same homicide,[19] confining the offender sample to those who were in fact convicted,[20] or by lowering the maximum age included in the sample.[21] There is legitimate rationale for *all* these adjustment strategies; there are no precise data available in aggregate form to provide the foundation for any of the computations (except population by sex) required to develop the alternative measures. Thus, no single number can provide anything but a rough indication of the incidence and trends in homicide and forcible rape participation.

But despite the crudeness of the data, and the arbitrary charac-

[16] Police "clear" a crime when they have identified the offender or have sufficient evidence to charge him or actually take him into custody. In 1975 reported clearance rates were 78 percent for reported murders, 51 percent for forcible rape, 64 percent for aggravated assault and 27 percent for robbery (U.S. Dept. of Justice, FBI 1975, p. 37).

[17] Clearance rates for reported crimes in 1960 were 92 percent for murder, 73 percent for forcible rape, 76 percent for aggravated assault, and 39 percent for robbery (U.S. Dept. of Justice, FBI 1960).

[18] The national population aged 13–20 was 21,659,049 in 1960, 30,758,218 in 1970, and an estimated 33,590,000 in 1975 (U.S. Dept. of Commerce, Bureau of the Census 1960, 1970, 1975).

[19] A Chicago study for 1965–70 found that killings by multiple offenders occurred in 45 percent of the homicides involving offenders aged 15–24 but in only 10 percent of all other homicides (Block and Zimring 1973, p. 8).

[20] In 1974 in Manhattan about 84 percent of juveniles "contacted" by the police did not reach court, and, of those that did, only 14 percent were adjudicated as guilty (see Strasburg 1978, pp. 95–127, and Boland and Wilson 1978, pp. 27–28).

[21] The 1975 statistics show 1,531 (8.4 per 100,000) arrests for homicide and 3,698 (20.9 per 100,000) arrests for forcible rape in the 13–17 age group. By also considering the significantly larger arrest totals for 18–20-year-olds, we find 4,107 (14.6 per 100,000) arrests for homicide and 7,972 (28.3 per 100,000) for forcible rape in the 13–20 population (U.S. Dept. of Justice, FBI 1975, table 36).

ter of the methods used to measure rates, the sharp differences in trend noted since 1970 suggest a leveling off which is inconsistent with public perceptions about trends in youth violence.

B. Robbery

The rate of youth robbery is much higher than rape and homicide and while robbery victimization is concentrated among the young, the poor and minorities, it also threatens large numbers of the old, the middle class, and a broad representation of the community at large (Cook 1976, pp. 175–77; U.S. Dept. of Justice, Nat. Crim. Justice Inf. and Stat. Svc. 1976, pp. 16, 33, 48, 64, 80). Table 2 sets out arrest statistics by age group for robbery, focusing on the period 1960 through 1977. It shows extremely high relative growth in robbery participation from a rather large base in 1960. Robbery arrests increase more modestly between 1970 and 1975 and decline to 1970 per capita rates by 1977. The growth during the 1960s in reported arrests per 100,000 youth—109 percent—is substantial but understates the real growth in the incidence of this offense because clearance rates for all major offenses of violence have declined; thus the

TABLE 2

Trends in Robbery Arrest Rates for Offenders Aged 13–20, 1960–77

	Estimated Robbery Arrests per 100,000	Percent Change
1960	118	
1970	205	
Change (1960–70)		74
1975	254	
Change (1970–75)		24
1977	210	
Change (1975–77)		−17

Sources: U.S. Department of Justice, Federal Bureau of Investigation, *Uniform Crime Reports, 1960, 1970, 1975, 1977*; U.S. Department of Commerce, Bureau of the Census, *Characteristics of the Population: United States Summary* (1960, 1970); U.S. Department of Commerce, Bureau of the Census, *Current Population Reports*, Series P-25, No. 643 (January 1977) and No. 541 (February 1975).

number of arrests for every 100 reported crimes has correspondingly decreased (Zimring 1978, pp. 19–20). If one assumes, as
I have argued is improper, the same ratio of arrests to crimes for
the young as for the not-young, offenders in the 13–20 age
bracket are responsible for 245,000 robberies in 1975—55 percent of the aggregate officially reported rate of robbery.

There remains the thorny problem of *what kind* of robbery is
committed by the young and whether the dangerousness of this
offense is increasing over time. Victim surveys and self-report
studies indicate a persistent tendency for younger offenders,
particularly those uniformly classified as juveniles, to rob more
often in groups, to use fewer weapons, and to constitute less of a
death risk per 100 offenses than older offenders (Cook 1976, pp.
179–80). But only fragmentary data are available to flesh out the
aggregate national numbers to give us any clear reading on which
of the many forms of robbery are represented, in what measure,
in the aggregate total of any year's arrests. Official statistics do
not give weapon breakdowns by age of offender, even where the
offense results in an arrest (U.S. Dept. of Justice, FBI 1975).
Nor is there a special category of robbery with injury used in
police reporting.[22] The Philadelphia cohort study, whose sample
of offenses roughly corresponds with the beginning of the time
series we are analyzing (1960–63), reports relatively low weapon
involvement and modest average seriousness.[23] Chicago studies
concerned with the period 1965 through 1970 provide evidence
that robbery committed in the late teen years involved increasing
use of firearms and sharp increases in levels of lethality (Block
and Zimring 1973, pp. 7–10). A continuation of the Chicago
studies suggests an absolute reduction in the lethality of youth
robbery since 1970.[24] Victim survey data are too new to provide

[22] Information supplied by the FBI, Uniform Crime Reporting Division.

[23] The Philadelphia study, which followed the city's male population from birth
in 1945 to age 18 in 1963, found 7 percent of its index offenses (injury, theft, or
damage) involved the presence of a known weapon, while less than 2 percent of these
offenses resulted in death or hospitalization (Wolfgang, Figlio, and Sellin 1972, pp.
82–84).

[24] The lethality of youth robbery may have peaked in 1970 when 78 percent of
Chicago robbery homicides were attributed to offenders aged 15–24. That figure
dropped to 70 percent in 1971 and rose to 74 percent in 1973 and 1974 (Block 1977,
table 4-3).

the kind of time perspective on patterns of youth robbery that would suit current needs.[25]

Because the robbery arrest rate is moderating during the mid-1970s, it will be of special importance to find out whether the seriousness of youth robbery is abating as the rates are leveling off.[26]

C. Aggravated Assault

Most homicide is the outgrowth of violent interactions that would be classified by the police as aggravated assault if a killing did not result. For this reason, rates, patterns, and trends in assaultive violence are of special interest to students of criminality among the young. Unfortunately, translating official statistics on this offense into meaningful trends is a source of particular frustration. Table 3 tells us virtually all that the official aggregate

TABLE 3

Trends in Aggravated Assault Arrest Rates for Offenders Aged 13–20, 1960–77

	Estimated Aggravated Assault Arrests per 100,000	Percent Change
1960	96	
1970	155	
Change (1960–70)		62
1975	220	
Change (1970–75)		42
1977	213	
Change (1975–77)		−3

Sources: U.S. Department of Justice, Federal Bureau of Investigation, *Uniform Crime Reports, 1960, 1970, 1975, 1977;* U.S. Department of Commerce, Bureau of the Census, *Characteristics of the Population: United States Summary* (1960, 1970); U.S. Department of Commerce, Bureau of the Census, *Current Population Reports,* Series P-25, No. 643 (January 1977) and No. 541 (February 1975).

[25] Apart from the pioneering victimization surveys of the middle sixties, the Justice Department began systematic collection of victimization data in 1972 and 1973 (U.S. Dept. of Justice, LEAA 1974).

[26] While age-specific data are unavailable, the rate of robberies involving weapons declined for the total urban population during the 1975–77 period. See Appendix, table B.

statistics can tell us about aggravated assault by the young since 1960. The arrest rate for non-robbery assaults begins at a high base rate in 1960. Between 1970 and 1975, the arrest rate for aggravated assault increased even more quickly, on an annual basis, than during the preceding decade, in contrast to the flat trends in per capita arrests for homicide and rape. Since 1975, rates of assault arrest have remained quite close to the 1975 peak. Thus aggravated assault is the only violent offense to display sharp increases during the 1970s that have not been counterbalanced by declines since 1975.

The divergence of trends between aggravated assault as measured by arrests and homicide is both puzzling and important. Have non-robbery assaults become less lethal among the young? Has police policy shifted toward including less serious events in the assault category? Has the rate of serious aggravated assault remained relatively stable while the rate of less dangerous assault has increased?

The puzzle of divergent trends in assault and homicide is important because of the extraordinary leverage that assault and robbery have in determining trends in total "violent crimes." A 2 percent increase in the rate of reported aggravated assault is the numerical equivalent of more than 25 percent of all homicide arrests among the young in 1975 in any aggregate index of youth violence.

The heterogeneous nature of aggravated assault as an offense category is a particular problem for students of violent crime among the young. Some evidence of the extraordinary variety of assaultive behavior can be gleaned from age-specific data on assault arrests. Over 1,000 arrests of offenders aged 10 and under for aggravated assault are reported in the *Uniform Crime Reports* in 1975. The police statistics tell us that these are arrests for serious assault, but the same edition of the *Uniform Crime Reports* indicates only 17 homicide arrests in the national sample for that year in that age group. Table 4 compares homicide arrests and aggravated assault arrests during 1975 by age. From this, the conclusion one reaches about relationships between age and violent crime depends heavily on one's definition of violence.

TABLE 4

Homicide and Aggravated Assault Arrests by Age, 1975

	Under 10	11–12	13–14	15	16	17	18	19	20
Homicide	17	25	142	292	500	597	855	852	869
Aggravated assault	1,013	2,301	7,286	6,754	8,732	9,426	10,354	9,874	9,576
Total	1,030	2,326	7,428	7,046	9,232	10,023	11,209	10,726	10,445

Source: U.S. Department of Justice, Federal Bureau of Investigation, *Uniform Crime Reports, 1975.*

Arrest statistics indicate 2,300 aggravated assaults and homicide arrests in the age bracket 11–12 as compared to 10,000 such arrests for 17-year-olds. In this aggregate measure of total violent crime, 11–12-year-olds would appear responsible for a fourth of the aggravated assaults and homicides attributable to 17-year-olds. Yet the death risk from attack reflected in these statistics varies dramatically. Seventeen-year-olds are arrested for homicide twenty-four times as often as 11–12-year-olds even though they are approximately half the size of the younger population at risk. Assaultive violence among 17- and 18-year-olds produces about one-third more arrests than among the age group 11–15, but it is responsible for three times the number of homicide arrests.

This roundabout investigation of patterns of aggravated assault suggests that any comparison of arrests in this category over time or between jurisdictions is hazardous and that any index of violent crime which *includes* undifferentiated measures of aggravated assault will be rendered opaque by the mixture of serious and less serious events agglomerated in the overall pattern. The index of violent offenses, itself a reform from the even broader "crime index,"[27] requires further specification before it can be a useful social indicator. And much greater detail on the nature of assaults known to the police and resulting in arrest will be needed before trends in this offense can be meaningfully discussed.

With this national level survey as background, the remainder of this section provides a brief sketch of the distribution of youth violence among the youth population and provides some data on the impact of demographic shifts on likely future trends.

D. *Youth Violence and the Youth Population*

To the extent that official statistics mirror reality, serious youth violence occurs more often in cities than in non-urban areas, involves boys far more frequently than girls, and is concentrated among low social status, ghetto-dwelling urban youth.

[27] The 1967 President's Commission targeted the four violent crimes—willful homicide, rape, robbery, and serious assault—as a special area of concern (President's Commission on Law Enforcement and Administration of Justice 1967, pp. 3–4).

Table 5 shows the concentration of youth violence arrests by crime in large urban areas. Offenses of violence, particularly robbery, are intensely concentrated in the nation's large cities. The offense that displays the smallest relative concentration is aggravated assault, the catholic category. Whether this reflects a wide distribution of both life-threatening and less serious violence cannot be inferred. But it is worthy of note that homicide arrests are three times as frequent in big city youth populations whereas assault arrests are only twice as frequent. It is thus plausible that less serious patterns of assaultive violence are reflected in the arrest statistics for reporting areas outside major cities.[28]

Table 6 shows the distribution by sex of violence arrests. To some extent the dominance of males in arrest statistics may reflect a reluctance on the part of the police to arrest girls or to charge an arrested female with an offense of violence. But the persistence and magnitude of the difference between the sexes in violent crime suggest that this difference is something more than the product of chivalry in the criminal justice system.

Similarly, available statistics indicate that urban minority youth are disproportionately involved in violent crime, although

TABLE 5

Violent Crime by City Size, 1975
(Arrests per 100,000)

	250,000+ City Size	All Other Areas	Ratio of City/Other
Homicide	21.3	6.7	3.2
Rape	56	20	2.8
Aggravated assault	369	187	2.1
Robbery	678	110	6.2

Source: U.S. Department of Justice, Federal Bureau of Investigation, *Uniform Crime Reports, 1975.*

[28] See table 5. It should be noted, however, that fatal attacks stemming from robbery are reflected in the homicide arrest statistics while nonfatal robbery attacks are not reflected in the aggravated assault arrest statistics. Since robbery is more common in large cities, this statistical quirk may also influence the variations in ratios of homicide to assault.

the official statistics probably overstate the difference between the races (Zimring 1978, pp. 39–42). Table 7 shows the ratio of black to white arrest rates per 100,000 youths by crime for five cities in the census year of 1970. The violent offenses of homicide and robbery show heavier racial concentrations than property offenses of burglary and auto theft. How much of the racial differences noted with respect to violent offenses can be attributed to selective enforcement, differences in socioeconomic class, and other unaccounted variables has not been adequately

TABLE 6

Distribution of Violence Arrests for Persons under 18 by Sex and Offense (Excluding Rape), 1975

	Percentage Male	Percentage Female	Total Arrests
Homicide	90	10	1,373
Robbery	93	7	40,796
Aggravated assault	84	16	30,858

Source: U.S. Department of Justice, Federal Bureau of Investigation, *Uniform Crime Reports, 1975.*

TABLE 7

Ratio of Black to White Arrest Rates per 100,000 Youths by Crime in Five Cities, 1970*

	Black/White Ratio
Homicide	7.2
Robbery	8.6
Burglary	3.9
Auto theft	3.0

* Boston, Chicago, Cleveland, Dallas, Washington, D.C.

Source: Franklin Zimring, "Crime, Demography and Time in Five American Cities," paper prepared for the Hudson Institute Project on Criminal Justice Futures (May 1976).

investigated.[29] But the concentration of offenses of violence in urban areas among minorities is an important partial explanation for the explosion of violent youth crime in the 1960s. The fifteen years from 1960 to 1975 were characterized by a large increase in the youth population, an increasing concentration of the young in urban areas, and a huge increase in the minority youth population in core cities (Zimring 1975, chap. 3). These population changes occurred in a social setting when crime rates for all significant age groups were increasing.[30] Given generally higher crime rates as well as large increases in the population at risk, a substantial increase in violent youth crime was predictable. The increases that occurred between 1960 and 1970 were, however, much greater than the most sophisticated demographic projections would have predicted, because rates per 100,000 of major crimes of violence increased dramatically.[31] During the 1970s it is probable that age- and race-specific rates of urban youth violence did not increase and there is some evidence of a decrease in rate.[32]

Over the next decade, if we assume that the present concentration of violent crime continues, the declining youth population should be responsible for a smaller volume of total youth criminality. However, the volume of violent crime should be less responsive to the overall decline of the youth population because

[29] The Philadelphia cohort study did attempt to control its population data for differences in socioeconomic status and disposition of offenders (Wolfgang, Figlio, and Sellin 1972, pp. 47–52, 218–26).

[30] The FBI reported a 233 percent increase in total index crimes per 100,000 inhabitants over the 1960–75 period. The rate per 100,000 of violent crime (murder, forcible rape, robbery, and aggravated assault) rose 199 percent (U.S. Dept. of Justice, FBI 1975, table 2).

[31] See tables 1, 2, and 3.

[32] Clearance rates for homicide declined from 86 to 78 percent from 1970 to 1975. To the extent that this accurately reflects a trend in clearance rates for youth population, the 4 percent increase in arrests would reflect a 15 percent increase in offenses. Similarly, forcible rape clearance rates declined from 56 to 51 percent, and if this accurately reflects a trend for youth, the 1 percent rape increase would represent an 11 percent increase in offenses. By contrast, similar manipulations of 1960 and 1970 data would yield an estimated increase of 98 percent during that period for homicide offenses and 52 percent for rape. It is important to note, however, that clearance rates used in these computations are arbitrary and aggregate. Age-specific data is not available. Furthermore, given the changing racial composition of urban areas over the period 1970 to 1975, one would expect increasing aggregate youth violence even if race-specific rates remained constant (U.S. Dept. of Justice, FBI 1960, 1970, 1975, 1977). See Appendix, table C.

the population of urban-dwelling minority males will not decline dramatically in the 1980s (Zimring 1975, chap. 3). What one would expect, therefore, is a greater drop in the more democratically distributed property crimes than in such offenses as robbery and homicide. There is some evidence, however, that offenses of violence are decreasing, and that this decrease is due in large measure to declining rates of youth violence. Nationwide, the homicide rate in 1977 was down almost 10 percent from 1975 levels.[33] Since 1975, individual cities have reported sharp decreases in homicide and robbery rates.[34]

There is no persuasive reason to believe the recent decreases in youth violence can be attributed solely to demographic shifts. The same can be said for the moderating rate of very serious youth violence that appears to have characterized much of the 1970s. The 1960s witnessed a period when sharp increases in youth violence could not be explained solely by changes in the youth population. The 1970s witnessed moderating rates of violence per capita. We are left in the happy if scientifically frustrating circumstance of confronting good news which the present level of social science understanding cannot explain.

II. Measuring Youth Violence: Current Methods and Limits

Recent debate about social policy toward young offenders contains frequent references to estimates of the volume, seriousness, and concentration of serious youth violence. Unfortunately, references to the "facts" of youth crime are both highly selective and uncritical in much of the literature. This section surveys existing methods of measuring youth crime. The following section addresses the relevance of existing data to three key policy issues and recommends supplemental approaches to the measurement of youth violence that would contribute to informed public policy discussion.

[33] The national homicide rate fell from 9.6 per 100,000 in 1975 to 8.8 per 100,000 in 1976 (U.S. Dept. of Justice, FBI 1976, table 2).

[34] Philadelphia and Detroit showed dramatic decreases in estimated homicide and robbery rates between 1975 and 1977. In Philadelphia homicides dropped from 573 to 389. In Detroit homicide rates decreased from 47 to 37 and robbery rates decreased from 1,597 to 1,218 per 100,000 (U.S. Dept. of Justice, FBI 1975, 1977).

A. Official Statistics

The principal tool for measuring age-specific violence is the series of annual aggregate arrest statistics forwarded by local police departments and reported by the FBI. Supplemental tools include occasional "cohort" studies sampling subjects from the general population and using police arrest statistics as a measure of criminality (Wolfgang, Figlio, and Sellin 1972; Polk, Frease, and Richmond 1974, pp. 84–97; Shannon, unpublished), studies of juvenile court intake (Cohen 1975; Strasburg 1978), self-report studies which survey samples of the youth population and ask them to report on the frequency and seriousness of their criminal acts (Gold and Reimer 1975, pp. 483–517), and surveys of the victims of crime that include victim estimates of the age of offenders.[35] While the variety of different measures of youth crime is substantial, the data base that has emerged is insufficient.

In the best of years, official statistics on arrest rates for violent crimes are seriously flawed. Whatever biases are built into the policing process are passed on in official statistics (Gold and Reimer 1975). For nine out of every ten youth violence arrests, there is no detail on the seriousness of the particular offense.[36] Statistics forwarded by local departments on the incidence of crime are audited by the FBI, but there is evidence that statistics on arrests are not similarly scrutinized. All these well-known difficulties are compounded by dramatic shifts in the number of agencies reporting age-specific arrest statistics and the periodic omission of major cities that make year-to-year comparisons in youth violence a hazardous occupation (Zimring 1978, pp. 15, 22–23). One does not have to read far back in history for examples of "peculiar" years in youth arrest reporting statistics. The present analysis is concerned with 1975 and 1977 but not 1976 as the end years because the 1976 data do not include Chicago arrest data.[37] By contrast, the 1974 *Uniform Crime*

[35] Victim estimation of offender age is collected by the Bureau of the Census but not published in the major criminal victimization surveys (Dodge, Lentzner, and Shenk 1976, pp. 1–26).

[36] See text at pp. 72–73, above.

[37] Information supplied by the Chief of the Statistical Division, FBI Uniform Crime Reporting Bureau, September 1977.

Reports did include the city of Chicago but did not include arrests from a host of police agencies representing a population of more than 20 million who were temporarily omitted from the reporting sample.[38]

B. *Alternative Measures*

The most important new method of measuring American delinquency is a series of cohort studies that depend on birth or school statistics to capture a representative sample of an area's population and use police statistics to estimate the incidence and distribution of delinquent behavior as the sample gets older (Wolfgang, Figlio, and Sellin 1972, pp. 27–52). Such an enterprise will reflect whatever biases influence the police decision to arrest, but the use of individual offense narratives rather than aggregate arrest statistics allows the researcher to follow individual careers, to make specific assessments of the seriousness of individual acts that come to the attention of the police, and to mesh data from law enforcement records with data on educational attainment, socioeconomic status, and other presumed correlates of delinquent behavior (Wolfgang, Figlio, and Sellin 1972, pp. 39–52; Jensen 1976, pp. 379–87). A second further advantage of the cohort strategy is the opportunity to study nondelinquent youth of the same age. The first major American cohort enterprise, a study of Philadelphia youth born in 1945, was published in 1972. It is, at present, the single most important data base for assessing the incidence and distribution of youth violence (Boland and Wilson 1978; Jensen 1976; Strasburg 1978). Unfortunately, research of this character is expensive if sample sizes are to be sufficiently large to permit the study of relatively low incidence offenses, and even retrospective studies are time-consuming if performed with care. Thus the Philadelphia cohort that is frequently discussed in contemporary policy debates about youth violence turned 18 in 1963, when rates of youth violence were about half current levels. The expense associated with large sample cohort

[38] The 1974 national age-specific arrest data were based on reports from 5,298 agencies covering an estimated population of 134 million. In 1973, 6,004 agencies (155 million population) reported (U.S. Dept. of Justice, FBI 1973 and 1974, tables 30 and 34).

studies means that relatively few such studies exist. The effort necessary to perform cohort analysis suggests that unless patterns of youth violence are stable over time, cohort research may be "dated" by the time it is completed. Full-scale longitudinal studies can help solve this problem, but these sustained efforts have not yet become an established part of American criminology.[39] Still, the cohort approach is properly serving as a model for contemporary replications in American urban and rural areas. If such studies had been made earlier and more frequently, far more reliable information on trends in youth violence over time would currently be available.

Studies of juvenile court intake are faster, less expensive and less informative than full-blown cohort enterprises.[40] By definition, such studies encompass suspected offenders only, and typically involve relatively small samples of the juvenile intake and correspondingly low levels of violence arrests.[41] Most of the studies published to date depend solely on juvenile court records, and these records contain very little information on cases that are informally disposed of before juvenile court petitions are filed (Strasburg 1978, p. 88). For example, in Paul Strasburg's study of the Manhattan Juvenile Court, a substantial number of police arrests for index violence offenses were informally disposed of, a phenomenon that suggests the residual sample of violent offenses was biased to some extent. This type of policy decision in the juvenile court also suggests what the above discussion of "heterogeneous" juvenile violence has implied: many officially recorded youth violence arrests stem from less than heinous behavior. Studies of juvenile court intake

[39] For a discussion of longitudinal studies in the United States and elsewhere, see David Farrington's essay in this volume.

[40] See Cohen (1975) for analysis of juvenile processing in the Denver County, Colorado, Memphis–Shelby County, Tennessee, and Montgomery County, Pennsylvania, courts; see also Strasburg (1978, pp. 88–112) concerning Manhattan and Westchester Counties in New York and Mercer County in New Jersey.

[41] Strasburg's Manhattan County sample of 221 juveniles in 1974 came from 13,000 police contacts leading to 4,313 arrests leading to 2,124 petitions to juvenile court. The Westchester sample of 111 juveniles was chosen from 636 petitions resulting from 2,293 arrests from 6,000 police contacts; the Mercer County sample of 178 derived from 6,717 contacts, 2,720 arrests, and 2,363 petitions (1978, p. 96). Cohen's study covered all juvenile cases referred to the courts in 1975: 5,684 in Denver, 6,596 in Memphis–Shelby, 1,302 in Montgomery County (1975, pp. 15–20).

are relatively recent, and it is thus difficult to use the data generated from such studies to address trends in youth violence over
time.

C. Survey Research

Self-report studies of potential young offenders and the victims
of crime are another supplement to official statistics emerging in
the literature. "One shot" studies of adolescents, students, and
adults who report on their criminal activity have long been a
staple of American sociological research. An effort to assess the
criminal behavior of a national sample of American adolescents in
two different years, 1967 and 1972, was reported by Martin
Gold and David Reimer in 1975 (Gold and Reimer 1975). Asserting that "official data on delinquency are tied so loosely to the
actual behavior of youth that they are more sensitive to the
changes in the measurement procedures than they are to the
object of measurement," Gold and Reimer (p. 514) conclude that
per capita rates of delinquent behavior, other than alcohol and
drug-taking, declined during the period 1967 to 1972. Paul Strasburg in his review of violent delinquency finds the results of this
study "surprising and significant" (1978, p. 21), and concludes
that "these findings run counter to the trend in the FBI's *Uniform
Crime Reports* for the same five year period" (p. 22). In fact, at
least as pertains to violent youth criminality, there may be little in
the self-report study that casts doubt on official statistics. In the
first place, the national sample interviewed by Gold and Reimer
was small (1,395 youth between ages 11 and 18 including fewer
than 500 males over the age of 15) (1975, pp. 484–85). Second,
29 percent of eligible respondents were not interviewed, and more
than two-thirds of the non-interviews were the result of refusals
by the youth, or both the youth and his parents, to participate.
Whether "refusers" were more apt to be offenders is not known,
but the likelihood cannot be lightly dismissed. Third, particular
high risk groups were not heavily represented: there were fewer
than 30 black males over the age of 15 in the sample.[42] Given the

---

[42] Approximately 36 percent of the Gold and Reimer sample were over 15 and
only 87 of 1,395 in the sample population were black males (1975, pp. 484–85).

low incidence of serious youth violence it is therefore altogether appropriate that no serious offense of violence was listed in the schedule of behavior that the youth sample was asked to respond to.

Surveys of crime victims add important if imprecise perspectives to offender surveys and official statistics on youth violence. A recent national survey on crime victimization asked those who reported being victims of robbery and assault to estimate the age of the offender or offenders responsible where face-to-face confrontation made such an estimate possible.[43] This survey, with a much larger sample than any existing self-report offense studies, covered both offenses that were reported to the police and those not reported. For the majority of crimes that were not cleared by arrests, the survey provides some data on the approximate age of the offender and the characteristics of the offense. The number of victims is sufficiently large for an offense such as robbery to give something of a national portrait of the approximate age of offenders. The study provides some basis for concluding that younger offenders are less frequently armed, more frequently in groups, and more likely to pick "softer" targets than are older offenders (Cook 1976, pp. 178–80). The sample of offenses in the national crime survey was evidently not sufficiently large to provide confident estimates of how these patterns vary by city size,[44] and (as noted earlier) the victim surveys do not extend far enough back in time to provide an independent indicator of trends over time.

D. Linking Measurements

When all these supplemental measures are added to the existing base of official arrest statistics, an incomplete and occasionally inconsistent portrait of youth violence emerges. The small number of supplemental studies, the varying methodologies, and the inconsistent findings do not permit a national portrait of youth violence to be drawn in which the different indices are

---

[43] See n. 35.

[44] The victimization survey statistics on offenders cited by Cook are aggregate totals from the National Crime Panel Survey of twenty-six cities (Cook 1976, pp. 178–80).

joined together so that the whole exceeds the sum of its parts. Instead, the primary data used in any discussion of trends or patterns of youth violence come from aggregated arrest statistics, and supplementary methods of study are used to interpret or argue about what the aggregate statistics mean. Attempts to link the products of supplemental methods of study to official statistics almost always involve assumptions that seem unwarranted about the continuity of trends over time and the similarity of patterns in different areas.

Indeed, there may be no single "national" portrait of youth violence or any uniform set of trends that can be generalized across regions and different population groups. The ebb and flow of aggregated national totals may reflect a wide diversity of patterns and trends. To date, however, empirical studies of youth violence are insufficient in number and quality to test even this hypothesis. Thus, while data play an important role in current debates about whether there is a wave of violence in the suburbs, or growth in the number of young career violent offenders, or a "breakdown" in the juvenile justice system, the information base available at present is too tentative and too internally inconsistent to bring such issues to resolution. In the pages that follow, these deficiencies in information will be a major theme animating discussion of three issues that have emerged in recent literature and in public debate.

III. From Statistics to Policy? Three Key Issues

Any short list of significant issues concerning youth violence will be necessarily incomplete and reflect the biases of both the list-maker and the times. In this period of intense debate about public policy toward serious young offenders, three questions appear to deserve detailed discussion.

1. How concentrated is serious youth violence among sectors of the youth population and how successfully can we predict the recurrence of violence in individual cases?
2. What is the relationship between variations in social control policy and the incidence of youth violence?
3. To what extent can trends in violence by the young be

used as a leading indicator of future trends in aggregate
rates of violent crime?

It is my view that existing data are insufficient to provide
acceptable answers to these questions.

A. The Concentration and Predictability of Youth Violence

Self-report studies indicate that the vast majority of American
young people violate the law during adolescence. Official statistics on arrests and juvenile court intake suggest a pool of officially
identified and suspected offenders in the millions (Zimring 1978,
pp. 178–80). Yet any intervention strategy—punitive, preventive,
or rehabilitative—must necessarily be directed at smaller numbers
of young offenders. In some reform proposals, selectivity is
urged in relation to the seriousness of the most recent offense
committed by a particular adolescent that leads to his conviction
in juvenile or criminal court. In its pure form, this proportional
emphasis would focus, primarily, on the seriousness of the youth's
offense and would be more concerned with retributive justice
than with the prediction of dangerousness.[45]

A second approach, designed to enhance crime prevention,
would attempt to isolate the young, violent career criminal
regardless of his age. While detailed policy recommendations are
not put forward in current literature, the broad outlines of such
an approach were recently suggested by Barbara Boland and
James Q. Wilson:

> [p]erhaps there should be a two-track system, but with the
> tracks defined by the nature of the criminal career rather
> than by the age of the offender. One system would deal,
> largely by non-custodial means, with routine, intermittent

[45] The American Bar Association's proposed juvenile justice standards classify
juvenile offenses according to criminal penalties applicable to adults. An offense
normally punishable by death or life imprisonment is a class one juvenile offense
punishable by a maximum of two years' confinement in a secure or nonsecure facility
or three years' conditional freedom. An offense normally punishable by a prison
term of six months or less is a class five juvenile offense, punishable by a maximum
of two months in a nonsecure facility if the juvenile has a prior record (a class one,
two, or three offense or three class four or five offenses) or conditional freedom for
six months (Institute of Judicial Administration and American Bar Association, Juvenile Justice Standards Project 1977a, Parts V–VI).

offenders or those with short criminal records. The other
would deal with serious, intensive offenders and would
almost invariably employ close supervision or custody.
(1978, p. 34)

To have any significant impact on violent crime, such an
approach would require a substantial number of young career
offenders who (*a*) are responsible for a large share of violent
crime and (*b*) can be identified in advance. Empirically, such a
two-track system works best when violent criminality is heavily
concentrated among a small segment of juvenile offenders and is
persistently committed by those offenders, and when such future
violent criminality can be predicted from a particular pattern of
present offense or prior criminal history.

The available evidence on these related topics is ambiguous.
Clearly, it is far less decisive than the recent Boland and Wilson
treatment of the subject would lead a reader to conclude. The
most often quoted finding of the Wolfgang, Figlio, and Sellin
study is that "the vast majority of *serious* crimes" in the sample
were committed "by the approximately six percent [of the sample]
who are chronic offenders" (Boland and Wilson 1978, p. 32).
At first glance, this 6 percent statistic suggests extreme concentration and appears to imply a high capacity to predict serious
future criminality. First impressions can be misleading however.
Six percent of a population of young males is a large number of
offenders indeed, too large for a general application of intensive
social control measures. Further, the 6 percent incidence of
chronic offensivity is associated with a rate of violent criminality
approximately half that of more recent years.[46] Finally, chronic
offenders in the Philadelphia study are defined in terms of total
"index offense" arrests, and the majority of these arrests are for
nonviolent property offenses. One searches the original cohort
study in vain to find strong evidence of a large number of identifi-

---

[46] The average estimated annual arrest rate per 100,000 youths aged 13–20 was
249 for the four violent crimes during 1960 to 1963, the period when the Philadelphia
cohort passed through the ages of 15–18. The annual rate was an estimated 491 per
100,000 for the period 1974 to 1976 (U.S. Dept. of Justice, FBI 1977).

able youthful offenders specializing in violence. Wolfgang, Figlio, and Sellin concluded (1972, p. 250):

> The offense transition matrices appear to be independent of offense number, and in fact, the same process seems to operate at each stage in the offense histories. There is no "break" after which the offenders specialize along some discernible pathways. Indeed, with the exception of a small tendency of like offense repetitions (particularly for theft offenses), the choice of the next offense follows the first offense probability vector as mentioned above.

This is an unpromising finding for those who are interested in the early identification of career violent offenders.

Other studies have been more successful in finding concentration and (to a lesser degree) specialization in criminal careers, but only through the judicious use of hindsight rather than forward predictions of dangerousness. The RAND Corporation study of 49 repetitively violent offenders currently incarcerated as adults for robbery found that those serious adult offenders had had extensive juvenile careers and a large number of offenses including a substantial number of robberies (Petersilia, Greenwood, and Lavin 1977). It was, of course, impossible in a sample selected for its serious adult criminal careers to know what factors could have predicted the kind of criminal involvement which that particular group experienced, because individuals with careers of youth violence could not be included in the sample unless they had persisted in repetitively violent behavior in developing years. (It is of more than passing interest that this RAND study also can *not* be cited as evidence that juvenile offenders are apprehended less frequently per 100 crimes—as Boland and Wilson have attempted to do [1978, p. 25]—because of the bias built into the sample selection. Since only individuals who have been repetitively apprehended as adults are included in the RAND sample, the sample consists of a prescreened group of unlucky as well as persistently criminal offenders. Because juvenile records were not considered in drawing the sample, the same propensity to be apprehended cannot be assumed for the sample's juvenile as opposed to adult criminal careers.)

There is, at present, insufficient evidence of the extent to which youth violence is extensively concentrated in a relatively small pool of career offenders. Further, no particular offense or series of offenses is an efficient predictor of future violence in a representative sample of young offenders. The younger the age at first arrest, and the more frequent the number of arrests or convictions, the greater the propensity toward future criminality, violent and nonviolent. To date, however, there is little evidence of the kind of intense specialization that would create maximum impact for a program that was focused on repetitively violent offenders.

Yet it would be foolish to deny, or deny the importance of, the intense concentration of serious violent crime among poor, minority, urban-dwelling males. In strict logical terms, groups do not have crime rates. Individuals either violate laws or they do not. Thus, to speak of blacks, males, 16-year-olds or any other aggregate population that shares a common demographic quality as having a "crime rate" is misleading. It is particularly misleading because the labels listed above produce an incomplete and dangerously distorted portrait of the actual distribution of serious youth violence. A primary future research task relating to the concentration of youth violence is to disaggregate the macrovariables used in common discussion and to examine the large variations that exist *within* demographically similar groups with different rates of criminal activity.

In logical terms the search for the answer to the question, "How concentrated are crime rates?" would lead to the individual level. But it is also important to know how many young offenders and what proportion of the population within the larger demographic socioeconomic subgroups are responsible for much of reported serious violent youth criminality. Simply combining sex, age, race, and socioeconomic status is a dangerously incomplete method for addressing the real concentration of youth crime. Any such limited approach both overstates the general propensity toward crime among the group under study and understates the concentration of offenses among particularized subgroups aggregated into the larger whole. At minimum, geographic and more refined social status and achievement measures must be added to the creditable cohort studies initiated in Philadelphia.[47] This kind of information is important even if it will not produce clear predictable pictures of career violent offenders on which intensive social control measures can be based.

Research of the kind described above will also provide information on the onset, duration, and intensity of careers in violent crime. The questions are clear: When do adolescents turn to violent crime? Are there patterns of specialization associated with violent young offenders or is there frequent crime "switching"? What is the frequency of commission of violent crime for those young offenders who persistently commit such acts? How long do violent young offenders persist in committing offenses? These empirical questions are high priority candidates for research support. It is also important to recognize how little is presently known about such topics. All too frequently, contemporary discussions of youth crime policy assume we know much more about these topics than a detailed review of existing research reveals. One of the most important contributions of future study will be a shift in focus away from "the violent young offender" to the variety of different types of violent offenders who may have importantly different criminal careers.

B. Does Social Control Make a Difference?

Most disputes about whether juvenile and criminal courts have failed to cope effectively with youth violence contain implicit assumptions about the effects of alternative (usually more punitive) mechanisms of control in reducing the incidence of violent crime. At the heart of such debate are questions about the deterrent and incapacitative effects of sanctions, particularly incarceration, and the marginal benefits that could be expected from policies that place a higher priority on crime control.

Yet evidence on the marginal effects of increased incarceration is tentative, not specific to youth, and subject to differing interpretations. After a long period of neglect, social and policy

---

[47] See Wolfgang, Figlio, and Sellin (1972, pp. 47–65) measuring socioeconomic status and educational background of the cohort members.

scientists have begun to address the issue of measuring the deterrent and incapacitative effects of punishment. To date, the results have been mixed (National Academy of Sciences 1978).

So far, the rekindled interest in deterrence and incapacitation has been confined to the study of sanctions delivered by the criminal courts. The impact of variations of social control strategy on youthful offenders is a neglected area of research. Paradoxically, it may be possible to gain more insight about the marginal deterrent impact of sentence severity by studying variations in social response to youth crime than by studies of variations in sanctioning policies directed at adult offenders. The fact that young offenders age out of the juvenile justice system in New York on their sixteenth birthday but are retained until the age of 18 in Pennsylvania[48] is a natural opportunity to explore whether juvenile and criminal courts deliver substantially different levels of punitive sanctions and whether whatever difference is noted has any impact on age-specific patterns of violent criminality. The existence of waiver provisions in the great majority of states may be seen as somewhat confounding this type of analysis, but recent research has shown that for an offense such as robbery, very few juvenile offenders are waived to criminal courts.[49]

To date, there has been no systematic study of the general deterrent impact of variations in sanctions available for young offenders and only occasional pilot studies on the incapacitative impact of sanctions presently delivered by juvenile courts. Studies by Stevens Clarke (1974), and John Conrad and his associates[50] tend to suggest that the incapacitative effects associated with present policies affect a low proportion of total youth crime, but little specific analysis has been done on the issue of youth violence (Van Dine, Conrad, and Dinitz 1977).

[48] N.Y. Jud. Law §712(a), (b) (McKinney) (1976); Pa. Stat. Ann. tit. 11 §50-102(1) (Purdon) (1972).

[49] Joel Eigen (1977) has found that fewer than 2 percent of the juveniles arrested for robbery are waived to adult courts.

[50] A study of the Columbus, Ohio, cohort and effects of incapacitation of chronic offenders has now been published (Hamparian, Schuster, Dinitz, and Conrad 1978).

If the sanctions delivered to young offenders make relatively little difference in crime rates, the juvenile justice system can make decisions which balance retributive community needs against policies of avoiding stigma and facilitating chances for young offenders to develop within the community. If the crime preventive potential of variations in sanctions is high, policy toward youth violence faces harder choices. In such a setting, the juvenile justice system must balance the interests of potential victims against the interests of young offenders, for the state has a positive obligation to protect both groups. In either case, it is far better to build toward estimating the deterrent and incapacitative potentials of various alternative strategies toward young violent offenders than to operate juvenile and criminal court systems essentially in the dark. If hard choices are to be made, they should be based on data rather than on conjecture. Here, as in the discussion of the concentration and predictability of violent crime, current commentaries on the topic tend to assume there is more reliable evidence available than is the case.

C. Youth Violence as a "Leading Indicator"

Intuitively, there is reason to believe that the involvement of adolescents in violent criminality may serve as a leading indicator of future trends in aggregate rates of violence in much the same way that certain indices of economic behavior are believed to forecast future trends in the general economy. The peak ages for serious violent crime occur in late adolescence and early adulthood, some years after youth participation in violent crime becomes substantial. If trends among a particular cohort of offenders in their younger years are predictive of relative rates of violence in their later years, one would expect that the earliest indications of an upward or downward shift in aggregate violence could come from reliable data on trends in violence among early and middle adolescents.

But more than intuition is needed to test this hypothesis. Careful and systematic study that encompasses both the period of explosive growth in violence and the more recent leveling-off phenomenon is a necessary element in a balanced agenda of youth crime research. Cursory inspection of aggregate arrest data reported to the FBI does not provide strong support for the "leading indicator" hypothesis. Males aged 21–24 show increasing violence arrest rates during the 1960s, followed by a pattern of moderation (1970–75) and decline (1975–77) that parallels the younger population at risk.[51] But the age categories, time periods, and arrest samples are not sufficiently refined to provide a fair test of the "leading indicator" thesis. Studies of a series of samples in individual cities are a more promising if more expensive approach. Such studies are well worth the effort. In an area where aggregate trends are difficult to predict and almost impossible to explain, any development of plausible leading indicators would be a major advance. And if youth violence rates are not a good predictor of offense rates in the same population some years hence, the implications for criminological theory would be profound.

IV. Conclusion

This is a difficult but interesting period for students of youth violence. The upward trend during the 1960s in violent youth criminality remains largely unexplained even as we are experiencing a period when the fever chart of officially reported violent youth crime is moderating. Youth violence is volatile; it is still too early to declare any victory in the war on violent youth criminality. But it is worthy of note that rates of some forms of violent youth criminality have been stable for a longer period than the intense policy debate about juvenile and criminal justice would suggest.

The gap between public perceptions and recent trends may be explained on a number of grounds. Even if the rate of youth violence is coming down on a per capita basis, the expanding youth population has led, until quite recently, to an expanding number of offenses.[52] The non-young may therefore be unconcerned with

[51] See Appendix, table D.

[52] Arrest rates for violent youth crimes may have decreased (table 1, homicide and rape) or increased more slowly since 1970 than before (tables 2 and 3, robbery and aggravated assault), but the youth population aged 13–20 expanded from 30,758,214 in 1970 to an estimated 34,300,000 in 1975. Therefore, the total number of arrests increased between 1970 and 1975. See Appendix, table E.

rates of per capita criminality if their own chances of becoming victims of youthful offenders are increasing on a statistical basis. More important, I suppose, is the gap between symbol and substance that pervades public discussion of crime and criminal justice. The violent young offender remains a threat on the streets of our cities. But the *image* of the violent young offender that animates policy and political debates is not simply a faithful reflection of statistical realities. It also reflects a complex amalgam of generational, racial, and other societal conflicts which pervade urban American life. In the end, fear of the young will moderate only if these larger social anxieties can be ameliorated. Yet any sustained decline in youth crime may contribute to a more general abatement in social tensions. If this occurs, it will be the most important benefit that fluctuations in the rate of crime can produce in the coming decade.

APPENDIX

TABLE A

Arrest Rates and Totals, 1975

	Estimated Arrests per 100,000		Total Arrests Reported	
	13–17	18–20	13–17	18–20
Robbery	233	289	41,275	30,433
Aggravated assault	182	283	32,198	28,904

Source: U.S. Dept. of Justice, FBI *Uniform Crime Reports, 1975*.

Known Robberies by Weapon, Total Urban Population, 1975–77 (Rates per 100,000)

	1975	1977	Percent Change
Strong-armed	113	98	−13
Firearm	140	108	−23
Knife/cutting instrument	41	35	−15
Other weapon	25	23	−8

Source: U.S. Dept. of Justice, FBI *Uniform Crime Reports, 1975, 1977.*

TABLE C

Clearance Rates (Percent)

	Homicide	Forcible Rape	Robbery	Aggravated Assault
1960	92	73	39	76
1970	86	56	29	65
1975	78	51	27	64
1977	75	51	27	62

Source: U.S. Dept. of Justice, FBI *Uniform Crime Reports, 1960 1970, 1975 and 1977.*

Trends in Violent Crime Arrest Rates for Offenders Aged 21–24, 1960–77

	Estimated Arrests per 100,000			
	Homicide	Forcible Rape	Robbery	Aggravated Assault
1960	13.7	29.8	121	154
1970	24.3	35.4	186	218
Change (1960–70)	77%	19%	54%	42%
1975	25.7	36.4	198	276
Change (1970–75)	6%	3%	6%	27%
1977	22.8	38.8	166	276
Change (1975–77)	−11%	7%	−16%	0%

Sources: U.S. Dept. of Justice, FBI *Uniform Crime Reports, 1960, 1970, 1975 and 1977.*

TABLE E

Total Arrests of Persons Aged 13–20

	1960*	1970†	1975‡
Homicide	973	3,197	4,107
Forcible Rape	3,088	6,421	7,972
Robbery	15,141	46,806	71,708
Aggravated Assault	12,341	35,384	62,002

* Estimated 12,868,000 aged 13–20 in *Uniform Crime Reports* sample population of 106,348,846.

† Estimated 22,892,000 aged 13–20 in *Uniform Crime Reports* sample population of 151,604,000.

‡ Estimated 28,186,744 aged 13–20 in *Uniform Crime Reports* sample population of 179,191,000.

Source: U.S. Dept. of Justice, FBI *Uniform Crime Reports, 1960, 1970, and 1975.*

REFERENCES

American Broadcasting Company. 1978. "Youth Terror: The View from behind the Gun." Television documentary presented 28 June.

Block, Richard. 1977. *Violent Crime: Environment, Interaction and Death.* Lexington, Mass.: Lexington Books.

Block, Richard, and Franklin E. Zimring. 1973. "Homicide in Chicago, 1965–1970," *Journal of Research in Crime and Delinquency* 10:1–12.

Boland, Barbara, and James Q. Wilson. 1978. "Age, Crime and Punishment," *Public Interest* 51:22–34.

Clarke, Stevens H. 1974. "Getting 'em Out of Circulation: Does Incarceration of Juvenile Offenders Reduce Crime?" *Journal of Criminal Law and Criminology* 65:528–35.

Cohen, Lawrence. 1975. *Delinquency Dispositions: An Empirical Analysis of Processing Decisions in Three Juvenile Courts.* Albany: Criminal Justice Research Center.

Cook, Phillip J. 1976. "A Strategic Choice Analysis of Robbery." In *Sample Surveys of the Victims of Crime,* ed. Wesley Skogan. Cambridge, Mass.: Ballinger.

Dodge, Richard W., Harold R. Lentzner, and Frederick Shenk. 1976. "Crime in the United States: A Report on the National Crime Survey." In *Sample Surveys of the Victims of Crime,* ed. Wesley Skogan. Cambridge, Mass.: Ballinger.

Eigen, Joel. 1977. "The Borderlands of Juvenile Justice: The Waiver Process in Philadelphia." Ph.D. dissertation, University of Pennsylvania.

Gold, Martin, and David J. Reimer. 1975. "Changing Patterns of Delinquent Behavior among Americans 13 through 16 Years Old: 1967–1972," *Crime and Delinquency Literature* 7:483–517.

Hamparian, Donna, Richard Schuster, Simon Dinitz, and John Conrad. 1978. *The Violent Few: A Study of the Dangerous Juvenile Offender.* Lexington, Mass.: Lexington Books.

Institute of Judicial Administration and American Bar Association, Juvenile Justice Standards Project. 1977a. *Standards Relating to Dispositions.* Cambridge, Mass.: Ballinger.

———. 1977b. *Standards Relating to Juvenile Delinquency and Sanctions.* Cambridge, Mass.: Ballinger.

Jensen, Gary F. 1976. "Race, Achievement and Delinquency: A Further Look at Delinquency in a Birth Cohort," *American Journal of Sociology* 82:379–87.

National Academy of Sciences. 1978. *Report of the Panel on Deterrence and Incapacitation.* Washington, D.C.: U.S. Government Printing Office.

New York Times. 1978a. "Beyond the Teen-Age Gun." Editorial, 28 June, p. 30.

———. 1978b. "Boy, 15, Who Killed 2 and Tried to Kill a Third, is Given 5 Years." 29 June, section 1, p. 1.

———. 1978c. "Carey, in Shift, Backs Trial in Adult Court for Some Juveniles." 30 June, section 1, p. 1.

Petersilia, Joan, P. W. Greenwood, and M. M. Lavin. 1977. *Criminal Careers of Habitual Felons.* Santa Monica, Calif.: RAND Corporation.

Polk, Kenneth, Dean Frease, and F. Lynn Richmond. 1974. "Social Class, School Experiences, and Delinquency," *Criminology* 12:84–96.

President's Commission on Law Enforcement and Administration of Justice. 1967. *Task Force Report: Juvenile Delinquency and Youth Crime.* Washington, D.C.: U.S. Government Printing Office.

Shannon, Lyle W. Unpublished. "Assessing the Relationship of Adult Criminal Careers to Juvenile Careers." Racine, Wis.

Strasburg, Paul A. 1978. *Violent Delinquents: A Report to the Ford Foundation from the Vera Institute of Justice.* New York: Monarch.

Time. 1977. "The Youth Crime Plague." 11 July, pp. 18–30.

U.S. Department of Commerce, Bureau of the Census. 1960. *Characteristics of the Population: U.S. Summary.* Washington, D.C.: U.S. Government Printing Office.

———. 1970. *Characteristics of the Population: U.S. Summary.* Washington, D.C.: U.S. Government Printing Office.

————. 1975. *Current Population Reports*, Series P-25, No. 541. Washington, D.C.: U.S. Government Printing Office.

————. 1977. *Current Population Reports*, Series P-25, No. 643. Washington, D.C.: U.S. Government Printing Office.

U.S. Department of Health, Education, and Welfare. 1975. *Vital Statistics of the United States, 1973*. Rockville, Md.: National Center for Health Statistics.

U.S. Department of Justice, Federal Bureau of Investigation. 1960. *Uniform Crime Reports*. Washington, D.C.: U.S. Government Printing Office.

————. 1970. *Uniform Crime Reports*. Washington, D.C.: U.S. Government Printing Office.

————. 1973. *Uniform Crime Reports*. Washington, D.C.: U.S. Government Printing Office.

————. 1974. *Uniform Crime Reports*. Washington, D.C.: U.S. Government Printing Office.

————. 1975. *Uniform Crime Reports*. Washington, D.C.: U.S. Government Printing Office.

————. 1976. *Uniform Crime Reports*. Washington, D.C.: U.S. Government Printing Office.

————. 1977. *Preliminary Annual Release—Uniform Crime Reports*. Washington, D.C.: U.S. Government Printing Office.

U.S. Department of Justice, Law Enforcement Assistance Administration. 1974. *Crime in Eight American Cities*. Washington, D.C.: U.S. Government Printing Office.

U.S. Department of Justice, National Criminal Justice Information and Statistics Service. 1976. *Criminal Victimization Surveys in Chicago, Detroit, Los Angeles, New York and Philadelphia*. Washington, D.C.: U.S. Government Printing Office.

U.S. Department of Justice, Office of Juvenile Justice and Delinquency Prevention. 1978. *The Serious Juvenile Offender: Proceedings of a National Symposium*. Washington, D.C.: U.S. Government Printing Office.

Van Dine, Stephen, John Conrad, and Simon Dinitz. 1977. "The Incapacitation of the Chronic Thug." Paper presented at the American Society of Criminology meeting, Atlanta, Georgia, November.

Wolfgang, Marvin E., Robert M. Figlio, and Thorsten Sellin. 1972. *Delinquency in a Birth Cohort*. Chicago: University of Chicago Press.

Zimring, Franklin E. 1975. *Dealing with Youth Crime: National Needs and Federal Priorities*. A Policy Report to the Coordinating Council on Juvenile Justice and Delinquency Prevention.

————. 1976. "Crime, Demography and Time in Five American Cities." Paper prepared for the Hudson Institute Project on Criminal Justice Futures.

————. 1978. *Confronting Youth Crime: Report of the Twentieth Century Fund Task Force on Sentencing Policy Toward Young Offenders*. New York: Holmes and Meier.

Zimring, Franklin E., Joel Eigen, and Sheila O'Malley. 1976. "Punishing Homicide in Philadelphia," *University of Chicago Law Review* 43: 227–52.

David H. Bayley

Police Function, Structure, and Control in Western Europe and North America: Comparative and Historical Studies

A B S T R A C T

This essay examines comparative and historical studies of the function, structure, and control of the police in Western Europe and North America, assessing what is known about variations in each and whether explanations for these variations have been convincingly demonstrated. Study of the nature of police work has employed three quite different measures of function—the number of personnel assigned to different specialized units, the kind of occasions that trigger police mobilizations, and the nature of outcomes from mobilizations. The bulk of police personnel appears always to have been assigned to patrol. Though policing is a many-faceted undertaking, state imposition of tasks on the police has declined in all countries during the past century. Adequate historical or comparative data are not available on whether as large a portion of patrol officers' time is taken up with service tasks in other times and places as in the modern United States. Because measures of function differ so significantly, there is no agreement about the factors that might explain variations. Little empirical testing of explanatory hypotheses has been done. National structures of policing are usually described in terms of the system for covering territory and the spatial location of command. The United States is the only country that has failed to enact legislation embodying principles for the establishment and evolution of a national system of policing. Centralization is a useful concept for describing individual cases, but is misleading when applied comparatively unless the geographical scale of the units compared is taken into account. Centralization does not appear to be the wave of the future in the national systems of Western Europe and North

David H. Bayley is Professor, Graduate School of International Studies, University of Denver.

America. Nor, contrary to accepted opinion, does centralization appear to be related to the character of government or the performance of the police. Control refers to active authority over the police by nonpolice persons. Control mechanisms in democracies vary considerably in terms of centralization and the kind of personnel involved. Centralization is unrelated to whether control is exercised by politicians or civil servants. Writing about control of the police tends to be moralistic, failing to distinguish conceptually between politics and policing or to include careful empirical analysis.

This essay examines what is known about the function, organization, and control of the police in Western Europe and North America. These three subjects have been selected because they are central to what people usually want to know about any police.[1] The essay considers whether we have any knowledge about these aspects of policing other than descriptions of particular cases. In order to do this, exclusive attention is given to studies that are either comparative or historical. Only studies that look at policing at several times or places can lead to the development of generalizations about it. Comparative and historical study, which is too often regarded as an academic luxury, especially by practitioners, is essential if any subject is to be understood generically, that is, in the variety of its occurrence. Only by studying multiple instances can explanations be tested about why things are one way rather than another.

This assessment of what is known about what the police do, how they are organized, and who controls them is based on studies published in English because these studies are most available to the readers of this volume. Since a great deal of research on the police has been published in other languages, conclusions drawn here may not adequately reflect all that is known about these features of policing.

The discussion of each aspect of policing follows a common format: first, the range of variation among contemporary systems in Western Europe and North America is described, along with what is known about their evolution, and, second, theories that

[1] Among the many other aspects of policing that might have been selected for study here are recruitment, deployment, impact on crime, rectitude of conduct, and relations with the larger criminal justice system.

have been put forward, if any, to explain these variations are reviewed. Section I, on police functions, discusses three different measures of the nature of police activity that have been widely used, namely, formal assignments, occasions for police acts, and outcomes. What is known about the variation in police function according to each measure is indicated. A schematic summary of the relationships among these measures of activity and the factors that explain variations in each is presented at the end. Section II discusses police organization, focusing on patterns of national coverage and command control. The value of using the concept of centralization in comparing the structure of police forces is sharply criticized. Section III reviews different national approaches to control of the police, distinguishing the agency of control from the territorial organization of control. The essay concludes by assessing the contribution made by comparative and historical studies to what is known about police function, organization, and control and suggests an agenda for future research.

I. Scope of the Police Function

Police work is not confined to protecting life and property and enforcing the law. Various neat but commodious classification schemes have been suggested to cover the range of police activities.[2] None of these schemes does justice to the richness of police work. Here is a nearly exhaustive list of police functions, specifying at least one country where each is performed: (1) protecting life and property (U.S.); (2) enforcing the criminal law (Britain); (3) investigating criminal offenses (France); (4) patrolling public places (Germany); (5) advising about crime prevention (Canada); (6) conducting prosecutions (Britain); (7) sentencing for minor offenses (Germany); (8) maintaining order and decorum in public places by directing, interrupting, and warning (U.S.); (9) guarding persons and facilities (France); (10) regulating traffic (Norway); (11) controlling crowds (Germany); (12) regulating and suppressing vice (U.S.); (13) counseling juveniles (Netherlands); (14) gathering information about

---

[2] American Bar Association 1973; President's Commission on Law Enforcement and Administration of Justice 1967, chap. 4; Webster 1973, pp. 13–14; Wilson 1968, p. 18; Bayley 1975b, pp. 3–27.

political and social life (France); (15) monitoring elections (Italy); (16) conducting counter-espionage (France); (17) issuing ordinances (Germany); (18) inspecting premises (Germany); (19) issuing permits and licenses (Britain); (20) serving summonses (Norway); (21) supervising jails (Norway); (22) impounding animals and lost property (Britain); (23) advising members of the public and referring them to other agencies (Scotland); (24) caring for the incapacitated (U.S.); (25) promoting community crime-prevention activities (Scotland); and (26) participating in policy councils of government (France).

While no police organization does all these things, many do most of them. And bewildering as the variety is, the list ignores housekeeping functions required to maintain the organization.

The critical question is how much attention has been given to each of these functions by police at different times and places. Resolving this, by undertaking enumerative studies, would seem to be straightforward in principle but it is not. The problem is conceptual, not methodological. To study what the police do, one must decide who the police are. Yet classifying people as police depends on what they are doing. It is hardly an advance in knowledge, for example, to survey police forces and find out that all of them enforce the law. Of course they do; if they did not, we would probably not call them police. On the other hand, not all people who enforce the law would be designated police. Are customs agents, for example, police? Even more complicating, many persons commonly classified as police do not spend even a majority of their time enforcing the law.

A determination of what the police do is not, therefore, initially an empirical matter. To the extent that being "police" implies doing some of the functions listed above, then what the police do is fixed by definition. The relation between identifying the police and specifying their functions would be tautological. Consequently, before studying variations in emphasis given by the police to different activities, it is necessary to be clear about what is meant by "police." While defining "police" is also important to an analysis of police structure and control, it is not conceptually required, as it is for function. That is, police are defined largely by what they do but never by how they are organized and rarely by how they are controlled.

An adequate definition of "police" should be sufficiently un-ambiguous to allow observers to recognize most instances of it without dispute. It should also fit commonly held conceptions of "police." Departing too much from core meanings is confusing and requires endless qualifications. Finally, to be useful as a basis for empirical study, the definition should be simple in the sense that it associates "police" with only a few activities. The more detailed the definition, the fewer instances of police will be found. Conversely, the fewer criteria that are included as defining "po-lice," the more varied and heterogeneous will be organizations that qualify as police. This makes generalizing difficult and frustrates the search for explanation.

This is the definition I employ: police are a group authorized in the name of territorial communities to utilize force within the community to handle whatever needs doing. This formulation ties police to government in its most common contemporary form, namely, with a territorial mandate; it excludes armies, except when they use force domestically; it excludes private regulatory forces because they are not authorized in the name of the commu-nity; and it also excludes persons whose enforcement responsi-bilities are restricted to specific portions of the law; finally, it does not tie policing to enforcement of law. This definition will not resolve all arguments about whether particular groups are really police; the world is rich in variety and there will always be borderline cases (see Banton 1974, pp. 662 ff.).

Understanding what is meant by "police," and therefore how they can be recognized for study, we can now examine fairly how they vary in function in different times and places. Studies of what the police do have employed three very different measures of the nature of activity: (1) the formal assignments of personnel, (2) the nature of occasions for police action, and (3) the nature of outcomes from encounters. Assignments are what the police say they are undertaking; occasions are the situations police en-counter when they are mobilized; and outcomes are the actions police take in any situation. To determine assignments, information must be collected about the amount of time devoted by police personnel to different functional specializations within the organization. To measure occasions, one must examine the nature of situations commanding attention regardless of the formal assignments of the personnel involved. Definition of the nature of the situation may be taken either from the public who asked for help or the police who responded. And to measure outcomes, what the police have done in each situation must be determined. All of these are appropriate but very different indicators of the nature of police work. Failure to distinguish them, which has been chronic, leads to great confusion if data of different sorts are used together—a classic case of comparing apples and oranges.

A. Formal Assignments

It is impossible to discuss variations in all types of work listed above. Instead, I shall focus on those that have attracted most attention, namely, criminal investigation, patrolling, traffic regulation, and auxiliary administration. A word of explanation is needed about the meaning of patrolling and auxiliary administration, since they are more ambiguous designations than criminal investigation or traffic regulation. Patrolling suggests an activity but it is actually a mode of deployment. Patrol personnel frequently do not patrol at all, but are kept as a static reserve. The British refer to patrol personnel as "general duties" officers, a much more apt characterization. The designation "patrol" is so common, however, that I have chosen to use it. Patrol personnel should be understood here to be personnel, usually uniformed, who are available for general assignment. What precisely they do when mobilized will be discussed later. Auxiliary administration refers to tasks of government performed by the police that do not fall directly within the criminal law.

Our knowledge of variations in formal police assignments from place to place in the modern world is a matter of impression only. There are no comparative studies providing estimates about relative emphasis on the four specializations discussed here—criminal investigation, patrolling, traffic regulation, and auxiliary administration. This is very curious considering how simple it would be to make tabulations of the number of personnel assigned to different specializations within police organizations.

Although hard data are lacking, two impressions about variations in police assignments are commonly accepted. First, the bulk of police personnel everywhere is assigned to patrol and always has been. Second, the amount of auxiliary administration undertaken by the police—issuing firearms licenses, registering aliens, making background checks on prospective government employees, certifying deaths—has always been greater among continental European than Anglo-Saxon police (Fosdick 1969b, chap. 1; Smith 1940, chap. 1; Bayley 1975b, pp. 330–40). Among continental countries, France and Germany seem to have done the greatest amount of auxiliary administration, Belgium and the Netherlands next, and the Scandinavian countries least. These impressions need to be tested.

Several writers have speculated about why the amount of auxiliary administration varies from place to place. Fosdick (1969b) and Coatman (1959) argue that differences are accounted for by philosophy of government and legal tradition. Continental countries, building on Roman law, have historically had a more paternalistic philosophy of government. The state, embodied in the monarch, has had responsibility for the proper running of the community. In Britain, Canada, and the United States, on the other hand, the state has never been trustee for the community. Acting within the much narrower conception of the responsibility of the state found in the Common Law, these governments do not intervene in social life unless specifically directed to do so. Government in this tradition is best which governs least, not best which governs most helpfully. Consequently, whereas the continental police have shared the state's residual power to regulate where necessary, British, Canadian, and American police have performed only those auxiliary administrative tasks they were expressly given. They have not created administrative work out of general authorization; they have been given specific tasks because no one else was around to do them (Fogelson 1977, pp. 16–17).

Fosdick also thought that size of population, at least for city police forces, might affect the amount of auxiliary administration (1969b, p. 14). Bruce Smith went further and showed that in the United States auxiliary administrative functions in cities tended to increase with population (1940, p. 113). Even this simple hypothesis has not been followed up in subsequent research. The stumbling block lies not with the measurement of population, but with the failure to collect comparative information about functional specialization as measured by formal assignments.

Neither Fosdick, writing in 1915 and 1920 nor Smith, in 1940, did much more than speculate about factors that might be relevant to variations in assignment emphasis. And succeeding generations have not done any better. Rather than analysis based on careful inspection of facts, writers offer lists of possible explanations. Fosdick's own included—in addition to size of population—economic conditions, character of industry, homogeneity of population, and national character. This is hardly an example of parsimonious theorizing. He lamely concluded, and it is a fair statement of our knowledge today of the reasons for variations in functional emphasis: "Sometimes there are other factors, perhaps equally important, which alter the police problem or which, in specific instances, combine with the factors already mentioned to produce special situations and corresponding tasks" (1969b, p. 14). The failure is not Fosdick's or Smith's; they went as far as any have gone.

In both Western Europe and North America the amount of auxiliary administration seems to have declined over the past century (Fosdick 1969b, chap. 1; Richardson 1974, chaps. 3, 4, 5; Stead 1957; Walker 1977, p. 8). Historians attribute this to enormous growth in the general administrative capacity of government. Other bureaucracies have developed to do things previously entrusted to the police.

It would be a mistake to conclude that the decline in the amount of auxiliary administration by the police has simplified police work, making it more coherent. Most historians, certainly those who study the American experience, would agree with Fogelson that the "catchall" nature of policing has remained. Two factors account for this paradox.

First, police activities designed to prevent crime have expanded considerably, especially during the past seventy-five years. In the nineteenth century prevention was achieved by capturing, punishing, and warning. With the twentieth century, crime prevention became less passive, not only a reaction to crimes that had already occurred. Police began to stress solving problems before crime grew out of them. Special units were developed to work with potentially wayward persons, such as juveniles, parolees, repeat offenders, emotionally disturbed, unemployed, minorities, abused children, and violent families. Thus, duties assigned to the police by the state concerned with noncriminal administration probably declined, but duties assigned by police commanders concerned with crime prevention probably increased. This movement may have been more marked in the United States, and perhaps Canada, than in Britain and Europe where the idea of prevention had been developed and accepted earlier. Unfortunately there is little chance that these impressions can be proved conclusively. Proof would require counting the time spent by police personnel in different tasks from year to year and cannot be done from historical sources.

Second, the public's requests for police assistance, which are now the prime instigator of police activity in Western Europe and North America, are as unrelated to criminal law enforcement as were state directives in the past. Where in the nineteenth century the police, American forces especially, lamented non-crime-related duties assigned them by government, they now complain about non-crime-related duties assigned them by the public. So while instigation of police activity may have shifted from state to citizen, the nature of activity may be equally diverse and equally tangential to law enforcement.

There is an interesting parallel between what happened to auxiliary administration over the past one hundred years and the current debate in police circles about what to do with service work. In the former, nonpolice bureaucracies took over much of the administration, in part responding to police complaints about being overburdened and distracted. Today some police officers are again urging concentration on law enforcement and the handing over of tasks not directly concerned with serious criminality to other agencies. Whether or not this occurs, now is the time to collect information on the composition of police specialization so that in the future it will be possible to determine whether anything has really changed.

B. *Occasions for Action*

The need for getting behind formal assignments in determining the nature of police work is obvious. Personnel in any specialized unit may devote time to work formally assigned to other units. This is particularly true for patrol personnel. They often regulate traffic and do auxiliary administration, such as checking potential safety hazards or serving legal papers. It is necessary, therefore, to obtain information about the daily activities of all personnel regardless of formal assignment. This has been very difficult to do in the past, requiring inspection of individual diaries or logs. With the advent of computer management in police forces, it becomes much easier. Command-and-control computer systems can record the kinds of events personnel become involved in and the kinds of action they take. The study of police functions is on the verge of a knowledge-explosion.

The search for historical trends must also avoid confusing formal specialization with real activity. All police forces during the past one hundred years developed a host of specialized units—traffic, criminal investigation, community relations, juvenile counseling, riot control, and so forth. Only patrol personnel represent a continuation of the omnicompetent tradition in policing. But it would be dangerous to infer from specialization that relatively more attention is being given to those specialties. Consider traffic control. Although traffic regulation as a specialization emerged with the development of the motor car, traffic congestion had been a preoccupation very much earlier (Richardson 1974, chap. 7). Have more personnel-hours been devoted to traffic management in the age of the automobile than in the age of the horse? We simply do not know. Similarly with criminal investigation. Most historians agree that the "new police" created by Peel in 1829 devoted little attention to detection; arrests were made immediately upon commission of a crime or not at all. Therefore it would seem reasonable to conclude that creation of criminal investigation units in England in the latter part of the nineteenth century did mark a shift in work emphasis. In the United States, however, police stressed detection, especially the recovery of stolen property, throughout their history. The American public, unlike the British, did not fear the plainclothes policeman. In London during the 1830s and '40s there was a public outcry against taking the Bobby out of uniform for criminal investigation, while in New York about the same time there was resistance to putting the officer into one (Critchley 1967, pp. 16–62; Miller 1977, pp. 36–37). In the American case, then, detective specialization would not seem to indicate a substantial change in function.

The most elaborate and extensive studies of the occasions for police action have focused on patrol personnel. This is appropriate since the majority of police personnel are assigned to patrol, and patrol is the most amorphous of specializations; what is actually done cannot be deduced from the formal assignment. The proportion of criminal to noncriminal situations patrolmen become involved in varies considerably. Reiss and Black, in their celebrated study of patrol mobilization in the United States, found that the vast majority (87 percent) were instigated by citizens rather than officers (Reiss 1967, p. 17; Reiss 1971, chaps. 1, 2). As many as half of these did not involve criminal matters. Data from elsewhere in the United States suggest that the proportion is often much lower. One study of Syracuse, New York, found that only 20 percent of calls from the public involved criminality; in a city in California about 33 percent involved criminality (Cumming, Cumming, and Edell 1965, p. 279; Webster 1973, pp. 13–14). There have been fewer studies in Europe of the occasions for patrol action than in the United States. The few that have been done indicate that a larger proportion of patrol work in Europe involves criminality: in Britain, 35 percent; in Norway, 57 percent (Home Office 1973, p. 11; Hauge and Stabell 1974). In the Netherlands a survey of the public showed that 14.5 percent of their contacts with the police during the preceding three years had involved criminal matters, and an additional 25 percent related to traffic infractions (Junger-Tas 1978, p. 5).

It is now accepted on both sides of the Atlantic that patrol officers spend a larger proportion of their time acting as "peace officers" than as "law officers," in Michael Banton's seminal phrase (1964). Unfortunately, without more information, especially from Europe, it is impossible to document this from place to place. An international study of the occasions for patrol mobilizations and encounters is urgently needed.

If contemporary data of this sort are fragmentary, they are nonexistent historically. One or two courageous historians have ventured opinions about the proportion of patrol work involved with criminality, but they recognize the weakness of retrospective analysis.[3] Conclusions are inevitably impressionistic, drawing on biographical accounts, or inferential, from arrest statistics and deployment patterns.

Despite the paucity of evidence on variations in the nature of patrol work, considerable thought has been given to factors that might account for differences. The following paragraphs describe the four best-developed lines of speculation.

1. The more responsive and sympathetic the public believes the police to be, the more likely they are to bring non-crime matters to police attention (Clark 1965; Newman 1978, pp. 29–39). The public's view may be shaped by circumstances within the control of the police themselves, such as demeanor and training. On the other hand, some studies have investigated the hypothesis that structural factors are involved over which the police have no control. For example, urban patrol personnel may be more heavily engaged in crime-related events than rural officers because urban people are less willing than rural ones to approach the police for mediation and services. The more impersonal the police appear and the less well integrated the police are into the life of the community, the less willing people are to call for their help except in times of extreme need (Cain 1973, chap. 2).

2. The fewer the number of police per unit of population, the more police must concentrate on crime-related events, neglecting

[3] Richardson, for example, says, "We do not have this kind of evidence for the nineteenth century, although it seems safe to say that the nineteenth century patrolman spent more of his time dealing with family squabbles, troublesome drunks, lost children, and stray horses than he did on safe cracking and bank robberies" (1974, pp. x–xi).

what they deem to be nonessential work (Cain 1973, p. 22; Miller, 1977, pp. 36–37).

3. The greater the emphasis given by a police organization to crime prevention, the more likely it is that non-crime-related requests for assistance will be taken seriously (see Fogelson 1977; Walker 1977; Richardson 1974; Carte and Carte 1975). Organizational philosophy, especially when translated into organizational rewards for individual officers, affects what police attend to.

4. The less tolerant the public is of diverse life styles, especially as displayed in public places, the more enforcement-oriented— though not necessarily crime-related—activity they will require of the police. Putting the point more generally: police attention to legal infractions is affected by what the public indicates it wants (see Reiss 1971; Miller 1977; Fogelson 1977; Storch 1976; Lofland 1973).

These propositions are only hypotheses; they have not been tested. Nor are they likely to be as long as data on variations in the character of police work remains patchy. So far, considerably more energy has been devoted to speculating about why there are variations than in determining the pattern of them.

C. Outcomes

The third measure of the nature of police work is outcomes from encounters. This perspective, which has probably attracted more attention than the other two put together, is founded on the recognition that police action is discretionary. Characterizing police work requires determining what the police did, not what they were called upon to cope with. Studies of outcomes employ the terminology of "peace officer" and "law officer," denoting differences in dominant style for handling events of a particular sort. I do not intend to discuss this rich and important work because it falls within the purview of Professor Bittner's essay in this volume. I shall simply note that when James Q. Wilson compares varieties of police behavior, he is referring for the most part to outcomes (1968). So, too, are Michael Banton (1964), Maureen Cain (1973), James Walsh (1972), Jerome Skolnick (1966), and Donald Black (1971). While there are more international studies of outcomes than of occasions, they are still very rare.

Because outcomes are conceptually different from assignments and occasions, requiring another strategy for measurement, the explanations for variations in the nature of police work by those who have studied outcomes are different from the explanations of those who have studied assignments and occasions. Variations in outcomes have been explained by the extent of social integration of the police into a community (Banton 1964; Cain 1973); scale and character of community (Banton 1964; Cain 1973; Punch and Naylor 1973, pp. 358–60); salience of various role-setting groups in the lives of policemen (Cain 1973; Skolnick 1966); organizational rewards (Manning 1977; Rubinstein 1973; Skolnick 1966); formal assignments (Reiss 1971); occasions (Reiss 1971; Reiss and Bordua 1967; Black 1971); laws and formal rules (President's Commission on Law Enforcement and Administration of Justice 1967); proactive versus reactive instigation (Skolnick 1966; Reiss 1971; Reiss and Bordua 1967; Black 1971); social and political environment (Wilson 1968); reactions of non-police actors in encounters—suspects, complainants, and the audience (Reiss 1971; Sykes and Clark, undated; Black 1971); aspirations and fears of officers (Skolnick 1966; Walsh 1972); and national character (Fosdick 1969b; Bayley 1975a; Miller 1977; Morrison 1974).

So many explanations have been put forward to explain the nature of police work because different measures have been used. One would not expect the same factors to account for variations in all of them. At the same time, these measures of police work are not wholly independent of one another. They are interrelated in two ways. First, changes in one affect changes in the others. For example, assignments influence the kinds of occasions that come to the attention of the police. Similarly, the kind of event brought to the police shapes what the police can do. Second, independent factors affecting one measure of the police function may affect others. For example, public opinion about the need to enforce certain laws influences both formal assignments and outcomes. National traditions may affect what the people bring to the police as well as what the police do.

The conceptual and empirical points that have been made about

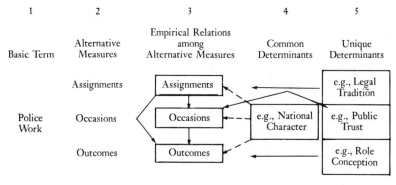

Fig. 1

the three measures of police work are illustrated in Figure 1. The relation between column 1 and column 2 is definitional. "Assignments," "occasions," and "outcomes" are distinguishable meanings of "police work." The relations shown among the boxes in column 3 are empirical, as are the relations between columns 3, 4, and 5. Separating common from unique determinants helps to organize the wealth of hypotheses suggested to account for differences in "police work." Legal tradition, for instance, probably impinges only on assignments; public trust only on occasions. But reactive or proactive instigation may affect both occasions and outcomes, while national character influences assignments, occasions, and outcomes.

II. Structure of Policing

I shall examine two aspects of the structure of policing—the pattern for covering territory and the location of command. The unit of analysis will be countries, as opposed to municipalities, provinces, or regions, because countries are the political entities that create systems of policing.[4]

Most countries in Western Europe and North America cover any unit of territory with a single police force. While there may

[4] For summaries of characteristics of coverage and direction in all the countries of Western Europe and North America, readers should consult Becker, *Police Systems of Europe* (1973); Cramer, *The World's Police* (1964), Dorey and Swidler, *World Police Systems* (1975); and Coatman, *Police* (1959). Bruce Smith's *Police Systems in the United States* (1940) is still as useful a single work on American police forces as can be found. For the structure of police systems up to 1915, Raymond Fosdick's *European Police Systems* (1969b, orig. pub. 1915) and his *American Police Systems* (1969a, orig. pub. 1920) are excellent.

be more than one force in a country, their jurisdictions do not overlap. The exceptions are Italy, Spain, and the United States. Decentralized political systems, even federations, do not necessarily have multiple coverage. Canada and Germany, for example, have laid down principles in law for determining which police force will have jurisdiction in any area. On the other hand, highly centralized political systems sometimes create competing police forces throughout their territory. Spain has done so with the Guardia Civil and the Policia Armada; Italy with the Carabinieri, and the Guardie di Pubblica Sicurezza. All national governments, federal or otherwise, create investigatory and enforcement units to deal with matters touching uniquely on central government responsibilities. These do represent an overlay in policing, but whether the duplication is substantial depends on operating agreements worked out in each country. Comparatively, the activities of the FBI in the United States seem to represent more intrusive duplication than those of the Royal Canadian Mounted Police or of Germany's Federal Criminal Police Bureau.[5]

All countries in Western Europe and North America except the United States have enacted statutes specifying principles for the way in which coverage is to be organized. Such legislation usually provides for adaptation over time, specifying what kind of police an area may have and the circumstances under which new forces may be created. A crucial feature, again lacking in the United States, is that new forces displace old ones, even though the forces involved may have been created by different levels of government. The United States has no general principles for organizing coverage. Almost any government can create police, unconstrained by considerations of geographical scale, overlapping jurisdiction, optimum size, or efficiency. The United States, as Bruce Smith noted almost forty years ago, does not really have a system of policing. Instead there is a hodgepodge of autonomous forces created by various levels of government according to parochial considerations. American police coverage is made up of patches on patches rather than tailored to fit.

This is not to suggest that countries with principles regulating

[5] The Royal Canadian Mounted Police also serves on a contract basis as the police of some provinces and municipalities.

police creation and development are without friction. In Italy the Carabinieri and the Guardie di Pubblica Sicurezza have competed bitterly for over a century, often working at cross-purposes. In the Netherlands, where the law authorizing creation of new forces is open-ended, fragmentation of police coverage has been increasing. Only in the United States has confusion in coverage been deliberate.

The second aspect of structure to be examined is the location of command. Is command located at one place, several, or many? This is what people have in mind when they ask how centralized a police system is. Here I will be looking only at the location of police command authority over operations. The structure of supervision over the police itself will be taken up in the next section.

As Raymond Fosdick noted more than fifty years ago, continental European countries tend to be more centralized with respect to command than Anglo-Saxon countries. In France, Italy, and Spain, direct orders can be issued from national police headquarters to local chiefs of police. There are variations, however, even in continental Europe. In Germany police command is decentralized, being exercised by the states that make up the federation. In the Netherlands, only the State Police (Reischpolicie) can be directed from The Hague; the Municipal Police (Gemeentepolitie) are organized into autonomous commands under mayors. The Norwegian Police Act, 1936, vests authority over the police, including the power to direct operations, in the Ministry of Justice. By convention, however, the ministry has never interfered with day-to-day operations, limiting its directions to matters of general policy.

Generalizations about command centralization in Europe are complicated by the practice of dividing control functionally. In several countries, police forces come under the direction of central authorities with respect to criminal investigation and prosecution, although they are independent with respect to everything else. In other words, chiefs of police can deploy their forces and maintain order as they choose, but when they apply the law their actions must conform to national regulations.

Canada and the United States are the extreme cases of decentralized command. Canada has about seven hundred autonomous municipal police forces, several provincial forces, and the Royal Canadian Mounted Police. In the United States the situation is so chaotic that no one knows for sure how many police forces there are. Bruce Smith thought there were about 40,000, but his celebrated figure has recently been challenged. Current estimates are about 25,000 (U.S. Department of Justice 1970).

In practice, command is never, or only very fitfully, exercised centrally over local operations even in the most centralized countries. Statements about differences in centralization are almost always based on the ease with which command can be appropriated by higher levels rather than on how often it actually occurs. It would be instructive, and would perhaps deflate some myths, if studies were made of the relations between different levels of command in countries contrasting in formal structure. Of course what happens in practice is affected by legal arrangements. But how much? There is no research that answers this question.

I have followed tradition in describing the location of command in terms of centralization and decentralization. This practice is useful in discussing single cases, but when comparisons are made among multiple cases it can generate misleading conclusions. Statements about differences in centralization are meaningless unless the geographical scale of the units compared is specified. What sense does it make to point out that France is more centralized than the United States when France is about four-fifths the size of Texas? The Netherlands has 143 police forces, making it much more centralized than the United States, but it is only half the size of West Virginia. Centralized Italy is smaller than decentralized Norway. Moderately centralized Germany is about the size of Oregon. A police system that is centralized in a small country may be smaller than one part of a decentralized system in a larger country.

Because both scale of jurisdiction and the structure of command affect the dynamics of control and responsiveness, debates about desirable combinations of centralization and decentralization are meaningless in the abstract. Yet politicians, experts, and the public unthinkingly employ these terms when arguing the merits of police structures in vastly different territorial units. To argue against command centralization in a city, for example, by invoking the rigidities of France is absurd. In order for discussions about the structure of command in police systems to escape present fatuity, studies must be undertaken to compare the effects of various degrees of centralization in areas of different size. Do differences in centralization in units of the same geographical size affect such matters as responsiveness to local problems, efficacy of supervision, individuation of justice, and unit costs? Perhaps there are thresholds in scale: decentralization in units below a certain size may always be cumbersome and counterproductive, while centralization in units above another size may be similarly inefficient. Such questions are rarely formulated, let alone answered.

One reason why the concept of centralization exerts such fascination is that it is assumed to be related to the character of government, especially the quality of police relations with citizens. Actually, centralized police systems are not necessarily more authoritarian than decentralized ones, even accounting for differences in scale. Quite small police forces have been brutal and unresponsive, while forces that are centralized by American standards have enviable reputations for considerateness and constraint. Moreover, the characters of governments change but police structure appears very durable. This seems to have been the European experience. Perhaps because beliefs about the relation between the structure of policing and the character of government—and the character of police operations—are so strong, there has yet to be a careful test of it. Americans, especially, continually assume that structure critically influences the proportion of freedom in government. What is needed are comparisons among countries of scale, centralization of police structure, character of government, and performance indicators of police activity.

Arguments for a link between police centralization of command and the character of government often confuse where control is located with who exercises that control. Command may be decentralized but political authority completely unrepresentative, with no legal checks on executive action. Conversely, command may be centralized but government both democratic and responsible to law. Conceptually, the territorial organization of police command is distinct from the nature of control over police operations.[6]

Viewed historically, significant changes have occurred in the structure of national police systems. Although the trends are mixed, tendencies are in the direction of reducing the number of separate commands, usually through amalgamation, and creating central coordinating services. It would be straining, however, considering Western Europe and North America together, to believe that something called centralization is the wave of the future.

Following enactment of national police laws in Norway in 1936 and Sweden in 1965, both countries replaced local police with larger consolidated commands. There are now 53 municipal forces in Norway, an area slightly larger than New Mexico, and 180 sheriff's (Lennsmen) jurisdictions. In Sweden there are 119 police districts. Britain has gradually consolidated police forces over the past two centuries, accelerating the pace sharply since 1962. From 125 in that year, the number has now been reduced to 43. In the Netherlands, by contrast, there are 143 forces today where there were 70 in 1945. Municipalities are allowed to create their own forces, replacing the central government's state police, when their population exceeds 25,000. In France, a formally centralized system, reorganization has created new commands. In 1971 four commands were made out of the old Paris prefecture of police.

In Germany, Canada, and the United States, no trend is dis-

[6] One of the best formulations of this point comes from the British Royal Commission on the Police (1962, p. 45): "British liberty does not depend, and never has depended, upon any particular form of police organization. It depends upon the supremacy of Parliament and on the rule of law. We do not accept that the criterion of a police state is whether a country's police force is national rather than local—if that were the test, Belgium, Denmark, and Sweden should be described as police states. The proper criterion is whether the police are answerable to law and, ultimately, to a democratically elected parliament. It is here, in our view, that the distinction is to be found between a free and a totalitarian state. In the countries to which the term police state is applied opprobriously, police power is controlled by the government; but they are so called not because the police are nationally organized, but because government acknowledges no accountability to a democratically elected parliament, and the citizen cannot rely on the courts to protect him. Thus in such countries the foundations upon which British liberty rests do not exist."

cernible. After World War II, Germany replaced Hitler's centralized police system with control by the constituent states. Although the central government now maintains a border security force and a riot police formation, Germany has reinstituted the system of state autonomy in police affairs that was a condition for German unification in 1871 (Fosdick 1969b; Liang 1970; Dawson 1914; Finer 1962; Pollock 1938). Information is not available indicating trends in the number of subordinate commands allowed by the states. In the United States and Canada some consolidations have taken place. These have not been many, and they have probably been offset by creation of commands in new towns and suburbs (Walker 1977; Kelly and Kelly 1976). In the United States, starting at the turn of the century, state police forces were created, followed shortly by the Federal Bureau of Investigation. Neither development can be characterized as significant command centralization. Old commands were not superseded nor was general police authority always given (Smith 1940, pp. 164–65).

A much clearer movement has been the development in all countries, especially during the past seventy-five years, of centralized servicing facilities. Sometimes these have been designed to ensure proper coordination and have been given supervisory authority. More commonly, they provide technical assistance, expertise, record-keeping, and training facilities that subordinate forces may utilize if they wish. National or state regulations prescribing standards for police operations have frequently been enacted. Whether control follows, however, has to be determined case by case, since it depends on whether oversight is meaningful and leverage compelling. Comparative research would be very instructive: through what means can central service authorities influence local activities and on what kind of matters? For the most part, central services seem to have arisen primarily because of practical needs felt by subordinate forces. They are rarely undertaken for the sake of control. Moreover, they may have the effect of making local control stronger by augmenting the capacity of small forces to cope effectively with modern problems of criminality and disorder (Smith 1940, p. 318).

III. Control of the Police

What kinds of persons, located at what points in political systems, have active supervisory power over the police? I put the question this way because forms of control over the police are manifold: they include the power of appointment, dismissal, and promotion; providing budget and supervising expenditures; laying down enforcement priorities; granting legal authority; fixing rewards and punishments; and publicizing police affairs. Control, therefore, is exercised by many agencies—courts, legislatures, cabinets, civil service commissions, ministries, and the press. Though the breadth of control mechanisms should be kept in mind, I am simplifying the discussion by focusing on control in the form of explicit and active authority to supervise and direct police activities. Who can exercise effective direction of the police when they choose? The emphasis on self-activating, direct, and explicit supervision excludes groups that have the ability to influence, sometimes profoundly, but do so as a part of other activities, such as legislating or adjudicating. The courts, then, to which the police are accountable in some measure in every country of Western Europe and North America, will not be discussed, since their control is episodic and reactive.

Patterns of control of the police vary considerably in Western Europe and North America.[7] In Britain, control is in the hands of the "Police Authority" in each force area except London. The "Police Authority" is an appointed body two-thirds of which is composed of elected members of local government councils and one-third of magistrates. Control in Britain can be characterized, therefore, as being situated at local levels of government and exercised largely by political persons. In France, on the other hand, supervision is national and bureaucratic. Any local control is exercised only by delegation from the central government. Moreover, it is carried out primarily by permanent civil servants, such as prefects. Although ultimate authority does reside in the national parliament, no structure has been provided for direct contact between politicians and command personnel, except for the Minister of the Interior and the Director-General of the Na-

[7] For basic reference materials see n. 4.

tional Police. Supervision is carried out by the bureaucracy of the Ministry of the Interior, working both through the central office of the national police and the prefects of each local government area. Such national and bureaucratic control is the dominant continental pattern, being found also in Italy, Spain, Norway, Sweden, Denmark, and the Netherlands. In Germany, control is bureaucratic as well, but it emanates from the states, an intermediate level of government. Sweden and Denmark are unique in having established advisory boards of elected persons at national and local levels, but their advice is not binding.

Control of the police in the United States is local and political. Considering that there are several layers of police in the United States, it is perhaps better to say that control is exercised wherever police command is exercised, which means primarily locally, and most often by elected persons. Some may argue that contact between a chief of police and politicians is not always direct, being mediated by a manager of public safety, a professional city manager, or occasionally a police board. The judgment is a relative one. Politicians are in much closer contact with command personnel in the United States than anywhere on the European continent. In Canada, control is decentralized, and it is exercised by appointed police commissioners, some of whom are elected officials. In effect, direct supervision by politicians is mediated by a single layer of other persons, neither wholly elected nor wholly bureaucratic.

Granting that systems of control over the police in Western Europe and North America are varied, several generalizations can be made:

1. Although all the countries of the sample are democracies, some with longer and more respectable pedigrees than others, there is no single pattern of supervision. It is not possible to say that democratic government requires a particular mode of control. Put more generally, the structure of supervision of the police does not appear to be tied to the character of government. This proposition needs to be tested over a broader range of political systems. It is instructive to note, however, that Fosdick came to the same conclusion just before World War I when monarchical and non-

democratic regimes were more in evidence in Europe (1969b, pp. 231–34).

2. It does not appear that repressiveness of a police system is a function of the place at which political supervision is exercised. A centralized political regime may not necessarily be more repressive in police policy than a decentralized one (Bayley 1975b, p. 369). This point parallels an earlier proposition, namely, that repressiveness is not related to centralization of command.

3. National structures of supervision tend to be congruent with the structure of police command. Supervisory control and command initiative are located at the same places in the territorial structure of government. My own guess is that the location of political authority—national, intermediate, local—determines the structure of police command, certainly not the other way around.[8] There are some incongruous systems. In the Netherlands, apart from the state police in rural areas, command coincides with municipalities but supervision is exercised from The Hague. This is true also in Norway.

4. Patterns of supervision over the police are relatively unchanging over time. Americans have insisted throughout their history on local control. Canadians, too, have eschewed national control, though they have stressed intermediate supervision by the provinces more than Americans have state control. Germany, apart from the Hitler interlude, has had supervision of the police by the states of its federal system since 1871. France's system of central supervision by appointed civil servants is to be found before the Revolution. The Italian system, quite similar to the French, began at unification over a hundred years ago, building on Piedmontese precedents that were even older (Bayley 1975a, p. 37).

This is not to suggest that there have been no changes in patterns of supervision. There have been and they can be labeled significant in the sense that they involved intense struggles over considerable periods of time. However, though momentous by

[8] Incongruity between the structures of police command and external supervision may represent fault lines that require adjustment. If the locus of political authority in a country shifts away from local units, for example, there may be a tendency for command initiative to follow (Bayley 1975b, p. 368).

local standards of opposition, they have not represented a change in character by international standards. This is an excellent example of how comparison provides perspective. A genuine revolution in control was certainly accomplished in the United States between 1890 and 1960. Control in all aspects had been exercised by political machines, negating even centralized command within cities. During the twentieth century political control became attenuated, sometimes absent altogether, in hiring, promotion, discipline, and operational command. Indeed, some observers now argue that the police have became too autonomous and insufficiently responsive to public opinion, especially within ethnically distinct neighborhoods. So change has certainly been real, even though it has not challenged two characteristics of American control of the police, namely, close contact by elected officials with the command hierarchy and extreme decentralization.

Though excellent historical studies tracing mutations in forms of control are now available in English for Britain and the United States, and to a lesser extent for Canada, there are none for continental European countries, apart from Stead's fine book, *The Police of Paris* (1957; also see Carte and Carte 1975; Fogelson 1977; Richardson 1974; Walker 1977; Critchley 1967). In explaining patterns of control over the police, these histories reinforce the point that political philosophy and government tradition are crucial, and that they are distinctive nationally.

5. Throughout Western Europe and North America control of the police is seen as requiring a balance between impartiality under law and responsiveness to community direction. The police are a peculiar executive agency of government. Like all administrative departments, they are accountable to the community that has authorized them to act. Unlike other executive agencies, however, they do not simply carry out particular policies stated in law; they are responsible for enforcing law generally. Political responsibility and the rule of law intersect at the police.

Recognition of this dual responsibility has grown slowly in Western Europe and North America with different countries starting from different places. In Europe the notion of state responsibility to the common interest, rather than to representative opinion, emerged very early. Popular control of the police was, therefore, anathema. The British shared this view, making police-men crown officers, like magistrates and justices of the peace, and insulating them from partisan politics. In the United States, however, the police were considered instruments of representa-tive government. And government was politics for Americans, not administration under law as was the case in Europe.

During the past century and a half there has been a convergence in the philosophies of police control of Europe and North America. In Europe fairness was gradually seen to be enhanced by making government responsive to public opinion. As a result, the franchise has been steadily widened. Across the Atlantic, where political participation had always been very open, impartiality was under-stood to be enhanced by lessening direct political control. Police were urged to develop a sense of professional responsibility to law transcending local interests. Throughout North America and Western Europe the ideal is now very nearly the same, though mechanisms for achieving balanced control vary considerably as befits national traditions.

Control of the police has been discussed thus far in terms of formal structures. Anyone familiar with administration knows that what really goes on may be very different. Some scholars have suggested, for instance, that in Britain and the United States the police are much more autonomous than they appear (Robinson 1974, pp. 277–316; Banton 1975, pp. 24–25; Wilson 1968, chap. 8; Reiss 1971, chap. 4). There has been almost no research, how-ever, into the interaction between police and erstwhile supervising agencies. How often do such authorities inquire into departmental affairs? How often do they meet and who sets the agenda? Do the police seek out their advice? On what sort of issues? What do members discuss when they meet? Are policies formulated explicitly or are they submerged in ad hoc discussion?

While it is clearly important to determine the nature of control over the police, paying particular attention to the role of politi-cians, it is no less important to examine the role of the police in politics. Police and politics have a reciprocal relationship. Space does not permit a full discussion of this meaty topic, so three comments must suffice. First, since police activities in politics are one indication of the character of political life, writing about them tends to be emotional. Some of the most superficial, careless, and tendentious studies of the police have been done on this subject. Second, the police affect political life in many ways besides spying, intelligence gathering, and crowd control. Attention needs to be given, in addition, to police supervision of elections, granting of licenses for parades and meetings, use of the criminal law to harass dissidents, actions that antagonize public opinion and undermine the legitimacy of regimes, and lobbying and voting en bloc. Equally destructive of discriminating analysis is the easy identification of any police activity as politics, which is the argument from the radical left. It thereby becomes impossible to discover differences in the impact of the police on political life in different times and places. Third, I suggest the following negative hypothesis about the relation between the police and politics that contradicts accepted beliefs: the salience of the police in a country's political life is not related either to the extent of penetration by politicians into policing or to the degree that external control of the police is centralized. Bureaucratic control of the police may impel police intrusion into politics as much as political control. Politicians are not the only politically interested persons. French experience would be to the point. Decentralized supervision, too, may produce as much partisan intrusion as centralized control. Certainly American experience suggests this.[9]

The relation between the police and politics is much more complex than is commonly assumed. Careful nonpolemical comparative research, sensitive to conceptual problems in separating "police" from "politics," is sadly lacking.

IV. Conclusion

Specific gaps in our knowledge—both descriptive and explanatory—have been mentioned in the course of discussing the function, structure, and control of the police. Here is a summary list of topics needing attention, presented in the hope that it may

[9] Bayley 1969, pp. 16 ff.; Bayley 1975b; Berkley 1969; Bowden 1978; Bramstedt 1945; Bunyan 1976; Coatman 1959; Emerson 1968; Mosse 1975; Payne 1966; Center for Research on Criminal Justice 1977.

serve as a research agenda for people who are concerned with increasing knowledge of policing and are prepared to do so comparatively or historically.

A. Functions
   1. Variation in functions as represented by the number of personnel assigned to different organizational specializations
   2. Nature of work performed by all personnel regardless of specialized assignment
   3. Nature of occasions for police mobilizations
   4. Nature of outcomes from mobilizations
B. Structure
   1. The real texture of command and supervisory relations among different structural levels
   2. The effect of variations in command centralization in jurisdictions of the same geographical scale on features of police performance such as authoritarianism, responsiveness, rectitude, and efficiency
   3. Evolution of central supervision, control, and servicing within countries
C. Control
   1. Whether the character of government affects the nature of control over the police
   2. Whether centralization of control over the police affects police repressiveness
   3. Evolution of control mechanisms over the police in non–English-speaking countries
   4. The nature of real as opposed to legal supervision of the police by bodies entrusted with such authority
   5. Impingement of the police on political and social life
   6. Whether the character of supervision of the police affects the extensiveness of the police role in politics

Reviewing the studies that throw light on the function, structure, and control of the police, what can one say about the state of the art with respect to comparative and historical research? Historians have been much more productive than comparativists.

There are many more longitudinal than cross-sectional studies. Historical interest, especially in the past ten years, has grown enormously. The blind eye, as Charles Reith characterized historical interest in the police thirty years ago, is beginning to show discernment (1952). Understandably, writing in English has concentrated on Britain and the United States with only glimmerings of interest in Canada or Ireland. Stead, *The Police of Paris* (1957), and Liang, *The Berlin Police Force in the Weimar Republic* (1970), are wonderful exceptions. The problem with historical scholarship is that it tends to be topically diffuse, not focusing carefully on particular features of police affairs so that explanations are naturally suggested. This may be inevitable in early stages of interest. Wilbur Miller's *Cops and Bobbies: Police Authority in New York and London, 1830–1870* (1977), which is both historical and comparative, shows what can be done to generate insightful explanations if analytical focus is maintained. So, too, do Fogelson's *Big-City Police* (1977), Samuel Walker's *A Critical History of Police Reform* (1977), and James F. Richardson's *Urban Police in the United States* (1974), though they examine only the American experience.

While specialized histories of the police are at last being written, general histories still give the police scant attention. Indexes of standard histories of countries in Western Europe and North America show few references to them. Until the late 1960s most national histories failed to mention the police at all. The major exceptions were countries with histories including notorious authoritarian periods, such as Russia and Germany.

Comparative work on the police is still very thin. Moreover, with one or two exceptions, it tends to be narrowly descriptive. Indeed, the bulk of comparative material on the police is in the form of reference books, surveys of features of contemporary systems.[10] Such works are valuable, providing useful facts on foreign police systems, but they need to be quickly superseded by analytical research. The other prominent group of comparative writings deals with the police and politics. Apart from Coatman's *Police* (1959) and Bramstedt's *Dictatorship and Political*

[10] See n. 4.

Police (1945), these works are more polemical than insightful, concerned with alleged abuses of police power. Often they do not focus so much on the police, at least according to the definition proposed earlier, as on practices of authoritarian control.

The great puzzle concerning comparative and historical work on the police is why superb initial scholarship did not generate continuing interest. The great classics are Raymond Fosdick's *European Police Systems* of 1915 (1969b) and his *American Police Systems* of 1920 (1969a) and Bruce Smith's *Police Systems in the United States* (1940). They are comparative in the international sense, apt at tracing evolutionary changes, precise and careful conceptually, persistent in providing explanations, and pointed in making recommendations. They set a standard that has yet to be approached.

There are several reasons why comparative work on the police, particularly internationally, has not been abundant.

First, the climate of opinion in academic circles has not been congenial. For some people study of the police is associated only with technical questions of administration. It is considered dull and "applied." For others, exactly the reverse is true. Police are worth studying only as a part of making larger political diagnoses. They are important as a distasteful sidelight to abusive political control. Then, too, American academics, like their fellow citizens, have perhaps allowed the low status of the police, especially in the criminal justice system, to obscure the pervasive power they wield.

Second, comparative study among countries requires skill in foreign languages. It is less demanding to study the history of one country's police than to compare several countries' police at any one time. Furthermore, as one shifts from country to country, the amount of background material that must be mastered grows oppressively. How many researchers are prepared to compare Canada, Sweden, and Germany?

Third, documentation on the police is not usually found in the holdings of even very good libraries. Individual researchers are forced to collect materials themselves from each force they study. At the present time there is no bibliographical center in the world committed to maintaining an international working collection of police material. Elementary questions about pay scales, legal liabilities of officers, recruitment procedures, deployment tactics, training, and statutory powers cannot be answered by going to a single collection. The greatest contribution that could be made toward comparative study of the police would be establishment of an international data collection, even if limited to serial reports in the public domain. The situation is only marginally better comparatively within countries, with each country's situation depending on how active the national government has been in exercising oversight. American collections, for example, of material about domestic police forces are hardly better than collections of international materials.

Fourth, permission has to be obtained, often from a hierarchy of authorities, to gain access to police records and personnel. Sometimes this is easy to get, often it is not. Research on democratic countries will always be more extensive, or at least more soundly documented, than elsewhere. There can, of course, be problems anywhere, since all bureaucracies try to protect themselves. In my experience, however, the police in Western Europe and North America are not noticeably more closed than other institutions. In fact, it has seemed to me that, when it comes to observing operations and evaluating accomplishment, the police are more open than universities. The police are often anxious to inform, if only to tell what they think of as their side of the story. They suffer almost universally from both a lack of appreciation and a sense of neglect. Serious study of their activities is welcomed by many forces, not only as a cost of public responsibility, but as long-delayed recognition of their social importance. They are more flattered than threatened at being singled out for thoughtful examination.

In sum, the field of comparative and historical research on the police in Western Europe and North America is still in its infancy. Concepts are ill-defined and a good deal of polemics are to be found. In place of explanations there are lists of factors that might exert an influence. Vague theorizing substitutes for sound descriptive research into patterns of variation. For the practitioner, the field is bound to seem disappointing—sometimes stimulating no doubt but giving little that can be carried away and applied. For the scholar, at least the scholar who has sense enough to recognize the importance of the police in national life, the field offers almost unlimited possibilities for making a contribution.

REFERENCES AND SELECTED BIBLIOGRAPHY

American Bar Association. 1973. *The Urban Police Function*. New York: American Bar Association.

Banton, Michael. 1964. *The Policeman in the Community*. New York: Basic Books.

———. 1974. "Police." *The New Encyclopaedia Britannica* (Fifteenth edition). Chicago: Encyclopaedia Britannica.

———. 1975. "A New Approach to Police Authorities," *Police* 7: 24–25.

Bayley, David H. 1969. *The Police and Political Development in India*. Princeton: Princeton University Press.

———. 1975a. *A Comparative Analysis of Police Practices*. United Nations Asian and Far East Institute for the Prevention of Crime and Treatment of Offenders, Resource Material Series, No. 10. Tokyo, Japan.

———. 1975b. "The Police and Political Development in Europe." In *The Formation of National States in Europe*, ed. Charles Tilly. Princeton: Princeton University Press.

Becker, Harold K. 1973. *Police Systems of Europe*. Springfield, Ill.: Charles C. Thomas.

Berkley, George E. 1969. *The Democratic Policeman*. Boston: Beacon Press.

Black, Donald J. 1971. "The Social Organization of Arrest." *Stanford Law Review* 23: 1087–1111.

Bowden, Tom. 1978. *Beyond the Limits of the Law: A Comparative Study of the Police in Crisis Politics*. London: Penguin Books.

Bramstedt, E. K. 1945. *Dictatorship and Political Police*. New York: Oxford University Press.

Bunyan, Tony. 1976. *The Political Police in Britain*. New York: St. Martin's Press.

Cain, Maureen. 1973. *Society and the Policeman's Role*. London: Routledge & Kegan Paul.

Carte, Gene E., and Elaine H. Carte. 1975. *Police Reform in the United States: The Era of August Vollmer, 1905–1932*. Berkeley: University of California Press.

Center for Research on Criminal Justice. 1977. *The Iron Fist in the Velvet Glove.* Berkeley, Calif.: Center for Research on Criminal Justice.

Clark, John P. 1965. "The Isolation of the Police: A Comparison of the British and American Situations." Unpublished paper.

Coatman, John. 1959. *Police.* London: Oxford University Press.

Cramer, James. 1964. *The World's Police.* London: Cassell.

Critchley, T. A. 1967. *A History of Police in England and Wales, 900–1966.* London: Constable.

Cumming, Elaine, Ian M. Cumming, and Laura Edell. 1965. "Policeman as Philosopher, Guide and Friend," *Social Problems* 12:276–86.

Dawson, William H. 1914. *Municipal Life and Government in Germany.* London: Longmans, Green.

Dorey, Marcia A., and George J. Swidler. 1975. *World Police Systems.* Boston: Northeastern University Press.

Emerson, Donald E. 1968. *Metternich and the Political Police.* The Hague: Martinus Nijhoff.

Finer, Herman. 1962. *The Major Governments of Modern Europe.* New York: Harper & Row.

Fogelson, Robert M. 1977. *Big-City Police.* Cambridge, Mass.: Harvard University Press.

Fosdick, Raymond B. 1969a. *American Police Systems.* Montclair, N.J.: Patterson Smith. Originally published 1920.

———. 1969b. *European Police Systems.* Montclair, N.J.: Patterson Smith. Originally published 1915.

Glueck, Sheldon. 1974. *Continental Police Practice in the Formative Years.* Springfield, Ill.: Charles C. Thomas. A report made to Colonel Arthur Woods, then Police Commissioner of the City of New York.

Gurr, Ted R., Peter N. Grabosky, and Richard C. Hula. 1977. *The Politics of Crime and Conflict: A Comparative History of Four Cities.* Beverly Hills, Calif.: Sage Publications.

Haller, Mark H. 1970. "Police Reform in Chicago: 1905–1935," *American Behavioral Scientist* 13:649–66.

———. 1976. "Historical Roots of Police Behavior: Chicago, 1890–1925," *Law and Society Review* 10:303–23.

Hauge, Ragnar, and Harald Stabell. 1974. *Politivirksomhet: En Undersokelse fa Follo Politikammer.* Oslo: Institut for Kriminologi of Strafferett.

Hinz, Liesolotte. 1974. "Police and Sociology in West Germany," *Police Journal,* 1974: 161–72.

Home Office (Policy Research Services Unit). 1973. *Study of Urban Workloads—Interim Report.* London: H.M. Stationery Office.

Junger-Tas, J. 1978. *The Dutch and Their Police—Experiences, Attitudes and Demands.* The Netherlands: Ministry of Justice, Research and Documentation Centre.

Kelly, William, and Nora Kelly. 1976. *Policing in Canada*. Toronto: Macmillan of Canada.

Lane, Roger. 1967. *Policing the City: Boston, 1822–1885*. Cambridge, Mass.: Harvard University Press.

Liang, Hsi-Huey. 1970. *The Berlin Police Force in the Weimar Republic*. Berkeley, Calif.: University of California Press.

Lofland, Lyn H. 1973. *A World of Strangers: Order and Action in Urban Public Space*. New York: Basic Books.

Manning, Peter K. 1977. *Police Work: The Social Organization of Policing*. Cambridge: M.I.T. Press.

Miller, Wilbur R. 1977. *Cops and Bobbies: Police Authority in New York and London, 1830–1870*. Chicago: University of Chicago Press.

Morrison, W. R. 1974. "The North-West Mounted Police and the Klondike Gold Rush," *Journal of Contemporary History*, April, pp. 93–106.

Mosse, George L., ed. 1975. *Police Forces in History*. Beverly Hills, Calif.: Sage Publications.

Newman, Graeme R. 1978. "Social Institutions and the Control of Deviance: A Cross-National Opinion Survey," *European Journal of Social Psychology* 7:29–39.

Payne, Howard C. 1966. *The Police State of Louis Napoleon Bonaparte, 1851–1860*. Seattle: University of Washington Press.

Pollock, James K. 1938. *The Government of Greater Germany*. New York: D. Van Nostrand.

President's Commission on Law Enforcement and Administration of Justice. 1967. *The Challenge of Crime in a Free Society*. Washington, D.C.: U.S. Government Printing Office.

Pringle, Patrick. n.d. *Hue and Cry: The Story of Henry and John Fielding and Their Bow Street Runners*. London: William Morris.

Punch, Maurice, and Trevor Naylor. 1973. "The Police: A Social Service," *New Society*, 17 May, pp. 358–60.

Radzinowicz, Leon. 1957, 1968. *A History of English Criminal Law and Its Administration from 1750*. Vols. 2, 3. New York: Macmillan, 1957. Vol. 4. London: Stevens, 1968.

Reiss, Albert J., Jr. 1967. *Studies in Crime and Law Enforcement in Major Metropolitan Areas*. Vol. 2. Washington, D.C.: U.S. Government Printing Office.

———. 1971. *The Police and the Public*. New Haven: Yale University Press.

Reiss, Albert J., Jr., and David J. Bordua. 1967. "Environment and Organization: A Perspective on the Police." In *The Police: Six Sociological Essays*, ed. David J. Bordua. New York: Wiley.

Reith, Charles. 1948. *A Short History of the British Police*. London: Oxford University Press.

————. 1952. *The Blind Eye of History: A Study of the Origins of the Present Police Era*. London: Faber & Faber.

Richardson, James F. 1970. *The New York Police: Colonial Times to 1901*. New York: Oxford University Press.

————. 1974. *Urban Police in the United States*. Port Washington, N.Y.: Kennikat Press.

Robinson, Cyril D. 1974. "The Mayor and the Police—the Political Role of the Police in Society." In *Police Forces in History*, ed. George L. Mosse. Beverly Hills, Calif.: Sage Publications.

Royal Commission on the Police. 1962. *Final Report*. London: H.M. Stationery Office.

Rubinstein, Jonathan. 1973. *City Police*. New York: Farrar, Straus & Giroux.

Shanley, Mark, and Marjorie Kravitz. 1978. *International Policing: A Selected Bibliography*. Washington, D.C.: National Institute of Law Enforcement and Criminal Justice.

Silver, Allan. 1967. "The Demand for Order in Civil Society: A Review of Some Themes in the History of Urban Crime, Police and Riot." In *The Police: Six Sociological Essays*, ed. David J. Bordua. New York: Wiley.

Skolnick, Jerome H. 1966. *Justice without Trial*. New York: Wiley.

Smith, Bruce. 1940. *Police Systems in the United States*. New York: Harper & Bros. 2d rev. ed., 1960.

Stead, P. J. 1957. *The Police of Paris*. London: Staples Press.

Storch, Robert D. 1976. "The Policeman as Domestic Missionary: Urban Discipline and Popular Culture in Northern England, 1850–1880," *Journal of Social History*, Spring 1976: 481–509.

Sykes, Richard E., and John P. Clark. n.d. "A Theory of Defence Exchange in Police-Civilian Encounters." Unpublished paper.

U.S. Department of Justice, Law Enforcement Assistance Administration. 1970. *Criminal Justice Agencies in Pennsylvania*. Washington, D.C.: U.S. Government Printing Office.

Walker, Samuel. 1977. *A Critical History of Police Reform*. Lexington, Mass.: D. C. Heath.

Walsh, James Leo. 1972. "Research Note: Cops and 'Stool Pigeons'—Professional Striving and Discretionary Justice in European Police Work," *Law and Society Review* 7:299–306.

————. 1975. "Police Career Styles and Counting Cops on the Beat—the Sources of Police Incivility." Paper presented to the American Sociological Association.

Webster, John A. 1973. *The Realities of Police Work*. Dubuque, Iowa: Kendall/Hunt.

Wilson, James Q. 1968. *Varieties of Police Behavior*. Cambridge, Mass.: Harvard University Press.

Malcolm W. Klein

Deinstitutionalization and Diversion of Juvenile Offenders: A Litany of Impediments

ABSTRACT

Deinstitutionalization and diversion of juvenile offenders have been prominent goals of recent juvenile justice reform efforts. Both are attempts to replace formal, institutional processing with various forms of community treatment. Legislatively mandated, theoretically justified, and responsive to a professional consensus that the conventional juvenile justice system is seriously deficient, both kinds of program enjoy broadly based support. For all that, however, neither program has often been established in accordance with its premises. They have not been meaningfully evaluated and their effectiveness, accordingly, cannot be shown. The words "diversion" and "deinstitutionalization" refer to both ideas and programs. Whether deinstitutionalization and diversion programs truly embody the ideas which underlie them is a critical question in any attempt to evaluate their effectiveness. This essay presents a paradigm for reviewing the degree to which social programs represent the ideas underlying them. It then applies a critical portion of this paradigm, "program integrity," to recent developments in diversion and deinstitutionalization and finds, overall, that neither kind of program has been very effectively implemented. Five specific impediments to proper implementation, along with definitional ambiguities and unintended program consequences, are set forth as the principal

Malcolm W. Klein is Professor of Sociology, and Senior Research Associate, Social Science Research Institute, University of Southern California.

I am indebted to a large number of colleagues who have shared in the analysis and evaluation of the issues covered in this essay. The principal shapers of my thoughts and protectors of my sanity have been LaMar T. Empey, Solomon Kobrin, and Katherine S. Teilmann. An earlier version of the essay yielded valuable comments from Delbert Elliott, LaMar T. Empey, Maynard Erickson, Frank Hellum, James C. Howell, Solomon Kobrin, Suzanne B. Lincoln, Lloyd Ohlin, Katherine S. Teilmann, Frank Zimring, and the editors of this volume. These reviewers will, I hope, recognize some improvements in this final version.

reasons for this failure of implementation. None of these impediments is necessarily insurmountable; they are merely unsurmounted to date. Neither diversion nor deinstitutionalization programs can as yet claim success.

There is every reason to expect diversion and deinstitutionalization programs for juvenile offenders to be well and fully implemented across the nation. As parts of a social movement, riding the crest of recent history, they have been legislatively sanctified, theoretically justified, and socially promoted; and they seem responsive to a professional consensus on the failures and frustrations of current systems and reforms.

Both diversion and deinstitutionalization have had the advantage of a federally orchestrated development during the 1960s and 1970s. The overture was the 1961 Juvenile Delinquency Act; crescendos occurred in 1967 (President's Commission on Law Enforcement and Administration of Justice), 1968 (the Juvenile Delinquency Prevention and Control Act), and 1974 (the Juvenile Justice and Delinquency Prevention Act).[1]

Accompanying this increasing federal involvement in the delinquency arena was the development of several significant sociological theories, most notably opportunity structure theory and labeling theory. These theories, the products of activist academics with concern for understanding and shaping public policy, infused the federal legislation with academically respectable rationales and offered the promise of consistent guidelines for program development.

Further justified by growing frustrations with rapidly rising delinquency rates and the seeming inability of the formal justice system to ameliorate the situation, the movement toward community treatment became connected with offshoots of the civil rights movement during the 1970s. This was a two-pronged development. The first prong was the overrepresentation of blacks

---

[1] The movement from "traditional federalism" to "active federalism" in delinquency prevention and control is summarized effectively in the first chapter of the DSO final report to OJJDP (Kobrin and Klein 1979). By way of illustration, in speaking specifically of the deinstitutionalization developments, Judge Gill refers to the "Gung Ho approach of the drafters of this 1974 Act" (1976, p. 6).

and other minorities in the populations of arrested, adjudicated, and incarcerated youths. The second was the growing assignment of rights to adolescents in what has been a protective and paternalistic society.

Ohlin and his colleagues (Ohlin, Miller, and Coates 1977), in much the same vein, note three sources of the criticisms aimed at the Massachusetts training schools prior to their closing: (1) a community treatment ideology (reflected in my reference to the new federal involvement and reliance on opportunity structure and labeling theories), (2) high recidivism rates (reflected in my reference to growing dissatisfaction with the existing system), and (3) the children's rights movement. The last, in part a "spillover" from the civil rights developments of the past two decades, has been well described by Sarri and Vinter (1976, p. 165):

> Minority groups continue to press their claims for equality, equity, and fairness. They have met with grudging recognition and some notable successes. Having no broad political base and lacking powerful allies, however, children will probably become the nation's last oppressed minority. But the responsiveness that other minority groups have kindled can be argued as inevitably working in their favor. Children must secure recognition in law as persons with substantive rights, and the gains won for others must be extended to them.

It is the basic contention of this essay that juvenile diversion and deinstitutionalization, two major reform movements in juvenile justice, have seldom in fact been implemented. This failure of implementation has occurred for both diversion and deinstitutionalization despite their impressive pedigrees, the powerful theoretical rationales which underlie them, and the strength of the social and political movements to which they are a response. This failure in implementation has been exemplified by programs being established where they were not needed, in ways that effects could not be objectively assessed or in ways that have not properly implemented the basic tenets of diversion and deinstitutionalization. As Dunford's (1977, p. 350) recent review of diversion programs notes:

> . . . we have good reason to be concerned that diversion as conceived by its creators and proponents, both in and out of government, will never receive a fair test. It is evident that the practice of diversion may be rejected, not because it could not fulfill its promise, but because it was never given a chance to do so.

My personal concern is not specifically with the failure of diversion and deinstitutionalization as reforms: most reforms are later revealed to be oversold and merely episodes in extended temporal cycles. Rather, my perspective is that of the social evaluator who has seen the claims for evaluation subverted by inadequate program implementation. Nonetheless, the materials to follow should provide grist for the mills of both the reformer and the social science evaluator. The reformer wants his program to fulfill its promise. The evaluator wants the program so constructed that he can determine the degree to which it has fulfilled its promise. Most attempts at diversion and deinstitutionalization, contrary to much professional belief, have been frustrating both sets of desires.

In order to increase our understanding of this situation, this essay concentrates on impediments to program implementation.[2] The intent is not to emphasize the negative for its own sake, but to document the reasons for the relative nonoccurrence of deinstitutionalization and diversion and show that adequate tests of the ideas underlying them may yet be mounted. To this end, this essay is based on a review of over two hundred published re-

[2] Readers wishing to encounter a more positive approach should refer to Romig's recent volume (1978), a valiant attempt to isolate variables which show promise of relating to positive program outcome. Romig's well-organized review of a wide variety of approaches to delinquency treatment is unfortunately marred in some instances by inadequate attention to the methodological flaws in the studies covered. Most notably, these flaws have to do with the selection of client groups and inadequate experimental controls, as in the Sacramento 601 Diversion Project (Baron, Feeney, and Thornton 1973) and Stratton's San Fernando study (1975). Far more discouraging is the final report of the American Public Welfare Association (1978), which announces that association's desire to provide assistance in program implementation to all comers, while deliberately burying in Appendix B (and mentioning nowhere else) data indicating that its program efforts were in fact *harmful* to the juvenile clients in the program.

ports, articles, chapters, and books, along with a variety of un-published works.[3] By far the greater number of these are con-cerned principally with diversion rather than with deinstitutional-ization.

It should be noted, however, as this essay shows, that much of what can be said for diversion applies equally to deinstitutional-ization. Indeed, a number of deinstitutionalization programs, while so labeled, turn out on inspection to be diversion programs, often closer to the ideal of diversion than the so-called diversion programs. The literature on the two reforms occasionally seems to confuse them unknowingly.[4] The confusion is in many ways legitimate. The rationales and programs of diversion and dein-stitutionalization have so much in common that "confusion" comes close to identity. Thus there is much to be gained by considering these two reforms jointly.

There are important differences between the two, however, and here the confusion is regrettable. These differences are strik-ing enough that at some points I speak only to deinstitutionaliza-tion, or only to diversion, when reviewing certain issues. An early reviewer of this paper has made the interesting suggestion, with which I agree, that deinstitutionalization has been resisted, while diversion has been coopted.

The remainder of this essay is divided into five sections.[5] Section I defines terms and describes sources of data. Section II

---

[3] An extensive literature review eventually meets a point of diminishing returns. Thus the references at the end of the essay constitute less than half the items re-viewed. Many other items became redundant merely because they were read later rather than earlier. Absence from this list of references does not imply a less worthy item; indeed some of those listed are, very frankly, of questionable merit.

[4] Hickey's (1977) extended programmatic statement on the proper jurisdiction for status offenders wanders back and forth between deinstitutionalization and diversion as though they were both part of the same package. Empey's (1973) comments on the California probation subsidy program imply that probation subsidy accomplished state-level deinstitutionalization by means of county-level diversion. His coverage of Youth Service Bureaus, in the same article, falls in the section on deinstitutionaliza-tion, even though these bureaus were always intended as diversion and prevention mechanisms. Finally, it can be noted that the major federal initiative in deinstitu-tionalization, a multimillion dollar effort to which we shall return shortly, clearly confuses deinstitutionalization with diversion strategies, a confusion exacerbated by the program staffs at a number of sites funded under that initiative.

[5] A clarifying postscript and an appendix reviewing impact studies follow the con-cluding section.

presents the basic paradigm around which my argument revolves. Section III presents the major impediments to what I have termed "Program Integrity," and Section IV warns of additional impediments which might arise from unintended program consequences. A brief conclusion constitutes Section V.

I. Defining the Programs

The critical distinction between deinstitutionalization and diversion is that the former must refer to juveniles who are incarcerated or who clearly would be under normal circumstances. The confusion between the terms comes about because the goals of deinstitutionalization are often approached through treatment programs identical or similar to those employed in connection with many diversion programs. But if the procedures are similar, the goals are still separable and we will benefit from maintaining this separation in the discussion to follow.

Deinstitutionalization, as the term is used here, refers to three procedures for reducing the number of incarcerated juveniles: (1) removal of inmates from secure institutions at a rate clearly greater than has normally occurred, (2) removal of juveniles from secure detention and temporary custody at a rate clearly greater than has normally occurred, and (3) preventing the placement in secure institutions, detention, and temporary custody of juveniles who normally would have been placed there in the past.

Before attempting the far more difficult task of defining diversion, the deinstitutionalization programs providing the bulk of material for my discussion of deinstitutionalization should be mentioned.

The first is the Community Treatment Program (CTP) initiated by the California Youth Authority in 1961.[6] Consistently monitored by Youth Authority researchers, the CTP has used classification schemes to place several thousand wards in a variety of community settings who would otherwise have been placed in state institutions. Although all these community placements seem obvious examples of deinstitutionalization, Lerman's (1975)

---

[6] A useful review of the CTP has been provided by Palmer (1974), and an intensive critique can be found in a recent book by Lerman (1975).

analysis makes it clear that the increasing use of detention and incarceration to "treat" those youngsters who do not respond satisfactorily to community treatment programs raises serious questions about the level of deinstitutionalization actually attained.

The second major program is generally known as the Massachusetts Experiment. In 1972, following two years of attempts at reform within the juvenile correctional system, the Commissioner of the Massachusetts Division of Youth Services rather abruptly closed almost all secure facilities, forcing a level of deinstitutionalization not before seen in this country. The results have been carefully documented and assessed by Ohlin and his colleagues at Harvard, and described by numerous others who have found much to say about both the process and the outcome of this "experiment."[7]

Finally, there are the materials from the national Deinstitutionalization of Status Offenders (DSO) program. This program was composed of a series of statewide and county programs funded in 1976 across the country by the Law Enforcement Assistance Administration's (LEAA) Office of Juvenile Justice and Delinquency Prevention (OJJDP). Eight have been the subjects of intensive data collection by evaluation teams at each site, coordinated by the national evaluation team at the University of Southern California (Kobrin and Klein 1979).

These programs—CTP, the Massachusetts Experiment, and DSO—differing in time, source of initiation, context, and target populations, provide a felicitous triangulation on the processes and problems of implementing deinstitutionalization reforms. No comparable set of rich but accessible materials is available for the analysis of diversion. The diversion literature is vast, heterogeneous, and inconsistent in quality. While some useful overviews are now available (Rutherford and McDermott 1976; Gibbons and Blake 1976; Neithercutt and Moseley 1974; Bohnstedt et al. 1975; National Center for Juvenile Justice 1977; U.S. Depart-

[7] Of particular value to understanding what happened are the Harvard team's summary report (Ohlin, Miller, and Coates 1977) and a series of five books, the second of which, *A Theory of Social Reform* (Miller, Ohlin, and Coates 1977), is particularly pertinent to our concern with impediments to program implementation.

ment of Justice 1976; Klein et al. 1976), it is nonetheless necessary in this essay to refer to a wide variety of materials.

In contrast to deinstitutionalization, a consideration of diversion is complicated by definitional ambiguity. For some, diversion refers not only to turning offenders away from the justice system but also to turning them away from a deeper to a shallower level of the system (sometimes referred to as "minimization of penetration").[8] Other writers attempting to settle on useful definitions have contributed other nuances, other terms, and other variations in order to stress particular intentions. Thus we have "new diversion" (Vorenberg and Vorenberg 1973), "true diversion" (Cressey and McDermott 1973), and minimization of penetration as terms standing in deliberate opposition to normal release processes such as station adjustment or "screening," rejection of petitions, and informal probation.

One trend in all this, therefore, has been to insist that diversion must mean something other than the usual practices of the various components of the justice system.

A second trend has been to define diversion as implying the cessation of system involvement; i.e., a diverted youngster must be freed of any control by the system. This means in practice that he cannot be reinserted if he fails in treatment or rejects treatment and that the treatment must not be connected to or controlled by the police, probation, or courts.[9]

A third major trend has been to insist, by definition, that diversion be not only *from* the system but also *to* some alternative handling of each case. This handling is supposed generally to occur in the community and, in practice, has usually meant some form of counseling. This trend would prohibit diversion to non-treatment despite some available data that treated divertees may

---

[8] Cressey and McDermott (1973, p. 71) have found diversion to a lower level, i.e., away from court, a far more acceptable motive among practitioners. With minimization of penetration, they note, "the juvenile doesn't get mucked about as much, or as well, as he would if penetrated to the maximum."

[9] Cressey and McDermott (1973) found this requirement of "true" diversion, total separation from the system with no strings attached, very uncommon. The California Youth Authority survey of seventy-four diversion projects (Bohnstedt et al. 1975) found that 46 percent of them *were* controlled by police or probation. Thus, this second definitional trend is not mirrored in practice.

actually suffer from treatment. Seen another way, this trend speci-
fies as diversion clients only those for whom community treatment is appropriate, a judgment in which it is generally conceded
we are very inept.

These three definitional trends—diversion as different from
usual practice, diversion as divorced from system involvement,
and diversion as a referral to a community alternative—represent
three significantly discrepant views. Taken together, they constitute a rather ambiguous definition of diversion. There is, however, one definitional ingredient implicit in the foregoing which
can fairly be insisted upon. Diversion means to turn away from,
and one cannot turn someone away from something toward which
he was not already heading. Diversion programs must handle
only youngsters who otherwise would enter, or penetrate further
into, the justice system. We must have some reasonable certainty
that they would do so; 6-year-old clients, many first offenders,
and many minor offenders do not offer that reasonable certainty.
Nowhere in the literature reviewed for this essay have I found
substantial disagreement with this point. It is only in practice that
it is often ignored, a fact which is of course central to a major
thesis here, that diversion has not been implemented.

Where ambiguity is rife and different definitions seem to reflect
different goals, the best we can probably achieve is a mutual understanding of the pivotal issues in the defining process, so that
misunderstandings will be minimized. *For the purposes of this
chapter, for the points I wish to make,* I would like the reader first to
understand that the meaning *I* attribute to diversion emphasizes a
client population that would otherwise be inserted into the system
(or further into it) in the absence of the diversion program;[10] that
the meaning *need not* include treatment of any sort as an alternative—one can have diversion with or without referral elsewhere;
and that the meaning *need not* exclude programs initiated by or
controlled by components of the justice system (I find the locus

[10] This, therefore, excludes the usual screening at the police level which is generally thought to involve up to half of all arrested juveniles. The diverted offenders
should come from the other half, those normally screened *into* further processing.

of control less important than the way it is exercised and its implications for the placement of the client population).

In other words, for me the essential point is the turning away, far more than it is turning by whom or to what. I would prefer to leave the latter to the evaluators, as relevant to the question, "Which form of diversion is the most valuable?" However, my preference is not the same as that adopted by most professionals in the field, especially some of those who have mounted diversion programs. This essay discusses the impediments to diversion as they use the term as well as the way I do.

II. Context: Tests of Program Implementation and Impact

Had this essay been concerned primarily with the impact of diversion and deinstitutionalization programs, it would have been easier to write, shorter, and misleading: diversion and deinstitutionalization have been comparatively unimplemented despite the plethora of programs which go under those names. Figure 1 is presented as a paradigm upon which my argument is based.

Level I of the paradigm deals with the conceptual (or theoretical) rationale for the program.[11] The ideas basic to diversion and deinstitutionalization programs usually involve notions of label-

Paradigm of Intervention Programs

	Ideal Formats	(Format Realities)	Tests
Level I:	Program Rationale	(alternative rationale) ◄———#1	
	↓ #4		◄------#4
Level II:	Program Activities	(alternative activities) ◄———#2	
	↓ #5		◄------#5
Level III:	Program Outcomes	(alternative outcomes)◄———#3	

Fig. 1. The paradigm is deliberately incomplete. It omits feedback loops (e.g., outcomes change activities) and context variables in the program environment. The simplicity of the paradigm is chosen in order to highlight the meaning of the five tests.

[11] I am concerned less with the issue of whether one sees this as theory, conceptual scheme, rationale, or ideology and more with the existence of an understanding that programs are based on ideas and, to the extent that they are so based, the activation and success of the programs provide validation of those ideas.

ing, association with antisocial peers, dehumanization, and civil rights.

Level II deals with the activities which actually constitute the program—who does what to whom, and how. Not only should the activities make "sense" in their own right, they should reflect the rationale stated on Level I.

Level III concerns outcomes. These can be highly varied, of course. With respect to diversion and deinstitutionalization, they usually fall within three categories: (1) impact on clients, either behavioral or cognitive; (2) system rates, such as reduction in system penetration and proportions incarcerated; and (3) changes in system structure, such as the closing of institutions, development of new treatment units, or alterations in liaison between components of the system. The reader particularly interested in tests of program outcomes is referred to the Appendix for a brief summary.

The paradigm draws a distinction between the Ideal Format and Format Realities. Experience with social programs reveals that ideals and hopes often give ground to what are seen as necessary adjustments to reality. Thus there are goal displacements: reduction in recidivism is discarded in favor of numbers of clients served; change in client self-concept is replaced by client satisfaction with the program; reduction in detention rates is supplanted by increase in services provided during detention or by reduction in length of detention.

Similarly, manifest functions often take a back seat to latent functions. Funds allocated for the treatment of diverted offenders become more important as guarantors of the organizational stability of the treatment agency; tractable clients are given precedence over less tractable clients because the former provide better "success" statistics; probation and police officials clash over the credit for diversion of more serious offenders, not because of differences in program rationales, but because each needs credit in connection with annual budget hearings.

Given the pressures derived from goal displacement and the many latent functions which may be served by social programs, it is not surprising that ideal formats yield to realities. Alternate rationales are soon espoused; easier, less risky alternate program activities are approved, and alternate goals and outcome measures are accepted. The result, too often, is the "success" of a program that no longer resembles its original design. The original rationale and the program designed to articulate it do not truly become implemented. Thus, the test of rationale and program is not undertaken, although many program audiences believe the test has been made.

If we understand the paradigm to represent the potential for this displacement process, then certain tests implicit in the paradigm can be made explicit. Figure 1 indicates five important tests, three dealing with components of the ideal format and two with the functional relationships between the components.

Test 1—*Adequacy of Rationale.* How adequate is the rationale? Is it logical, internally consistent, parsimonious? Can it be implemented in programs? Is it sufficiently well articulated that it can be debated by reasonable people?

Test 2—*Level of Implementation.* How fully do the program activities become implemented?

Test 3—*Outcome Achievement.* How well do program outcomes achieve the criteria established for them, i.e., how much "success" is achieved?

Test 4—*Program Integrity.* How well and directly do the program activities articulate and flow from the rationale, i.e., how well satisfied are we that these activities represent the operational meaning of the ideas behind the program?

Test 5—*Outcome Integrity.* To what extent do the program activities lead to the measured outcomes? Were they sufficient to achieve these outcomes? Can we be reasonably certain that they, and not something else, led to the outcomes?

In the literature on diversion and deinstitutionalization, one seldom encounters Test 1, a concern for the adequacy of program rationales. Consequently Test 4, the relationship between rationale and activities (Program Integrity), is also seldom undertaken.[12] Test 3, achievement of desired outcome, has received some

[12] I am reminded of a site visit to a program in a southwestern city which had been established and funded as an exemplar of the "National Strategy" of HEW's Youth

attention. Test 5, relating outcomes to activities (Outcome Integrity), has been undertaken in a number of instances, but almost never with an adequate research design or intent. A recent California Youth Authority survey of seventy-four diversion projects (Bohnstedt et al. 1975) found that only one-third had ongoing evaluation activities. Among these, the average evaluation budget was only $2,000, one of them being as low as $65.

The bulk of the writing currently available refers most directly to Test 2, Level of Implementation. It describes the activities undertaken. But the major concern of this essay is with Test 4, Program Integrity, the degree to which program rationales have been articulated in action programs. If they have, then adequate tests of the efficacy of diversion and deinstitutionalization are possible and have been undertaken in many instances. But if rationales are not reflected in the actual programs—if Program Integrity is low—then such tests (Test 5) have not really been possible and those that have been proffered are probably inappropriate.

The latter case is the true case: diversion and deinstitutionalization rationales have yet to be tested adequately because they have yet to be implemented properly. Something else has been tested—alternative rationales, alternative activities, alternative outcomes and criteria—but not diversion and deinstitutionalization.

III. Implements to Proper Program Implementation

The definitional ambiguities noted earlier constitute, in themselves, a substantial impediment to the incorporation of program rationales in program activities. The remainder of this essay discusses five additional major categories of impediments: insufficiently developed program rationales, inappropriately selected client groups, development of insufficient and narrowly conceived social services and treatment strategies, professional resistance to

---

Development and Delinquency Prevention Administration. Although the program had been independently evaluated by the criteria associated with that strategy (rationale), the director could not name, nor did he recognize, a single component of the strategy. His program's activities were based on his rationale and his staff's predilections and were totally divorced from YDDPA's National Strategy. Program Integrity was low, although other values of the program may well have been higher.

reform attempts, and placement of programs in inappropriate settings.

A. Theoretical Rationales

The theoretical rationales underlying diversion and deinstitutionalization programs could presumably give these programs both direction and strength. Well-articulated rationales can lead directly to integrated programs capable of providing tests of the underlying idea systems and their utility. Yet this has not happened. Rather, as Rutherford and Bengur note in their review of alternatives to incarceration (1976), there has been a tendency toward "ad hoc policymaking."

LaMar Empey's major review and statement of a decade ago (1967) seems equally applicable today. He noted that major impediments to successful program implementation have been (a) our lack of knowledge and (b) our unsystematic approaches. In the absence of adequate theory, he suggests, we develop no systematic strategies, but only "a strategy of activity."

As evidence that the situation has not changed substantially, consider Miller's (1978, p. 13) overview of the rationales for the organizational structures of programs funded under the DSO program:

> Many of the problems that were encountered can be traced to the fact that most of the programs were funded and implemented with only indistinctly drawn organizational features. New projects were combined with or superimposed upon ongoing ones and formerly independent agencies were tied into networks of service delivery with other agencies, both public and private. Methods of coordination, spheres of responsibility and the division of labor among the parts of these complicated systems were not always apparent. An argument could certainly be made that a flexibly structured approach to the delivery of human services is preferable to one that requires precisely defined organizational features, on the grounds that such flexibility will have a payoff in performance that a more bureaucratic approach would sacrifice. However, indistinctly defined boundaries and

responsibilities are not synonymous with the flexibility this argument has in mind. The lack of clarity encountered in the DSO programs meant that their activity often took place in an atmosphere of turbulence and uncertainty, a fact that should definitely influence the way the findings are read. The idea of conducting an *organizational* evaluation was sometimes conceptually out of phase with the somewhat unorganized state of the programs.

I suspect that a separate and full paper could be written about the reasons for the failure of substantial theoretical or conceptual frameworks to provide proper guidelines for diversion and deinstitutionalization programs. Let me briefly suggest just two.

First, differential association theory, which stresses both the interpersonal and social contexts for the development of criminal and delinquent patterns, suggested ameliorative action mostly by implication. Further, the nontheorists' understanding of the theory has been simplistic—"keep good kids away from bad kids." This is not sufficient for adequate program development.

Second, labeling theory, too, has been simplistically understood—"don't stigmatize kids, lest they live up to the stigma"— while its underlying structure has defied clear explication. It is described by its adherents not as a theory but merely as a perspective, thus absolving them of the requirements of theory construction. The implicit structure of labeling theory is complex; few have had the patience to attempt clarification in the context of action programs.[13]

Thus, the two theoretical approaches most consistently invoked as initiating and directing diversion and deinstitutionalization efforts have not been mined adequately for their practical wealth.

Earlier in this essay, a good deal of attention was devoted to the problems of definition. We can fairly say that definitional ambiguity constitutes one major impediment to achieving adequate tests of diversion and deinstitutionalization. Now, we can add the second major impediment: available theoretical structures al-

[13] These points, and an attempt to deal directly with them in the context of diversion, are set forth more fully in Katherine S. Teilmann et al. (n.d.). Empey (1973) provides a useful critical overview.

ready used to justify these social movements have not been used well to construct the programs embodying the movements. In terms of my paradigm, the rationales have not led directly to the programs; the programs do not mirror or implement the rationales.

B. Client Targeting

The clients served by diversion and deinstitutionalization programs often are not those to whom program rationales most clearly apply. The problem applies both to diversion and to deinstitutionalization, although less so to the latter. Reviewing deinstitutionalization first, I find that the Massachusetts Experiment presents no problem. The rationale referred to all juveniles incarcerated in the admittedly inadequate state institutions. When the institutions were closed, the target population was indeed directly addressed.

In California, the CTP was designed to test various alternatives to incarceration for a wide variety of youngsters according to a conceptually derived classification system. Here, again, client populations presented no major problem. The juvenile classification scheme was applied (and modified in light of experience) and to that extent planned treatment alternatives were coupled with the specified types of offenders.

The DSO projects present a somewhat different picture because appropriate client targets were not clearly defined by the federal legislation, nor were they uniformly defined in the various state statutes. Clients were to be those status offenders who were incarcerated at the time of program initiation or who would normally be detained or incarcerated. This requires, first, a consistent and satisfactory definition of what constitutes a status offender. It also requires some means of identifying those status offenders, out of the many available, who would otherwise be detained or incarcerated. Neither the definition nor the identification was achieved with any uniform success in the various DSO sites.

The complexities of the definitional problem are surprising. The federal legislation, and much of the professional testimony in the Senate hearings which led to it, seemed to assume that there are people called "status offenders." Yet available criminological data suggest the opposite, that those who commit status offenses also commit delinquent offenses. Further, different jurisdictions characterize different acts as status offenses; some jurisdictions do not legislatively distinguish between status and delinquent acts; in some jurisdictions, but not in others, violation of probation in which the probation results from a status offense is considered a *delinquent* act.[14]

The problem was so complex that OJJDP, in connection with the DSO initiative, commissioned a special study to consider problems raised by nonstandard definitions (Foster et al. 1975). A thirty-page report identified various status, delinquent, and nonoffender categories. A total of forty-six classifications resulted, including seventeen detention and commitment categories. For the most part, the report had no effect on the selection of target groups in the DSO projects.

In one site, Pima County, Arizona, the conception of eligible "status offender clients" was so broad that it threatened a serious dilution of resources among delinquents, status offenders, and dependent and neglected children (Kobrin and Klein 1979). In another, Connecticut, clients could only be those arrested for a status offense who had never been charged with a delinquent offense, or been on probation in connection with a prior offense, or had delinquent charges associated with the status charge for which the arrest was made (Logan et al. 1978). This is as close to a "pure" status offender as one can come. It is also almost totally divorced from the realities of juvenile behavior and of police and court processing of that behavior.

It is fair to say that the eight DSO sites evaluated by the University of Southern California research team failed to yield a consistent or perhaps even comprehensible population of clients. At best, one could probably refer to these clients as a mélange of varying cohorts of mild offenders.

As to identifying those status offenders who would otherwise

---

[14] The latter issue has been of particular concern to juvenile court judges for whom probation can serve as an important control measure (Gill 1976).

have been detained or incarcerated, the picture is even worse. A serious attempt was made in only one site: paradoxically, Connecticut. Most sites cared little for restricting themselves to truly potential detainees, preferring to follow the conventional wisdom that early identification (e.g., first contact with the justice system) and treatment are appropriate. "Our goal," as one judge put it, "must be to prevent adult criminals from developing by early apprehension and treatment of juvenile offenders" (Tamilia 1976, p. 8). And again, this same judge stresses, one must "provide for a far more extensive early location and intensive treatment of learning disabilities, health, and mental problems of children. There is an absolute link between these problems and delinquency."

The result, of course, is that deinstitutionalization programs are applied to a set of clients not likely to have been institutionalized in any case. When we add this to the definitional problem, and then look at client eligibility, a truly damaging picture begins to emerge. For example, the report from the Clark County, Washington, DSO site finds that 47 percent of potential clients were ineligible (Schneider, Cleary, and Reiter 1978a). In Connecticut, the final DSO report (Logan et al. 1978) indicates that 40 percent of the potential clients were definitionally excluded. Of the remaining 60 percent, only 58 percent actually entered the program, yielding a final program entry cohort of only 35 percent of the eligibles. The report's author comments, "This does not seem like much of an effort when we recall . . . that 35% of status offense detainees were out by the end of the next day even prior to the DSO program" (Logan et al. 1978, p. 198). This narrowly limited clientele, the report continues, yields a typical DSO client who is a girl diverted from detention despite the fact that "there is evidence suggesting that prior to the DSO program she might not have been detained in the first place" (Logan et al. 1978, p. 295). The conclusion is obvious: to the extent that clients are inappropriately defined and eligibility is restricted, deinstitutionalization programs cannot be successfully implemented.

The situation is even worse for diversion programs. The available literature reveals few serious attempts to develop client populations which would consistently have been inserted further into the system but for the activities of the program. Exceptions include a prescriptive document from the Michigan State Police (Shepherd and Rothenberger 1977) which warns against including minor offenders as diversion clients; a Baltimore court intake project (National Pretrial Intervention Service Center 1974) which concentrates on 15- to 17-year-olds charged with all but the most serious offenses; several projects of the Sheriff's Department in Los Angeles which attempt to involve more serious offenders (Berger et al. 1977);[15] and new juvenile legislation in the state of Washington which *requires* diversion in delinquency arrests if the offender's prior record contains nothing worse than three misdemeanor charges.

That there are so few exceptions is not surprising, given the conceptual and definitional problems noted earlier. It can be accounted for relatively easily. The emphasis on early identification and treatment—early in age or in system contact (Binder 1976; McAleenan 1976; Gonsalves 1975)—results in clients not likely yet to be caught up in the justice system. One of the nation's largest police departments orders that "referral agencies should be used wherever possible with the beginning offender" (Carter and Klein 1976, p. 10). Thus many "diversion" programs quickly become prevention programs, more characterized by referrals from schools, welfare agencies, and parents than by referrals from the police or courts (McAleenan et al. 1977; Statsky 1974; Humphreys and Carrier 1976; National Advisory Commission 1973; Dennison, Humphreys, and Wilson 1975).[16] Also, areas with adequate referral resources tend to be middle-class areas with fewer youngsters whose prior records or serious offenses propel them on toward court. The danger is that diver-

[15] These projects rely heavily on the juvenile officers' judgments about whether juveniles would have been petitioned toward court. The judgment is positive in two-thirds of the cases, but a careful analysis of the descriptive information about the juveniles forces some skepticism about these post hoc judgments. Still, the sheriff's cases tended to be less mild, on the average, than those in most other projects.

[16] In one instance (Dennison, Humphreys, and Wilson 1975), the diversion personnel participated with local police in "truancy sweeps" in which school-age juveniles not in school were gathered up all over town and deposited at the schools by the police. These youngsters were included as diversion clients by the program staff.

sion with referral comes to be an opportunity disproportionately available to the advantaged (Carter 1978a; Pitchess 1976; Hackler 1976).

The outcome is clear. One critical review determined that the problem of inappropriate clients makes assessment of impact quite nebulous (Neithercutt and Moseley 1974). Another found that selection criteria in eight of twelve sites "insured the placement of relatively minor first and non-serious offenders into the community-based programs." Further, "the chances of incarceration would have been slight" (Rutherford and Bengur 1976, p. 15). Perhaps the extreme is provided by the Miami police department's claim that its diversion program "has served more than 1200 of the 1500 youngsters who *were warned and dismissed*" by the department (Anon. 1978, p. 2, emphasis added).

To judge whether a diversion program is selecting clients who would otherwise be processed formally, one can look at such matters as the age, gender, prior record, and offense seriousness of program clients. In contrast to released youngsters, diverted clients should be older (predominantly 15 to 17) and male (perhaps in a 5 to 1 or greater proportion to females); a higher proportion should have prior juvenile records and the present offense should be at least moderately serious. Status offenders should be in the minority.

In our review of thirty-five police diversion programs, colleagues and I (Klein and Teilmann 1976) found no such trend. Indeed, with respect to age and gender, clients who were referred tended to be younger and there were proportionately more females than among released offenders.

As a standard to which to compare other programs, we found one police command was determined to avoid diverting those they referred to as "cream puff" cases (Klein 1975). The mean age of clients referred was 15.8, with the modal age at 17. Almost all cases led to a formal arrest. Fifty percent had prior records. In the weakest part of the picture, one-quarter of the youngsters were female. This standard is almost never met elsewhere.

In eight other available reports, the projects most nearly resembling the "standard" project were three subprojects run by the enforcement agency that ran the standard (Berger et al. 1977). Twenty percent of the cases were female, only 17 percent were arrested for status offenses, and two-thirds were judged after the fact as being petitionable cases. However, mean age was only 15 and 55 percent had no prior records.

Consistent reporting of the relevant data is hard to find, but the following are available: Proportion of females in other projects is reported as 30 percent (McAleenan 1976), 35 percent (Humphreys and Carrier 1976), 41 percent (Berg and Shichor 1977), and finally 39 percent in a broad review of many California programs (Bohnstedt et al. 1975). Mean or median age is reported in two studies as 13.1 years (McAleenan 1976) and 14 years (Humphreys and Carrier 1976). Age ranges are reported as 6 to 17 (Binder, Monahan, and Newkirk 1976), 9 to 15 (Theuriet 1974), and 4.5 years and up (McAleenan 1975). Other age reports include 27 percent over 15 years (Berg and Shichor 1977), 6 percent under 10 years (Bohnstedt et al. 1975), and 13 percent under 10 (McAleenan 1976).

Only two reports (Humphreys and Carrier 1976; McAleenan et al. 1977) specify the proportion of cases referred into the program by the justice system—41 and 43 percent—although a number of others indicate that the system is not the primary source of referrals. Only the California review (Bohnstedt et al. 1975) reports the proportion of status offenders—51 percent overall. Finally, three other reports deal with the number of referred juveniles who had *no* prior records: 43 percent (Humphreys and Carrier 1976), 77 percent (McAleenan 1976), and 91.5 percent (Berg and Shichor 1977).

Once again, the conclusion seems unavoidable: among projects reporting on the characteristics of diversion clients, no reasonable case can be made that these projects are carrying out diversion as its rationale suggested they should. The bulk of "diversion clients" are young people who are normally counseled and released by the police, if indeed they have any dealings with the police. With clients like these, we cannot truly be testing the efficacy of diversion.[17]

C. Service Delivery and Modalities

Two major program impediments are associated with delivery of services: the level of that delivery and its appropriateness or flexibility. On balance, the picture for both deinstitutionalization and diversion is one of too little service and service too narrow in its character. I will look at level of service first, starting with deinstitutionalization programs and then moving on to diversion. Then, in the same order, I will discuss the diversity, or its absence, in both types of programs.

In commenting on the national review of community corrections, Vinter, Downs, and Hall (1975, p. 68) concluded that "community-based residential facilities are not—in the overwhelming majority of states—handling juvenile offenders on a scale consistent with either the recommendations of several national commissions and advisory bodies or the opinions of state correctional executives." Echoing comments heard about the Massachusetts Experiment, they find one reason for this is the inability of staff in institutions to adjust to deinstitutionalization: "Existing staff are often ill-suited to perform these tasks because they call for different competencies than do institutional duties, as well as different orientations and commitments" (p. 22).

Lerman's (1975) critique of the CTP provides another interesting example: staff members unable to make progress through client counseling in the community reassert control by ordering temporary confinement. Reviewing a sixteen-month period, Lerman's analysis of CTP data reveals a 10 to 1 ratio of time placed in confinement to time in direct service, 6 to 1 if noncriminal confinements alone are used. For a deinstitutionalization program to rely so much more heavily on confinement than

[17] This is not to say that the programs are, ipso facto, not of value. Perhaps as prevention programs they have some promise, and most assuredly as continuing sources of funding and public justification for agency activities, important latent functions, they are fulfilling notable social needs.

on direct services to clients says little for the amount of direct service offered.[18]

Data on the level of service delivery in DSO programs are, as of this writing, too fragmentary and anecdotal to merit reporting. It seems likely, nonetheless, that once again it is the diversion programs which present the more discouraging picture. As early as 1969, a survey of justice system referrals throughout Los Angeles County (Klein 1976a) found only forty-two referrals from the police, as compared to over six thousand from correctional and court personnel. Periodic updates (Klein 1976b) indicate minor improvement since then, but service levels appear to remain somewhat low and restricted in character.[19]

Only a few specific reports provide data on level of service delivery. Berger and his colleagues (1977) report that a number of diverted court cases never received their planned contact, tutoring, or counseling. McAleenan's final report on a three-year project (McAleenan et al. 1977) noted that "negative terminations"—failure to complete the service plan—ranged from 11 to 39 percent during the three years. Dunford (1977, p. 338) describes a project in which 38 percent of the diverted clients received *no* service. Dunford observes that programs, dependent for survival on financial stability, need to provide less service to more clients in order to justify increased funding. The resulting low level of services hardly distinguishes this treatment from that offered under the high case-load probation services to which diversion was to be an alternative.

Finally, Elliott's major evaluation study (1978) of three diversion sites reports that 12 percent of the juveniles screened out of the programs reported receiving some services anyway. Yet of those diverted and referred to treatment resources, only 35 percent reported actually receiving treatment. And of those referred on to court, only 27 percent reported being treated. Elliott

[18] True, staff often feels in such circumstances that confinement is a form of service. But at the level noted by Lerman, the argument seems specious.

[19] When new legislation in California prohibited secure detention of status offenders in 1977, requests for proposals were sent to the various community agencies which had lobbied vigorously for this legislation. Reflecting the reaction elsewhere, Los Angeles County received only one response.

concludes, "The assumption that youth diverted or referred to court get some kinds of services appears unwarranted. Most youth report getting no services" (1978, p. 5).[20]

Turning to the question of type of service rendered, the Massachusetts Experiment provides a fair model. The breadth and variety of services eventually developed in the community were comparatively impressive (Bakal 1973). Of equal import is the finding by the Harvard evaluators that diversity of program services was directly related to recidivism levels. Regions of the state which developed a greater variety of community programs were the regions which also manifested lower subsequent recidivism rates. The Harvard report suggests a causal relationship (Coates, Miller, and Ohlin 1978).

Diversity was less common in CTP where the rationale was based on intra- and interpersonal dynamics calling for a variety of counseling methods as the primary treatment strategy. Other major strategies such as advocacy or skill development were deliberately downplayed.

Perhaps I should digress briefly to remind the reader that "treatment" or service can take many forms. We live in a nation in which the psychotherapeutic models combine with a strong emphasis on free will and individual responsibilities ("Freud and the Frontiersman" would make a felicitous catch phrase) to stamp us with a unique character as a service-oriented society. We locate problems primarily within the individual rather than within his environment; we locate the responsibility for dealing with the problems within the individual as well; thus we rely upon counseling and other treatment or change strategies which focus upon the individual and his role in bringing about change.

But other broad categories of treatment strategy are available. Strategies of *advocacy* stress acting on behalf of the client to reform institutional intransigence. Strategies of *opportunity enhancement* seek to increase vocational, educational, and other oppor-

---

[20] The skeptic should not seek comfort from the fact that these data came from youth reports. In similar research, my colleagues and I have found a reasonably close correspondence between client reports of receiving service and agency records of service connections obtained.

tunities for youth involvement. Strategies of *skill development* include tutoring programs, sex and grooming information programs, job training, role-playing, and paraprofessional training. While the emphasis is on the individual, it is on his behavioral capacities as opposed to his psychodynamic shortcomings.

These four categories—counseling, advocacy, opportunity enhancement, and skill development—do not exhaust the repertoire of treatment strategies available to diversion and deinstitutionalization programs, but they do indicate the diversity of activities available. The matter is further complicated in the context of programs for status offenders, such as DSO, where definitional problems interact directly with program rationale and activities. If status offenders constitute a relatively discrete category of persons, then specific treatment activities can be devised for them. If not, then a broad repertoire of treatments, perhaps bridging all four of our main categories, seems called for.

The 1974 Juvenile Justice and Delinquency Prevention Act clearly implies the existence of status offenders as a discriminable category. But the data available so far suggest quite the opposite. Thomas's court data from two cities (1976), Klein's report of gang data from five cities (1971), and reports from Philadelphia (Wolfgang, Figlio, and Sellin 1972) and Arizona (Erickson 1979) suggest that juvenile offenders reveal few patterns and constitute, rather, a "cafeteria style" of offense behavior. Today's status offender is tomorrow's burglar and vice versa.

The problem is further illustrated in the OJJDP attempt to establish a status offender classification system (White 1976), Isenstadt's review of definitions and statutes (1978), and Rojek's analysis of Pima County DSO client data (1978). The last revealed that only 8 percent of 515 self-report respondents were "pure" status offenders; three-fourths of them admitted to status, misdemeanor, *and* felony offenses.

Status offenders, at best, are marginal types. In a ten-state review, the Arthur D. Little organization noted this definitional marginality and the result, for status offenders, that "service needs are mostly unrelated to that label" (1977). To its credit, OJJDP recognized this problem and heeded the legislative admonition to include among DSO treatment alternatives a wide variety of residential and nonresidential programs for status offenders. The national evaluation design allowed for seven categories of treatment programs and, within those, twenty-four service variations including advocacy; recreational, educational, legal, and employment services; removal from home; and a host of others.[21]

The initial descriptive data on the DSO program services are now becoming available. They indicate an overwhelming preponderance of counseling and short-term crisis intervention strategies. The variety of treatment activities advocated in the legislation, in program guidelines, in special OJJDP reports (Arthur D. Little, Inc. 1978), and in the national evaluation design, and implicit in the available data on the nature of the status offense phenomenon simply did not become implemented. Whether under the auspices of public or private agencies, DSO treatments reflect the still dominant—and narrow—American social service orientation to counseling as the appropriate treatment for juvenile misbehavior. Advocacy, opportunity enhancement, skill development, and other possible strategies are underused.

Given that much of the DSO programming resembles diversion programming, it should not be surprising to find a similar record in diversion programs as we now turn to a review of them. Diversion program activities described in the literature consist mostly of counseling activities—individual, group, or family counseling, but counseling (e.g., Dunford 1977). Klein and Teilmann (1976) and the CYA review of seventy-four projects (Bohnstedt et al. 1975) similarly revealed predominantly counseling forms of treatment. The Public Systems Incorporated review (1974) reveals the same trend and attributes it to a medical model which it considers both inappropriate and unfair for large numbers of diverted offenders.

Counselors and agency administrators seldom accept that counseling has limited value in delinquency programs. McAleenan

[21] Details can be found in research forms 1A and 1B in the DSO National Evaluation Design cited earlier, available on request from the Office of Juvenile Justice and Delinquency Prevention, LEAA.

(1975) reports the archetypal comment of one agency person, "I can't believe that fifteen minutes of counseling with me wouldn't help a child." Yet as early as 1939, the famous Cambridge-Somerville study began to accumulate evidence that delinquency is generally not amenable to the counseling strategies we have devised to date.[22] The latest and most comprehensive review has been provided by Romig (1978) in an interesting attempt to separate out those treatment activities that might show promise.

Romig's exercise is very discouraging. Emphasizing studies with experimental designs and a counseling focus, he reports such conclusions as the following:

A. Casework (10 studies): "The results were conclusively negative. Casework was *not effective* in the rehabilitation of delinquent youth" (1978, p. 7, emphasis in original). Further, "Programs that emphasize diagnosis and recommendations will only fail. Programs that provide direct services will fail, unless there is follow-up that gives the individual the skills to work out his or her own problems" (1978, p. 9).

B. Behavior modification (14 studies): Not very useful because delinquent behavior is a complex and variegated phenomenon. Behavior modification requires simple and specific behavior as its targets.

C. Group counseling (28 studies): ". . . did not result in significant behavior changes." In some cases it improved institutional adjustment, but this "did not transfer outside the institution" (1978, p. 68).

D. Individual counseling and psychotherapy (10 studies): Nine studies were negative and one positive.

E. Family counseling (12 studies): These studies show more promise, especially where they stress specific

---

[22] For those whose response to such statements is often that impact on clients is a long-term affair and thus not apparent in most project evaluations, McCord (1978) has provided the most devastating data yet. Her follow-up analysis of the Cambridge-Somerville clients more than thirty years later provides evidence that equivocal and negative impacts can be permanent.

parenting skills—communication, problem-solving, and disciplining.

With counseling our primary activity and showing so little positive impact, and with a program rationale (labeling, differential association, or opportunity structure) that clearly calls for diverse program activities rather than just counseling, we must again reach the same conclusion: Diversion has not truly been an implemented program.

D. Professional Resistance

Social reforms, almost by definition, must encounter resistance. Such resistance is most likely to come from those with a "stake in the game." The resistance to diversion and deinstitutionalization programs has come primarily from juvenile justice professionals, people more comfortable with the status quo. Professional resistance has characterized deinstitutionalization programs more than diversion programs, the latter being more prone to transformation and cooptation. Accordingly, we will look first at forms of resistance to deinstitutionalization.

Juvenile court judges tend to be reluctant to relinquish jurisdiction over offenders and seem concerned that any loss of hegemony threatens present levels of jurisdiction. Status offenders illustrate the problem. The desire to remove status offenders from the jurisdiction of the juvenile court (a process called divestment, divestiture, or dejuridication) has been expressed by such prominent bodies as the National Council on Crime and Delinquency (Hickey 1977) and the National Advisory Commission on Criminal Justice Standards and Goals (1973). Opposition—stiff opposition—emanates primarily, but again not exclusively, from those sitting on the juvenile court bench (Gill 1976; Tamilia 1976; Gagliardo 1971; Isenstadt 1978; Gilman 1976).

A useful "line-up" of the players on both sides has been provided by Isenstadt (1978). Basically, the issues revolve around preferences for civil rights priorities versus protectionist priorities. One side sees status offender statutes as "void for vagueness" and inevitably discriminatory; the other sees the court, by virtue of authority and knowledge, as the best repository of the capacity to help minors in trouble:

1. Status offenders have "inherent problems with authority" (Gill 1976, p. 7).
2. ". . . the courts are the most stable branch of government and have the greatest capacity to acquire long-term empirical knowledge about problems such as delinquency" (Tamilia 1976, p. 9).

The impact of court resistance on implementation of deinstitutionalization is suggested by the Arthur D. Little study of progress in ten states (1977) and illustrated most dramatically in Connecticut. In that state, the presiding judge of the state juvenile court also served as president of the National Council of Juvenile Court Judges. Both the judge and the council have stood firmly for retaining jurisdiction. Carter's (1978b) analysis of changes in institutionalization rates in all DSO sites reveals that the Connecticut rate was least affected by the DSO program. The Connecticut rate rose slightly, while in eight other sites the rate dropped to zero.

Logan's analysis of specific DSO client data in Connecticut (Logan et al. 1978) reveals that the DSO program did not accelerate the already existent trend toward fewer commitments to secure institutions; thus the DSO program in that state seems not to have affected court practices in status offender placement. In the judicial district handled by the aforementioned presiding judge of the state, when compared to the other two districts, more eligible DSO clients were retained under court control rather than being given to the DSO program.

The Connecticut experience makes the point, but it is an extreme case. In no other DSO site was the court so adamant and so great an impediment to program initiation. At the other extreme is the case of the Pima County, Arizona, site. There, the DSO program was mounted several years after the judge of the juvenile court had already mandated and completed the process of status offender deinstitutionalization!

The jurisdictional issue primarily involves juvenile court judges. A second form of resistance comes from the other professionals who wish to retain control over juvenile offenders. For deinstitutionalization, the greatest resistance comes from the correctional staff who must deal with the most recalcitrant youths in the justice system. Although others may become involved,[23] it is correctional personnel whose institutional control is directly threatened by deinstitutionalization. Certainly Lerman's (1975) critique of the use of confinement in the CTP is a reflection of this problem. Parole staff, when unable to affect the behavior of resistant Youth Authority wards by means of the designated treatment activities, found their authority questioned and responded with confinement of the wards. As this recurred, Lerman suggests, it became a legitimated organizational response with, in my terms, an alternate rationale that "custody is treatment."

The Massachusetts Experiment provides a striking case study. The dominant theme is the correctional staff's resistance to loss of control over their wards. Staff intransigence was based on its investment in custodial practice and ideology (Ohlin, Miller, and Coates 1977). Indeed, in the two years prior to the abrupt closing of the institutions, strenuous efforts were made to introduce treatment reforms in far less radical fashion—training sessions, introduction of individual changes such as more liberal hair and dress codes for clients, hiring of special consultants, and so on. Had staff acceptance of change been greater, there probably never would have been a Massachusetts Experiment.

Ohlin and his colleagues (Miller, Ohlin, and Coates 1977) concluded, however, that the custodial system in the Massachusetts institutions was too well entrenched. Corrections is a system embedded in other systems; major changes such as deinstitutionalization cannot be wrought by chipping away. In California, it

---

[23] Examples include educators in the Silverlake Experiment (Empey and Lubeck 1971) and social scientists in reacting to the UDIS report (Murray, Thomson, and Israel 1978). This latter is particularly interesting as it seems to represent the investment that even the "disinterested" scientist may have in maintaining the conventional wisdom about the ineffectiveness of correctional programs. Judge Whitlatch documents police, probation, and private agency resistance to his attempts to reduce pretrial detention (Whitlatch 1973).

should be remembered, the chipping away process has been going on since the early 1960s through CTP and probation subsidy, yet the institutional system still thrives.

Can deinstitutionalization be accomplished through gradualism, or must it be by edict (either legislative or administrative)? The answer provided by the Harvard researchers is direct: "Thus the answer to the inevitable question—would DYS reform have been accomplished without all the fuss?—is that eliminating the fuss would probably also have eliminated many of the substantive reform achievements" (Miller, Ohlin, and Coates 1977, p. 29).

Resistance to diversion programs has typically taken the form of retaining control by cooptation. In diversion, it is primarily the police whose desire to maintain control has been most prominent. They wish, understandably, to keep the strings attached (Public Systems Incorporated 1974). For example, three programs evaluated by Berger et al. (1977) were originally proposed by a large police department's juvenile bureau, designed by the bureau, and in each of the three cases administered by a sergeant, although the program emphasis was on community referrals. Hunsicker (1976) describes the extreme case in her report of a program which hires diversion counselors, sends them to the police academy, and then installs them as in-house diversion counselors who are also sworn police officers.

Cressey and McDermott sought out instances of "true" diversion, that is, cases in which the program was divorced from the justice system with no strings attached. They did not succeed: "This study did not encounter a single agency that was requesting funds for this form of diversion" (1973, p. 33).

Their finding is not surprising. The police are reluctant to rely on other agencies to achieve what they, the police, see as pivotal concerns in controlling crime. One police agency has put the case succinctly:

Also an appealing aspect of juvenile diversion is the fact that it gives to the police additional control over juvenile dispositions. . . . The use of diversion allows the police to investigate a case, and when a decision is made to divert the offender, to gain control over the disposition. (Shepherd and Rothenberger 1977, p. 16)

Of course, this penchant for control is only an impediment to "true diversion," not to all forms of diversion. I noted earlier that I was less concerned with who controls programs than with what this might portend for their success. Should "true diversion" prove more successful than system-integrated forms, or should a consensus evolve that the proper diversion rationale is one encompassing only "true diversion," then police control mechanisms will indeed constitute serious impediments to implementation.

The test is facilitated by considering the forms that police control has taken. Summarized elsewhere (Klein et al. 1976), these have included: (a) in-house counselors, (b) police-based agencies, (c) police selection of referral agencies, (d) police purchase-of-service contracts, (e) police initiation of programs, (f) police use of feedback forms from agencies, (g) police involvement on advisory boards or Boards of Directors, and (h) police in role of program coordinators.

Many diversion programs cannot succeed without the cooperation of police officials and line officers. And if such cooperation is contingent upon police control, "true diversion" is not possible. Thus we have a paradox, at least at the level of police diversion: success in implementation may be dependent on acceptance of altered rationales (Dunford 1977; Rivera and King 1975; National Center for Juvenile Justice 1977; Kobrin and Klein 1979).

The unintended consequences of resistance can be, in the long run, most detrimental to the young offenders around whom these issues of control are played. In Massachusetts, stable residential communities would not accept the group homes required by deinstitutionalization, so most of these homes had to be established in less satisfactory surroundings (Serrill 1975). In Chicago, police resistance to diversion via court decentralization and early screening led to increased detention levels (Rivera and King 1975). In California, the new 1977 law prohibiting secure detention of status offenders led to a dramatic police response: up to 50 percent of status offenders formerly arrested and dealt with by release, referral, or petition were now ignored by the police, while a small percentage of others were relabeled as dependent or delinquent in order to obtain secure detention.[24]

Clearly, such forms of resistance can impede program implementation. However, lest the picture be painted too darkly, it should be stated that the literature does not document widespread, wholesale program debilitation through professional resistance. Certainly there are enough instances to justify careful attention and analysis, and the development of prescriptive procedures (Miller, Ohlin, and Coates 1977; Downs 1976). The most dramatic case of intransigence is offered by the correctional staff in Massachusetts. The single most intransigent case, however, is probably within the traditionalist structure of the juvenile court, where ideology has the backing of social and political clout (Rubin 1976). Judges, no less than police, correctional personnel, and social agencies, develop strong preferences for control of client populations. Judges, moreover, through act and implication, can make law.

E. Program Location

The basic issue here is simple, yet it is raised by every serious attempt to mount intervention programs. It applies equally to diversion and to deinstitutionalization. Should the program activities be located in amenable surroundings, where the climate for change is favorable and success seems likely? Or should they be located where change is not yet underway, where the climate for change is uncertain and success less predictable? Program administrators generally opt for the former, and independent evaluators for the latter.

From the viewpoint of figure 1, the paradigm which is the fulcrum of this essay, programs launched where change is already underway are of little value. The rationale-to-activities-to-outcome sequence cannot be mounted where the activities are

---

[24] Full discussions of these matters are forthcoming in reports prepared under grants administered by Katherine S. Teilmann and Malcolm W. Klein.

already established. A "new program" cannot be new under such circumstances. The problem is the same where major change has not yet taken place but seems about to do so. In such a situation (in the absence of experimental controls), it is all but impossible to attribute subsequent change to the new program if such a change seemed likely to have occurred anyway.[25]

The literature on diversion is full of examples of program location where "success" was likely in any case. Most commonly, however, this was as much the result of "cream puff" client populations as of placement where trends were already underway. The DSO program offers the best illustration and I will limit my comments to that experience. The legislation which led to the DSO projects was passed in 1974. The projects themselves started in early or mid-1976. The climate is effectively established in the following summary:

> Experience at the state level indicates the movement
> toward deinstitutionalization is of relatively recent origin,
> and that efforts were underway in a number of states *prior to*
> passage of the Juvenile Justice Act. Before 1971, state
> legislative action regarding status offenders had not
> progressed beyond the creation of a statutory distinction
> often involving the phrase "in need of supervision." There
> were no juvenile jurisdictions that restricted either detention
> or institutional placement of status offenders. Between 1971
> and 1973 there were seven states that established prohibitions
> on institutional commitments: Alaska, Maine, Nevada, New
> Mexico, South Dakota, Texas, and Wisconsin. In 1974,
> when the Juvenile Justice Act became effective, Maryland

[25] A fine, illustrative case in point comes from a project mounted by Legis 50 (n.d.). The project was designed to test the value of providing professional staff to legislative committees concerned with juvenile justice matters. The five state legislatures selected for the project constituted a virtual guarantee of success—and thus a poor test of the underlying rationale—by virtue of their being selected according to the following criteria: "(a) Urgency of juvenile justice issues on the state's legislative agenda; (b) Commitment of bipartisan support for resolving the problem; (c) Indications of legislative willingness to take positive action in the area of juvenile justice; (d) Readiness of the legislature to consider professional staffing for major committees to improve its effectiveness as a policy-making branch of state government."

and New Jersey became the first states to prohibit both detention and institutionalization. During this same year Illinois, Iowa, and Massachusetts joined those states with limitations on institutional placements only. Thus by 1974 there were 12 states that had already begun the process of deinstitutionalizing status violations. While anticipation of federal effort may have promoted state activity during this initial period, the major impact of the Juvenile Justice Act seems to have been in accelerating the process after 1974.

During the three year period from 1975 through 1977, actions were taken in 32 juvenile jurisdictions to limit the incarceration of status offenders. Among the 10 states that had previously limited only correctional placement, five also placed restrictions on detention. For the 18 jurisdictions initiating activity for the first time during this period, 12 states placed prohibitions on institutional commitments only, one state restricted detention while allowing post-adjudication commitment, and 15 jurisdictions limited both detention and correctional placement of status offenders. In five jurisdictions these limitations were not made fully effective until 1978.

In the seven years prior to the 1978 state legislative sessions the "score" for specialized treatment of status violations amounted to 17 states having limited correctional placement, one state having restricted detention only, and 22 jurisdictions having barred both detention and institutional commitment. The most intense period of change has occurred in the last three years under the influence of the Juvenile Justice Act provisions.[26]

Thus, by the time the federal legislation was enacted, the movement to deinstitutionalize status offenders had started. The legislation clearly accelerated progress; the program just as clearly capitalized on both. Unfortunately, to capitalize on the movement also meant limiting the conclusions that could be drawn

---

[26] This statement is excerpted from a draft paper by DSO project director Frank Hellum. A more extensive analysis is presented in the paper and will be employed in the national evaluation team's final report on the DSO program. Meanwhile, I am grateful to Mr. Hellum for permission to use the passage above.

from the large-scale DSO program. Where OJJDP chose the sites for DSO projects, it chose in such a fashion as to increase the chances of seeming "success," at the expense of testing deinstitutionalization rationales.

Of eight evaluated project sites, five pertinent local evaluation reports are available. In Connecticut (Logan et al. 1978) change was minimal. But beyond that, the final report indicates that the court referral trends of the project period merely extended an ongoing, two-year trend and could not therefore be attributed to the impact of DSO program activities.

In Pima County (Tucson, Arizona), Judge Collins had fully instituted deinstitutionalization two years prior to program initiation. Further, the critical DSO program activity (known as "mobile diversion") had been implemented in the year prior to DSO funding. With full deinstitutionalization already a fact and the maintaining activity already developed and functioning, the Pima County DSO project could not have provided a test of the federal deinstitutionalization program (Kobrin and Klein 1979).

In Alameda County, much of the referral process and mechanism was in place and functioning long before DSO funds were sought. The success already claimed would seem to guarantee a "success" for DSO. Further, 24 percent of the client population was defined as ineligible and, significantly, this 24 percent was characterized by a higher recidivism rate. Statistics look better if the tougher cases are eliminated (Isaacs and Baron 1978).

In Spokane County (Schneider, Cleary, and Reiter 1978b), analyses in the final report substantiated detention decreases but found these merely a continuation of a trend already established in 1974 and 1975. Had the data for 1974 and 1975 been available prior to the award of program funds, there is the presumption—certainly the hope—that such funds would not have been given to Spokane. A congratulatory letter would have been far more appropriate. The report concluded that there is no need to invoke DSO program activities as an explanation of the decreases.

In Clark County (Schneider, Cleary, and Reiter 1978a), the final report attributes greater impact to the DSO program, but still notes that deinstitutionalization was already underway owing to anticipation of the program. Thus the program may be credited at best with accelerating earlier activities.

If these five DSO reports are reinforced by the three remaining reports now in preparation, critics can legitimately be expected to assail the location of the projects in sites which provided so poor a test of the program rationales. While second guessing has an unfortunate "I told you so" flavor, it is nevertheless true that, at the time of proposal review and grant award, OJJDP was poorly equipped to make data-based decisions. Decisions were in part political and in part philosophical and humanitarian, but in no part scientific. The recommendations of a consultant research team were all but ignored.[27] Thus the ultimate conclusion may be that, owing to the impediment of inappropriately chosen project sites, the national DSO program could not have demonstrated procedures for deinstitutionalizing status offenders.

IV. Unintended Consequences

Critics of American treatment propensities have noted from time to time that exclusive or predominant concern with effecting change in clients draws energy and attention away from effecting change in the "root causes" of human difficulties, such as poverty, urban decay, an inequitable class structure, or moral decay. The common analogy is that of applying a Band-Aid to a pervasive illness. Seen from this viewpoint, diversion and deinstitutionalization programs, if successful, would have the unintended consequence of prolonging the ills they seek to ameliorate by failing to attack underlying social problems.

All social programs run the risk of yielding unintended consequences; unwanted side effects are not the province solely of medical practitioners. The question for us, in the current context, is whether diversion and deinstitutionalization are producing side effects of sufficient magnitude that the very recognition of these side effects might also become an impediment to the continuation of the programs. In addition to the Band-Aid problem three un-

[27] The recommendations included, as a major choice criterion, the data base and capabilities of the proponent sites.

intended consequences of some magnitude emerge from a review of the available literature.

A. Alternative Encapsulation

In reviewing the relationships between community structure and social services for delinquents, Irving Spergel (1976) reminds us that moving youngsters from secure institutions into local alternatives may amount to nothing more than developing "community incarceration." Coates, Miller, and Ohlin (1978) note the same problem: "Instead of having 'institution kids' we now have a new group of 'agency kids' " (p. 173). Some aspects of social structure can be just as restrictive of freedom, and just as oppressive, as the walls of a detention center. In similar fashion, my colleagues and I concluded from a review of police diversion programs that the tendency to divert offenders from one system to another may merely substitute new stigma for old. As we noted then,

> There is a danger that the attempt to remove young offenders from the juvenile justice system may do so merely by inserting them into another system which might be characterized as the mental health, welfare, or social service system. So long as it is felt that diverted offenders, or deinstitutionalized offenders, need service or treatment when we turn them away from the justice system, then ipso facto we are inserting them into an *alternative* system which may be equally pervasive or *encapsulating*. For all we know, it may be equally stigmatizing although admittedly less costly. (Klein et al. 1976, p. 109)

Two other concrete instances of this pattern have recently emerged. In the DSO project in Pima County, Arizona, the evaluators' analysis reveals a low rate of termination of agency referrals of very minor offenders: "This again reflects the concern of many critics of diversion that once a referral is made, the recipient agency will virtually always attempt to provide a service whether it is necessary or not" (Rojek 1978). Agencies need clients. Case workers are trained to believe that they have the capacity to help troubled young people; the appearance of a client walking through the agency doorway may activate the assumption that help is needed.

And to reinforce the point, we have Elliott's finding from several diversion projects that services provided through diversion are no less stigmatizing than those provided through the court. Even worse, he concludes, "From a labeling perspective, it appears that receiving help or treatment from agencies is more stigmatizing than being arrested and processed in the justice system" (Elliott 1978, p. 10).

If Elliott's findings are confirmed elsewhere,[28] certainly one implication will return us directly to the strategic and definitional issues raised earlier. Diversion without referral, diversion away from but not to, must be given greater consideration by funders and practitioners alike.

B. Relabeling

Alternative encapsulation includes the deliberate absorption of juvenile justice clients into other bureaucracies. In contrast, relabeling involves the deliberate alteration of a juvenile's status to retain control. The ambiguous labels used in the juvenile justice system to classify young people allow for a good deal of reclassifying in this manner. Such reclassifications can be manipulated by workers in justice and social service agencies to permit or justify their decisions about appropriate dispositions and treatment. The relabeling process is clearest in the case of status offenders who can be relabeled downward as dependent and neglect cases or upward as delinquent offenders. The amount and direction of relabeling can be determined as much by agents of the system as by the behavior of the clients. A few examples should suffice.

1. Gilman (1976) reports the case of the 1975 Florida law which relabeled status offenders as dependents, and two-time adjudicated ungovernable cases as delinquents.

---

[28] My colleagues and I are now pursuing relevant data analyses—the question will not remain unanswered.

2. Schneider et al. (1978b) report that in the Spokane DSO project an increase in the number of status offenders handled by the program and court can be accounted for by relabeling both delinquents and neglect cases as status offenders (appropriate program clients).

3. In the most blatant case of all, a report on a Santa Clara, California, project[29] indicates that police were trained by program staff to relabel juveniles contacted by them in order to provide "program credit for expanding efforts to divert such juveniles" (Nielson and Berkowitz 1972).

4. In an ongoing assessment of the impact of a new California law which prohibits secure detention of status offenders, my colleagues and I have found evidence of consistent, albeit only moderate, levels of relabeling of status offenders in both directions, upward to delinquency and downward to dependent/neglected. We have also found evidence of the shifting of some cases into the mental health system via referral to county departments of mental health and to mental hospitals. This was not a matter of deliberate diversion or alternative encapsulation resulting from a desire to avoid a particular label; it was a matter of deliberate relabeling in order to maintain detention and control.

C. Net-Widening

It was Roscoe Pound, I believe, who warned us many decades ago against the dangers of the "overreach of the law." The particular form that this overreach takes in our context is the phenomenon known as net-widening, the gathering of yet larger numbers of clients into the justice system by "spreading the net wider." It is ironic that diversion away from the system should result in a system with an even greater reach.

I recall visiting a southern state which was applying for DSO project funds. The new director of the correctional program for the state cited a distinct advantage of being able to turn all status

[29] Ironically, the title is "*Pre-Delinquent* Diversion Project" (emphasis mine).

offenders out of the state institutions: it would allow his department to use the freed up bed space to bring in predelinquent
youngsters for prevention programs the director's staff would de-
vise at the institutions. Why he felt that institutionalization of
predelinquents was an adequate alternative use of bed space was
not made clear.

This gentleman's plan was not implemented, but a variation
seems not uncommon within the community. Reviewing the
problem nationally, Vinter, Downs, and Hall conclude, "A state
can arrive at a high level of deinstitutionalization either by adding
to the number of offenders in community settings, or by reducing
its institutional population. Our findings suggest that deinstitutionalization is more often achieved through the first approach"
(1975, p. 77).

Similarly, the review by Rutherford and Bengur of alternatives to incarceration concludes that "programs appear to be
serving a supplementive rather than an alternative role" (1976,
p. 30). Young and Pappenfort, in their review (1977), also find
net-widening of the same nature even in the use of alternatives
to secure detention while awaiting court appearances. In DSO
the same pattern is appearing in the early project reports. In
Spokane County an increase in the number of status offenders
handled by the program *and* the court is attributed to a wider
police net (Schneider, Cleary, and Reiter 1978b). In Pima County,
noting that only 41 percent of the DSO clients actually came
from the justice system, the evaluator comments, "It is not inconceivable that a diversion project can become the dumping
ground for marginal youthful offenders" (Rojek 1978, p. 5).

These comments may apply to many deinstitutionalization programs. They almost certainly apply to most diversion programs
(remembering, of course, that in practice diversion is a more accurate term for many deinstitutionalization programs). The program and literature review undertaken by the National Center
for Juvenile Justice reiterates the point: "The fundamental requirement for any police diversion program is the prevention of
processing children who otherwise would be released" (1977,
p. 13).

The evidence for net-widening in diversion programs has already been presented in the section on client targeting earlier in this essay. Two projects report that only 42 and 43 percent of their referrals, respectively, come from the justice system; another reports 67 and 57 percent of the referrals coming from the justice system in a program in which the police officers themselves say that only a quarter of the cases were diverted from formal processing. Such data leave little doubt of the dimensions of the situation. Far too many referrals come from sources—most often the schools—that are not justice related. Recall also that in over thirty police diversion programs, the youngsters diverted were younger than those released outright. The epitome, however, may have been the case documented by Blomberg (1977), in which a diversion program providing family counseling by probation officers included, by design, the younger siblings of the targeted offender, siblings who had no prior delinquent or "predelinquent" history.

V. Conclusions

In this essay, I have provided a litany of impediments to the implementation of diversion and deinstitutionalization programs. The thrust of the argument derives from the paradigm presented in Section II. In that paradigm, test number 4, Program Integrity, considers whether program activities implement and embody program rationales. Diversion and deinstitutionalization fail the test.

At the first level, rationales, ambiguity is rife—leaving the way open for more convenient but inappropriate alternative rationales. At the second level, program activities, major impediments are identified as follows: definitional ambiguity; inadequate rationales; inappropriate client targeting; inadequate or inappropriate service delivery; professional staff resistance; inappropriate program location; and backlash from several unintended consequences.

With respect to diversion the conclusion seems inescapable: we have not provided the rationale of diversion a reasonable opportunity to be tested. The single impediment of inappropriate client targeting has been sufficient to prevent the test.

To the extent—and it is considerable—that DSO has been diversion in deinstitutionalization clothing, the DSO rationale also has not been tested. Further, program location, partly inadvertently and partly to insure "success," has prevented a fair test of the DSO rationale.

The California Treatment Program, while it has continued for many years with some limited success and some notable problems, has not resulted in truly significant deinstitutionalization levels in the state or county facilities. Nor has the state's probation subsidy program significantly relieved institutional pressures.[30] Of course, it was not their purpose to close the institutions.

The Massachusetts Experiment, on the other hand, has succeeded in emptying the institutions, leaving only a few offenders in secure placement.[31] It has done this, current reports from the Harvard researchers indicate, at no major cost in increased recidivism or serious delinquency (Coates, Miller, and Ohlin 1978). The Harvard group has concluded that gradualism could not have achieved what the sudden and arbitrary edict did. Is there a lesson in this?

Placed in the context of recent events, there may well be. Deinstitutionalization of status offenders on a statewide basis is now underway in many locations throughout the nation. It is being brought about, in response to the 1974 Juvenile Justice and Delinquency Prevention Act, by "sudden and arbitrary" legislation. State after state has adopted legislation restricting detention, institutionalization, or both—especially with reference to status offenders.

Not that this legislation occurs in a vacuum; in California and elsewhere, it seems to follow upon several years of gradual increases in deinstitutionalization levels, to legitimate these in-

[30] Reports on the probation subsidy indicate a steady reduction in state incarceration levels for several years, followed by an increase toward the end of the program. There were concomitant increases in local jail use for juveniles.

[31] In a personal communication (6 Dec. 1978), Ohlin has indicated that even in Massachusetts there are still a few problems. A small number of twelve-bed facilities have been established for intensive, long-term treatment of offenders who have failed elsewhere. These facilities are on the grounds of state mental hospitals!

creases, and to accelerate them. The acceleration occurs because "the law's the law" and the hesitant are not permitted so easily to hesitate.

And while there may be backlashes—California's recent re-establishment of very limited secure detention is an example—the pattern seems to be that deinstitutionalization by edict or law is the most effective route. Since this has occurred as a response to the federal carrot, it may also be fair to suggest that major financial incentives provide the surest guarantee of progress in the face of a hesitant and often resistant justice system. To overcome the impediments to appropriate implementation, especially to encourage concentration on appropriate clients, perhaps once again the financial incentive, coupled with careful monitoring of the handling of identified impediments, might finally provide the tests we have not yet seen.

Finally, we might add a note about the legislative process which could yield bills of greater clarity and thrust. A review of the 1974 Juvenile Justice and Delinquency Prevention Act and much of the testimony related to it reveals the "innocence" of much of the thinking that influenced the form of the legislation. I speak specifically of innocence with respect to relevant social science information and skill. Future legislation could well benefit if greater attention were given to what is known about delinquency and delinquency reduction; it could well benefit from analyses of likely program impediments and of procedures for anticipating and reducing them; it could well benefit from more current expositions of the values and promise of available evaluation procedures and paradigms. Certainly the various impediments noted in this paper need not constitute insurmountable obstacles to better programming or program assessment.

Postscript

In earlier draft form, this essay was reviewed by a number of individuals very familiar with the issues raised and with a number of the programs cited. I want to comment briefly on the comments of these reviewers because, in aggregate, they reflect some of the major complexities inherent in the issues raised in the essay.

Allowing for a bit of stereotyping, the reviewers' comments put them into three categories.

Some find little fault with the essay and agree that it's time to demonstrate the need to try again; i.e., diversion and deinstitutionalization programs have not been properly implemented for a variety of reasons and therefore the success claimed for them is misleading. Success cannot yet be assessed. These reviewers take my stance to be that of the disinterested evaluator, value-free except for the pragmatism of effectiveness.

Others feel that I have been too harsh. They remind us that juvenile offenders are often hard to handle and that a good deal of empathy is due those who take on the task of treatment. Establishing and sustaining social programs is enormously difficult; program directors and their staffs face awesome financial and professional problems, and early "burn out" is consequently common. The press of business leaves little opportunity to indulge the abstractions of the theorist or the demands of the evaluator. Many of the impediments to program implementation are unavoidable responses to reality, not the result of malevolent intent or selfish interests.

Finally, some urge that I have not placed blame with sufficient clarity, or with sufficient intensity. Programs are often concerned more with their own maintenance and growth than with identifying and serving appropriate clients. Legislators often frame bills for purposes other than to provide clear guidelines for amelioration of well-defined social problems. Worthy reforms are subverted by unworthy motivations, and public accountability for the use of public funds is sorely missing. Political manipulations, organizational malevolence, and professional malfeasance are not uncommon; these are preventing the implementation of worthwhile experiments in social reform and they must be taken to task.

There is validity to these opposing views, and there is certainly some appeal in being (a) disinterested, (b) understanding, and (c) zealous. I personally prefer the disinterested stance. I am skeptical of those who find excuses in explanations, and suspicious of those who find malevolence in excuses.

Reforms tend to be illusory; they only look like reforms if one's vision is curtailed. This certainly applies to diversion and deinstitutionalization. Therefore my aim in this essay has not been to decry the poor implementation of reform.

Nor am I much moved by those who cite the difficulties of implementation. These become excuses to switch to alternate rationales, alternate program activities, and alternate measures of outcome. The distinction between explanation and excuse must be maintained; the former can lead to new effort, while the latter leads to stagnation.

And disinterest does not equate with noninvolvement; it merely provides a different judgmental context. I have devised and carried out delinquency programming. I know it's tough out there on the streets and in the organizational mazes. But if conceptual rationales exist to guide program decisions, many of the short-term pressures can be understood in terms of their value for longer-range goals. The rationales, and commitment to them, have largely been missing in many diversion and deinstitutionalization programs. And so has the commitment to valuing them, in the longest-range view of all, as exercises in knowledge building for what such knowledge may yield in the future.

If my reviewers want me to lay "blame" somewhere, then it must be on those agencies of federal, state, and local government which have provided the impetus and the funding for these programs. Their emphasis has been so much on the providing that they have come up short on conceptualizing and on maintaining accountability. In the spirit of the paradigm presented in this essay, it should be possible to develop and implement programs which have well-developed conceptual rationales of some intellectual merit and which permit adequate assessment of the effectiveness of the programs and their rationales. It is incumbent upon the funders to move for clarification of confounding confusions, e.g., the nature of status offenders, the appropriate clients for diversion programs, and the identification of debilitating organizational imperatives. Such clarification should inform future legislation and provide structure for program initiatives. At least on the federal level, some steps in these directions can be discerned.

But they have been few and, I fear, idiosyncratic. They can and should be encouraged; their absence is so easy to document that their presence should also prove highly visible.

APPENDIX: PROGRAM IMPACT

Have diversion and deinstitutionalization programs succeeded? I cited earlier the California Youth Authority review of seventy-four diversion programs, most of which were managing to exist without evaluation. Klein and Teilmann (1976), in reviewing thirty-five police diversion projects, found many with no evaluation, others with minimal evaluation. The evaluations they did find were so insubstantial that the police officers doing the diversion were often unaware of them, and their programs were almost invariably unaffected by them.

Neithercutt and Moseley (1974) found the quality of evaluation so low that only two of twenty-two reviewed programs could properly yield an acceptable test of program success. Gold (1975) has even gone so far as to suggest, "a badly done evaluation is a valuable political asset." Most programs have been able to justify themselves in the absence of acceptable data. Indeed, LEAA commissioned a "prescriptive package," a how-to-do-it monograph on diversion (National Center for Juvenile Justice 1977), even though senior officials were aware that adequate tests of the efficacy of diversion had not been carried out.

In 1973, a federally funded study of deinstitutionalization published by the Urban Institute (Koshel 1973, p. 43) concluded, "at this point the subject of the deinstitutionalization of juvenile delinquents probably does not warrant additional federal funds for the purpose of establishing demonstration projects." The conclusion reflected principally the limited knowledge of the impact of the new program. Yet just one year later the federal delinquency legislation resulted in the establishment of a dozen such demonstration projects across the country. With respect to both diversion and deinstitutionalization, then, there is adequate testimony to the low priority of impact evaluation in decisions about program initiation. What are these impact evaluations?

With reference to diversion, the first set are those which measure change in clients, i.e., juvenile offenders. Ordinarily this refers to officially recorded recidivism, although self-reported delinquency and attitudinal or other cognitive changes are also involved. Of those studies reporting on client change, three cite positive findings (Klein 1974; Ku and Blew 1977; Baron, Feeney, and Thornton 1973), two cite negative findings such as an increase in delinquency (Lincoln 1976; Elliott 1978), and eight cite equivocal findings (Lincoln et al. 1977; Elliott 1978; Klein 1974; Binder 1976; Stratton 1975; Berger et al. 1977; Carter and Gilbert 1973; Forward, Kirby, and Wilson 1974).

Almost none of these studies employed random assignment of offenders to diversion and nondiversion conditions. One which did gives evidence of the interpretive difficulties one can encounter. My colleagues and I achieved random assignment to release (i.e., diversion without referral), community referral, and court petition conditions. A nine-month follow-up analysis (Lincoln et al. 1977), since extended to twenty-seven months, revealed significantly lower recidivism rates for referral than for petitioned offenders. This is a "success" statement. But the nonreferred, released offenders fared significantly better than both other groups; diversion without referral was more successful than diversion with referral. Further, self-report indices revealed no subsequent differences between the three groups; they each committed about the same amount of further delinquency, so that their further arrest differences probably reflected official reactions, not levels of delinquent behavior.

The picture does not become appreciably happier when the impact measure is a change in system rates, especially those reflecting minimization of penetration. Nejelski (1976), Elliott (1974), and Elliott, Blanchard, and Dunford (1976) argue strongly that this is perhaps *the* most important criterion for determining the success of a diversion program. LEAA's Office of Juvenile Justice and Delinquency Prevention has incorporated the criterion into the evaluation of its national initiative (U.S. Department of Justice 1976). Very few studies, however, have employed the rates criterion. The results to date reveal two cases of successful reduction of penetration rates (Baron, Feeney, and Thornton 1973; Carter and Gilbert 1973).

Finally, there is the question of changes in justice system structure as a result of diversion program activities. Only one report (Klein 1976b, p. 427) looks directly at this issue. The summary of this study of police diversion reports:

> While an analysis of past programming in the juvenile field does not make us hopeful, somewhat clearer evidence is available. A new program trying to move from outside to inside funding must compete with other priorities and it must establish itself within the permanent departmental structure. As to competition, we find little in our survey of existing diversion programs to suggest that they are anything but low priority items. Juvenile matters are

rather low on the police totem pole; diversion gets low priority even within that status.

Second, in very few departments have we detected *structural* changes to accommodate diversion. In most instances, new units are not established, additional staff are not assigned, work routines are not substantially altered, lines of supervision are not shifted, etc. This is significantly less true of large departments but it is nonetheless the dominant pattern. *Diversion has been appended rather than incorporated.* Among the police, we predict for it a short, inconclusive life.

If we turn to studies of deinstitutionalization, we find a somewhat different emphasis. As might reasonably be expected, more attention has been paid to system rate changes than to client impact. Indeed, in many instances it is merely assumed that removal from an institution must result in benefits for the offenders.

Our review has found six reports on client impact (Empey 1973; Empey and Lubeck 1971; Empey and Erickson 1972; Palmer 1974; Ohlin, Miller, and Coates 1977; Murray, Thomson, and Israel 1978); one of these, the Provo experiment, found a reduction in recidivism while the others reported equivocal findings. Seven projects reported on system rate changes, usually the reduction of detention or institutionalization rates. They are impressively ambiguous; several report a mixture of findings within a single project. There are no instances of clear success, but two DSO reports suggest some success mixed with negative (Peat, Marwick, Mitchell & Co. 1978) or equivocal (Schneider, Cleary, and Reiter 1978a) conclusions. There are two reports of equivocal findings (Carter 1978b; Sarri and Vinter 1976) and one of clearly negative findings (Lerman 1975). Two others, both from DSO sites, tend toward the negative, i.e., an *increase* in rates where a decrease was the goal (Logan et al. 1978; Schneider, Cleary, and Reiter 1978b). The National DSO evaluation, employing somewhat different data from some of the DSO sites, reports a comparison of detention figures for program and comparable pre-program periods. Five sites experienced a decrease in detention; three exhibited an increase. At all eight sites, the number detained is reported to have decreased by 24 percent, while numbers institutionalized decreased by 51 percent in the five sites for which data are appropriate or available. Neither figure is close to the 75 percent mandated by Congress (Kobrin and Klein 1979).

Finally, as with diversion, in only one instance were system changes studied. The instance is, of course, the Massachusetts Experiment (Ohlin, Miller, and Coates 1977), in which dramatic alterations were undertaken. Most notably, these were the closing of the institutions, the regionalization of the correctional program in the state, and major shifts in personnel allocation and placement. Surprisingly, however, this instance is an exception. The evaluations of deinstitutionalization do not, to date, document transformations of institutions, shifts of personnel, expansions of alternative or supplanting community agencies, or major budgetary changes. Clearly, this is in part because such changes have not been common. Admittedly, it may also be due to the failure of evaluators to seek out such changes, given their focus on client and rate impact. Blame can easily be shared.

A brief review of impact evaluation such as the foregoing, given its failure to reveal any consistent pattern of success, should lead to a simple and obvious conclusion: the projects evaluated to date yield little support for the efficacy of the concepts of diversion and deinstitutionalization, as implemented in these projects.

REFERENCES

American Public Welfare Association. 1978. *The Youth-Community Coordination Project: Final Report*. Washington, D.C.
Anon. 1978. "Miami Police Provide Social Services to Juveniles," *Target* 7:1–2.
Arthur D. Little, Inc. 1977. *Cost and Service Impacts of Deinstitutionalization of Status Offenders in Ten States*. Washington, D.C.: Law Enforcement Assistance Administration.
———. 1978. *Community Alternatives*. Washington, D.C.: Arthur D. Little.
Bakal, Yitzhak. 1973. *Strategies for Restructuring the State Department of Youth Services*. Washington, D.C.: U.S. Government Printing Office.
Baron, Roger, Floyd Feeney, and Warren Thornton. 1973. "Preventing Delinquency through Diversion," *Federal Probation* 37 (No. 1):13–18.
Berg, Dennis, and David Shichor. 1977. *Methodological and Theoretical Issues in Juvenile Diversion: Implications for Evaluation*, a paper presented at the National Conference on Criminal Justice Evaluation, Washington, D.C.
Berger, Dale E., Mark W. Lipsey, Laura B. Dennison, and Janet M. Lange. 1977. *The Effectiveness of the Sheriff's Department's Juvenile Diversion Projects in Southeast Los Angeles County*. Claremont, Calif.: Claremont Graduate School.
Binder, Arnold. 1976. *Diversion and the Justice System: Evaluating the Results*. Irvine, Calif.: University of California at Irvine (mimeo).

Binder, Arnold, John Monahan, and Martha Newkirk. 1976. "Diversion from the Juvenile Justice System and the Prevention of Delinquency." In *Community Mental Health and the Criminal Justice System*, ed. John Monahan. New York: Pergamon Press.

Blomberg, Thomas. 1977. "Diversion and Accelerated Social Control," *Journal of Criminal Law and Criminology* 68:274–82.

Bohnstedt, Marvin, et al. 1975. *The Evaluation of Juvenile Diversion Programs*. Sacramento: California Youth Authority.

Carter, Genevieve W., and G. Ronald Gilbert. 1973. *An Evaluation Progress Report of the Alternative Routes Project*. Los Angeles: University of Southern California Regional Research Institute in Social Welfare.

Carter, Robert M. 1978a. "The Diversion of Offenders." In *Corrections in the Community: Alternatives to Imprisonment—Selected Readings*, ed. George G. Killinger and Paul F. Cromwell, Jr. St. Paul, Minn.: West.

———. 1978b. *Evaluation of the Deinstitutionalization of Status Offenders Project through the System Rates Methodology*. Los Angeles: Social Science Research Institute, University of Southern California.

Carter, Robert M., and Malcolm W. Klein. 1976. *Back on the Street: The Diversion of Juvenile Offenders*. Englewood Cliffs, N.J.: Prentice-Hall.

Coates, Robert B., Alden D. Miller, and Lloyd E. Ohlin. 1978. *Diversity in a Youth Correctional System: Handling Delinquents in Massachusetts*. Cambridge, Mass.: Ballinger.

Cressey, Donald R., and Robert A. McDermott. 1973. *Diversion from the Juvenile Justice System*. Ann Arbor, Mich.: National Assessment of Juvenile Corrections, University of Michigan.

Dennison, Laura, Laud Humphreys, and Duke Wilson. 1975. "A Comparison: Organization and Impact in Two Diversion Projects." Paper presented at the 1975 meeting of the Pacific Sociological Association, Victoria, British Columbia.

DeShane, Michael, Gerald F. Blake, and Don C. Gibbons. n.d. *Background Paper: Juvenile Diversion Issues and Strategy*. Portland, Ore.: Portland State University (mimeo).

Downs, George W., Jr. 1976. *Bureaucracy, Innovation, and Public Policy*. Lexington, Mass.: Lexington Books/D. C. Heath.

Dunford, Franklyn W. 1977. "Police Diversion: An Illusion?" *Criminology* 15:335–52.

Elliott, Delbert S. 1974. *Evaluation of Youth Service Systems: FY 1973*. Boulder, Colo.: Behavioral Research and Evaluation Corporation.

———. 1978. *Diversion: A Study of Alternative Processing Practices*. Final report to the Center for Studies of Crime and Delinquency, NIMH. Boulder, Colo.: Behavioral Research Institute.

Elliott, Delbert S., Fletcher Blanchard, and Franklyn W. Dunford. 1976. *The Long and Short Term Impact of Diversion Programs.* Boulder, Colo.: Behavioral Research and Evaluation Corporation.

Empey, LaMar T. 1967. *Alternatives to Incarceration.* Washington, D.C.: U.S. Government Printing Office.

———. 1973. "Juvenile Justice Reform: Diversion, Due Process, and Deinstitutionalization." In *Prisoners in America,* ed. Lloyd E. Ohlin. Englewood Cliffs, N.J.: Prentice-Hall.

———. 1978. *American Delinquency: Its Meaning and Construction.* Homewood, Ill.: Dorsey Press.

Empey, LaMar T., and M. L. Erickson. 1972. *The Provo Experiment.* Lexington, Mass.: Lexington/D. C. Heath.

Empey, LaMar T., and Steven G. Lubeck. 1971. *The Silverlake Experiment: Testing Delinquency Theory and Community Intervention.* Chicago, Ill.: Aldine.

Erickson, Maynard L. 1979. "Some Empirical Questions concerning the Current Revolution in Juvenile Justice." In *The Future of Childhood and Juvenile Justice,* ed. LaMar T. Empey. Charlottesville, Va.: University of Virginia Press.

Forward, John R., Michael Kirby, and Kathleen Wilson. 1974. *Volunteer Intervention with Court-Diverted Juveniles.* Boulder, Colo.: University of Colorado.

Foster, Jack D., et al. 1975. *Status Offenders: A Working Definition.* Lexington, Ky.: Council of State Governments.

Gagliardo, Angelo J. 1971. "Are Youth Bureaus the Answer?" *Juvenile Court Journal* 22:57–59.

Gibbons, Don C., and Gerald F. Blake. 1976. "Evaluating the Impact of Juvenile Diversion Programs," *Crime and Delinquency* 22:411–20.

Gill, Thomas D. 1976. "The Status Offender," *Juvenile Justice* 27 (No. 3):1–10.

Gilman, David. 1976. "How to Retain Jurisdiction over Status Offenses: Change without Reform in Florida," *Crime and Delinquency* 22:48–51.

Gold, Martin. 1975. "The Politics of Delinquency Treatment and Research," *Criminal Justice Newsletter* 6 (14 Aug. 1975):4–5.

Gonsalves, Lee. 1975. "A Diversion Program With L.A. Police," *Youth Authority Quarterly* 28:34–37.

Hackler, James. 1976. "Logical Reasoning versus Unanticipated Consequences: Diversion Programs as an Illustration," *Ottawa Law Review* 8:285–89.

Hickey, William. 1977. "Status Offenses and the Juvenile Court," *Criminal Justice Abstracts* 9 (No. 1, March 1977):91–122.

Humphreys, Laud, and Joseph M. Carrier. 1976. *Second Annual Evalua-

tion Report: Pomona Valley Juvenile Diversion Project. Claremont, Calif.: Pitzer College.

Hunsicker, Patricia Ann. 1976. "Police Help Youth." In *Back on the Street: The Diversion of Juvenile Offenders,* eds. Robert M. Carter and Malcolm W. Klein. Englewood Cliffs, N.J.: Prentice-Hall.

Isaacs, John, and Roger Baron. 1978. *An Evaluation of Selected Aspects of the Alameda County Deinstitutionalization of Status Offenders Program.* Menlo Park, Calif.: SRI International.

Isenstadt, Paul M. 1978. "An Overview of Status Offenders in the Juvenile Justice System." In *Introduction to Juvenile Delinquency: Text and Readings,* ed. Paul F. Cromwell, Jr., et al. St. Paul, Minn.: West.

Klein, Malcolm W. 1971. *Street Gangs and Street Workers.* Englewood Cliffs, N.J.: Prentice-Hall.

————. 1974. "Labeling, Deterrence, and Recidivism: A Study of Police Disposition of Juvenile Offenders," *Social Problems* 22:292–303.

————. 1975. *Alternative Dispositions for Juvenile Offenders.* Los Angeles, Calif.: University of Southern California.

————. 1976a. "On the Front End of the Juvenile Justice System." In *Back on the Street: The Diversion of Juvenile Offenders,* ed. Robert M. Carter and Malcolm W. Klein. Englewood Cliffs, N.J.: Prentice-Hall.

————. 1976b. "Issues and Realities in Police Diversion Programs," *Crime and Delinquency* 22:421–27.

Klein, Malcolm W., and Kathie S. Teilmann. 1976. *Pivotal Ingredients of Police Juvenile Diversion Programs.* Washington, D.C.: National Institute for Juvenile Justice and Delinquency Prevention, Law Enforcement Assistance Administration.

Klein, Malcolm W., K. Teilmann, J. Styles, S. Lincoln, and S. Labin. 1976. "The Explosion in Police Diversion Programs: Evaluating the Structural Dimensions of a Social Fad." In *The Juvenile Justice System,* ed. Malcolm W. Klein. Beverly Hills, Calif.: Sage Publications.

Kobrin, Solomon, and Malcolm W. Klein. 1979. *Final Report: National Evaluation of the Program for the Deinstitutionalization of Status Offenders.* Los Angeles, Calif.: University of Southern California.

Koshel, Jeffrey. 1973. *Deinstitutionalization—Delinquent Children.* Washington, D.C.: Urban Institute.

Ku, Richard, and Carol Holliday Blew. 1977. *A University's Approach to Delinquency Prevention: The Adolescent Diversion Project.* Washington, D.C.: U.S. Government Printing Office.

Legis 50. n.d. *The Model Committee Staff Project in Juvenile Justice.* Englewood, Colo.: Center for Legislative Improvement.

Lerman, Paul. 1975. *Community Treatment and Social Control: A Critical*

Analysis of Juvenile Correctional Policy. Chicago: University of Chicago Press.

Lincoln, Suzanne Bugas. 1976. "Juvenile Referral and Recidivism." In *Back on the Street: The Diversion of Juvenile Offenders,* ed. Robert M. Carter and Malcolm W. Klein. Englewood Cliffs, N.J.: Prentice-Hall.

Lincoln, Suzanne Bugas, K. Teilmann, M. Klein, and S. Labin. 1977. "Recidivism Rates of Diverted Juvenile Offenders." Paper presented at the National Conference on Criminal Justice Evaluation, Washington, D.C.

Logan, Charles H., J. Bacewicz, S. Rausch, N. Rich, and H. Hauschild. 1978. *An Evaluation of Connecticut's Deinstitutionalization of Status Offenders Project.* Storrs, Conn.: University of Connecticut (mimeo).

McAleenan, Michael. 1975. "The Politics of Evaluation in a Juvenile Diversion Project." Paper presented at the Pacific Sociological Association meetings, Victoria, British Columbia.

———. 1976. *The West San Gabriel Valley Juvenile Diversion Project: Annual Report, Second Year.* Los Angeles, Calif.: Occidental College.

McAleenan, Michael, et al. 1977. *Final Evaluation Report, the West San Gabriel Valley Juvenile Diversion Project.* Los Angeles, Calif.: Occidental College.

McCord, Joan. 1978. "A Thirty-Year Follow-up of Treatment Effects," *American Psychologist* 1978:284–89.

Miller, Alden D., Lloyd E. Ohlin, and Robert B. Coates. 1977. *A Theory of Social Reform: Correctional Change Processes in Two States.* Cambridge, Mass.: Ballinger.

Miller, Jon. 1978. *The Organizational Properties of Seven Programs for Deinstitutionalization of Status Offenders.* Los Angeles: University of Southern California.

Murray, Charles A., Doug Thomson, and Cindy B. Israel. 1978. *UDIS: Deinstitutionalizing the Chronic Juvenile Offenders.* Washington, D.C.: American Institutes for Research.

National Advisory Commission on Criminal Justice Standards and Goals. 1973. *Corrections.* Washington, D.C.: U.S. Government Printing Office.

National Center for Juvenile Justice. 1977. *Police Diversion of Juveniles: Program Development Guidelines.* Pittsburgh: National Center for Juvenile Justice.

National Pretrial Intervention Service Center. 1974. "Baltimore Pretrial Intervention Program." In *Portfolio of Descriptive Profiles on Selected Pretrial Criminal Justice Intervention Programs.* Washington, D.C.: American Bar Association.

Neithercutt, M. G., and William H. Moseley. 1974. *Arrest Decisions*

as Preludes to ?: An Evaluation of Policy Related Research. Vol. 2.
Davis, Calif.: National Council on Crime and Delinquency.

Nejelski, Paul. 1976. "Diversion: The Promise and the Danger," Crime
and Delinquency 22:393–410.

Nielson, Raymond C., and Joyce Berkowitz. 1972. Santa Clara County
Pre-Delinquency Diversion Project: Quarterly Report, July 1, 1972–
October 1, 1972. Report to the California Council on Criminal Justice.

Ohlin, Lloyd E., Alden D. Miller, and Robert B. Coates. 1977. Juvenile
Correctional Reform in Massachusetts. Washington, D.C.: U.S. Government Printing Office.

Palmer, Ted. 1974. "The Youth Authority's Community Treatment
Project," Federal Probation 38 (No. 1):3–14.

Peat, Marwick, Mitchell & Co. 1978. Comparative Cost Analysis of
the Deinstitutionalization of Status Offenders Program. Report to the
Social Science Research Institute, University of Southern California.

Pitchess, Peter J. 1976. "Law Enforcement Screening for Diversion."
In Back on the Street: The Diversion of Juvenile Offenders, ed. Robert M.
Carter and Malcolm W. Klein. Englewood Cliffs, N.J.: Prentice-
Hall.

Public Systems Incorporated. 1974. California Correctional System Intake
Study. Sacramento, Calif.: Office of Criminal Justice Planning.

Rivera, Ramon J., and Richard M. King. 1975. Juvenile Court Decentralization: Implications for Communities in Effecting Juvenile Justice in
Cook County. Berwyn, Ill.: Youth in Crisis Project.

Rojek, Dean G. 1978. Evaluation of Status Offender Project, Pima County,
Arizona. Quarterly Progress Report submitted to the National Insti-
tute of Juvenile Justice and Delinquency Prevention. Tucson, Ariz.:
University of Arizona.

Romig, Dennis A. 1978. Justice for Our Children. Lexington, Mass.:
Lexington/D. C. Heath.

Rubin, H. Ted. 1976. "The Eye of the Juvenile Court Judge: A One-
Step-Up View of the Juvenile Justice System." In The Juvenile Justice
System, ed. Malcolm W. Klein. Beverly Hills, Calif.: Sage Publica-
tions.

Rutherford, Andrew, and Osman Bengur. 1976. Community-Based Alternatives to Juvenile Incarceration. Washington, D.C.: National Institute
of Law Enforcement and Criminal Justice.

Rutherford, Andrew, and Robert McDermott. 1976. Juvenile Diversion.
Washington, D.C.: National Institute of Law Enforcement and Criminal Justice.

Sarri, Rosemary C., and Paul Isenstadt. n.d. Remarks, Presented at the
Hearings of the House of Representatives Select Committee on Crime,

April 18, 1973. Ann Arbor, Mich.: National Assessment of Juvenile Corrections, University of Michigan.

Sarri, Rosemary C., and Robert D. Vinter. 1976. "Justice for Whom? Varieties of Juvenile Correctional Approaches." In *The Juvenile Justice System*, ed. Malcolm W. Klein. Beverly Hills, Calif.: Sage Publications.

Schneider, Anne L., Colleen M. Cleary, and Paul D. Reiter. 1978a. *The Clark County, Washington, Deinstitutionalization of Status Offenders Evaluation Reports*. Eugene, Ore.: Institute of Policy Analysis.

————. 1978b. *Final Evaluation Report on the Spokane Project to Deinstitutionalize Status Offenders*. Eugene, Ore.: Institute of Policy Analysis.

Serrill, Michael S. 1975. "Deinstitutionalization," *Corrections Magazine* 2 (entire issue).

Shepherd, Jack R., and Dale M. Rothenberger. 1977. *Police Juvenile Diversion: An Alternative to Prosecution*. East Lansing, Mich.: Michigan Department of State Police.

Social Science Research Institute, University of Southern California. 1976. *National Evaluation Design for the Deinstitutionalization of Status Offender Program*. Washington, D.C.: U.S. Government Printing Office.

Spergel, Irving A. 1976. "Interactions between Community Structure, Delinquency, and Social Policy in the Inner City." In *The Juvenile Justice System*, ed. Malcolm W. Klein. Beverly Hills, Calif.: Sage Publications.

Statsky, William P. 1974. "Community Courts: Decentralizing Juvenile Jurisprudence," *Capital University Law Review* 3:1–31.

Stratton, John G. 1975. "Effects of Crisis Intervention Counseling on Predelinquent and Misdemeanor Juvenile Offenders," *Juvenile Justice* 26:7–18.

Tamilia, Patrick R. 1976. "Toward a More Credible Juvenile Justice System in the United States," *Juvenile Justice* 27 (No. 2):3–11.

Teilmann, Katherine S., M. Klein, S. Lincoln, S. Labin, P. Landry, and C. Maxson. n.d. *Diversion, Delinquency, and Labels*. Lexington, Mass.: Lexington/D. C. Heath. (forthcoming)

Theuriet, Linda. 1974. *Study of Youth Diversion Services in Los Angeles County*. Report prepared for the Los Angeles County Administrator's Office.

Thomas, Charles W. 1976. "Are Status Offenders Really So Different?" *Crime and Delinquency* 22:438–55.

U.S. Department of Justice, Law Enforcement Assistance Administration, Office of Juvenile Justice and Delinquency Prevention. 1976. *Program Announcement: Diversion of Youth from the Juvenile Justice System*. Washington, D.C.: U.S. Government Printing Office.

Vinter, Robert D., George Downs, and John Hall. 1975. *Juvenile Corrections in the States: Residential Programs and Deinstitutionalization: A Preliminary Report*. Ann Arbor, Mich.: National Assessment of Juvenile Corrections, University of Michigan.

Vorenberg, Elizabeth W., and James Vorenberg. 1973. "Early Diversion from the Criminal Justice System: Practice in Search of a Theory." In *Prisoners in America*, ed. Lloyd E. Ohlin. Englewood Cliffs, N.J.: Prentice-Hall.

White, Joseph L. 1976. "Status Offenders: Which Side of the Road?" *Criminal Justice Review* 1:23–43.

Whitlatch, Walter G. 1973. "Practical Aspects of Reducing Detention Home Population," *Juvenile Justice* 24(No. 2):17–19.

Wolfgang, Marvin E., Robert M. Figlio, and Thorsten Sellin. 1972. *Delinquency in a Birth Cohort*. Chicago: University of Chicago Press.

Young, Thomas M., and Donnell M. Pappenfort. 1977. *Secure Detention of Juveniles and Alternatives to Its Use*. Washington, D.C.: U.S. Government Printing Office.

Daniel Glaser

A Review of Crime-Causation Theory and Its Application

ABSTRACT

Crime control policies are inextricably connected to efforts to
understand the causes of crime. As theories of crime causation
change, so—imperfectly and with delay—do efforts to contain,
prevent, and respond to criminal acts. A tendency to isolate crime
control policy from theory has recently developed, influenced in
part by the belief that "nothing works," that we do not know how
to reduce the future criminality of convicted offenders. The
tendency is unfortunate and uninformed. Research and theory in
many disciplines and from many perspectives have identified a
number of basic notions about crime which can inform criminal
policy. Those basic notions—including concern for social ties,
social learning, and perceived risks and opportunities—can be
integrated into a theory of "differential anticipation" which provides
a sound foundation for sensible and hopeful public policies.

There have always been many explanations for crime, often
coexisting peacefully but sometimes stridently debated. When
uncertainty prevails about the wisdom of any approach, however,
when nothing seems to work, many persons become indifferent
to explanatory theories. This is a common stance today.

A concern with the social bonds of offenders is often absent in
criminal justice agencies because public officials—as well as
many criminologists—have abandoned crime-causation theory.
There is a widespread retreat from behavioral science to a simple
faith that somehow sentencing and correction can minimize
recidivism if offenders receive their "just deserts." Rehabilitation

Daniel Glaser is Professor of Sociology, University of Southern California.

services are neglected, allegedly because the monumental Lipton, Martinson, and Wilks (1975) survey of 1945–67 correctional treatment evaluations (hereafter called "the Survey") found that "nothing works." Such a conclusion is warranted, however, only if the Survey's findings and more recent evaluative research are assessed without carefully considering the causes of crimes, and without examining what actually occurs in programs that are said to provide particular types of rehabilitative assistance.

Changes in the relative influence of alternative crime-causation theories have repeatedly fostered revisions in criminal law, in correctional practices, and in other efforts to prevent crime. But many of these shifts are cyclical, so that one era's explanations for lawbreaking and its consequent government policies go out of fashion, then later come back as modern ideas. Such fluctuations have been especially evident in recent years. Thus, in the first half of the twentieth century, acceptance of predominantly psychiatric theories of crime causation fostered indeterminate sentencing and parole, for these theories suggested that rehabilitation of offenders can be accurately forecast by correctional officials, especially when aided by specialists trained to diagnose prisoners psychologically. Meanwhile, biological explanations of the most shocking and puzzling crimes generated statutes on sexual psychopaths, defective delinquents, and habitual criminals— laws that permitted lifelong confinement, partially on the basis of psychiatric testimony in a civil commitment hearing. The criminal law's more stringent requirement of proof beyond a reasonable doubt could thereby be avoided. Replacement of all these perspectives by a return to the utilitarian view that most criminals are rational calculators, however, has in the past decade stimulated a return to early nineteenth-century policies of definite sentencing.

Explanations of crime derive from more abstract philosophies or from theories in the social sciences that are concerned with much more than lawbreaking (Glaser 1956). Causal explanation is evident, although often not explicit, even in the crime control efforts of practitioners who deride "theorists." Explanatory theory cannot disappear, for it is inherent in human thinking, even in that of persons who disavow it. We theorize whenever we explain, and we theorize scientifically whenever we offer explanations that observation could prove erroneous (Glaser 1976; Walker 1977).

Unless theory is made explicit, it cannot have cumulative growth and improvement. The foundations of any science are the basic statements of its theory—its principles. If evidence inspires increasing confidence in their validity and utility, they gradually acquire the status of scientific laws (Hempel 1965). This essay briefly reviews the history of leading crime-causation theories and shows that research reveals prospects of some of them developing into lawlike principles for better guidance of criminal justice policies.

To serve this essay's argument that causal theory is germane to public policy on crime, Section I reviews major historical interpretations of offenses from the eighteenth through the middle of the twentieth centuries. Section II assesses theories of the past few decades and proposes a theory of "differential anticipation" which integrates all still viable explanations of willful lawbreaking into a "differential anticipation theory." Section III illustrates how that theory can help us make sense of some evaluations of correctional programs, even some of those on which the Survey was based. It argues that certain correctional practices do seem to work for some offenders, and that these practices can be made more effective if our policies reflect the substantial knowledge and useful insights that presently available theory provides.

I. The Major Historic Theories

Explanations for crimes can be found in the most ancient of human writings, but my concern here is primarily with eighteenth- and early nineteenth-century utilitarian explanations of conduct, with late nineteenth- and early twentieth-century biological determinism and Marxist perspectives, and with psychodynamic, sociocultural, and multicausal theories of the first half of the twentieth century.[1]

Ancient and medieval thought ascribed a large variety of

---

[1] For fuller discussion of these theories, but with somewhat diverse assessments of them, see Vold (1958), Mannheim (1960), and Schafer (1969).

events, including many crimes, to the influence of demons and witches. Yet many societies have also believed that some humans are disposed to pursue illegal profit or pleasure unless fearful of punishment for it. This interpretation of much crime as rational gain-seeking came to the forefront in the works of Beccaria and other eighteenth-century writers in so-called Classical legal philosophy. Bentham and his Utilitarian followers portrayed humans as rational calculators aiming to maximize happiness and minimize distress. Accordingly, early nineteenth-century criminal law in western Europe and America tried to prescribe a punishment for each offense just severe enough for a rational person to conclude that the gain from a crime would not be worth the penalty (Phillipson 1923).

This "Age of Reason" was an outgrowth of seventeenth-century Cartesian dualism, a view of the mind as independent of the human body. By the mid-nineteenth century, however, the theory of evolution fostered doubts, not only about the uniqueness of the human species, but also about the separateness of body and mind. Differences between humans and beasts were now considered highly variable and a matter of degree. Lombroso (1912) and other late nineteenth- and early twentieth-century criminologists ascribed much crime to atavism, to the hegemony of beastly instincts in criminals. Offenders were seen as either incapable of reason or as unable to control their animal impulses.

Although theories of biological determinism have lost much of their former prominence, they have never disappeared; instead, they have had repeated transformations. The so-called criminal stigmata, the bumps that Lombroso pointed out in the skulls of some prisoners, were shown by Goring (1913) to be as frequent in Britain's armed forces and in its university students as in its convicts. The mental-testing movement of the early twentieth century, however, fostered a neo-Lombrosian school that ascribed crime to low intelligence from a biologically inherited defect not closely related to physiognomy. Support for this view was strengthened by studies showing that crime sometimes runs in families (Dugdale 1877; Goddard 1912; Estabrook 1916) and is more common in identical than in fraternal twins (Lange 1930;

Mednick and Christiansen 1977, chaps. 4, 5). It was then diminished by nonbiological explanations for differences in I.Q. scores,[2] and especially by the competition of new ideologies and research that ascribed crimes to the social, economic, and cultural environments of offenders.

Criminologists who were Marxists at the turn of the century, such as Bonger (1916) and Ferri (1897), noted the correlation of crime rates with poverty and blamed poverty on capitalism. In the United States during the 1920s and 1930s, Shaw and McKay and their associates (Shaw 1929; Shaw and McKay 1942; Thrasher 1927) compiled statistics and spot maps which showed that juvenile arrests, juvenile court cases, and delinquent gangs were concentrated in the slums of our largest cities, where also were to be found the most poverty, disease, and other social problems. They also published and interpreted life histories of offenders which conveyed the impression that it is as normal for a slum boy to become delinquent as it is for a Parisian boy to learn French. Their thesis was that delinquent subcultures are shared and transmitted by almost all slum youths and are nurtured by the visibility of much adult professional crime which operates more openly there than in better residential areas.

The theory of slum subcultures derives from the following principle of sociocultural relativity: social separation fosters cultural differentiation. This law explains, for example, why so many people who historically were from a single society and shared a common speech, but then became two or more geographically separated groups, eventually developed different accents or dialects and other cultural divergences. Similarly, subcultural explanations for high delinquency areas contend that the relative isolation of slum youths gives them a set of shared values and customs that differ from those in more affluent parts of the city with which they have little contact.

Theories inspired by Freud, and to a lesser extent by Adler, Rank, and Jung, challenged this sociological view. Psychiatrists, psychoanalysts, and clinical psychologists have been concerned

[2] For reviews of the early literature on intelligence and crime, see Zelany (1933) and Ferentz (1954).

not with statistical variations in crime rates but with efforts to explain why specific individuals committed particular crimes. When they interpret crimes, they stress the offender's emotional dynamics and experiences with parental figures during early childhood (Aichhorn 1935; Eissler 1949; Redl and Wineman 1951). Their two major premises may be summarized as:

1. All persons have selfish and grasping impulses, evident most clearly in infancy, but normal personality development enables noncriminals to express such impulses in socially acceptable ways.
2. Traumas, conflicts, and guilt feelings are often unconscious, especially during the first years of life and inhibit normal personality development in offenders.

These clinicians are asked for advice primarily on the cases most puzzling to others, or on those from homes affluent enough to pay for private psychological services; consequently, their generalizations about crime tend to be based on an atypical sampling of offenders. Furthermore, since their explanations postulate unconscious causal mechanisms, often in formulations that are unique for each case, their theories are either difficult or impossible to test scientifically.

Many textbook writers and a prominent team of criminological researchers, the Gluecks (1950, 1964), concluded that the only tenable explanation for crime is that crime has many causes, an assertion they usually call multicausal theory. They identify important explanatory factors, but do not interrelate them, and attempt to validate this theory by one or both of two methods. First, they present case histories in which all unusual stresses and all deviations from what is presumed to be normal biological development, family life, or social and economic conditions are alleged to have caused criminality.[3] Second, they tabulate the traits of offenders and presumed nonoffenders, and assume that all significant statistical differences between them are indications of the causes of crime.[4] Failure to interrelate conceptually the

[3] Classic studies of this type include Healy (1924) and Burt (1938).

[4] Classic studies of this type include Healy and Bronner (1936) and Glueck and Glueck (1950).

causal variables in multicausal theory may be said to make it impossible to prove the theory wrong and hence makes the theory unscientific (in Popper's sense that a scientific theory is one that might be empirically proved erroneous).[5]

Nevertheless, Sutherland's theory of differential association (e.g., Sutherland and Cressey 1978) insists that the many separate alleged causes contribute to crime only if they bring the offender into contact with persons who communicate ideas favorable to lawbreaking and have more influence over him than do those who transmit anticriminal views. Multicausal theory tends to view humans as objects in a field of forces, pulled one way or another by the cumulative effect of the separate influences. By contrast, Sutherland's theory sees humans as learning from others, especially in intimate groups, such as the family and juvenile gangs. Thus, the many attributes and circumstances that multicausal theorists say create crime are in Sutherland's theory linked to crime only if they foster an offender's differential association with criminal rather than anticriminal sources of social learning.

II. Recent Theories

Criminology continually attracts recyclers. In recent years, all the theories just described have reemerged, but usually with important revisions.

The image of humans as rational calculators returned in purest form in economic theories of crime. Gary Becker's famous essay (1968) prompted many economists to develop equations that predict offense rates from their statistical relationships to economic rewards from crime, risks of punishment, and prospects of legitimate employment (Ehrlich 1973; Votey and Phillips 1974).

Some post–World War II theories combine ideas from earlier psychological and sociological perspectives in complex ways but superimpose the image of humans as rational calculators. Thus, the hypothesis that frustration automatically evokes aggression, and that aggression invariably reflects frustration, was promulgated in this simplistic form in 1933 by experimental and social psychologists (Dollard et al. 1939). It thereafter became common

[5] On empirical falsifiability as the key requirement of science, see Popper (1959).

in clinical psychology and social work. Derived from an older conception, sometimes called the hydraulic theory of behavior because of its analogy to the physics of fluids and gases under pressure, the hypothesis postulates that each human has a relatively fixed amount of emotional drive that must be released in one way or another. When expression of this drive is blocked, it builds up until it reaches a "bursting point" and explodes in emotional acts, some of which may be criminally assaultive.

Several variations of such "strain theory" have been developed by sociologists. Merton suggests that persons who cannot achieve culturally prescribed goals (such as economic success) by socially approved means develop the state of normlessness called "anomie" (Merton 1957, chaps. 4, 5; Clinard 1964). Anomic groups, according to Merton's theory, adopt one of four types of deviant conduct that reduce strain:

1. They abandon socially approved ways of achieving the culturally endorsed goals (e.g., by committing theft or fraud for economic success).
2. They "retreat" from society's preferences by blotting out both goals and means (e.g., by alcohol or other drug abuse, with indifference to living conditions, as is common on skid rows).
3. They become indifferent about achieving goals yet are hyperconformist about means of pursuing them (e.g., by stressing "proper" procedures, dress, and speech, as though these are the goals).
4. They become revolutionary and try to revise society's goals and means (e.g., by seeking to establish anarchistic communes that nurture mutual aid rather than competitive striving).

Cloward and Ohlin (1960) converted Merton's idea (that anomie fosters deviance) into an "opportunity theory" of youth crime to explain prominent variations in delinquent subcultures. According to opportunity theory, the youths in traditional slums who fail in the school and in the employment paths to legitimate adult roles, but who have access to older professional offenders as mentors or even as employers, develop criminal subcultures that transmit rationalizations and technical knowledge about crime. But, this theory asserts, when such juveniles have little access to successful adult criminals (e.g., as frequently occurs when they reside in public housing or in new slums), their delinquent subcultures glorify conflict for its own sake (evident in fighting gangs), because they need to create some opportunity to achieve a sense of adulthood, and they can readily do this by assertions of masculinity (e.g., showing physical strength, aggressiveness, sexual prowess, coolness under stress). What Cloward and Ohlin call the "double failures," persons who fail in both legitimate and criminal pursuits, are said to develop retreatist subcultures in which the greatest value is given to experiencing distinctive moods through alcohol or other drugs.

Research to test the Cloward and Ohlin theory found that almost all urban gangs are oriented to conflict but also engage in considerable theft and drug use (Short and Strodtbeck 1965). Other research, however, demonstrates that most delinquency occurs in small friendship groups rather than in gangs (Lerman 1967). It can readily be observed that these small groups vary greatly in the extent of their property or drug crimes. Cloward and Ohlin portrayed and explained what the sociologist Max Weber called "ideal types," patterns of thought that differentiate groups, even if few or no persons in any group have its pattern in pure form (Runciman 1978). Thus, if appropriately qualified to fit particular mixed cases, the Cloward and Ohlin ideal types can help us to understand much of the variation in behavior encountered in delinquents. (In some ways, this kind of theory is analogous to the idealized laws of the physical sciences that are formulated in terms of frictionless surfaces and perfect vacuums but which must be qualified to take friction and air resistance into account when applied to the real world.)

Sociological studies in the 1960s estimated delinquency rates not only from police or court statistics but also from self-report studies. Juveniles were asked about conduct that might constitute a criminal offense and about their personal backgrounds, attitudes, and other topics. The responses (that validation efforts, even with a lie detector, indicate are remarkably candid) show that delinquency is much less concentrated in particular social classes than arrest or court records suggest.[6] The findings are consistent with Hirschi's (1969) control theory of delinquency, which portrays humans as rational calculators (he asserts that everyone would be delinquent if they "dared") but also adopts the psychoanalytic view of all persons as inherently delinquent. He describes humans as not so much deterred by fear of government penalties as by bonds with conventional society, and that these bonds have four components: attachment to conventional persons that would be strained by delinquent acts, conventional pursuits that would be jeopardized by offenses, the time required for noncriminal activities, and anticriminal beliefs.

Also prominent in sociology in the past fifteen years has been labeling theory (H. Becker 1963; Lemert 1967; Schur 1971), a reformulation from earlier literature on delinquent subcultures (similar to attribution theory in psychology [Kelley 1971; Jones et al. 1972]). Labeling theory asserts that (1) when someone is called delinquent or criminal, persistence in lawbreaking follows because the label causes conventional persons to reject and only lawbreakers to accept the labeled person and (2) the offender feels deserving of his label and acts in ways that confirm it. Such a process of cumulative criminalization can be illustrated in the careers of some recidivist offenders, but research suggests that the more frequent result of being labeled a criminal is an increase in law-abiding conduct.

Persons who have what Hirschi calls conventional bonds, but who are revealed to have engaged in delinquency or crime, usually react to public exposure by assiduously striving to regain "good" reputations. The label also often mobilizes intensive assistance for them from the conventional persons with whom they have bonds. Thus the opposite of labeling theory is the older theory implicit in traditional judicial practice, that lawbreakers who have a stake in conformity can be deterred from recidivating

---

[6] Important literature on the implications and validity of self-report data on offenses, as contrasted with police statistics, include Short and Nye (1957–58, 1958), Erickson and Empey (1963), Clark and Tifft (1966), Hardt and Peterson (1968), Erickson (1972), Farrington (1973), Teilmann (1976), and Petersilia (1977).

by giving them a stigmatizing label such as "criminal" or "delinquent." This may explain why most first offenders, especially older ones who have strong family ties and stable work records, do not recidivate after the stigma of an arrest or even a prison sentence (Thorsell and Klemke 1972; Rogers and Buffalo 1974; Glaser 1978; Kitchener, Schmidt, and Glaser 1977).

A differential control theory would account for the contrasting effects of labeling. Such a theory would recognize, first, that most persons have some conventional bonds that they dare not jeopardize by serious crimes. When such people commit offenses, they try to keep their crimes secret; if caught and labeled for their offenses, they are unlikely to repeat. Middle-class housewives who shoplift epitomize this pattern (Cameron 1964). But the differential control theory would note, secondly, that some persons with weak conventional ties have their strongest bonds with other offenders (even if these, too, are weak) and that for this reason they often dare not decline to join in criminal activity with their associates (Hirschi 1969, p. 156; Linden and Hackler 1973). Finally, such a theory would imply that inflexible labels which cannot be hidden eventually or compensated for by gaining a good reputation, tend to weaken whatever conventional bonds the labeled persons may have and to strengthen their criminal bonds.

At the same time that these new theories in sociology were being developed, new trends in psychology also affected criminology. Skinner's influential reformulations of older ideas and the research that he stimulated indicate that (1) behavior which is gratifying in a given kind of circumstance tends to be repeated in that type of circumstance, whereas behavior which is not gratifying ceases, and (2) gratifying behavior that is punished generally ceases only while the punishment cannot be evaded or endured, and recurs thereafter unless alternative behavior becomes gratifying in this type of circumstance (Skinner 1953; Bandura 1969). This theory, like Cloward and Ohlin's, conveys an image of persons who follow the most gratifying course of conduct available in their learning experience, but whose options are limited by the alternative opportunities they encounter. Since Skinnerian psychologists stress social approval as one of the major sources of positive reinforcement for behavior, their perspective today is often called a social learning theory and is quite compatible with the central ideas in most economic and sociological theories on crime. The frustration-aggression hypothesis is not needed in social learning theory, however, because of evidence that reactions to frustration are not automatic but are learned instead from social models, and that the only modes of reaction that persist are those that receive positive reinforcement (Bandura 1973).

Another noteworthy development in psychology during the past two decades has been a resurgence of biological explanations for crime, although markedly different from those at the turn of the century and based on much more rigorous research. Psychiatrists long used the terms "psychopath," "sociopath," and "antisocial personality disorder" to designate persons who seem devoid of conscience and unable to learn from punishment, but these labels were so inconsistently applied and interpreted that they fell into disrepute. Research since 1957, however, shows that offenders whom tests, interviews, or other procedures classify as deficient in guilt feelings (and, hence, are called "psychopaths") tend to differ in autonomic nervous system reactions from persons who show more guilt feelings. Psychopaths average a lesser drop than most other persons in skin resistance to electricity following a sudden noise or electric shock (the galvanic skin response, or "GSR") and also average a slower return from any change that they do evince. Furthermore, their adrenal glands may be deficient in producing or in releasing the hormone epinephrine; injection of this hormone makes their GSR more like that of nonpsychopaths who are less affected by such injections. However, the hormone's effect is demonstrable only on nonviolent psychopaths. Also, there is evidence that these GSR patterns are hereditary. Yet it should be stressed that none of the statistically significant correlations reported here shows nearly an invariant relationship; although the distribution of GSR differences in relationship to criminality is not well charted, many persistent criminals lack the nervous system arousal pattern associated with psychopathy and many other persons with this pattern acquire no criminal record (Hare 1970; Glaser 1978, pp. 142–47).

Psychologists generally interpret the correlation between GSR reaction and apparent deficiency in guilt feelings as evidence that, from infancy on, psychopaths are handicapped in learning from punishment. This conclusion is inferred in two ways. First, psychopaths are not aroused as much as others by shock. Thus, repeated experiments show that while presumed psychopaths do about as well as others in cognitive tests, they do not average as much increase of speed as others do if given an electric shock following each wrong response on a finger maze puzzle or other testing device. Second, and what some consider the strongest argument, GSR changes in psychopaths following pain do not end as quickly when the pain is removed as they do in others. It is inferred from this "slow recovery rate" that psychopaths experience less of the sudden relief from anxiety that others get as reinforcement for becoming obedient after punishment for misconduct. Such reduction of discomfort is believed to be the positive reinforcement of greatest influence in shaping our conduct. Thus psychopaths may not only experience less guilt than others but also may enjoy slower release than others from whatever disturbed feelings they do develop from wrongdoing. Theirs is described as a sluggish autonomic nervous system, slow to emotional arousal and also slow to return to normal, but not necessarily slower in thinking, which is a function of the central nervous system (Mednick and Christiansen 1977, chaps. 12, 13, 17).

Weak reaction of the autonomic nervous system, hence failure to develop normal fears and anxieties, may conduce to crimes of deception. In one well-known experiment (Schachter 1971), psychology students in one class thought they were testing a new tranquilizer, and in the next class were given an apparent opportunity to cheat when grading their own examinations. Students given a placebo cheated significantly less than those given the tranquilizer, chlorpromazine, which reduces fear and anxiety.

The psychopathy and tranquilizer studies suggest that if biological conditions produce crime, they do so only indirectly, by reducing—not eliminating—the capacities to learn from punishment or to apply the inhibitions that are learned. There is also evidence of more direct relationships between crimes and physiological disturbances. Thus, many conditions that create irritability are associated with assaultive offenses. For example, several studies suggest that about half the violence by women occurs in the four days before and the four days during menstruation, when many women have endocrinal imbalances that make them irritable (Ellis and Austin 1971; Shah and Roth 1974). Men, too, are more likely to become violent when irritable.

Of course, most women are not violent during premenstrual and menstrual periods, and most persons using tranquilizers do not cheat. Social learning apparently controls behavior more powerfully and consistently than the physiological states that affect moods. Indeed, some have speculated that the social learning which stresses hard work and instills strong drives for achievement may accelerate physiological reactions, and that social reinforcement of indolence may slow them. Thus there may be intricate relations between biology and culture.

Growing evidence suggests that most impediments to school performance, from low intelligence[7] to poor education of parents, are highly correlated with delinquency. Such findings reflect two major changes that have occurred in the United States with rapid urbanization and industrialization:

1. The duration of schooling has increased about one year per decade, so that (according to the Census) the median for persons 25 years of age or over rose from around eight and a half years of school in 1940 to more than twelve in 1970.

[7] Hirschi and Hindelang (1977). Note that an extra male chromosome (the XYY genetic type), believed in the 1960s to be a major biological cause of violent crime, was later shown to occur in only about one in a thousand males but to be more common among prison inmates than in the general male population, perhaps because it (and other sex chromosome anomalies) tends to be associated with lower intelligence. Also, like most other school handicaps, it is correlated more with nonviolent than with violent crime. For detailed data, see Borgaonkar and Shah (1974).

2. Our society has become increasingly age-segregated and hence the home and the workplace have become less influential for adolescents as sources of instruction in conventional adult roles; among the causes are:

   a) more common breakup of marriages;
   b) more mothers working outside the home;
   c) later entry of youths into employment;
   d) drastic reduction of family businesses;
   e) the commercialization of recreation and its catering to age-specific markets; and
   f) modern appliances, as well as new types of food and clothing, that decrease household chores.

These trends reduce the contact and collaboration between adolescents and adults outside of school, and the larger schools are often more impersonal. Thus, good school experiences may be more crucial than ever for preventing delinquency because other institutions have become less influential in creating social bonds between children and grownups, and in preparing youth for a legitimate adult occupation and lifestyle. Almost all types of difficulties in school are highly correlated with both arrests and self-reported delinquency but, once students are arrested, their prospects of further arrests decline if they drop out of school, especially if they then marry, get a job, or both (Elliott and Voss 1974). Apparently, conflict with teachers or other school maladjustment impedes student acquisition of conventional adult roles, but when difficulties in school become extremely severe, dropping out and acquiring a job or a spouse, or both, increase a youth's conventional bonds and adulthood.

Differential association, social learning, opportunity, and control theories can be integrated on a very abstract level as *differential anticipation* theory (Glaser 1978, pp. 126–27), which asserts: a person refrains from or commits crime because of his or her anticipations of its consequences, but the anticipations are determined by (1) the person's total conventional and criminal social bonds; (2) the person's prior social learning experiences that have provided skills, tastes, and ideas conducive to gratification in criminal or in alternative pursuits; and (3) the person's perceptions of needs, opportunities, and risks when interpreting momentary circumstances.

Differential anticipation theory can be a useful explanation for intentional crime and delinquency. The theory is *not* applicable to crimes of strict liability, negligence, or recklessness (in most cases), or to those committed in ignorance of the law or by mentally irresponsible persons. Differential anticipation theory assumes that the three factors it distinguishes are important in every intentional offense, and that these three factors are listed in the order of their relative importance in most cases.

An integrated theory has the advantage that it can explain a large and diverse range of offenses. It is therefore preferable to a multicausal theory which merely lists broad factors without suggesting the manner in which they are interrelated. Differential anticipation theory is more than what Homans derogates as a mere "orienting statement" (Homans 1967; Walker 1977, pp. 41–42), for it offers specific explanations for particular cases of lawbreaking. It can encompass specific criminal behavior patterns and justify particular correctional policies (some of which are indicated in the following section).

III. Implications and Applications

Differential anticipation theory lacks the precision of most laws in the physical sciences, but its component principles are sufficiently supported by empirical research and by other well-established causal explanations in the social sciences to warrant considerable confidence in its validity. Its three principles provide major guidance for criminal justice policies, but their application to specific issues and situations requires deduction and testing of more concrete generalizations. The following pages illustrate some of the lessons of differential anticipation theory for particular types of criminal justice policies and programs.

A. Social Bonds

Failure to take into account the social bonds of offenders is the most glaring source of ineffectiveness in sentencing and in correctional and crime-prevention policies when dealing with juvenile and young adult offenders, but it also has important significance for predominantly adult lawbreakers who engage in organized and white-collar crime. According to arrest reports and self-report studies, peak arrest rates for the FBI's Index Crimes of theft, burglary, auto theft, robbery, assault, and rape occur during the teen years, and murder arrests peak at age 20 but are almost as high at 18 and 19 (Glaser 1978, p. 75). This age range is in that vaguely defined span of life known as adolescence, the period between childhood dependence and adult independence. These are years of frequent conflict between juveniles and their adult authority figures at home and in school; for many youths, they are a time of weakened social bonds with adults and of new and often intense but unstable relationships with peers. Yet, as previously noted, research indicates that the ties between juveniles and their parents, teachers, and nondelinquent peers are the strongest controls against serious delinquency (Hirschi 1969; Glaser 1978, chap. 8).

It will be argued here that ambiguous and inconsistent results have resulted from tests of the deterrent effects of alternative government penalties and of various rehabilitation programs, and that these results occur because the penalties, programs, and tests neglect to consider the diverse effects of sentencing and correctional practices on the social bonds of offenders.

To test whether punishments deter, researchers try to find out whether the recidivism rates of released offenders vary with differences in the speed, certainty, or severity of the penalties imposed. For probationers, however, certainty of arrest for a new offense depends in large part upon the closeness of surveillance provided by the probation officers. The Survey seems to provide validation for traditional deterrence theory in all five studies in which "youthful subjects were randomly assigned to various forms of intensive supervision and to standard supervision." The Survey concludes: "A clear finding is that intensive probation supervision is associated with reduction in recidivism among males and females under 18 years of age" (Lipton, Martinson, and Wilks 1975). Yet in the one study comparing probation with incarceration, first offenders given probation had significantly lower recidivism rates than similar offenders who were imprisoned and then paroled; there were no differences for those with prior convictions. Likewise, in the only somewhat comparable study, first offenders under 20 years old were less recidivistic with suspended sentences than with imprisonment, and there were no significant differences for older ones. Furthermore, there was much less marked and consistent relationship between intensity of supervision and recidivism rates for parolees of any age, and for older probationers, than for young probationers with no prior record (Lipton, Martinson, and Wilks 1975).

If these findings are analyzed in terms of social bonds rather than deterrence, it will be noted that intensity of supervision is usually measured by the small size of caseloads rather than by the amount of actual surveillance. Indeed, the probation staffs are most likely to learn of new crimes committed by their clients from police reports rather than from their own observations. Also, with probationers—especially young ones—intensive supervision programs focus on building rapport between staff and clients rather than closer surveillance. It is doubtful, however, that staff members develop very close bonds with many offenders, since they differ markedly from most of their clients in age, education, social class, and ethnicity, and they are perceived by the clients as potentially punitive. Even intensive supervision involves at most only a few hours of contact per month with each person.

Social bonds may explain the Survey's contradictory findings on the effects of intensity of supervision for different clientele. Young first offenders generally have stronger conventional ties and weaker criminal bonds than either parolees (of any age) or probationers with a prior record. Thus, intensive supervision of the young first offenders protects or enhances these ties; probation or suspended sentences prevent both impairment of conventional bonds and criminalization from jail or prison life. In contrast, however, persons who have been previously convicted usually have had so much detention or jail life and years of conflict with the law that the ordinary variations in intensity of parole or probation supervision cannot significantly affect their weakened conventional and strengthened criminal bonds. Finally, in older offenders, with or without a prior record, both conventional and criminal bonds are likely to be too firmly established to be nearly as susceptible to alteration in one way or another by these variations in correctional treatment as are the more flexible bonds of young first offenders.

The probable effects of correctional measures on social bonds also help to explain another set of contrasting results with alternative penalties for different types of offenders. In the 1961–69 phase of the California Youth Authority's "Community Treatment Project," youths in state custody for the first time were quickly screened to remove from the study about 25 percent of the boys and 5 percent of the girls whose crimes were so violent that it was presumed the public would demand severe penalties for them. The remainder were randomly divided into an experimental group paroled immediately to intensive parole supervision (eight to twelve persons per officer), and a control group confined an average of eight months before parole under regular supervision (caseloads of seventy or more).

About half the Community Treatment Project's clients were diagnosed as "neurotics," because they did not seem highly committed to delinquency, and they were considered more mature than others, since they appeared to be less impulsive and manipulative. These were the youths with strongest conventional bonds, and they had lower recidivism rates both during and after supervision if in the experimental rather than the control group. However, about a fifth of the clients, the "power oriented," were the most enculturated in delinquency and the most defiant or manipulative toward authority figures. They appeared to have the strongest delinquent subcultures, tried to take advantage of permissiveness in parole staff, and had lower recidivism rates if in the control rather than the experimental group. No clear advantage for either group was evident for the roughly 30 percent diagnosed in residual categories (Palmer 1974). (Unfortunately, although Lerman's evaluation of this study [1975] is much more lucid than the official reports and although it incisively criticizes some features, it does not analyze the typologically differentiated or the four-year post-discharge data that are cited here and are to be supplemented by two books of later findings by the project staff.)

Although most prisons seem to strengthen bonds among criminals and to impair whatever ties they may yet have with conventional society, control theory implies that prisoners who can nevertheless maintain or augment their ties with law-abiding persons will be less likely to commit further offenses. Holt and Miller's California study (1972) found that inmates who could maintain family ties through staff facilitation of visits to the institution, including conjugal visits for married prisoners, had better success rates on parole. In California, also, recidivism reduction at both youth and adult institutions was associated with the services of the M-2 Sponsors organization in arranging visits of conventional persons to prisoners who would otherwise get few or no visits (Lewis 1976; M-2 Sponsors, Inc. 1978). In Massachusetts, short furloughs for inmates when their release dates are imminent are associated with significantly lower recidivism rates (LeClair 1977).

The pertinent research cited indicates that concern with maximizing the conventional bonds of offenders and minimizing their ties with other lawbreakers can contribute to the reduction of recidivism. Programs with this purpose appear to be most influential on young lawbreakers who have not yet been greatly involved in delinquency, but even the incarceration of hardened convicts can be made somewhat less criminalizing if administrators bear in mind the effects of social bonds on the probable post-release anticipations of prisoners. Replacement of large institutions by small homes, as was done with juvenile corrections in Massachusetts (Ohlin, Miller and Coates 1977; Miller, Ohlin and Coates 1978), and reduction in the size and regimentation of others, are steps in this direction. Many more significant changes, such as greater use of restitution and of public service penalties, may also be developed if the effects of correctional practices on social bonds are imaginatively considered.

B. Social Learning

What life teaches us depends on our experiences, and especially on who influences us and serves as our model. Most ideas of good and bad, and conceptions of one's own worth, are acquired in intimate interaction with close personal associates such as family and friends. Also, the most intense gratifications tend to be from social approval. Therefore, social learning is much more relevant than book learning to understanding and controlling criminals, although their academic achievement affects their social learning opportunities. Indeed, comparison of what is learned in school by delinquents with what is learned by nondelinquents suggests that the contrasts of greatest significance for the success of each in legitimate pursuits are illustrated not only by their grades or their scores on achievement tests but also by subtle aspects of their social habits and skills.

Apparently because of their failure and humiliation in formal relationships with adults, especially in school, delinquents seem to become habituated primarily to informal modes of interaction. It is noteworthy that among the best predictors of nondelinquency is participation in formal organizations, such as high-school extracurricular groups, and in a college preparatory curriculum. Nondelinquents generally are more oriented to learning the formal style of interaction prevailing in large organizations, where most employment occurs today. Delinquents spend more time than nondelinquents "hanging out" with friends, and much less time on homework, extracurricular activities, or employment (Hirschi 1969). Informal adolescent groups have loose schedules and vague conduct rules, and they provide immediate reinforcement for "horsing around," teasing, threatening physical violence, and other expressive rather than task-oriented communication. In contrast, high-standard classrooms and formal groups reinforce efficient speech, analytic thought, punctuality, diligence, dependability, and other achievement-oriented behavior. Incidentally, these differences increasingly cut across class lines, for delinquency is becoming less linked to social class and more to school and home relationships, especially if self-reported rather than police data on delinquency are the basis of comparison (Loeb

1973; Tittle 1978; Hirschi 1969, chaps. 9, 10). In summary, delinquents tend to be found in adolescent groups that encourage lifestyles which impede achievement in school or work, and non-delinquents are more often encouraged when still young in habits that later lead to adult occupational success.

Insensitive to these contrasts and to their consequences, many schools adopt "social promotion" policies by which teachers are encouraged to be indifferent to the informality and low achievement of any students who do not impede the work of the more academically successful youths. Indeed, schools often foster contrasting subcultures among their students by track systems that separate the high from the low achievers. Research indicates that this separation fosters delinquency among the low achievers (Kelly 1974).

Unfortunately, efforts to correct the academic and learning deficiencies of offenders seldom give much attention to their handicaps from the lifestyles they have learned. Many schools in correctional institutions and manpower training centers in the cities continue the informality, indolence, and social promotion policies to which most of their students have become accustomed. Their teachers often expect (and therefore get) a level of performance which neither matches that in the regular school system nor meets the requirements of typical employment.

Concern for social learning may explain why the Survey reveals no consistent patterns in the results of evaluation studies which compared the recidivism rates of offenders assigned to a school with the rates of other ostensibly similar lawbreakers. Such studies do not investigate the mode or conditions of instruction, or recognize bias in the analysis; for example, they fail to consider that some prisons may keep the most criminalistic inmates within the most secure part of the buildings (which is where the school is also located) and place the best-risk inmates elsewhere. A clue that such research inadequacies may explain the inconclusiveness of these studies is provided by the Survey's finding of a relationship between lower recidivism rates and increase in academic grade while in prison (rather than mere attendance at school); for youthful offenders it found that voca-

tional education—whether in prison or on probation—was associated with less recidivism (Lipton, Martinson, and Wilks 1975,
pp. 184–207).

McKee (1972, 1978) found that California prisoners who
received vocational training (especially over 1,000 hours) in
auto repair, welding, machine shop, or sheet metal work had
distinctly higher post-release earnings and less recidivism than
similar prisoners without such training or with types of training
irrelevant to their job opportunities (e.g., shoe repair, dry clean-
ing, and masonry). Tropp (1978) reports that Department of
Labor studies find the most consistent post-program success of
delinquents in federally subsidized vocational training that provides hard physical labor, rather than in trade schools with
typical classroom atmospheres and often the social promotion
policies by which regular schools may have already made these
students incompetent for the labor market. Physical labor programs can simulate the standards of adult employment and appeal
to adolescent pride in showing manliness. Several studies show
programmed instruction also to be especially conducive to reduced
recidivism rates, particularly if provided to delinquents in the
community (Cohen and Filipczak 1971; Odell 1974; Hackler and
Hagan 1975). Programmed instruction rewards students individ-
ually for each mastered lesson and all proceed at their own pace.
Previous underachievers often advance rapidly.

In summary, there is much evidence that if an awareness of
differential social learning is combined with a sensitivity to
differential social bonds, efforts toward crime prevention and
reformation of offenders can be more successful.

C. Perceived Opportunities

The consideration of consequences that guides willful conduct
varies greatly in duration and quality. It is brief and impulsive
when we act in anger or panic, but long and careful when we act
deliberately. There also are variations in the extent to which any
thoughts that direct our behavior are focused on immediate
expectations or on the long-run consequences of contemplated
actions. An individual's view of his circumstances reflects not

only objective opportunities but also personal surmises of alternative possibilities. It is because past experiences influence these current assessments that people generally persist in activities that gratified them, and eventually abandon pursuits that proved frustrating. These effects of prior learning and current opportunities help to explain the previously noted inverse correlation between juvenile delinquency rates and school achievement and employment qualifications and, also, the fact that increases in a community's unemployment rates tend to be followed by increases in its crime rates (Glaser and Rice 1959; Ehrlich 1973).

Most juvenile and young adult criminal careers appear to be intermittent and unspecialized (Wolfgang, Figlio, and Sellin 1972; Petersilia, Greenwood, and Lavin 1977). Offenders change their pattern of conduct suddenly with shifts in their circumstances and moods, or with the dynamics of social interaction. For example, much serious crime is committed with little forethought when challenges to engage in an offense are made or implied by others and "face" would be lost by backing down (Short 1974; Short and Strodtbeck 1965). Often some impulsive reactions in a brief moment suffice to inflict long-term damages and regrets. Nevertheless, some stability in behavior eventually develops: the longer the period in which an ex-offender has no delinquent or criminal record, the greater is the prospect that no recidivism will occur, and conversely, the longer and more continuously lawbreaking is pursued, the greater is the probability that the criminal will persist in it (Kitchener, Schmidt, and Glaser 1977).

A number of studies indicate that immediate, tangible assistance to alleviate a released offender's desperate economic plight reduces the probability of recidivism. Maryland in 1971–74 and California in 1973–74 paid parolees up to $60 and $80 per week, respectively, if unemployed during the first three months out of prison. In both states, the assisted parolees had less recidivism and a better work record than similar releasees in a control group lacking this aid. The difference occurred primarily in lower rates of new property crimes, was most evident in parolees previously convicted of property rather than of violent crimes, and was most marked for younger parolees with some prior work history (Reinarman and Miller 1975; U.S. Department of Labor 1977).

Throughout the United States a person is ineligible for unemployment payments unless he earned a minimum amount (varying from one state to another) in two separate quarters of the preceding year and unless the employer made payments to the state unemployment compensation fund for these earnings.[8] Therefore, those imprisoned (or hospitalized) in all of the preceding year cannot receive such benefits, regardless of how much their previous employment contributed to these funds. As a result of the cited experiments, California enacted a law, effective in 1978, which gives prisoners credits for work and good conduct while incarcerated that will result in payments if they are unemployed during the one-year parole that all receive under California's new sentencing law.

The U.S. Department of Labor's enthusiasm over the results of the Maryland experiment led it to finance similar projects in Georgia and Texas during 1976. Initial remarks by federal officials on the results suggested that the programs in these two states made no difference, since about 40 percent of the parolees were rearrested within a year whether in the treatment or the control groups. The first of several planned reports on these projects now permits us to infer reasons for the disappointing outcome, although data are now available only on Georgia.[9] Georgia had three experimental groups, each receiving payments for different periods and employment conditions. It also had three control groups, of which one received job-procurement aid (e.g., counseling, money for tools) and two received no aid. All groups except one of those with no assistance were interviewed three times during the year after their release; all six were followed through state records to tabulate what earnings were reported to the Unemployment Insurance Division for them, and what new arrests were registered by law enforcement agencies.

The most informative finding of the Georgia study applies to all releasees, whichever group they were in: "at best, through the year, for each four who went to work, there were six without employment." Many jobs were temporary and median earnings

---

[8] For examples of the varying state qualifying formulas, see Hickey (1977).

[9] Stephens and Sanders (1978). This paragraph and the next two reflect valuable comments by Lois W. Sanders on a first draft of this section.

were well below the poverty level. Only during the last quarter of the follow-up year was the median higher than the project's maximum unemployment compensation payment of $70 per week. For every five persons in the total of over two thousand in this study, one received wages during each of the four quarters of the year, two had earnings in three or fewer quarters, and two had no earnings in any quarter. The interview responses suggest, however, that during each quarter approximately 10 percent of these releasees earned wages that were neither reported by employers nor the basis of payments to the state unemployment compensation funds.

In such a low-income environment, the $70 weekly unemployment compensation was apparently so high as to be a disincentive for some even to seek work, but for others it permitted more selectivity with regard to the wage level and security of the jobs accepted. Thus, the experimental groups (eligible for compensation payments) had the highest rates of both unemployment and arrest during the first quarter out, but they also had the highest total earnings during the year. Those assisted by project staff in getting employment had the lowest-paying jobs, while those not eligible for aid who found their own jobs earned more, on the average, and had the lowest arrest rates. Arrests among the unemployed were more often for crimes to obtain money than were the arrests of the others. About half of these Georgia releasees were under 25 years old.

Possibly the optimum method of reducing recidivism by expanding the conventional opportunities of releasees is by some combination of (1) guaranteed employment by government-subsidized private firms or by government itself; (2) trade training in which support payments to the students are based on demonstrated gains in knowledge or skill; and (3) unemployment compensation payments provided on some more restricted basis than in this experiment. At any rate, it is clear that reliable knowledge for better policy guidance in this area will come only from further types of rigorous experimentation. But such optimum aid for *all* unemployed persons, regardless of crime record, would doubtless not only prevent offenses but would provide many other public benefits.

Theoretically, assistance during economic crises should reduce recidivism if the aid is timely and tangible enough to foster persistence in job seeking by the "intermittent" offenders who are marginal in conventional and criminal bonds; it would be less likely to alter the probable low crime rate even in adversity of those with a strong "stake in conformity" or the high crime rate of the minority of convicts who are "intensive" or truly "career" criminals (Petersilia, Greenwood, and Lavin 1977).

In 1961 the U.S. Bureau of Prisons established urban halfway houses to which prisoners are transferred in the last three months before parole. Many states and a few county jails have since developed similar programs; others release inmates daily from prison to jobs or school in nearby communities. The Survey labeled all these release arrangements "Partial Physical Custody" and found no clear pattern of results from five evaluations of halfway houses and seven of prison work release programs (Lipton, Martinson, and Wilks 1975, pp. 269–80). However, there were markedly lower violation rates for previously recidivist young auto thieves paroled from the federal centers in their home areas than for those paroled from a distant reformatory. This category had higher failure rates than other federal prisoners regardless of how released. However, a place for food, shelter, and company, with immediate staff counseling or control while they seek or start jobs during their first few months out, apparently has more significant impact on such youths' prospects of establishing firm conventional bonds than it does for other types of offenders (Hall, Milazzo, and Posner 1966).

A 1975 survey of halfway-house evaluations discovered only two controlled experiments, both of which showed no differences in recidivism rates between residents and their control groups, as well as seventeen quasi-experiments in which eleven found residents had less recidivism than their comparison groups (Seiter et al. 1977). Massachusetts experienced less recidivism for halfway-house than for comparison cases, especially for prisoners with little previous employment experience (LeClair 1975; Landolfi 1976a, 1976b). Two other studies found that jail-operated halfway-houses reduced recidivism rates, especially for unskilled and unmarried men with prior convictions (Rudoff and Esselstyn 1973; Jeffery and Woolpert 1974). On the other hand, a controlled experiment with work release from Florida prisons found no difference in recidivism rates between experimental and control cases (Waldo and Chiricos 1977).

This array of findings suggests that immediate social and economic aid, and possibly control and counseling through a halfway house in the community of future residence, can make a significant difference in the prospects of some prisoners who have not yet been very successful at crime or employment and are not utterly disabled by addictions. Obviously, however, more qualitative investigation and quantitative checks are needed to know the optimum modes of such aid and control for various types of offenders.

All the expansions of conventional opportunities described here were limited in duration and scope. Not one was analyzed with great probing of what tangible aid was provided, for whom it was most significant, and why. The studies suggest, however, that expanding offenders' chances for success in legitimate endeavors may often be as important as reducing their prospects of "getting away with" further lawbreaking. Since the government can usually supply employment or other aid to an offender much more easily than it can reduce his prospects of gaining income illegally, in what circumstances is it most cost-effective to try to reduce recidivism by aid? Search for better answers to this question should benefit from guidance by a theory that helps to pinpoint the types of aid, of beneficiary, and of distribution procedures that most augment the recipient's perception of greater opportunities in noncriminal pursuits than in lawbreaking.

IV. Conclusion

A few basic ideas on crime causation have recurred in history. The general principles that best survived the tests of time and of research can be summarized as differential anticipation theory. These principles are largely supported by correctional evaluation studies; they demonstrate that lower recidivism rates for many offenders can be achieved by measures that strengthen their conventional bonds, effectively train them for legitimate occupations, and improve their opportunities for gaining economic self-sufficiency. Differential anticipation theory also supports efforts to reduce opportunities in crime by any of a large variety of methods (e.g., target-hardening, fines, probation, incarceration) whenever their benefits to society in crime prevention offset their social and economic costs. The theory can improve this benefit-cost estimation, however, by stimulating and guiding decision-makers to design sentences and correctional practices that, as much as possible, (1) minimize the bonds among criminals and the extent to which they are criminalized by each other, and (2) maximize the bonds of offenders to conventional persons, and their conventional learning and opportunities.

The discussion and illustrations presented here deal mainly with the most frequent clientele of correctional agencies, the largely unspecialized and unprofessional ordinary offenders. If space permitted similar attention to other types of lawbreakers, such as white-collar criminals, sex offenders, or drug-law viola-tors, the specific services recommended would be considerably different, but the general principles presented would not be basically altered.

Crime-causation theory that is derived from the most relevant and adequately proven abstract behavioral science theory, is continually made explicit, and is rigorously tested by practical application remains the best hope for increasing valid and useful knowledge on how to cope with lawbreaking. Etiology, the study of causation, is frequently moribund, but it never expires; if instead of trying to kill it we strive to give it new health, efforts to reduce delinquency and crime can only benefit.

REFERENCES

Aichhorn, August. 1935. *Wayward Youth*. New York: Viking.
Bandura, Albert. 1969. *Principles of Behavior Modification*. New York: Holt, Rinehart & Winston.
———. 1973. *Aggression*. Englewood Cliffs, N.J.: Prentice-Hall.

Becker, Gary S. 1968. "Crime and Punishment: An Economic Approach," *Journal of Political Economy* 76:169–217.

Becker, Howard S. 1963. *Outsiders*. New York: Free Press.

Bonger, Willem A. 1916. *Criminality and Economic Conditions*. Boston: Little, Brown.

Borgaonkar, Digamber S., and Saleem A. Shah. 1974. "The XYY Chromosome: Male—or Syndrome?" In *Progress in Medical Genetics*, vol. 10, ed. Arthur G. Steinberg and Alexander G. Beam. New York: Grune & Stratton.

Burt, Cyril. 1938. *The Young Delinquent*. London: University of London Press.

Cameron, Mary Owen. 1964. *The Booster and the Snitch*. New York: Free Press.

Clark, John P., and Larry L. Tifft. 1966. "Polygraph and Interview Validation of Self-Reported Deviant Behavior," *American Sociological Review* 31:516–23.

Clinard, Marshall B., ed. 1964. *Anomie and Deviant Behavior*. New York: Free Press.

Cloward, Richard A., and Lloyd E. Ohlin. 1960. *Delinquency and Opportunity*. New York: Free Press.

Cohen, Harold L., and J. Filipczak. 1971. *A New Learning Environment*. San Francisco: Jossey-Bass.

Dollard, John, L. Doob, N. Miller, O. H. Mowrer, and R. Sears. 1939. *Frustration and Aggression*. New Haven: Yale University Press.

Dugdale, Richard L. 1877. *The Jukes*. New York: Putnam.

Ehrlich, Isaac. 1973. "Participation in Illegitimate Activities: A Theoretical and Empirical Investigation," *Journal of Political Economy* 81:521–65.

Eissler, K. R., ed. 1949. *Searchlights on Delinquency*. New York: International Universities Press.

Elliott, Delbert S., and Harwin L. Voss. 1974. *Delinquency and Dropout*. Lexington, Mass.: D. C. Heath.

Ellis, Desmond P., and Penelope Austin. 1971. "Menstruation and Aggressive Behavior in a Correctional Center for Women," *Journal of Criminal Law, Criminology and Police Science* 62:388–95.

Erickson, Maynard L. 1972. "The Changing Relationship between Official and Self-Reported Measures of Delinquency: An Exploratory-Predictive Study," *Journal of Criminal Law, Criminology and Police Science* 63:388–95.

Erickson, Maynard L., and LaMar T. Empey. 1963. "Court Records, Undetected Delinquency and Decision Making," *Journal of Criminal Law, Criminology and Police Science* 54:456–69.

Estabrook, A. H. 1916. *The Jukes in 1915*. Washington, D.C.: Carnegie Institution of Washington.

Farrington, David P. 1973. "Self-Reports of Deviant Behavior: Predictive and Stable?" *Journal of Criminal Law and Criminology* 64: 99–110.

Ferentz, Edward J. 1954. "Mental Deficiency and Crime," *Journal of Criminal Law and Criminology* 45:299–307.

Ferri, Enrico. 1897. *Criminal Sociology*. New York: Appleton.

Fleisher, Belton M. 1966. *The Economics of Delinquency*. Chicago: Quadrangle Books.

Glaser, Daniel. 1956. "Criminality Theories and Behavioral Images," *American Journal of Sociology* 61:433–44.

———. 1976. "The Compatibility of Free Will and Determinism in Criminology: Comment on an Alleged Problem," *Journal of Criminal Law and Criminology* 67:486–90.

———. 1978. *Crime in Our Changing Society*. New York: Holt, Rinehart & Winston.

Glaser, Daniel, and Kent Rice. 1959. "Crime, Age, and Employment," *American Sociological Review* 24:679–86.

Glueck, Sheldon, and Eleanor H. Glueck. 1950. *Unravelling Juvenile Delinquency*. New York: Commonwealth Fund.

———. 1964. *Ventures in Criminology*. Cambridge: Harvard University Press.

Goddard, H. H. 1912. *The Kallikak Family*. New York: Macmillan.

Goring, Charles. 1913. *The English Convict*. London: H.M. Stationery Office.

Hackler, James C., and John L. Hagan. 1975. "Work and Teaching Machines as Delinquency Prevention Tools: A Four-Year Followup," *Social Service Review* 49:92–106.

Hall, Reis H., Mildred Milazzo, and Judy Posner. 1966. *A Descriptive and Comparative Study of Recidivism in Pre-release Guidance Center Releases*. Washington, D.C.: U.S. Bureau of Prisons.

Hardt, Robert H., and Sandra J. Peterson. 1968. "Neighborhood Status and Delinquency Activity as Indexed by Police Records and a Self-Report Survey," *Criminologica* 6:37–47.

Hare, R. D. 1970. *Psychopathy: Theory and Research*. New York: Wiley.

Healy, William B. 1924. *The Individual Delinquent*. Boston: Little, Brown.

Healy, William B., and Augusta F. Bronner. 1936. *New Light on Delinquency and Its Treatment*. New Haven: Yale University Press.

Hempel, Carl G. 1965. *Aspects of Scientific Explanation*. New York: Free Press.

Hickey, Joseph A. 1977. "State Unemployment Insurance Legislation Changes in 1976," *Monthly Labor Review* 100:46–51.

Hirschi, Travis. 1969. *Causes of Delinquency.* Berkeley: University of California Press.

Hirschi, Travis, and Michael J. Hindelang. 1977. "Intelligence and Delinquency: A Revisionist Review," *American Sociological Review* 42: 571–87.

Holt, Norman, and Donald Miller. 1972. *Explorations in Inmate-Family Relationships.* Research Report 46. Sacramento: California Department of Corrections.

Homans, George C. 1967. *The Nature of Social Science.* New York: Harcourt, Brace & World.

Jeffery, Robert, and Stephen Woolpert. 1974. "Work Furlough as an Alternative to Incarceration: An Assessment of Its Effects on Recidivism and Social Costs," *Journal of Criminal Law and Criminology* 65:405–15.

Jones, Edward E., D. Kanouse, H. Kelley, R. Nesett, S. Valins, and B. Weiner. 1972. *Attribution: Perceiving the Causes of Behavior.* Morristown, N.J.: General Learning Press.

Kelley, Harold H. 1971. *Attribution in Social Interaction.* Morristown, N.J.: General Learning Press.

Kelly, Delos H. 1974. "Track Position and Delinquent Involvement," *Sociology and Social Research* 58:380–86.

Kitchener, Howard, A. Schmidt, and D. Glaser. 1977. "How Persistent Is Post-Prison Success?" *Federal Probation* 41:9–15.

Landolfi, Joseph. 1976a. *An Analysis of Recidivism among Residents Released from the Pre-Release Centers Administered by Massachusetts Halfway Houses, Inc.* Boston: Massachusetts Department of Corrections.

———. 1976b. *Charlotte House Pre-Release Center for Women.* Boston: Massachusetts Department of Corrections.

Lange, J. 1930. *Crime as Destiny.* New York: Boni.

LeClair, Daniel P. 1975. *An Analysis of Recidivism among Residents Released from Boston State and Shirley Pre-Release Centers during 1972–1973.* Boston: Massachusetts Department of Corrections.

———. 1977. *The Effect of the Home Furlough on Rates of Recidivism.* Boston: Massachusetts Department of Corrections.

Lemert, Edwin M. 1967. *Human Deviance, Social Problems and Social Control.* Englewood Cliffs, N.J.: Prentice-Hall.

Lerman, Paul. 1967. "Gangs, Networks and Subcultural Diversity," *American Journal of Sociology* 73:63–72.

———. 1975. *Community Treatment and Social Control.* Chicago: University of Chicago Press.

Lewis, Roy V. 1976. *M-2 Project Evaluation: Final Parole Followup of Wards in the M-2 Program.* Sacramento: California Youth Authority.

Linden, Eric, and J. C. Hackler. 1973. "Affective Ties and Delinquency," *Pacific Sociological Review* 16:27–46.

Lipton, Douglas, Robert Martinson, and Judith Wilks. 1975. *The Effectiveness of Correctional Treatment: A Survey of Treatment Evaluation Studies.* New York: Praeger.

Loeb, Rita. 1973. "Adolescent Groups," *Sociology and Social Research* 58:13–22.

Lombroso, Cesare. 1912. *Crime: Its Causes and Remedies.* Boston: Little, Brown.

McKee, Gilbert J., Jr. 1972. "A Cost-Benefit Analysis of Vocational Training in the California Prison System." Doctoral dissertation in economics, Claremont Graduate School.

————. 1978. "Cost Effectiveness and Vocational Training." In *Justice and Corrections*, ed. N. Johnston and L. D. Savitz. New York: Wiley.

Mannheim, Hermann. 1960. *Pioneers in Criminology.* Chicago: Quadrangle Books.

Mednick, Sarnoff, and Karl Christiansen, eds. 1977. *Biosocial Bases of Criminal Behavior.* New York: Gardner Press.

Merton, Robert K. 1957. *Social Theory and Social Structure.* New York: Free Press.

Miller, Alden D., Lloyd E. Ohlin, and Robert B. Coates. 1978. *A Theory of Social Reform.* Cambridge, Mass.: Ballinger.

M-2 Sponsors, Inc., of California. 1978. *Successful Habilitation of Ex-Offenders.* Hayward, Calif.: M-2 Sponsors.

Odell, Brian N. 1974. "Accelerating Entry into the Opportunity Structure: A Sociologically-Based Treatment for Delinquent Youth," *Sociology and Social Research* 58:312–18.

Ohlin, Lloyd E., Alden D. Miller, and Robert B. Coates. 1977. *Juvenile Correctional Reform in Massachusetts.* Washington, D.C.: U.S. Government Printing Office.

Palmer, Ted. 1974. "The Youth Authority's Community Treatment Project," *Federal Probation* 38:3–20.

Petersilia, Joan. 1977. *The Validity of Criminality Data Derived from Personal Interviews.* Rand Paper Series P-5890. Santa Monica, Calif.: RAND Corporation.

Petersilia, Joan, Peter Greenwood, and M. M. Lavin. 1977. *Criminal Careers of Habitual Felons.* Santa Monica, Calif.: RAND Corporation.

Phillipson, Coleman. 1923. *Three Criminal Law Reformers: Beccaria, Bentham, Romilly.* London: Dent.

Popper, Karl R. 1959. *The Logic of Scientific Discovery*. New York: Basic Books.

Radzinowicz, Leon. 1966. *Ideology and Crime*. New York: Columbia University Press.

Redl, Fritz, and David Wineman. 1951. *Children Who Hate*. New York: Free Press.

Reinarman, Craig, and Donald Miller. 1975. *Direct Financial Assistance to Parolees*. Sacramento: California Department of Corrections.

Rogers, Joseph W., and M. D. Buffalo. 1974. "Fighting Back; Nine Modes of Adaptation to a Deviant Label," *Social Problems* 22:101–18.

Rosanoff, A. J., L. M. Handy, and F. A. Rosanoff. 1934. "Criminality and Delinquency in Twins," *Journal of Criminal Law and Criminology* 24:923–34.

Rudoff, Alvin, and T. C. Esselstyn. 1973. "Evaluating Work Furlough: A Followup," *Federal Probation* 37 (June):48–53.

Runciman, W. G., ed. 1978. *Max Weber: Selections in Translation*. Cambridge: Cambridge University Press.

Schachter, Stanley. 1971. *Emotion, Obesity and Crime*. New York: Academic Press.

Schafer, Stephan. 1969. *Theories of Criminology*. New York: Random House.

Schur, Edwin M. 1971. *Labeling Deviant Behavior*. New York: Harper & Row.

Seiter, Richard P., H. E. Allen, E. W. Carlson, and E. C. Parks. 1977. *Halfway Houses*. Washington, D.C.: U.S. Department of Justice (reprinted 1978 by U.S. Government Printing Office under same title with authors listed alphabetically).

Shah, Saleem A., and Loren H. Roth. 1974. "Biological and Psychological Factors in Criminology." In *Handbook of Criminology*, ed. Daniel Glaser. Chicago: Rand McNally.

Shaw, Clifford R. 1929. *Delinquency Areas*. Chicago: University of Chicago Press.

Shaw, Clifford R., and Henry D. McKay. 1942. *Juvenile Delinquency and Urban Areas*. Chicago: University of Chicago Press. Rev. ed. 1969.

Short, James F., Jr. 1974. "Collective Behavior, Crime and Delinquency." In *Handbook of Criminology*, ed. Donald Glaser. Chicago: Rand McNally.

Short, James F., Jr., and F. Ivan Nye. 1957–58. "Reported Behavior as a Criterion of Deviant Behavior," *Social Problems* 5:207–13.

———. 1958. "Extent of Unrecorded Juvenile Delinquency: Tentative Conclusions," *Journal of Criminal Law, Criminology and Police Science* 49:296–302.

Short, James F., Jr., and Fred L. Strodtbeck. 1965. *Group Process and Gang Delinquency*. Chicago: University of Chicago Press.

Skinner, B. F. 1953. *Science and Human Behavior*. New York: Macmillan.

Stephens, Jack L., and Lois W. Sanders. 1978. *Transitional Aid for Ex-Offenders: An Experimental Study in Georgia*. Atlanta: Georgia Department of Offender Rehabilitation.

Sutherland, Edwin H., and Donald R. Cressey. 1978. *Criminology*. Philadelphia: Lippincott.

Teilmann, Kathleen S. 1976. "Sources of Bias in Self-Reported Delinquency." Ph.D. dissertation in sociology, University of Southern California.

Thorsell, Bernard A., and Lloyd W. Klemke. 1972. "The Labelling Process: Reinforcement and Deterrent?" *Law and Society Review* 6: 393–403.

Thrasher, Frederic M. 1927. *The Gang*. Chicago: University of Chicago Press.

Tittle, Charles R., W. J. Villemez, and D. A. Smith. 1978. "The Myth of Social Class and Criminality," *American Sociological Review* 43:643–56.

Tropp, Richard A. 1978. "Suggested Policy Initiatives for Employment and Crime Problems." In *Crime and Employment Issues*, ed. Leon Leiberg. Springfield, Va.: National Technical Information Service.

U.S. Department of Justice, Federal Bureau of Investigation. 1978. *Crime in the United States—1977*. Washington, D.C.: U.S. Government Printing Office.

U.S. Department of Labor. 1977. *Unlocking the Second Gate: The Role of Financial Assistance in Reducing Recidivism among Ex-Prisoners*. Research and Development Monograph No. 45. Washington, D.C.: U.S. Government Printing Office.

Vold, George B. 1958. *Theoretical Criminology*. New York: Oxford University Press.

Votey, Harold L., Jr., and L. Phillips. 1974. "The Control of Criminal Activity: An Economic Analysis." In *Handbook of Criminology*, ed. Daniel Glaser. Chicago: Rand McNally.

Waldo, Gordon P., and Theodore G. Chiricos. 1977. "Work Release and Recidivism: An Empirical Evaluation of a Social Policy," *Evaluation Quarterly* 1:87–108.

Walker, Nigel. 1977. *Behavior and Misbehavior: Explanations and Non-Explanations*. New York: Basic Books.

Wolfgang, Marvin E., Robert M. Figlio, and Thorsten Sellin. 1972. *Delinquency in a Birth Cohort*. Chicago: University of Chicago Press.

Zelany, L. D. 1933. "Feeblemindedness and Criminal Conduct," *American Journal of Sociology* 38:564–76.

Rubén G. Rumbaut and Egon Bittner

Changing Conceptions of the Police Role: A Sociological Review

ABSTRACT

Contemporary conceptions of the police and of the problems of
policing in the United States have been shaped by the political
upheavals and crisis of legitimacy that confronted all institutions
of government in the 1960s. Recent research has focused attention
on the structural aspects of discretion and peacekeeping in police
work, and on the emergence of the ideology of police-community
relations. Such studies have provided a critique of traditional police
rationales and have demonstrated the complexity and contradictions
inherent in the exercise of police power. Meanwhile, police reform
in the 1970s has become an established enterprise, increasingly
under the technical and administrative control of a class of
professional change-makers. The present direction of technologically
and legalistically determined reforms reflects an accelerated
movement away from concerns of "substantive rationality" to
those of "formal rationality" so that the reform process has become
depoliticized and lacks policy direction. While helping to insulate
the police from arbitrary political manipulation, this movement also
attenuates the aims of substantive political justice, including those
of police accountability, local community review, and control of
police discretionary policymaking powers. Moreover, the prevailing
forms of change-making in police organizations have not been
substantively aimed toward creating the informed, skilled, and
judicious police officer.

Rubén G. Rumbaut is Assistant Professor of Sociology, University of California
at San Diego. Egon Bittner is Professor of Sociology, Brandeis University.

239

Pressure for police reform has been a pervasive and prominent theme in the history of the police in the United States. In the late nineteenth century the agenda called for the liberation of the police from the corrupting influence of urban machine politics; in the period of the Wickersham Commission the central concern of reformers was the elimination of brutality and excessive violence (Fogelson 1977); in the 1960s the critics turned to the conflict between the police and the policed, particularly the minorities and the urban poor. All these reform efforts, and many others of lesser scope or prominence, were set into motion by external initiative; once the agenda had been set out, implementation was left to the police themselves. As a result, the products of reform were too frequently merely ceremonial.

This historical pattern of bringing reform to the doorstep of the police and leaving it there to be picked up has in recent years yielded to an alternative. Reform is still externally initiated—at least in the sense that everything that has been happening in recent years can be shown to bear the mark of impulses originating in the social upheaval of the 1960s—but now the details of proposed reforms are increasingly formulated and administered by a staff of technical specialists who are recruited from without the institution and who act as outsiders working within it. Thus, for the first time, police reform is coming under the control of people who are not police officials, people who cannot claim professional expertise in policing and who have not made long-range career commitments to it.

In this essay, we examine the changing conceptions of the police role which provide the contextual basis for reform. In Section I we first discuss two emerging insights into the police role—the range and type of police discretion and the extent of police involvement in peacekeeping activities not connected with law enforcement. We then consider various efforts at improved police-community relations and certain experiments in police patrol practices relevant to the exercise of police discretion, to peacekeeping, and to police-community relations. In Section II we review the major social science literature on the police role over the last twenty years. Section III then discusses the relationship between emerging insights into the police role and various problems of reform of police organization and practice.

I. The Police in the Crucible of the 1960s

Contemporary conceptions of the police and of the problems of policing have been shaped by the crisis of legitimacy that faced all institutions of government in the 1960s. The impact of that crisis upon the police is unclear. Too little time has passed since the end of that tumultuous decade to permit a sober assessment. The real significance of many events of the period is unclear; some things that seem important now may later be viewed as merely conspicuous. Matters are complicated by developments in the study of the police that occurred before the crisis of the 1960s, probably as an expression of the same trends and impulses that caused the larger upheavals. Finally, while some of the concerns regarding the police were products of the social ferment of the 1960s, others were probably reactions to it. Unfortunately the two cannot be easily disentangled. For example, the recent large-scale research and planning efforts were initiated—to a great extent, if not wholly—as the consequence of inquiries that expressed discontent with the police. Those inquiries—many of them the work of commissions at all levels of government—were politically inspired and politically intended; they sought to expose police wrongdoing in order to justify extending and intensifying democratic controls over police practice. While recent work in one sense continues those efforts, its technical emphasis and the selection of topics has had the effect of depoliticizing police change. Thus, in another sense, present-day research efforts have counteracted, or at least obscured, the reformist intentions that spawned them.

A. The Discovery of Police Discretion

One of the most important discoveries about the nature of police work was the realization that police officers make discretionary decisions, even very important decisions, in the course of their tours of duty. That should have caused no surprise, but the way the matter was frequently presented was that police officers were often making arbitrary decisions. Most persons whose opinions mattered could have deduced that from their occasional experiences as motorists accused, tried, and sentenced by a traffic officer. Other forms of "curbstone" justice might have been less well known, but their existence was scarcely a secret. That police officers were not doing what the law books said they should do, that is, literally enforcing the law, was viewed as a scandal or a blessing, depending on one's outlook, and by and large, as something one could not or should not do anything about, again depending on one's outlook. Thus, in part, the discovery of police discretion consisted in speaking openly about something that was known but not talked about. More important, however, was the characterization of discretion as not just an incidental and regrettable but an essential and unavoidable aspect of policing.[1]

The interpretation of police discretion as a structurally essential aspect of policing was of seminal significance. But influential writers (J. Goldstein 1960; LaFave 1965; and Davis 1969, 1975) treated the problem almost completely in reference to the criminal process within which they saw it operating. As Joseph Goldstein posed it, in being free either to invoke or not invoke the law, in situations in which the conditions for invoking it were met, the police officer rendered one part of the criminal process invisible and nonreviewable: the ministerial officer usurped the powers of the magistrate. Indeed, the officer claimed even greater power than the magistrate, for the officer could exonerate solely on the basis of his own view of the facts and judgment, and without explanation, while the judge could do so—in the very same case— only in accordance with rules of procedure and fact finding and in open court. As Goldstein, LaFave, and Davis saw it, the freedom to decide in police work resulted—in large part—from a variety of inadvertent and deliberate ambiguities and omissions

---

[1] In an extraordinarily important and influential paper, Joseph Goldstein (1960) gave this observation its first precise expression. By far the most copious documentation of the observation that police officers routinely transcended the ministerial responsibilities traditionally assigned to them was collected in the course of the American Bar Foundation's survey of the administration of criminal justice in the United States, carried out in 1956–57, the results of which were not published until much later (LaFave 1965).

in the way statutes and regulations are drafted, exacerbated by the absence of explicitly formulated law enforcement policies. Because of these shortcomings the police officer had to supply what—had it come from a more exalted functionary—would have been called jurisprudential policy. He had also to incorporate administrative considerations into his decision making from case to case.

From this perspective, a police officer confronting a boisterous drunk measures what he sees against the letter of the law while taking into account the larger aims of the administration of criminal justice and its underlying principles. He calculates how the case of this boisterous drunk fits into the overall demand conditions for police service and how the treatment of this case can be fitted into the general economy of resource distribution in the administration of justice, while also paying attention to the problems of alcoholism in society and to the dominant views concerning its seriousness. On the basis of such reckoning, of which the above is admittedly an exaggerated version, he might let the drunk stumble on without interference toward his uncertain destination. The police officer's decision would be unreviewable; there would be no record and no justification would be available or expected.

Legal commentators were alarmed by the seeming paradox of the superior powers of the ministerial, as compared to the magisterial, functionaries of the state. And, not surprisingly, their minds turned to rule-making and to policy formulation. They knew that the exercise of discretion could not be eliminated entirely, but they took it upon themselves to urge that its scope be severely curtailed. Although the question of the scope of that minimum range of discretion received some attention, it was apparently not regarded as a pressing problem. There existed, it seemed clear, a wide area of unregulated decision making that should be brought under control, long before one reached the limits of necessary discretion. Nor did they insist that the norms and policies be given the traditional legal forms.[2]

Of course the legal commentators were not naive and neither

---

[2] Professor Davis (1969) was particularly inventive in suggesting a variety of innovative forms of regulation and accountability that should be tried.

said nor implied that patrolmen actually review legal and policy considerations, nor did they propose that the promulgation of explicit norms and policies would automatically solve the problems of discretionary practice. Rather, they believed that the exercise of discretion was explainable in the light of such considerations, however implicit, unformulated, or routine they may be in practice. According to this view, the implicit norms and policies existed and were to a degree applied, even though not all police officers could explain their decisions in those terms. The legal commentators also realized that normative regulation of police practice would bring its own enforcement problems; but they rightly assumed that promulgation of explicit norms and principles would create a sense of certainty and clarity that would be welcomed by policemen and would give law enforcement a sense of stability and predictability it lacked. Their arguments were strong and sensible. They had, perhaps, too much confidence in rules, but this ought not to be held against them because the lawyer's trust in rules is a desirable counterweight to the skepticism of most others.

B. The Police as Peacekeepers

The significance of the discovery of discretion in criminal law enforcement was almost overshadowed by another discovery, however, which increased appreciation for the broad range of police discretion. The discovery concerned the distinction between law enforcement and the peacekeeping functions of the police. As in the case of the "discovery" of police discretion, the broad facts were known. Everyone knew that police officers perform all sorts of helpful services in addition to catching crooks. What was new was the significance claimed for peacekeeping in the overall composition of police work.[3] In the second half of

[3] While Cummings and her co-workers (1965) still thought that the helping function, though very time-consuming, was peripheral to the mandate of the police, Banton (1964) saw it clearly as an integral part of policing, even though it has nothing to do with criminal law enforcement. Herman Goldstein (1963, 1967, 1968), more than any other scholar, drawing on his experience in police administration, saw the full complexity of police work and emphasized the seriousness and importance of decision making in every part of policing. He emphasized that it is not merely the question of whether or not to make an arrest that involves discretion but rather that every situation in which the police become involved unavoidably contains choices.

the 1960s it was generally conceded (Niederhoffer 1967) that what Banton called peacekeeping made up the bulk of police work, that routine criminal law enforcement was the work of only a minority of police officers, and that the preponderant majority had few opportunities on a day-to-day basis to become involved in activities leading to arrests and prosecutions.

In the light of observations concerning peacekeeping the problem of discretion assumed a new cast. While there existed a certain amount of discretionary law enforcement, it was wedged between the most serious crimes, in which the decision to invoke the law was a foregone conclusion, and an array of decision making among which a certain number of arrests could be found that involved consideration of legality only in a special sense. In the latter, as Bittner (1967a) argued, the decisions to arrest and to charge are not made to enforce provisions of "the law"; instead, arrests can better be understood as one way of "handling" certain situations requiring control. The police officer does not implement existing penal laws; rather, he takes advantage of their availability in accomplishing other tasks, for example, keeping people out of harm's way. Thus, apart from a small number of genuine law enforcement decisions—especially in the area of the sumptuary offenses—police discretion concerns the handling of all situations in which force may have to be used. The police officer's judgment comes into play twice, first in deciding whether a coercive measure must be taken, and second in deciding whether physical force is called for. The first concerns the definition of a demand or a situation as proper police business; the second concerns the means for coping with the task.

The enlarged conception of the police mandate did little more than explicitly recognize what had been standing police practice. It brought into the open that police officers do not only decide whom to arrest but actually make many other important decisions that affect the vital interests of large numbers of people. Moreover, it has begun to make the public aware of the not yet fully understood fact that police work involves the routine exercise of coercion on occasions, in circumstances, and in ways for which no explicit legal authorization exists, coercion which is commonly justified on grounds of practical necessity and expert judgment.

Recognition that between four-fifths and nine-tenths of all police manpower and resources are committed to activities only tangentially related to criminal law enforcement does not, of course, lead automatically to displacement of criminal law enforcement from its position of primacy in the hierarchy of perceived responsibilities. Within police agencies a relatively trivial arrest still takes precedence over the skillful handling of a potentially dangerous situation in which no one is charged with a crime. It is not difficult to speculate why this should be so.

One prominent and plausible explanation is that placing criminal law enforcement at the center of the working patrol officer's concerns causes other concerns, such as handling situations without making arrests, to be interpreted as decisions *not* to invoke the law. Thus, police procedure receives the cast of objective and compelling necessity. One can say of any police procedure that executing it correctly and effectively calls for "going by the book," and one can say this even when actual practice is demonstrably arbitrary. So long as criminal law enforcement is paramount in the conception of the police task it will influence everything done. For example, heavy patrol surveillance of minority neighborhoods and of their inhabitants can be interpreted as preemptive crime prevention, even though it may be perceived as intolerably intrusive, oppressive, unjust, even racially biased, by the population exposed to it.

That the police do much more than catch crooks has long been known to those members of American society left behind in its march toward prosperity, for they have been most affected by such activities. To these people the police have represented the cutting edge of racism and oppression. Thus, in the 1960s, minorities and the poor found "the thin blue line" between themselves and their aims. Even though the police were not the real adversaries of civil rights activism, they were the adversaries' most exposed element, a position the police seemed to accept without qualm.

C. Police-Community Relations

The third conceptual innovation, police-community relations, resulted directly from the political upheavals of the second half of the 1960s. Just as discretion and peacekeeping were deeper perceptions of well-known but unacknowledged practices, so police-community relations was a peculiar invention, one that never played the role assigned to it, but which nevertheless left its imprint on police practices. The police-community relations device was intended to provide an ongoing process of communication and influence between the police and various segments of the community, especially the poor and oppressed (Hormachea and Hormachea 1971; Hewitt and Newman 1970; Norris 1973; Geary 1975). It was one of the several conciliatory responses of the "Establishment" to the deep-seated discontent that produced violent insurrection and urban street struggles. Despite the good faith efforts of some police officials, it remained largely a gesture.

To understand why police-community relations units and officers were unable to open channels of communication between the departments and the minority community, it must be remembered that, given their normally conservative disposition, many police were unsympathetic to the aims of the civil rights struggle even before it started. From the typical police perspective, the Warren Court decisions created an obstacle course of procedural protections for defendants in the criminal process. Connected with this was the wholesale outlawing by the Court of a large number of "Jim Crow" laws leading to, as many police officers perceived it, a plethora of unearned entitlements for poor people of color. The official solicitude for the underdog—with whom the police saw themselves locked in combat—increased during the Kennedy presidency and culminated in the War on Poverty of the Johnson administration. There was a general failure by the police to recognize that these apparent indulgences toward the black and poor were more apparent than real, that they represented little more than a trail of broken promises. Instead of seeing the protests of the 1960s as an expression of anger by deceived people, they saw them as an impudent demand for the good life on the part of people who would not work to earn it. Indeed, many police officers dealt with protest exclusively in terms of its outward form, without regard for its content. All that was seen was the breach of the peace; that was all that deserved attention. Hence, the widespread police aversion to the police-community relations programs reflected a pervasive conviction that there was nothing to talk about with the people with whom the dialogue was sought.

While the police-community relations efforts were more or less openly sabotaged by officers of all ranks, but especially by the line personnel, some aspects of the concept—in combination with the new appreciation for the importance of peacekeeping— found expression in innovative approaches to patrol work in the 1970s. These ideas were able to play a role in changing practices because the Police Foundation funneled large amounts of money to several strategically chosen large police departments to support research and experimentation with patrol practices.[4]

Innovations in patrolling were directed chiefly toward four related aims. All four were not recognized everywhere, nor were the recognized aims everywhere ordered in the same hierarchy of priorities. Still, reform of patrol practices was usually pointed toward, or had the effect of, (1) decentralizing command and control and increasing the amount of collaborative policy formation involving police officers of all ranks including those at the local, that is precinct or subprecinct, level; (2) creating an enhanced recognition of the importance and seriousness of peacekeeping, as distinct from criminal law enforcement; (3) aligning police services with perceived community needs through direct studies of social conditions and consultations with local community organizations of all kinds; and (4) evaluating the effectiveness of these attempts with, for the police, unprecedented rigor, by means of social scientific research techniques using measurable indices of performance and of the effects of changed practices.

---

[4] Certainly this would not have been possible without the readiness of a number of police officials, of whom Clarence Kelley as chief of the Kansas City Police Department was the leading example, to accept and advance such change.

The first two of these aims represent the embodiment in programs of the "discoveries" of discretion and of peacekeeping.
They were liberating in the sense that they let happen openly
and more effectively what was done anyway, albeit in unacknowledged and inefficient ways. The third aim represents a depoliticized version of the police-community relations aspiration. Deprived of the ideological edge of the civil rights struggle, the
aspiration centered upon practical and worldly issues involving
police protection and service. Still, unavoidably the contacts resulted in lowering somewhat the barriers between the police and
the policed. Before considering the fourth aim, we might mention
that most experiments in patrolling involved younger officers who
seemed to welcome the new orientation of their activities. Resistance to the experiments came, by and large, from older officers
who had already adopted previous methods, and whose own
career development might be jeopardized by these new ways of
doing police work. But opposition to the changes in patrol practices did not approach the vehemence of opposition to the concept of police-community relations. The damper which residual
resistance placed upon the enthusiasm of reformers was aug-
mented, however, by the testing to which the reforms were
routinely exposed. Change had to take forms that could be
assessed by using available research techniques; therefore changes
had to be given the character of time-limited projects, which
cannot readily be turned into structural reform.

Evaluation research on patrol reforms did more, however, than
introduce the sobering procedures of experimentation. The impact of evaluation was not merely that relatively insignificant
but "objectively" measurable results were favored over longer-
range and nonmeasurable effects. And it certainly was not a matter of putting limits on programs that might have degenerated
into a well-intentioned but diffuse deterioration of police service.
Perhaps the most important effect of the social scientific aspect
of the patrol reform was indirect. The presence of social scientists, research technicians, and research instruments, all directed
in the study of an activity that in the past had not rated official
notice, transformed the meaning of that activity into something

more serious and important. It would be a romantic delusion to think that patrolmen took all that science and research seriously; indeed, many found much of it to be busywork of meddlers. But no one could for long resist wholly the implication that policing might be a complex craft (or better yet, a profession), the practice of which rested, at least to some extent, on reason, knowledge, and skill.

II. Changing Conceptions of the Police

Even a simplified picture of the relations between the events of the 1960s and the concepts that then entered into the idea of policing in the United States contains a considerable degree of complexity. The new appreciation of the role of discretion and of the importance and legitimacy of peacekeeping, as well as the developments connected with the complex of police-community relations programs and patrol strategy reform, took shape partly under the influence of the political trends of the decade and partly in reaction to them. Of course, other major developments came to light and were debated in the past fifteen years. This recent history cannot be summarized in a brief review, but some sense of the prevailing ideas may be gained from the following selective discussion of recent scholarly publications about the police. These works have influenced the contemporary meaning of policing and have given intellectual substance to ongoing debates; they also cast further light on the notions of police discretion, peacekeeping and police-community relations.

A. Efficiency and the Police Occupational Environment

Jerome Skolnick's benchmark study of the Oakland Police Department, *Justice without Trial* (1966), undertaken during 1962–64, analyzed police discretion in its "operational environment" from the perspective of the sociology of law. The study helped to set the terms of the subsequent debate on police reform, at least in academic circles, especially on the issues of the legal accountability of the police and of their occupational morale. Skolnick's liberal democratic concern for "due process of law" in police practice echoed the concerns powerfully stressed at that time by the growing civil rights movement. Indeed, his research was initially intended as an investigation of the plea-bargaining system of "justice without trial." He first focused on the offices of the public defender and the district attorney, and then moved to the police as de facto chief invokers and interpreters of the criminal law whose work "constitutes the most secluded part of an already secluded system and therefore offers the greatest opportunity for arbitrary behavior" (1966, p. 14). Responding directly to the dialogue on police discretion and its control emerging mainly in law journals (J. Goldstein 1960; Kadish 1962; LaFave 1962), Skolnick's principal "theoretical concern is with the phenomenon of law and its enforcement" (1966, p. 15n). Following Banton (1964), he distinguishes "law officers" (detectives) from "peace officers" (patrolmen); unlike most other police studies of the 1960s which examined the "peacekeeping" work of patrol officers, Skolnick's is based on the discretionary "law enforcement" work of vice and narcotics detectives and his conception of the police role is developed against this background.

Skolnick sees the police as a class of authorities required to manage competing role expectations, caught in the dilemma of maintaining public order while remaining accountable to the "rule of law," to the procedural provisions of laws of search, proof, and arrest. While he observes that the "rule of law" is an ambiguous ideal and has no precise definition, he argues that in this context it refers essentially to "the reduction of arbitrariness by officials" (1966, p. 8). Order and legality are thus conflicting principles:

> The phrase "law and order" is misleading because it draws
> attention away from the substantial incompatibilities existing
> between the two ideas. . . . "Law and order" are frequently
> found to be in opposition, because law implies rational
> restraint upon the rules and procedures utilized to achieve
> order. Order under law, therefore, subordinates the ideal of
> conformity to the ideal of legality. The actual requirement
> of maintaining social order under the principle of legality
> places an unceasing burden upon the police as a social
> institution. Indeed, the police is *the* institution best
> exemplifying the strain between the two ideas. (1966, p. 9)

The exercise of police discretion and initiative—whether "delegated" or "unauthorized"—epitomizes the dilemma of law and order, says Skolnick, and the dilemma is complicated by police organizational pressures for "efficiency" and "productivity." Like other complex organizations, police departments need to control and evaluate the performances of their members. For detectives "clearance rates" have become the most significant measures of police efficiency and the basis for the distribution of organizational rewards. From their point of view, therefore, police see judicial constraints as impeding their capacity to "produce results." These external controls over police conduct emphasize legality as a means to the goal of efficiency, not vice versa. Indeed, one of the dominant concepts of "professionalism" promoted by police reformers in this century[5] is that of a "managerial" as opposed to a "legal" professionalism, based mainly on satisfying the demands for administrative efficiency in crime control rather than rewarding police compliance with legal "procedures designed to protect individual liberties" (1966, p. 239). Moreover "an 'order' perspective based upon managerial efficiency also tends to be supported by the civic community," particularly by political and business elites in the community concerned "not over violations of due process of law, but over a seemingly ever-rising crime rate and the inability of the police to cope with it" (p. 241). Skolnick argues that such a model of professionalism cannot resolve the dilemma of the police:

> The working policeman is well aware of the limitations of
> "scientific" advances in police work and organization.
> He realizes that his work consists mostly of dealing with
> human beings, and that these skills are his main achievement.
> The strictures of the rule of law often clash with the
> policeman's ability to carry out this sort of work, but he
> is satisfied to have the argument presented in terms of
> technological achievement rather than human interaction,
> since he rightly fears that the public "will not understand"

[5] See, for example, Fosdick (1920), Wilson (1950), and Wilson's (1957) account of the views of William Parker.

the human devices he uses, such as paying off informants, allowing "fences" to operate, and reducing charges, to achieve the enforcement ends demanded of him. (1966, p. 244)

Accordingly Skolnick places his hopes for liberal reform on political rather than technical approaches to the dialectic of "law and order":

[T]he prospects for the infusion of the rule of law into the police institution may be bleak indeed. As an institution dependent on rewards from the civic community, police can hardly be expected to be much better or worse than the political context in which they operate. . . . When prominent members of the community become far more aroused over an apparent rise in criminality than over the fact that Negroes are frequently subjected to unwarranted police interrogation, detention, and invasions of privacy, the police will continue to engage in such practices. Without widespread support for the rule of law, it is hardly to be expected that courts will be able to continue advancing individual rights, or that the police will themselves develop a professional orientation as *legal* actors, rather than as efficient administrators of criminal law. (1966, p. 245)

Adding to the fundamental ideological conflict of the police role depicted by Skolnick, the conceptions of public order held by police are ambiguous and vary with social conditions. Among the main influences shaping the police conception of order is the police organizational model, with its paramilitary structure, its stress on hierarchy, command, routine, and obedience to orders, all of which tend to discount the need for discretion and initiative in policing and to value crime control more than accountability to the rule of law. Skolnick's critique of the quasi-military model of the police—its pressure toward goal displacement in the interests of efficiency, internal discipline, and "production demands," and its effects on the work of members who are molded into soldier-bureaucrats—has been elaborated by subsequent organizational analyses of the police (Bordua and Reiss

1966; Niederhoffer 1967; Bittner 1970; Rubinstein 1973; Manning 1977).

Expanding on William Westley's earlier analysis, Skolnick's chapter on the "policeman's working personality" also provided a major contribution to the debate on the police occupational culture. He demonstrated that the policeman's situation in the community, defined by the constant threat of violence and the self-protective police identification of certain categories of citizens as "symbolic assailants," interlocks with the quasi-military police organization to engender an occupationally specific "style of life."

Westley's pioneering 1950 study in Gary, Indiana, merits attention because it constituted the first thorough sociological analysis of an American police organization and of the culture of the police as an occupation.[6] His focus was on the police job: how the job forms the man and forces the development of uniquely adaptive and occupationally derived norms and values. The police, Westley wrote, are a low-status occupational group expected to do the "dirty work" of the community. Paradoxically, theirs is a role of high public importance yet is accorded low public esteem, such that policemen come to regard themselves as an elite "pariah" class. In the course of their work—handling the intoxicated, the insane, the criminal, the diseased, the dead—the police are called to intervene in conflict situations covering the full range of human problems, and meet the public mostly "in their sorrow, their degradation, their evil, and their defeat" (1970, p. 105). As agents of order and control and as symbols of authority and interference —whether in regulating traffic, settling family fights, or testifying in court—theirs is usually an adversarial role, binding the police to isolation and secrecy. This shared occupational existence, including the daily round of "war stories" they tell each other about that common experience, builds and reinforces a cynical and suspicious occupational outlook on the public as "enemy" in a hostile and ungrateful community. In response Westley suggested, the police demand respect in their contacts with the public

[6] Westley's doctoral dissertation was completed in 1950, and circulated widely thereafter, but was not published until 1970 (Westley 1970).

and develop occupational norms which legitimate toughness and violence. Their occupational culture is transmitted and maintained through the various initiation rites that mold the rookie policeman, a process culminating in the rookie's recognition of the rules and values of the group as defining his own self-esteem.

To similar effect, Skolnick's later analysis concentrated on "certain outstanding elements in the police milieu, danger, authority, and efficiency, as they combine to generate distinctive cognitive and behavioral responses in police: a 'working personality' " (1966, p. 42), most saliently developed in the role of patrol officers. He argued that while these elements may be found in other lines of work, for example, among soldiers, teachers, and industrial workers, their combination was unique to the police role. Allowing for individual and group differences and specialties within the occupation, Skolnick stressed that he was referring solely to role conflicts and pressures which compel a "general disposition" among police "to perceive and to behave in certain ways," which in turn served psychologically to reduce cognitive dissonance (see Festinger 1957). Essentially, the "two principal variables" of the police role, *danger* and *authority*, plus the organizational demands for "production," were shown to lead to (1) social isolation from both the symbolically dangerous and the conventional citizenry, entrenching a "we-they" world view, (2) police solidarity, *esprit de corps*, a heightened sense of in-group loyalty which promotes secrecy and closed ranks, and (3) self-defensive conduct and a trained, persistent suspiciousness. Skolnick also provided evidence of political conservatism among police, arguing that their social role, not "authoritarian personality" variables, invites an emotional attachment to the status quo: "the fact that a man is engaged in enforcing a set of rules implies that he also becomes implicated in *affirming* them" (1966, p. 59). He concluded that these social psychological features of the police occupational environment, introjected by members to form a "working personality," further weaken the conception of the rule of law as a primary goal of police conduct.

Comparative studies of the British and American police done by Banton (1964) and Clark (1965) have generally confirmed this analysis, while noting that the processes bringing about the social isolation of the police officer differ in Great Britain and the United States. They report that the British policeman faces less danger than does his American counterpart. Similarly, Niederhoffer's (1967) study of police cynicism and authoritarianism views these not as psychological traits brought by recruits into the job but as part of the occupational ideology required by the police role and entrenched in the police system, impinging most strongly on the patrolman on the beat. But the mold of police culture and the psychology of the enlisted recruit obviously interact. Gray (1975) has shown how police selection processes screen and recruit individuals who demonstrate an "affinity" for both the formal police organization and the informal culture. Also along these lines, longitudinal research by McNamara (1967) and Van Maanen (1973, 1974, 1975), focusing on the occupational socialization of police recruits during the academy and field training process, has added to our understanding of the police culture and its organizational development, transmission, and management. These studies all make clear that policing will not be amenable to substantial changes by narrowly based reform programs aimed at modifying police attitudes, beliefs, and values independently of the powerful police organizational and cultural environment in which they function.

B. The Management of Law and Order

James Q. Wilson's 1965–67 comparative field study of the police role in eight communities in New York, Illinois, and California—*Varieties of Police Behavior* (1968)—coincided with the heightening of nationwide public protest and civil disorder, spanned the work of the President's Crime Commission, and showed awareness of the earlier discoveries of discretion and peacekeeping in routine police work. It is therefore not surprising that Wilson focused attention on the varied styles and uncertain management of police discretion, particularly at the level of the uniformed patrolman on the beat, who at once occupies the lowest ranking office in the police organization yet exercises the greatest practical discretion. And given this perspective, Wilson's work was also concerned with the nature and management of public order as central to the patrolman's role. This "order maintenance function" of police patrol "necessarily involves the exercise of substantial discretion over matters of the greatest importance (public and private morality, honor and dishonor, life and death) in a situation that is, by definition, one of conflict and in an environment that is apprehensive and perhaps hostile" (1968, p. 21). Setting aside traffic offenses, patrol officers encounter such problems of "order maintenance" far more frequently than occasions for "law enforcement," says Wilson, at least in the socially heterogeneous cities. It is this combination of features that defines the police role as unique, unlike any other occupation. The provision of "services" by the police—tasks that are intended strictly "to please the client" and that involve no "disorder," that is, no breach of the public peace or social conflict—is, for Wilson, "only a matter of historical accident and community convenience" and peripheral to the police function, hence omitted from his study.[7] Unlike earlier studies by such legal scholars as LaFave and Joseph Goldstein or by the legal sociologist Skolnick, Wilson's empirical study is among the first attempts to demystify the relationship of police work to "law enforcement"; as such it contributed to the beginnings of a more realistic sociological approach to the debate on the police role. For these reasons, and because it provides a useful pivot around which to consider later contributions to this debate, Wilson's analysis merits detailed review.

The police "order maintenance" function "places the patrolman in a special relationship to the law, a relationship that is obscured by describing what he does as 'enforcing the law' " (1968, p. 31). The police officer's response to incidents which occasion his intervention is routinely of the sort that Peter Manning (1977) has termed "situationally justified action." As Wilson puts it,

> To the patrolman, the law is one resource among many that he may use to deal with disorder, but it is not the only one or even the most important; beyond that, the law is a

[7] "There is no reason in principle why these services could not be priced and sold on the market . . . . One can just as easily imagine them sold by a private, profit-making firm ('Emergency Services, Inc.')" (Wilson 1968, p. 3).

constraint that tells him what he must *not* do but that is peculiarly unhelpful in telling him what he *should* do. Thus, he approaches incidents that threaten order *not in terms of enforcing the law but in terms of "handling the situation"* . . . keeping things under control so that there are no complaints that he is doing nothing or that he is doing too much. (1968, p. 31)

Wilson's rejection of the core role of the police as mere functionaries of the criminal law has been followed by more recent work in police sociology. Thus, Bittner notes:

> In the typical case the formal charge *justifies* the arrest a patrolman makes but is *not* the *reason* for it. The actual reason is located in . . . the need to "handle the situation," and invoking the law is merely a device whereby this is sometimes accomplished. . . . If criminal law enforcement means acting on the basis of, and in accordance with, the law's provisions, then this is something policemen do occasionally, but in their routine work they merely avail themselves of the provisions as a means for attaining other objectives. (1974, p. 27)

The point, Bittner argues, is that "all formal rules of conduct are basically defeasible," and that "new rules do not restrict discretion but merely shift its locus" (1970, pp. 3–4).

For Wilson, police discretion exists because rules prescribed for order maintenance situations are necessarily ambiguous or equivocal, involving competing interpretations, interests, and values, and often requiring the unreliable cooperation of "victims" if the law is to be invoked by the police officer. The role of the police conveys a quasi-distributive conception of justice and a situational orientation to action that differs sharply from the perspective of other actors in the legal system:

> To the judge, the defense attorney, and the legal scholar, the issue is whether a given individual was legally culpable as defined by a written rule. The individualistic, rule-oriented perspective of the courtroom is at variance with the

situational, order maintenance perspective of the patrolman.
. . . Thus the patrolman describes his activity as "playing
it by ear" and "taking each case as they come," *not* in terms
of "enforcing the law" or "making exceptions to the law."
(1968, p. 32)

Wilson leaves largely unexplicated the specific competences
which police officers employ in the "handling of situations," but
in some respects he anticipates Bittner's later (1970) analysis of
the capacity to employ coercive force as constituting the very
core of the police role:

To handle his beat and the situations and disputes that
develop on it, the patrolman must assert his authority. To
him, this means asserting his *personal* authority. . . . By
authority the patrolman means the right to ask questions,
get information, and have his orders obeyed. . . . The
patrolmen observed for this study almost always acted, and
said later they had acted, in such a way as to show
immediately "who was boss." (1968, pp. 32–33)

How is such authority itself to be policed and made accountable
to the polity? In the first place, can police administrators establish
policies to control the discretion of patrol officers on the beat?
Wilson addresses these questions by postulating four types of
situations, either "law enforcement" or "order-maintenance"
where the stimulus to police action is either "police-invoked" or
"citizen-invoked." Each type of case invites a different degree
of discretion by the patrolman, whose decision whether and how
to intervene depends on his evaluation of the "costs and benefits"
of various courses of conduct. The police administrator, on the
other hand, seeks to "manage" that discretion so that it falls in
line with his "policy"; this, in turn, reflects his interests in promoting a certain image and in strengthening his political position
to protect and obtain desired resources for the police agency.

It is mainly in *police-invoked law enforcement* situations—for
example, enforcement of laws dealing with traffic and vice
offenses—that the rate and form of police interventions can be
decisively controlled by the policy of the administrator. The ad-

ministrator achieves control over subordinates' discretion in these cases by imposing performance measures such as a quota of traffic tickets, or the closing down of a brothel or of a bookie operation. However, in *citizen-invoked order maintenance* situations, such as family quarrels and comparable disputes and public disturbances, the patrolman's great discretion cannot similarly be brought under departmental control. The other two types of situations involve "intermediate" cases. In *citizen-invoked law enforcement* situations, such as reports of burglary, auto theft, or shoplifting, the patrolman functions primarily as a report taker and information gatherer, and his attitude and discretion can be controlled to some extent by setting procedural guidelines on how such cases will be handled, especially in cases where the suspects are juveniles. In *police-invoked order maintenance* situations, such as public drunkenness or "disorderly conduct" cases where the police intervene on their own initiative, discretionary action can be influenced by the administrator only through general incentives to be "more aggressive" or to "take it easy."[8]

From this conceptual framework, Wilson proceeded to examine variations in the management of police discretion or "law and order" in eight cities. As a result he proposed a tentative typology of three major organizational styles of police activity—watchman, legalistic, and service—and tied the prevailing police "style" to the policies of the police administrator, local politics, and community structure. In Wilson's language, the "watchman style" emphasizes order maintenance rather than law enforcement as the principal police function. Watchman departments are characterized by low pay, minimum training, and high turnover, and entry to and promotion within these departments are controlled

[8] In this connection it may be pertinent to note some of the results of a study by Albert J. Reiss, Jr. (1971) of the police-citizen relationship in three cities—Boston, Chicago, and Washington, D.C. Also with a focus on the work of patrol officers, Reiss's analysis revolves around the distinction between the "reactive" and "proactive" character of police departments. He found that 87 percent of police-citizen transactions were citizen-mobilized (reactive), while only 13 percent were police-initiated (proactive), underscoring the largely "reactive" nature of police patrol activity. In turn, he suggests that this discretionary control exercised by citizens in mobilizing the police contributes to the maintenance of police legitimacy. Further, Reiss presents data indicating that more than eight of every ten incidents handled by patrol officers were regarded by police as noncriminal matters.

by the local dominant political party. A "legalistic style" emphasizes a strict law enforcement definition of the police role, patrolmen being induced to handle commonplace situations as if they
were matters for law enforcement rather than order maintenance,
and under pressure to produce many arrests and citations. Legalistic departments are characterized organizationally by strict
bureaucratic control and an ideological commitment to doctrines
of "police professionalism," and are well insulated from community influences seeking changes in police policies. The "service
style" emphasizes community and public relations. Here the
police (in contrast to the legalistic style) are less likely to respond to law enforcement and order maintenance situations by
making an arrest or otherwise imposing formal sanctions. Service
departments are usually located in homogeneous, middle-class
communities, not deeply divided along class or racial lines, and
are politically highly sensitive to community interests.

C. The Dominant Ideology of Criminal Law Enforcement

Wilson traces his conception of police work as concerned
chiefly with the problems of order and social control to the historical context which in the nineteenth century shaped the emergence of modern municipal police forces: "the fear of riot and
popular uprising was usually the reason for enlarging, profes-
sionalizing, and ultimately arming the police" (1968, pp. 31–32;
see Silver 1967). He suggests that the practical and political
requirements for public order preceded the passage of laws to
justify and legitimate police action.

> Police officers were originally "watchmen" whose task it
> was to walk their rounds and maintain order in the streets.
> To maintain order meant everything from removing
> obstructions on streets to keeping pigs from running loose
> to chasing footpads and quelling riots. Watchmen were not
> officers of the court charged with bringing to the bar of
> justice persons who had broken a law; that task was
> performed by constables, for a fee, and only on the basis of
> sworn warrants. These watchmen and later the police

handled many situations that had nothing to do with enforcing the law or getting evidence and as a result they often acted under vague laws or no laws at all; a city council would later set down as written law rules that common practice had already established as binding. (1968, p. 31)

Writing a decade later, Manning (1977) has similarly if more bluntly argued that the view of the police as an "appendage" of the law rather than as an "extension of the violent potential of the state" is a recent one. He contends that "the state and the law are not isomorphic," and emphasizes that "the legitimation of the police in terms of legal authority flows from the power of the state and citizens' deference to it rather than from law as an independent entity" (1977, pp. 40–41). Manning, however, who is interested in the process of the legitimation of power, goes much further than Wilson, whose concern is with disorder and the management of order:

> *The law serves as a mystification device or canopy to cover selectively, legitimate, and rationalize police conduct.* It does not prospectively guide police action, nor does it provide the principal constraint upon police practices. . . . There is little question that public policy is everywhere shaped by economic elites and disproportionately reflects their political and social interests. The police, as an instrumentality of public policy, are no exception. Policing cannot be other than a reflection of those interests that define the nature of the legitimacy on which they draw. (Manning 1977, pp. 101–2)

Why then, despite persuasive evidence and an evident consensus in the literature on police sociology to the contrary, does the popular conception of the police as law enforcers and crime fighters persist? The vivid and dramatic image of the police officer as a front-line soldier in the war on crime, which is at the center of what Manning has called the "police myth" (1977, pp. 323 ff.), continues to be cultivated and propagated in the popular media, as well as by government officials and the police themselves. In part this view is supported by the facts that the criminal process is principally set in motion by the police, and that the work of a proportionately small corps of investigative officers is directed to the identification and apprehension of suspects for criminal prosecution. But this position is undercut by the knowledge that criminal law enforcement activity is not characteristic of the everyday practices of the vast majority of police officers, and that, moreover, their work is more plausibly understood in other terms entirely (Bittner 1974, pp. 22–23).

Wilson has noted various ideological functions of this traditional view of the police role which help account for the fact that police managers aim to define the mission of their agencies and to deal with the community in terms of the "crime problem" rather than the "order problem." Crime, he writes, notably what is reported in the FBI's annual index, is seen by the public as "more serious" than disorder and "combatting crime" is a less controversial way of presenting the police role to the public than "maintaining order." When "enforcing the law," the police "can act more frequently within the legal fiction, as ministerial agents applying unambiguous, unequivocal rules to clear-cut cases" (1968, pp. 67–68).

Manning (1977, pp. 15–19) has argued that the traditional law enforcement view serves to promote a neutral and apolitical conception of police practice, concealing the fact that the police mandate is politically defined and that the police ineluctably function as an instrument of a political system. These are, says Manning, "dramatic dilemmas" which confront the police in the process of managing a "contradictory mandate." In his language, the police seek to mediate the structural contradictions of their "law enforcement" and "crime control" mandate, to manage the appearance of effectiveness, and to establish credibility and legitimacy with the public, through various presentational strategies. These impression-management strategies are organized around the rhetoric of professionalism, the use of sophisticated technology, and the statistical measurement of the crime rate. But by focusing attention on crime and arrest and clearance rates as their measure of success and legitimating theme, theirs is a "pyrrhic victory," since the police cannot in any fundamental sense control or prevent crime, and have thus tied themselves, so Manning suggests, to a largely self-defeating enterprise. He traces the origins of these strategies to the "three changes made in the 1930s" which were "fundamental to the alteration of the police role":

> The first was the linkage of criminal statistics with professionalism among the police. . . . Second, the police began to tie their own fate to changes in the crime rate as measured by these published figures. The crime rate became the responsibility of the police both in the sense of measuring, explaining and accounting for it, and for substantially reducing it. Third, the police began to symbolize their mission in terms of the technological means by which they were said to accomplish it. . . . They provided the police with a new set of symbols and rhetorics. They could now present their work as crime-responsible professional work based upon applied scientific knowledge and technology. . . . Within a hundred years of Peel's invention, a new version of policing with an American character had emerged. (1977, pp. 97–98)

This ideology of the police role as criminal law enforcement at once reinforces and is reinforced by the formal bureaucratic organization of police agencies. Wilson sees it this way:

> If order were the central mission of the department, there might be a "family disturbance squad," a "drunk and derelict squad," a "riot control squad," and a "juvenile squad"; law enforcement matters would be left to a "felony squad." Instead, there is a detective division organized, in the larger departments, into units specializing in homicide, burglary, auto theft, narcotics, vice, robbery, and the like. The undifferentiated patrol division gets everything else. Only juveniles tend to be treated by specialized units under both schemes, partly because the law requires or encourages such specialization. (1968, p. 69)

Bittner (1974, pp. 21–22) has suggested various ways in which the police organization perpetuates this view. In police training academies, criminal law and criminalistics are emphasized, police record keeping is almost wholly dedicated to law enforcement activities, making them the only documented output of police work; and, in the police structure of rewards and incentives, career advancement is closely related to initiative and ability in criminal law enforcement, "good pinches" weighing heavily in the evaluation of a policeman's performance. In short, the ideology of law enforcement and crime control has been deeply institutionalized in police organizations and stereotyped in the public consciousness.

D. The Capacity to Use Force as the Core of the Police Role

If the normative idealization of the police as a ministerial agency of the criminal law does not explain the specific nature of police competence—although it is in those terms that the application of police power is legitimated and granted public sanction—then on what alternative conceptual basis can the police role be defined? What distinguishes the role of the police from other occupational roles? Generally, as every city dweller knows who "calls the cops" as a method of handling problems, police intervention involves a powerful round-the-clock capacity to take decisive action in all kinds of emergencies. But more specifically, as Bittner proposed in a study of the functions of the police, "it makes much more sense to say that the police are nothing else than a mechanism for the distribution of situationally justified force in society" (1970, p. 39). This conception of the police role, which lends thematic unity to the immensely varied array of situations in which police intervene, was elaborated by Bittner as follows:

Whatever the substance of the task at hand . . . police intervention means above all making use of the capacity and authority to overpower resistance to an attempted solution in the native habitat of the problem. There can be no doubt that this feature of police work is uppermost in the minds of people who solicit police aid or direct the attention of the police to problems, that persons against whom the police proceed have this feature in mind and conduct themselves accordingly, and that every conceivable police intervention

projects the message that force may be, and may have to be,
used to achieve a desired objective. It does not matter
whether the persons who seek police help are private
citizens or other government officials, nor does it matter
whether the problem at hand involves some aspect of law
enforcement or is totally unconnected with it. . . . What
matters is that police procedure is defined by the feature
that it may not be opposed in its course, and that force can
be used if it is opposed. This is what the existence of the
police makes available to society. Accordingly, the question,
"What are policemen supposed to do?" is almost completely
identical with the question, "What kinds of situations require
remedies that are non-negotiably coercive?" (1970, pp. 40–41)

Moreover, as Bittner points out elsewhere, the policeman's mandate to use nondeadly force in a given situation is limited mainly
by his own sense of proportion; only deadly force is regulated
more stringently (1974, p. 35).

It is this feature that has been ignored in the polemical debate
on the role of the police, buttressed by the empirical studies of
the preponderance of police time spent on noncriminal matters
(see H. Goldstein 1977, pp. 24–25) in which the police are portrayed as "uniformed social workers" or the argument is advanced that police services unrelated to crime control should be
curtailed or handed over to the appropriate civilian specialists
who are more competently trained to deal with such problems.
"Unfortunately," Bittner notes,

this view overlooks a centrally important factor. While it
is true that policemen often aid sick and troubled people
because physicians and social workers are unable or unwilling
to take their service where they are needed, this is not the
only or even the main reason for police involvement. In fact
physicians and social workers themselves quite often "call
the cops." For not unlike the case of the administration of
justice, on the periphery of the rationally ordered procedures
of medical and social work practice lurk exigencies that call
for the exercise of coercion. Since neither physicians nor

social workers are authorized or equipped to use force to attain desirable objectives, the total disengagement of the police would mean allowing many a problem to move unhampered in the direction of disaster. (1970, p. 43)

In stressing the centrality of the police power to coerce provisional solutions by force Bittner does not imply that policing routinely consists of the actual exercise of coercion nor does he overlook the fact that officers are often ordered by their superiors to perform a variety of unrelated service, administrative, or menial chores. Rather, the issue is that situations are "policed" to the extent that force may have to be used in their official management. How and how often force is actually used are then problems for the evaluation, not the definition, of police work. Thus "good" police practice may be judged to involve strictly limiting the use of force and confining it to effecting restraint. Moreover, the proposed definition of the police function subsumes those forms of police activity traditionally understood as "criminal law enforcement":

> . . . the special role the police play in the administration of criminal justice has to do with the circumstance that "criminals"—as distinct from respectable and propertied persons who violate the provisions of penal codes in the course of doing business—can be counted on to try to evade or oppose arrest. Because this is so, and to enable the police to deal effectively with criminals, they are said to be empowered to use force. . . . But the conception of the police role in all this is upside down. It is *not* that policemen are entitled to use force because they must deal with nasty criminals. Instead, the duty of handling nasty criminals devolves on them *because* they have the more general authority to use force *as needed* to bring about desired objectives. (1974, pp. 35–36)

Understood in this light, the view of the police role proposed here demystifies police power by pointing to the illusion and pretense inherent in the prevailing conventional conception of the police role as "law enforcement" and "crime control." Bittner summarizes his argument as follows:

> In sum, the role of the police is to address all sorts of human problems when and insofar as their solutions do or may possibly require the use of force at the point of their occurrence. This lends homogeneity to such diverse procedures as catching a criminal, driving the mayor to the airport, evicting a drunken person from a bar, directing traffic, crowd control, taking care of lost children, administering medical first aid, and separating fighting relatives. (1970, p. 45)

This role definition implies a corresponding shift in efforts to reform and improve police practice. Thus, for example, if the mandate of the police is organized around their capacity and authority to use force, then any evaluation of their effectiveness must focus on "their methods as society's agents of coercion" (1970, p. 46). Bittner distinguishes two general and irreconcilable approaches to the problem of the police exercise of force: the "quasi-military model" and the "professional model" (1970, pp. 47–122). But he suggests that reform attempts will be confronted by various "structural character traits" of police work which are deeply rooted historically, thus not easily amenable to change. Briefly, these are as follows: (1) Deserved or not, police work has developed historically as a tainted occupation, stigmatized in the public mind because of its connection with evil, crime, and disorder, socially defined as "dirty work" the rest of us typically have no stomach for, and socially feared more than admired even in modern folklore for its repressive potential and shady imagery. These are persistent popular conceptions about the character of police work which are attached to the occupation as a whole. (2) Police work is bound to be often unjust and offensive to someone, partly because, with few exceptions, it can "accomplish something for somebody only by proceeding against someone else," and partly because it requires quick, often intuitive action and peremptory solutions to complex human problems and conflict. This structural pressure puts the police in a position where, as the popular police refrain goes, they are "damned if they do and damned if they don't." (3) Since its creation as a response to the threat posed by the "dangerous classes" (see Silver 1967), police work has reflected a whole range of public prejudices, principally in its concentration of coercive control and surveillance on the young-poor-black—with "considerable justification," as Professor Wilson feels obliged to inform us (1968, p. 40)— rather than the old-rich-white. As such, police work in a class society is inherently discriminatory and tends to have socially divisive effects (Bittner 1970, pp. 6–14, 44–46). The police have been structurally situated in this anomalous position as a result of a progressive historical process, most generally the legalization and pacification of the criminal justice process as administered by the courts, on the one hand, and the legitimation and institutionalization of the use of force as the exclusive monopoly of the police, on the other (Bittner 1970, pp. 15–35, 45).

E. Streetcorner Politicians: Police Responses to Paradoxes of Coercion

In his seminal essay "Politics as a Vocation," Max Weber saw long ago that "he who lets himself in for politics, that is, for power and force as means, contracts with diabolical powers . . . it is *not* true that good can follow only from good and evil only from evil, but that often the opposite is true. Anyone who fails to see this is, indeed, a political infant" (1946, p. 123). For Weber, the legitimate practice of coercion, of violence as a means, defines the tasks of politics and confronts its practitioner with inescapable "ethical paradoxes" which exact a moral price and "endanger the 'salvation of the soul' " (pp. 125–26). The police role is defined by such a contract: as curbside agents of the state, that is, of the community that effectively claims "the monopoly of the legitimate use of physical force within a given territory" (as Weber defined the modern state, p. 78), the police are "streetcorner politicians." This conception informs a noteworthy field study of police recently published by political scientist William Ker Muir, Jr. (1977). Muir is principally concerned with examining the consequences of the practice of coercion on police officers themselves—how police respond to violence and develop morally and intellectually in the job, how they manage the contradiction of seeking worthwhile ends with coercive means—while grappling anew with the larger and more elusive question, "What is a good policeman?" In this respect his work supplements that of Westley, Skolnick, Wilson, Reiss, and others.

Muir elaborates his conception of the situation of the police as follows:

> The policeman's authority consists of a legal license to
> coerce others to refrain from using illegitimate coercion.
> Society licenses him to kill, hurt, confine, and otherwise
> victimize nonpolicemen who would illegally kill, hurt, confine,
> or otherwise victimize others whom the policeman is charged
> to protect. But the reality, and the subtle irony, of being a
> policeman is that, while he may appear to be the supreme
> practitioner of coercion, in fact he is first and foremost its
> most frequent victim. The policeman is society's "fall guy,"
> the object of coercion more frequently than its practitioner.
> . . . If he is vicious, his viciousness is the upswing of the
> vicious cycle inherent in an extortionate relationship.
> (1977, pp. 44–45)

As a political actor who must perform in a world in which relationships are based on threat, the policeman as "oppressor must instinctively anticipate resistance from the oppressed. . . . The victimizer is always a potential victim of counter-threats, ever on guard against the moment his victim retaliates" (1977, p. 38). Thus the policeman, a victim of coercion, as Muir quotes Tocqueville's sharp observation about politicians in general, is "absorbed by the cares of self-defense" (p. 5). Muir's study, based on detailed ethnographic description of daily patrol rounds, revolves around the formulation of a typology of distinct police defensive responses to "paradoxes of coercion."

Muir observes that while much of the time spent on patrol involved a variety of routine activities (taking reports, driving the streets, etc.), the basic theme of police work consisted of coping with or looking for "critical incidents." Critical incidents or "rebellions" occurred in any situation in which the officer was actually or potentially threatened or attacked by a citizen. The likelihood of such rebellions increases under the following conditions: "(1) if the citizen were likely to suffer a *less severe injury* than he could inflict on the policeman or on persons with whom the policeman identified; (2) if the citizen were *less vulnerable to injury* than were the policeman and persons with whom the policeman identified; (3) if the citizen were *less remorseful* about any injuries he caused than the policeman; and (4) if the citizen were *less aware* of any injuries he causes than was the policeman" (1977, p. 59). These four types of actually or potentially dangerous situations—often reflected, respectively, in the policing of skid row confrontations, family beefs, crowd scenes, and juvenile capers—correspond to what Muir terms the four "paradoxes of coercive power": (1) the *paradox of dispossession* ("The less one has, the less one has to lose"); (2) the *paradox of detachment* ("The less the victim cares about preserving something, the less the victimizer cares about taking it hostage"); (3) the *paradox of face* ("The nastier one's reputation, the less nasty one has to be"); and (4) the *paradox of irrationality* ("The more delirious the threatener, the more serious the threat, the more delirious the victim, the less serious the threat") (1977, p. 44). In such recurrent street situations, in Muir's view,

> The citizen is, relative to the policeman, the more
> dispossessed, the more detached, the nastier, and the crazier.
> . . . The policeman is the one who is on the defensive. . . .
> What will distinguish one policeman from the other are the
> techniques he invests to defend himself in his position of
> comparative vulnerability. (1977, p. 45)

What can explain the development of "good" policemen in the context of such extortionate relationships? And how can the exercise of coercive power avoid or mitigate corruption and moral depletion? Muir again turns to Weber's analysis of the "ethical paradoxes" of coercion and their consequences for its political practitioner. For Weber, the "model of professional politician" combined two essential "virtues" or "psychological qualities": *passion* and *perspective* (1946, pp. 115, 128). Muir adapts these concepts to generate a typology of four ideal types of policemen, and hence of four types of police responses to the practice of coercive power (1977, pp. 50–58). "Passion" is a moral quality, a "capacity to integrate violence into ethics" through "principled" devotion to the general welfare, a guilt-free reconciliation of the use of force to achieve just ends. The absence of "passion" or of this "integrated morality" is a "conflicted morality," guilty about and irreconciled to the results of employing police violence. "Perspective" is an intellectual quality, composed of "objectivity" and a "sense of proportion," a trained and cognitively efficient police "judgment" of events and an "understanding" of human conduct, a capacity to grasp "the knowledge of tragedy with which all action, but especially political action, is truly interwoven" (Weber 1946, p. 117). The absence of such a "tragic perspective" leads to a "cynical perspective," to what Weber called a "radical Machiavellianism" where there would be no guilt about the use of force because there would be no conscience, and hence a ready and misanthropic justification of police violence would be possible. The combination of these two qualities prescribed by Weber—"warm passion and a cool sense of proportion forged together in one and the same soul" (1946, p. 115)—yields Muir's *"professional"* or "good" policeman. The model further leads to three types of "nonprofessional" policemen: "(1) *enforcers*—police who had passion, but lacked perspective; (2) *reciprocators*—police who had perspective, but lacked passion; and (3) *avoiders*—police who lacked both passion and perspective" (Muir 1977, p. 55). These three types represent varieties of the "corruption" of police authority—respectively, "brutality, banality, or cowardice." "Being a policeman changed attitudes. . . . The deals a patrolman has to make with the devil of coercion had unforeseen consequences for his perspective and passion" (p. 147).

Muir's typology is an *attitude model* which aims to evaluate and classify police officers on the assumption that an officer's attitudes ("passion," "perspective") are related to his police actions —a relation which Muir believes to be both logical and factual. Analysis of interview responses by a random sample of twenty-eight young police officers was the basis for classifying the officers into the four categories as a starting point for the study (begun in 1971); field observation of their development was reportedly conducted with each of the officers on an occasional basis over the next several years. Muir described a range of defensive reactions by these officers to the four "paradoxes of coercive power" in street situations (skid row, family beefs, crowd scenes, juvenile capers).

The *professional* response characteristically involved teaching through talk, talk which helped take charge of events, and a readiness to explain and exhort, to establish hope, understanding, and fear. In contrast, the *reciprocating* response depended on nurturing the citizen's sense of personal obligation to the police officer. It depended on the officer's touching some personal compulsion of gratitude, on the return of favors. The reciprocating response let people get away with illegal activity. It was essentially passive resistance to the coercion of others and depended on the citizens' conscious understanding of their moral obligations in the course of time. And sometimes, as in the family beef, the reciprocating response was extremely effective. The *enforcement* response was aggressive, somewhat like the professional response but more impatient and unenlightening, unresponsive to the possible changes going on inside the citizen's head and heart. Words were used as weapons or to incite, never to probe the soul. The *avoidance* response, almost invariably passive, ineloquent, unintimidating, was none of these. It was merely lifeless, unresponsive to human suffering (Muir 1977, pp. 144–46).

The study focuses on the complex dynamics of the intellectual development of police officers, of "judgment" and "understanding" in police work, and on specifiable conditions shaping "cynic" and "tragic" perspectives; and on their moral development in a context of inherent moral contradictions and broad moral discretion. "The young patrol officer exposed himself more often to more severe moral problems than any young professional I have ever encountered. An unremitting and unavoidable series of quandaries assaulted the policeman's power of decisiveness" (1977, p. 208). Muir concludes in this respect that such quandaries were frequent, morally probing and courting unpopular decisions, and requiring swift judgment in highly complex situations. And a major cause of this complexity was that the policeman was an instrument of a coercive legal order. A policeman, in practicing and contending with the techniques of threat, was always encountering the paradoxes of coercive power. Hence he was always tempted to simplify his moral choices, to be self-defensive, detached, remorseless, and irrational, and to justify segregating his police life from his personal life (pp. 211–13).

The balance of Muir's study is devoted to a consideration of some reform proposals, that is, of ways of deliberately changing some " 'natural' consequences of the policeman's lot." But in this regard Muir's proposals seem narrowly conceived and reveal the limitations of his attitudinal model. For Muir, police reform is a function of developing the proper "professional" qualities of "passion" and "perspective" in individual police practitioners through what he calls "language, learning, and leadership." The goal of the "good policeman" emerges here as a compromised quest in which the most effective remedy to the contradictions of coercive power is moral training and leadership, particularly as provided by field sergeants' skillful on-the-job teaching and through the role of the police chief in affecting "the inner perspectives and passions of the patrolmen in his department" (Muir 1977, p. 226). While these are matters of the utmost seriousness and merit no disparagement, Muir does not propose— and cannot, by the logic of his argument propose—changes in social structures that give rise to and are protected by the coercive power of the police; instead, dominant social arrangements are, at least implicitly, seen as given and irremediable features of the human condition. Muir's conservative approach to social planning is plainly stated:

> The proper solution to the problem of coercive power is
> not to eliminate the contradictory demands of civility and
> coercion but to provide the understanding and the moral
> strength which will enable policemen to harmonize the two.
> . . . The imperative in a free society must always be to

strengthen the human being. Discussion, understanding of the world and the job, and moral self-knowledge—these become the central instruments of shoring up the moral strengths of mankind. (p. 268)

Though his presupposition seems remote, Muir's formulation of the problem remains an original and timely contribution to the debate on the police role, wholly eschewing the prevailing official ideology of criminal law enforcement and the attendant view of police reform as a merely technical operation. By focusing attention on police work as a moral and intellectual problem—specifically on the dilemma of exercising "coercion for the general welfare in the face of personal danger without becoming radically Machiavellian" (1977, p. 279)—Muir underscores again the complexity and contradictions of the practice of "streetcorner politics."

III. Notes on the Politics of Police Reform

We have argued, though it is a vastly simplified picture, that contemporary conceptions of the police, and of their problems and their reform, were shaped in the crucible of the 1960s, that is, in the context of the intensified social conflict and diminished political consensus that confronted all institutions of government with a crisis of legitimacy. Particularly for the police, these social and political upheavals accentuated the adversarial character of their role. In a wave of governmental concern and reaction reminiscent of earlier periods of police history, notably the period of the 1920s which culminated in the Wickersham Commission, the 1960s saw a succession of presidential and other official commissions which both focused unprecedented public attention on the police institution and provided the rationale for a major mobilization of federal resources.[9]

---

[9] Police response to crime, civil disorders, violence, and campus antiwar protest was examined in the respective reports of the "Crime Commission" (President's Commission on Law Enforcement and Administration of Justice 1967), "Riot Commission" (National Advisory Commission on Civil Disorders 1968), "Violence Commission" (National Commission on the Causes and Prevention of Violence 1968a, 1968b, 1969), and "Campus Unrest Commission" (President's Commission

One early and structurally significant result of this politically motivated activity—in a politically charged "law and order" climate urging a "war on crime" alongside the "war on poverty" as a dual national strategy—was the creation of the Law Enforcement Assistance Administration (LEAA) under the 1968 Omnibus Crime Control and Safe Streets Act. LEAA established a funding infrastructure to funnel federal monies to local criminal justice agencies in the form of block grants to the states. At the same time, the National Institute of Law Enforcement and Criminal Justice (NILECJ) was formed within the LEAA structure as its national research and development arm. LEAA and NILECJ constitute by far the major external source of available funds for "improving" local police operations. Their allocation of funds has been principally justified on the premise that the problems of crime and policing are essentially technical problems to be remedied through the scientific application of increasingly sophisticated technology. This dominance of technocratic assumptions, values, and interests in the police-reform market has been criticized as misbegotten and counterproductive by social critics of diverse political persuasion. Among academics, Herman Goldstein, for example, whose recent book (1977) provides the most comprehensive and detailed review of police reform programs available, notes that the police have used federal funds to "acquire the long-established elements of the professional model, such as communications equipment, computers, vehicles, specialized units, and limited forms of training and education" (1977, p. 6). He goes on to argue:

> In fact, despite all the changes that have been made, most
> of the problems from which the police field has long
> suffered remain. . . . Except for a relatively small number

on Campus Unrest 1970). For an analysis of the politics of such commissions from 1917 to 1970, see Platt (1971).

Police corruption also received wide attention as a result of the investigations of the Knapp Commission (1973) in New York City. The last in this series of official statements was the voluminous task force report of the National Advisory Commission on Criminal Justice Standards and Goals (1973).

of notable breakthroughs, the police have generally been reluctant to challenge existing practices, to conduct research, and to engage in experimentation. (1977, p. 8)

James Q. Wilson is similarly critical:

Nearly ten years ago I wrote that the billions of dollars the federal government was then preparing to spend on crime control would be wasted, and indeed might even make matters worse if they were merely pumped into the existing criminal justice system. They were, and they have. In the next ten years I hope we can learn to experiment rather than simply spend, to test our theories rather than fund our fears. (1975, p. 208)

An eighteen-month LEAA-funded internal evaluation of the research and development programs financed by NILECJ during the years 1969–75 (White and Krislov 1977) underscores both the dominance of advanced technology in the Institute's budget and the limitations of an atheoretical, "narrow technological approach" to reform, especially apparent in NILECJ's hardware projects. The report shows that "research organizations, particularly Federal Contract Research Centers (e.g., the Mitre Corporation, the Rand Corporation, the Aerospace Corporation), have captured the lion's share of Institute resources through its entire history" and "received the largest percentage increase in funds as the Institute's budget grew over the years" (p. 57). The report also points out that programs funded by NILECJ during this period have reflected shifting research and development strategies and priorities over time, given "the political atmosphere and administrative conditions" in which it has functioned, with the Institute's programming responding to many different and often competing demands and expectations. Since its inception, "NILECJ's political heritage was without a broadly pluralistic base" (p. 16). For example, the report argues, academic social scientists "tend[ed] to be ideologically liberal," generally avoided involvement with NILECJ, and as a result "a major source of research competence was isolated from the federal effort in criminal justice research." In addition:

> LEAA (and consequently the Institute) lacked a range
> of constituencies from the start and has continued to attract
> an asymmetrical set of interest and pressure groups, mostly
> practitioners and other government fund-seekers. Conse-
> quently, the influence and direction from the user community
> has been one-sided. For most of LEAA's history, the police—
> traditionally well organized and considered synonymous with
> law enforcement—have provided the most visible and
> effective source of influence. (p. 16)

Another major source of external financing for innovative police programs has been the Police Foundation, a private organization established in 1970 by the Ford Foundation. The Police Foundation has favored a strategy of strict evaluation research directed mainly to selected patrol projects; though this strategy has often artificially narrowed the analysis of project results to whatever quantifiable effects can be measured by available social science research techniques, it has produced some notable and controversial studies. Best known is the Kansas City "Proactive-Reactive Patrol Deployment Experiment" (Kelling et al. 1974), a test of the traditional police practice of random "preventive patrol." The findings indicated no significant differences in the level of reported crimes or citizen perception of the police among three matched areas of the city which had received varying patrol coverage for one year—thus seriously questioning the validity of roving patrol and provoking a vehement controversy in police circles. Similar tests to assess the value of police "field interrogations" (Boydstun 1975) and of one-officer versus two-officer patrol car staffing systems (Boydstun, Sherry, and Moelter 1977) were carried out in San Diego, again eliciting controversy. In the patrol staffing project, evaluators concluded that one-officer cars were more cost-effective and safer (as measured by various empirical indicators, including number of officer injuries and resisting arrest cases) than two-officer cars, even though the latter were preferred by a majority of patrol officers sampled. This finding immediately came under attack by various police officer associations, who saw the report as undermining negotiations for manpower increases, and has recently come under fire in San Diego after the on-duty shooting death of a police officer assigned to a one-officer car.

These projects have focused on questioning traditional police methods; a few others have aimed to test new approaches, such as the Foundation-sponsored experiments in "team policing" in several cities (Sherman, Milton, and Kelley 1973; Bloch and Specht 1973), and the San Diego "Community Profile Development Project" (Boydstun and Sherry 1975). Despite a number of similar experiments in patrol innovation funded by LEAA or the Police Foundation, the Community Profile Development Project is rare in that it actually served as a catalyst for a long-term process of organizational change throughout the San Diego Police Department. Indeed, the research literature on police reform is marked by a dearth of detailed and critical accounts of actual programs of planned social change in police organizations, that is, of the *politics* of effecting reforms in police settings (H. Goldstein 1977, p. 307; Rumbaut 1978). Available descriptions of programs that have been implemented over the past decade have generally been written from official perspectives and for pragmatic purposes—for example, the various and useful NILECJ "National Evaluation Program" reports and "Prescriptive Packages"—rather than in an effort to probe and understand the dynamics of such enterprises in reform, and the ways in which new reforms may be subverted, resisted, compromised, or redefined in the process of being implemented.

Many of the recommendations contained in the various national commission reports have not been implemented. There has been a considerable lag between the formulation and testing of police reform proposals and their incorporation and acceptance in police practice. In large part, this gap underscores the nature of the resistance within police organizations to "outside" criticism and pressures for reform and control, especially in a situation where, even if the severe strains of the late 1960s have been relaxed, those who are to be "reformed" are expected willy-nilly to do the "reforming." Criticism of the police tends to be dismissed or derided by Panglossian police apologists and others within police agencies who see the critics and the reformists as uninformed "bleeding hearts" or "subversives." They answer that these "outsiders" and "ivory tower types" know nothing about "real police work" and seek capriciously to undermine policing and police officers by casting aspersions on their profession and their performance. Some leading police officials have argued that the mobilization of official resources prompted by public debate on the police coincides with the objectives and interests of their agencies, and have welcomed and promoted the reform process. But in the charged political ambience of the past decade, criticism even by public officials has had the effect of further alienating and polarizing the police, entrenching a distrustful and defiant posture, and stimulating organized reaction to protect their perceived interests and their image (see Alex 1976). Further, the growing strength and politicization of rank-and-file police associations and unions has resulted in increased resistance to control by police managers and policymakers (see Bent 1974, pp. 77 ff.). The context and process of reform, in short, have been exceedingly problematic.

Thus far we have briefly considered some *structural* developments in the social reform of the police that came into being in connection with the political upheavals of the past decade and which have influenced the direction of reform. One significant *ideological* development which achieved its formulation during this period, and which despite its failure has in some respects influenced the conception of many of the "community-oriented" patrol reform projects referred to above, was the development of police-community relations projects. Manning (1977) views police-community relations as an "alternative police myth" which complements the prevailing "crime control myth." Both ideologies "serve the same function of obscuring and mediating the conflicting expectations, audiences and demands made upon the police by middle-class groups" (p. 359). He elaborates:

To the middle classes, the police wish to symbolize crime control (of the lower classes), while their actions toward

the middle classes are in accord with the middle classes'
general moral and social position (that is, they maintain
good police/community relations). On the other hand, to
the lower classes, the police wish to symbolize, at least on
occasion, and as long as it is expedient (as long as there are
federal dollars to support the programs), police/community
relations, while their conduct is in actuality crime-repression
oriented. It is a contradictory set of expectations and actions.
(p. 360)

For Manning, the ideology of police-community relations "surfaces precisely when the quality of police service becomes a
public issue."

When what is considered to be crime reaches beyond lower
class areas (that is, when social conflict increases), the
segmentalization of audiences fails, and the targeting of
lower-class groups is insufficient to control the "crime
problem." PCR arises. Liberal and scholarly attention emerges
at the same point and for similar reasons. It is an ideological
obfuscation intended to mask the contradictions of policing
in this society. (p. 362)

These considerations of recent police structural and ideological
developments dovetail in some respects with an analysis of the
U.S. police put forth by the Center for Research on Criminal
Justice (1976). Arguing from a left-radical perspective that sees
the police primarily serving a class control function, the analysis
is concerned with interpreting the implications of the rapid
growth and expansion of police personnel and funds over the last
decade. The report distinguishes and documents two approaches
to new developments in policing: (1) a "hard" side based on
sophisticated technology and an increased capacity to use force—
the "iron fist"; and (2) a "soft" side based on new forms of
"community pacification and penetration," and programs to
legitimate and "sell" the police to the public—the "velvet glove."
The former includes the design and refinement of computerized
intelligence systems, command control centers, automated dis-
patch and communications technology, aerial surveillance, identi-

fication techniques, lethal and nonlethal weaponry, and paramilitary tactical units. The latter includes police-community relations units, special "sensitivity" and "conflict management" training, recruitment of women and black officers, and neighborhood team policing programs. LEAA and Police Foundation grants, respectively, are analyzed as the principal sources of funds for putting these two major emphases into practice.

In our review of changing conceptions of the police role in the 1960s we focused on the "discoveries" of discretion and peacekeeping as key conceptualizations which have emerged from and bestowed a sense of order to a sustained debate on the nature of the police role. Connected to a critique of the prevailing police ideology or mythology, the debate has had a demystifying effect for our understanding of policing and of the problems and prospects for its reform. First, the analysis of "peacekeeping" has undercut the imagery of crime control, revealing that "crime fighting" and "law enforcement" are less a description of what in fact police work consists of than they are its traditional *raison d'être*, a deeply embedded rationalization of society's curbside agency of coercive power, and occasionally an effective political scare tactic which can equate a "vote against police" with a "vote for crime." Second, the analysis of police "discretion" has undercut the myth of police work as a ministerial and apolitical activity, supposedly involving the nondiscretionary application of "the law" and hence inherently under legislative and judicial control and guidance; and it has undercut the associated professionalized imagery of policing as a value-free technical activity, involving the objective and expert application of science and technology in the neutral and rational interests of operational efficiency. Indeed, the analysis of discretion has focused attention on the politics and not just the techniques of police work, on the ways in which police officers, supervisors, and administrators make discretionary choices in their work constantly and unavoidably among diverse ends and means, and on the ways those choices are influenced by complex and intense situational interests, values, and pressures (see H. Goldstein 1977, pp. 93–126). The inquiry into the nature of the police role, then, as suggested by our preceding review of the literature, has alerted us to the diversity and complexity of police work, its ambiguous and problematic social context, its role conflicts and contradictions. Police must manage the competing demands and expectations of diverse audiences, and the paradoxes of order and legality, civility and coercion, means and ends, which inhere in the exercise of police power in a class society. The problems are built into the basic arrangements for policing in our society, and yet have been largely ignored or avoided by the reform movement; that is, reforms have not been based on conceptions which penetrate to the core of the police function and which confront the underlying problems, but rather on efforts, well intentioned to be sure, aimed at improving the accouterments of the police establishment.

Efforts to define and improve the quality of police practice, to place police work on a fully reasoned basis, and to develop skilled, informed, and judicious individual practitioners of a highly complex police vocation remain blocked by a set of structural and cultural constraints. Among those that lie within the possibility of control and change by the police, the principal obstacles are the currently existing organization of police departments and their insular and change-resistant occupational culture. In addition, concerns with defining and ensuring police accountability to the citizenry and with establishing new forms of political review and control over police discretion by local communities— concerns which peaked in the late 1960s amid widespread political protest—are attenuated by the present direction of technologically and legalistically determined reforms. We might briefly elaborate here a pertinent distinction between what we might call *formal rationality* and *substantive rationality*. The former addresses "how" questions and focuses on the *means* of human action; the latter addresses "why" questions and focuses on the *ends* of human action. An emphasis on one or the other approach to police problems has crucial consequences for the type and direction of proposed solutions. The tendency of a bureaucratic technical-rational orientation is to transform problems of politics and morality into problems of administration and technology. Such an orientation depoliticizes police reform by (1) taking the established social order and police objectives as given and beyond question, positing if need be a fictive community consensus on the social purposes of policing; (2) focusing attention away from the comprehensive, complex, and often conflicting sociopolitical context of policing and concealing dominant police values and interests (i.e., police politics) under the neutral cover of "techniques" and "facts"; (3) assuming that the social problems of policing, now narrowly defined as problems of engineering and administrative control, can be solved by scientific means, an assumption which moots the issue of police accountability to the public and further insulates the police from citizen evaluation and control; and (4) turning police reform into efforts to maximize the "efficiency" and "effectiveness" of police operations through the systematic application of technical expertise. This may account, in part, for the Sisyphean character of police reforms that have been based on little but the provision of more, better equipped, and better disciplined personnel, and should suggest the limitations of a technocratic police professionalism.

The problems of policing are not simply problems of finding "efficient" and "effective" means; they are problems of ends, of competing social values, interests, and priorities, the resolution of which raise fundamental moral and political issues to be decided by an informed citizenry, not only scientific or technical issues to be decided by experts and technocrats. Hence, the most hopeful prospect for substantive police reform is the influence an informed public can exert on the direction of change in police agencies. Such a prospect is at best uncertain. Meanwhile the present dominance of technocratic values and interests in police reform will likely continue to be achieved at the expense of democratic values and interests.

REFERENCES

Alex, Nicholas. 1976. *New York Cops Talk Back: A Study of a Beleaguered Minority*. New York: Wiley.

Banton, Michael. 1964. *The Policeman in the Community*. New York: Basic Books.

Bent, Alan E. 1974. *The Politics of Law Enforcement: Conflict and Power in Urban Communities*. Lexington, Mass.: Lexington Books.

Bittner, Egon. 1967a. "The Police on Skid-Row: A Study of Peace Keeping," *American Sociological Review* 32:699–715.

———. 1967b. "Police Discretion in Emergency Apprehension of Mentally Ill Persons," *Social Problems* 14:278–92.

———. 1970. *The Functions of the Police in Modern Society*. Washington, D.C.: U.S. Government Printing Office.

———. 1974. "Florence Nightingale in Pursuit of Willie Sutton: A Theory of the Police." In *The Potential for Reform of Criminal Justice*, ed. Herbert Jacob. Beverly Hills, Calif.: Sage Publications.

Bloch, Peter B., and David Specht. 1973. *Neighborhood Team Policing*. Washington, D.C.: U.S. Government Printing Office.

Bordua, David J., and Albert J. Reiss, Jr. 1966. "Command, Control and Charisma: Reflections on Police Bureaucracy," *American Journal of Sociology* 72:68–76.

Boydstun, John E. 1975. *San Diego Field Interrogation: Final Report*. Washington, D.C.: Police Foundation.

Boydstun, John E., and Michael E. Sherry. 1975. *San Diego Community Profile: Final Report*. Washington, D.C.: Police Foundation.

Boydstun, John E., Michael E. Sherry, and Nicholas P. Moelter. 1977. *One—or Two—Officer Units*. Washington, D.C.: Police Foundation.

Center for Research on Criminal Justice. 1976. *The Iron Fist and the Velvet Glove: An Analysis of the U.S. Police*. 2d rev. ed. Berkeley, Calif.: Center for Research on Criminal Justice.

Clark, John. 1965. "Isolation of the Police: A Comparison of the British and American Situations," *Journal of Criminal Law, Criminology and Police Science* 56:307–19.

Cummings, Elaine, Ian Cumming, and Laura Edell. 1965. "Policeman as Philosopher, Guide and Friend," *Social Problems* 12:276–86.

Davis, Kenneth C. 1969. *Discretionary Justice; A Preliminary Inquiry*. Baton Rouge: Louisiana State University Press.

———. 1975. *Police Discretion*. St. Paul, Minn.: West Publishing Co.

Festinger, Leon. 1957. *A Theory of Cognitive Dissonance*. Evanston, Ill.: Row-Peterson.

Fogelson, Robert M. 1977. *Big-City Police*. Cambridge, Mass.: Harvard University Press.

Fosdick, Raymond. 1920. *American Police Systems*. New York: Century.

Geary, D. P., ed. 1975. *Community Relations and the Administration of Justice*. New York: Wiley.

Goldstein, Herman. 1963. "Police Discretion: The Ideal Versus the Real," *Public Administration Review* 23:140–48.

———. 1967. "Policy Policy Formulation: A Proposal for Improving Police Performance," *Michigan Law Review* 65:1123–46.

————. 1968. "Police Response to Urban Crisis," *Public Administration Review*, 28:417–23.

————. 1977. *Policing a Free Society*. Cambridge, Mass.: Ballinger.

Goldstein, Joseph. 1960. "Police Discretion Not to Invoke the Criminal Process: Low Visibility Decisions in the Administration of Justice," *Yale Law Journal* 69:543–94.

Gray, Thomas C. 1975. "Selecting for a Police Subculture." In *Police in America*, ed. Jerome H. Skolnick and Thomas C. Gray. Boston: Educational Associates.

Hewitt, W. H., and C. L. Newman, eds. 1970. *Police-Community Relations*. Mineola, N.Y.: Foundation Press.

Hormachea, C. R., and Marion Hormachea, eds. 1971. *Confrontation: Violence and the Police*. Boston: Holbrook Press.

Kadish, Sanford H. 1962. "Legal Norm and Discretion in the Police and Sentencing Process," *Harvard Law Review* 75:904–31.

Kelling, George L., Tony Pate, Duane Dieckman, and Charles Brown. 1974. *The Kansas City Preventive Patrol Experiment: A Technical Report*. Washington, D.C.: Police Foundation.

Knapp, Whitman. 1972. *Commission to Investigate Allegations of Police Corruption: Summary and Principal Recommendations*. New York: Fund for the City of New York.

Knapp Commission. 1973. *Report on Police Corruption*. New York: George Braziller.

LaFave, Wayne R. 1962. "The Police and Nonenforcement of the Law," *Wisconsin Law Review*, 1962:104–37, 179–239.

————. 1965. *Arrest: The Decision to Take a Suspect into Custody*. Boston: Little, Brown.

Manning, Peter K. 1977. *Police Work: Essays on the Social Organization of Policing*. Cambridge, Mass.: MIT Press.

McNamara, John H. 1967. "Uncertainties in Police Work: The Relevance of Police Recruits' Backgrounds and Training." In *The Police: Six Sociological Essays*, ed. David J. Bordua. New York: Wiley.

Muir, William Ker, Jr. 1977. *Police: Streetcorner Politicians*. Chicago: University of Chicago Press.

National Advisory Commission on Civil Disorders. 1968. *The Kerner Report*. Washington, D.C.: U.S. Government Printing Office.

National Advisory Commission on Criminal Justice Standards and Goals. 1973. *Report on Police*. Washington, D.C.: U.S. Government Printing Office.

National Commission on the Causes and Prevention of Violence. 1968a. *To Establish Justice, to Insure Domestic Transition*. Washington, D.C.: U.S. Government Printing Office.

————. 1968b. *The Walker Report*. Washington, D.C.: U.S. Government Printing Office.

————. 1969. *The Skolnick Report.* Washington, D.C.: U.S. Government Printing Office.

Niederhoffer, Arthur. 1967. *Behind the Shield: The Police in Urban Society.* Garden City, N.Y.: Doubleday.

Norris, Donald F. 1973. *Police-Community Relations: A Program That Failed.* Lexington, Mass.: Lexington Books.

Platt, Anthony M., ed. 1971. *The Politics of Riot Commissions.* New York: Collier.

President's Commission on Campus Unrest. 1970. *The Scranton Report.* Washington, D.C.: U.S. Government Printing Office.

President's Commission on Law Enforcement and Administration of Justice. 1967a. *The Challenge of Crime in a Free Society.* Washington, D.C.: U.S. Government Printing Office.

————. 1967b. *Task Force Report: The Police.* Washington, D.C.: U.S. Government Printing Office.

Reiss, Albert J., Jr. 1971. *The Police and the Public.* New Haven: Yale University Press.

Rubinstein, Jonathan. 1973. *City Police.* New York: Farrar, Strauss & Giroux.

Rumbaut, Rubén G. 1978. *The Politics of Reform in a Police Bureaucracy: A Case Study in Social Intervention and Organizational Change.* Ph.D. dissertation, Department of Sociology, Brandeis University.

Sherman, Lawrence W., Catherine H. Milton, and Thomas V. Kelley. 1973. *Team Policing: Seven Case Studies.* Washington, D.C.: Police Foundation.

Silver, Allen. 1967. "The Demand for Order in Civil Society: A Review of Some Themes in the History of Urban Crime, Police and Riot." In *The Police: Six Sociological Essays*, ed. David J. Bordua. New York: Wiley.

Skolnick, Jerome H. 1966. *Justice without Trial; Law Enforcement in Democratic Society.* New York: Wiley.

Van Maanen, John. 1973. "Observations on the Making of Policemen," *Human Organization* 32:407–18.

————. 1974. "Working the Street: A Developmental View of Police Behavior." In *The Potential for Reform of Criminal Justice*, ed. Herbert Jacob. Beverly Hills, Calif.: Sage Publications.

————. 1975. "Police Socialization: A Longitudinal Examination of Job Attitudes in an Urban Police Department," *Administrative Science Quarterly* 20:207–28.

Vollmer, August. 1936. *The Police and Modern Society.* Berkeley: University of California Press.

Weber, Max. 1946. "Politics as a Vocation." In *From Max Weber: Essays in Sociology*, ed. Hans H. Gerth and C. Wright Mills. New York: Oxford University Press.

Westley, William. 1970. *Violence and the Police: A Sociological Study of Law, Custom and Morality.* Cambridge, Mass.: MIT Press.

White, Susan O., and Samuel Krislov, eds. 1977. *Understanding Crime: An Evaluation of the National Institute of Law Enforcement and Criminal Justice.* Washington, D.C.: National Academy of Sciences.

Wilson, James Q. 1968. *Varieties of Police Behavior: The Management of Law and Order in Eight Communities.* Cambridge, Mass.: Harvard University Press.

————. 1975. *Thinking about Crime.* New York: Basic Books.

Wilson, Orlando W. 1950. *Police Administration.* New York: McGraw-Hill.

————, ed. 1957. *Parker on Police.* Springfield, Ill.: Charles C. Thomas.

David P. Farrington

Longitudinal Research on Crime and Delinquency

ABSTRACT

Longitudinal research involves study, over time, of a group of people, or of samples from the same population, using records, interviews, or both. Studies which extend over a long period, which are prospective, and which include interviews with the subjects are especially useful. The longitudinal method has been used to investigate criminal careers, especially the incidence and prevalence of official delinquency at different ages, the peak age for convictions, the relationship between juvenile delinquency and adult crime, and offense specialization. It has also been used to predict the onset of convictions, recidivism, and the ending of criminal careers; to study the effects of penal treatments and other events such as marriage on delinquency; and to investigate the transmission of criminality from one generation to the next. Longitudinal and cross-sectional methods each have a part to play in research into crime and delinquency and each has its advantages and disadvantages. Major methodological questions concern the relative value of prospective versus retrospective research, and of interviews versus official records. Practical problems of longitudinal surveys include funding, staffing, attrition, and ethical issues. More prospective longitudinal research projects, including interviews, should be undertaken to provide basic information about the natural history of delinquent behavior and about the progression of detected offenders through the criminal justice system.

David P. Farrington is University Lecturer in Criminology, Cambridge University.

Longitudinal research involves repeated measures of the same people, or of samples from the same population. Its primary use has been to investigate the course of development, the natural history and prevalence of a phenomenon at different age levels, how phenomena emerge, or continuities and discontinuities from an earlier age to a later age. It has also been used to study the relationship between earlier and later events, the effects of particular events or life experiences on the course of development, and transmission of characteristics from one generation to the next.

This paper explores some of the uses and problems of longitudinal studies of crime and delinquency. Section I discusses major uses of longitudinal studies and presents major findings on such matters as patterns of delinquency and criminality, prediction of the beginnings or endings of criminal careers, and the effects of penal treatments. Although many questions can be investigated both longitudinally and cross-sectionally, Section I identifies several questions for which longitudinal research is particularly appropriate. Section II discusses methodological issues, including the comparative advantages of longitudinal and cross-sectional research, whether longitudinal research should be prospective or retrospective and whether it should be based on records or interviews. This section also discusses problems of sample size, staffing, funding, and attrition of subjects and identifies ethical difficulties. Section III, the conclusion, suggests several longitudinal projects which could greatly benefit our understanding of crime and delinquency.

This review is restricted to research in which the first and last measures are separated by at least five years, since the distinctive advantages and disadvantages of longitudinal surveys become clearer with the length of the research. Special attention is given to prospective rather than retrospective research, and to surveys including at least one interview, rather than those based only on records.

Only studies published in English are considered; in most instances these have been carried out in North America, Great Britain, Australia, New Zealand, or the Scandinavian countries.

While the focus of interest is on surveys including information about crime and delinquency, other classic long-term studies are also mentioned. Methodology is emphasized rather than substantive results, although some important findings are described. Comprehensive coverage of all the results and methodological issues of longitudinal research on crime and delinquency is of course not possible in a paper of this length.

I make frequent reference to the Cambridge Study, the major results of which are contained in three books (West 1969; West and Farrington 1973, 1977); a summary through 1977 is also available (Farrington and West 1979). The Cambridge Study is a prospective long-term survey of 411 males. When the survey began in 1961–62 it included all the boys of age 8–9 in six state primary schools in a working-class area of London. The boys were tested in their schools at ages 8, 10, and 14 and were interviewed outside school at ages 16, 18, and 21. Their parents were interviewed in their homes about once a year from the time the boys were 8 until their last year of compulsory schooling at age 15, and their teachers filled in questionnaires about them at ages 8, 10, 12, and 14. Information about the boys and about their parents and siblings has also been obtained from other sources, notably criminal records. The primary aim of the project is to investigate the development of delinquency, and to this end self-report measures of delinquency have been obtained at ages 14, 16, 18, and 21 to supplement the official records.

The Cambridge Study is a prospective survey, since the major outcome of interest (who would become officially delinquent) was not known when the earliest data were collected and coded. Furthermore, members of the research team have regularly made direct contact with the subjects and with their families over a long period. In these respects, the survey is unusual. Most longitudinal surveys of crime and delinquency are retrospective, and are based entirely on official records, notably from the police, penal institutions, hospitals, and schools.

The major longitudinal surveys on crime and delinquency are summarized in two tables. Table 1 shows surveys which have

TABLE 1

Longitudinal Surveys with More than One Contact

Principal Investigators	Sample
J. W. B. Douglas, M. E. J. Wadsworth (National Survey of Health and Development)—U.K.	5,362 children selected from all legitimate single births in England, Scotland, and Wales in one week of March 1946. Children or families contacted every 1–2 years since.
S. Glueck, E. T. Glueck—U.S.	510 men (average age 25) whose sentences in Massachusetts reformatory expired in 1921–22. Contacted 5, 10 and 15 years later.
S. Glueck, E. T. Glueck—U.S.	1,000 delinquents (average age 14) examined by Judge Baker Clinic in 1917–22. Contacted 5 and 15 years later.
S. Glueck, E. T. Glueck—U.S.	500 delinquents in Massachusetts correctional schools in 1939–44, and 500 matched nondelinquents. Contacted initially at average age 14, later at average ages 25 and 31.
S. R. Hathaway, E. D. Monachesi, R. D. Wirt, P. F. Briggs—U.S.	1,958 boys (average age 15) tested in Minneapolis in 1947–48 (88.5% of 9th grade school children in Minneapolis). Selected samples contacted 4 and 8 years later.
S. R. Hathaway, E. D. Monachesi—U.S.	5,701 boys (average age 15) tested in Minnesota schools in 1953–54 (28% of 9th grade school children in Minnesota). Selected samples contacted at average ages 19 and 28.
T. S. Langer, J. C. Gersten (Family Research Project)—U.S.	1,034 children aged 6–18 randomly selected in Manhattan, New York City. Mothers and about a quarter of the children interviewed in 1967–68 and again 5 years later. Similar study of second sample of 1,000 children aged 6–18 in households receiving aid to dependent children, in same area.
M. M. Lefkowitz, L. D. Eron, L. O. Walder—U.S.	875 children aged 8–9 interviewed in 1959–60 (3rd grade population of Columbia County, New York) and again 10 years later.
W. McCord, J. McCord, E. Powers (Cambridge-Somerville Study)—U.S.	325 boys (average age 10) chosen in 1937–39 in Massachusetts, nominated by schools as difficult or average. Given social work treatment for 5 years on average. Also nontreated group of 325. Attempted reinterview began in 1975.
F. J. W. Miller, S. D. M. Court (Thousand Families Study)—U.K.	1,142 children: all those born in Newcastle in May–June 1947. Children (and families) contacted at least once a year up to age 15, finally at age 22.
D. J. West, D. P. Farrington (Cambridge Study in Delinquent Development)—U.K.	411 boys aged 8–9 in 1961–62: all those of that age in 6 London schools. Boys contacted every 2 years up to age 21, families every year up to boy's age 15.

involved at least two contacts with the subjects or their families separated by at least five years. All are, at least in some respects, prospective. They vary from having only one initial and one follow-up contact (e.g., Langner, Gersten, and Eisenberg 1977; Lefkowitz et al. 1977) to having regular contacts over a period of ten years or more (e.g., Miller et al. 1974; Wadsworth 1979). Investigators who contact their subjects directly almost invariably supplement this with searches of records.

Table 2 presents major longitudinal surveys in which one interview is preceded, followed, or both, by a search in records. A survey is included in this table only if the sample was defined at one time and followed up at least five years later. Table 2 also includes surveys in which subjects were contacted more than once but the total period of contact, before the follow-up in records, was less than five years (e.g., Havighurst et al. 1962; Tait and Hodges 1971).[1]

Longitudinal surveys based entirely on records are much more common than those including interviews, and are too numerous to attempt to summarize in a table.

I. The Uses of Longitudinal Research in Crime and Delinquency

In discussing the advantages and uses of longitudinal surveys on crime and delinquency, I pay particular attention to prospective surveys involving direct contact with the subjects and frequent data collection. The longitudinal method has been used to study criminal careers, or the natural history and prevalence of delinquency at different ages. It has also been used in predicting the onset and ending of criminal careers, in investigating the effects of penal treatments on such careers, and in studying the transmission of criminality from one generation to the next. This section discusses important uses of longitudinal research and presents major findings.

[1] Reports of the projects listed in tables 1 and 2 can be found in the list of references under the names of the principal investigators. Surveys were included in the tables only if their reports contained significant information about crime and delinquency. The Appendix to this paper contains fuller details about the inclusion and exclusion of projects.

TABLE 2

Longitudinal Surveys with One Contact Only

Principal Investigators	Sample
M. M. Craig—U.S.	303 boys aged 5–6 in New York in 1952. Interviewed mothers, 10-year follow-up in records.
O. S. Dalgard, E. Kringlen —Norway	All male twins born 1921–30 in Norway. In 1966, tried to interview 139 with at least one member convicted.
I. Dootjes—Australia	388 boys aged 9–12 interviewed in 1957 and followed up in records to 1967.
M. Fitzsimons—U.S.	158 children referred by teachers for poor adjustment in Michigan in 1936–39. Tried to contact in 1954.
S. Glueck, E. T. Glueck— U.S.	500 women in Massachusetts reformatory whose parole expired 1921–24. Tried to contact 5 years later.
R. J. Havighurst, P. H. Bowman—U.S.	487 children in midwest city contacted at age 11–14 in 1951–54, followed up in records, by mail and by telephone to 1960.
E. F. Hodges, C. D. Tait (Maximum Benefits Project)—U.S.	179 children in 2 Washington schools given preventive casework, age 8–11 in 1954–57. Followed up in records to 1962.
S. A. Mednick, B. Hutchings—Denmark	1944 boys born in Copenhagen hospital 1936–38. Tried to interview selected samples more than 30 years later.
S. A. Mednick, B. Hutchings—Denmark	311 individuals intensively examined in 1962. Followed up in records for 13 years.
K. Polk—U.S.	1,227 high school boys (Pacific N.W. county) completing questionnaire in 1964. Subsamples interviewed in 1967. Followed up to the present, using postal questionnaires.
L. N. Robins—U.S.	524 children treated in St. Louis child guidance clinic in 1924–29, and 100 control public school children from the same period. Tried to interview more than 30 years later.
L. N. Robins—U.S.	235 black males born in St. Louis in 1930–34 and located in elementary school records. Tried to interview in 1965–66.
M. Roff—U.S.	40,000 children age 7–11 rated by peers and teachers in early 1960s (Minnesota and Texas). Followed up in delinquency records.
L. W. Shannon—U.S.	333 out of 1,352 children born in 1942, and 566 out of 2,099 children born in 1949, interviewed (Racine, Wis.). All followed up in records to 1973.
D. H. Stott, D. M. Wilson—U.K.	700 delinquents in Glasgow, Scotland, rated by teachers in 1957–59. Followed up in records to 1968.

J. R. Thurston, J. F. Feld-husen—U.S.	192 aggressive and 192 socially acceptable children identified by 3d, 6th, and 9th grade teachers in Eau Claire County, Wis., in 1961–62 and interviewed. Followed up in records for 10 years.
H. A. Witkin—Denmark	4,591 men born in Copenhagen 1944–47 with known heights at least 6 feet. Tried to interview at age 26.
M. E. Wolfgang, R. M. Figlio, T. Thornberry—U.S.	974 boys born in Philadelphia in 1945 (random sample of 9,945 residing there at least from age 10 to 18). Tried to interview at age 26, followed up in records from 7 to 30.

A. Prevalence

How prevalent are arrests and convictions? What proportion of the population experiences one or the other? No doubt because annually published figures show low incidences, it was assumed for many years that only a small minority of the population was convicted, even in high delinquency areas. Theorists were castigated because they predicted "too much" delinquency (see, e.g., Matza 1964). Longitudinal surveys have shown that a substantial minority of the male population has been or will be arrested or convicted, and that in some areas nonarrested or nonconvicted males are or will be the statistically deviant ones.

The British National Survey of Health and Development found that 18 percent of males and 2.5 percent of females were convicted or officially cautioned before their 21st birthdays (Douglas et al. 1966; Wadsworth 1979). The exclusion of minor traffic violations reduced the prevalence figure for males to 15 percent. Higher prevalence figures have been obtained in other British surveys. In their representative sample of children born in Newcastle in 1947, Miller et al. (1974) found that 22 percent of males and 3.7 percent of females had been convicted by their 17th birthdays. The Cambridge Study found that 20 percent of males were found guilty in court for the more serious (indictable and akin-to-indictable)[2] offenses by their 17th birthdays, and

[2] In England, indictable offenses are more serious than non-indictable ones, not unlike the distinction between felonies and misdemeanors in the United States. Akin-to-indictable offenses are non-indictable but are generally comparable to indictable offenses.

31 percent by their 21st birthdays (West and Farrington 1973, 1977).

In Philadelphia, Wolfgang (1973) found that 35 percent of a cohort of males were arrested before their 18th birthdays, and 43 percent before their 27th birthdays. There was a very marked racial differential. Fifty percent of the nonwhites and 29 percent of the whites were arrested by age 18. In another Philadelphia cohort study, in a high delinquency, predominantly black area, Savitz (1970) found that 59 percent of boys living in Philadelphia for the full period between their 7th and 18th birthdays had juvenile court records. In Wisconsin, Shannon (1978) discovered that almost 70 percent of males and 24 percent of females had at least one recorded police contact for a nontraffic offense by age 31.

Obtaining comparable rates in different countries is difficult because of differences in official processing. Unlike the United States, the vast majority of arrests of adults in England are followed by court appearances and convictions. In the Scandinavian countries, juvenile delinquency is dealt with by the child welfare authorities rather than by the police and courts. Perhaps because of this, the prevalence of official delinquency in these countries seems to be somewhat lower than in England or the United States. Janson (1977) followed up records of all 15,000 children born in 1953 and living in the Stockholm metropolitan area in 1963, and reported that 9 percent of the boys and 1 percent of the girls had an official delinquency record by age 16.

The prevalence of arrests and convictions can also be estimated by studying cohorts taken from official records published annually. One problem with official criminal statistics is that persons convicted in one year cannot be linked up with those convicted in another. Prevalence can, however, be estimated if the number of first offenders among those convicted at any given age in any given year is known. In studying the prevalence of juvenile convictions among males born in 1946, it would be necessary to add first convictions of 8-year-olds in 1954, 9-year-olds in 1955, and so on up to 16-year-olds in 1962. But this method is inferior in some ways to a true longitudinal survey of one cohort. The population of 8-year-olds in 1954 differs from the population of 16-year-olds in 1962, because of immigration, emigration, and deaths. Using the figures published annually by the (London) metropolitan police for people arrested for the first time at different ages for indictable offenses, Little (1965) followed up people born in 1942 and discovered that the prevalence of these arrests up to age 20 was 20 percent for males and 2.5 percent for females.

Prevalence can also be calculated by using criminal statistics for only one year. The prevalence of convictions up to age 20 in 1962 could be estimated by adding together the incidence of first convictions of 8-year-olds in 1962, 9-year-olds in 1962, and so on up to 20-year-olds in 1962. A major shortcoming of this method is that it produces a reliable estimate only if the incidence of convictions has remained constant over the years. Both in England and the United States, the incidence of convictions has increased substantially in the last twenty years. Little (1965) demonstrated that, for arrests of males up to age 20, the prevalence estimated from the 1962 statistics was 23 percent, and from the 1952 statistics was 15 percent. These figures can be contrasted with the 20 percent derived from the cohort born in 1942 and hence reaching age 20 in 1962. The longitudinal analysis gives the more accurate estimate; the cross-sectional analyses indicate that prevalence is increasing.

Using the 1965 English *Criminal Statistics*, McClintock and Avison (1968) estimated that the cumulative lifetime risk of a conviction for a more serious (indictable or akin-to-indictable) offense in England was 31 percent for males and 8 percent for females. These figures seem high. One problem with this kind of cross-sectional survey based entirely on records is that the information about who is or is not a first offender is often unreliable (Walker 1971). Many recidivists are probably recorded as first offenders, leading to a prevalence estimate which is too high. Perhaps because of this, the British Home Office ceased to publish annual figures for first offenders at each age in their supplementary statistics at about the time that the prevalence estimates of McClintock and Avison became known.

Even higher prevalence estimates have been obtained in the United States by studying one year's statistics. On the basis of the 1965 *Uniform Crime Reports*, Christensen (1967) estimated that the lifetime probability of being arrested for a nontraffic offense in the United States was 50 percent for males and 12 percent for females. The prevalence was higher for nonwhites than for whites, and higher in cities than in suburban or rural areas. Christensen estimated that more than 90 percent of nonwhite males living in cities would be arrested for a nontraffic offense during their lifetimes. Using Kentucky juvenile court records for 1960, Ball, Ross, and Simpson (1964) estimated the prevalence of court appearances for delinquency to be 20.7 percent for boys and 5.2 percent for girls, and Monahan (1960) obtained similar estimates from juvenile court records in Philadelphia (22.3 percent for boys, 6.0 percent for girls). Prevalence estimates obtained in Scandinavian countries by this method have generally been lower. On the basis of the 1968 criminal statistics for Denmark, Christiansen and Jensen (1972) estimated that the lifetime prevalence of convictions was 12 percent for males and between 1 percent and 2 percent for females.

Because of the doubtful assumptions which have to be made about the constancy of offending and about the proportion of convictions which are for first offenses, prevalence estimates derived from one year's statistics are less accurate than those obtained by following a cohort in a longitudinal survey. Wolfgang (1974, p. 79) has written that the main interest in his Philadelphia cohort study was to determine the probability of becoming officially recorded as a delinquent, because cross-sectional studies did not provide adequate estimates.

B. Peak Age

Longitudinal surveys can establish the peak age for arrests or convictions. This is usually between 15 and 18. The official criminal statistics show the peak age in each year, but that does not necessarily coincide with the peak age in any given cohort. In England, researchers (e.g., McKissack 1967, 1973) have noted that the peak age for convictions, as shown by the official statistics, often coincides with the last year of compulsory schooling, and it has been suggested that there is a causal relationship between them. Before World War II, when the minimum school leaving age was 14, the peak age for convictions was 13. In the postwar years, when the school leaving age was raised to 15, the peak age became 14. The school leaving age was raised to 16 in the 1970s, and the current peak age (when convictions and cautions for indictable offenses are added together) is 15 for males, although it is 14 for females (Home Office 1978). Because of an increasing tendency in the past ten years for the police to caution persons under 17 rather than prosecute them, the peak age for conviction is now 17 for both males and females. Approximately 7 males and 1 female per 100 aged 17 are convicted for serious offenses each year.

The boys in the Cambridge Study were mostly born in 1953, and so reached 14 in 1967, the last year in which the peak age for conviction in the official statistics was 14. However, the peak age for conviction in this sample was 18, with the next highest incidence at age 17 (West and Farrington 1973, 1977). This result would not have been different if cautions had been added to convictions, because these boys were juveniles at a time when police policy in London was to prosecute nearly all apprehended juvenile offenders rather than to administer official cautions. The disparity between the peak age and the school leaving age, which was 15 for most boys, casts doubt on the idea of a causal relationship between them.

Similar results would have been obtained if a cohort had been followed in the official statistics. The incidence of convictions of 14-year-old boys in 1967 (3.5 per 100) was less than that of 17-year-old boys in 1970 (5.9 per 100) and that of 18-year-old boys in 1971 (5.7 per 100). Again, this pattern is not substantially affected when cautions are added to convictions. As was true with prevalence, longitudinal results are different from cross-sectional results when the incidence of convictions is not steady over the years. Furthermore, in relation to the theory linking school leaving age and peak age, the longitudinal results are more relevant.

Finally, the peak age for first arrests or convictions may or may not coincide with the peak age for arrests or convictions. While the peak age for convictions in the Cambridge Study was 18, the peak age for first convictions was 14. In the Philadelphia cohort study of Wolfgang, Figlio, and Sellin (1972), the peak age for both arrests and first arrests was 16.

C. Delinquent Generations

Just as it has been argued that there is a peak age for delinquency, it has been suggested that there may be peak periods or generations. Using the official criminal statistics, Wilkins (1960) followed up cohorts of persons born in England between 1925 and 1949, and found that those born in 1939–40 showed unusually high conviction rates for indictable offenses at all ages (up to 1957). He argued that persons born between 1936 and 1942 were an unusually delinquent generation, and linked this to the experience of being a child during World War II. Similar results were later obtained in other countries, notably Denmark (Christiansen 1964), Poland (Jasinski 1966) and New Zealand (Slater, Darwin, and Richie 1966). However, Walters (1963) argued that Wilkins's results reflected two trends of the 1950s, namely, the increasing reluctance of the police to prosecute those aged 8–11, and the increasing conviction rates of those aged 17–20. When later criminal statistics became available, Rose (1968) showed that the trends identified by Walters were continuing, and that the generation born during and just before World War II was not unusually delinquent. The major problem was to decide whether trends in criminal statistics reflected changes in police policies or in offending behavior, and this was impossible on the basis of the statistics alone.

D. Juvenile Delinquency and Adult Crime

What is the relationship between juvenile delinquency and adult crime? The question has important implications for crime control policy. Retrospective studies of persistent adult criminals (e.g., Hammond and Chayen 1963; Taylor 1960; West 1963) suggest that a substantial proportion had no juvenile or early

adult convictions. If this is true, then perhaps we need not officially process so many juvenile offenders, especially in view of
the negative effects of contact with the juvenile justice system
(e.g., Farrington 1977; Gold 1970). However, studies of adult
criminals are limited by the unreliability and unavailability of
earlier records. Prospective longitudinal surveys are needed to
establish the relationship between juvenile and adult delinquency,
and the prevalence of "latecomers to crime."

The Cambridge Study (Farrington 1979a; Farrington and West
1979) found that 61 percent of the juvenile official delinquents
were reconvicted as young adults (i.e., before their 21st birthdays). In contrast, only 13 percent of those who were not convicted as juveniles were convicted as young adults. From the
reverse perspective, 46 percent of convicted young adults had not
been convicted as juveniles. Comparable figures have been obtained in the United States. In a long-term Chicago survey of boys
making their first juvenile court appearance in 1920, McKay
(1967) found that 60 percent were arrested as adults, including
40 percent who were convicted. A Detroit survey of boys born
in 1941 (Chaitin and Dunham 1966) showed that 40 percent of
juvenile delinquents were reconvicted before age 21. In Philadelphia, Wolfgang (1973, 1974) discovered that 44 percent of
juvenile delinquents were rearrested before age 27, and conversely
that 34 percent of adult offenders had not been arrested as juveniles.

The Cambridge Study found that the number of juvenile convictions was significantly related to the number of adult convictions (West and Farrington 1977). However, nearly a quarter
of those with two or more adult convictions had not had juvenile
convictions. As others have shown (e.g., Sellin 1958; Wolf 1965),
boys first convicted at the earliest ages tended to become the most
persistent offenders as adults. The small group first convicted
between ages 10 and 12 averaged more than six convictions by their
21st birthdays, and half were still being reconvicted at age 19
or 20. These results may suggest that prevention and treatment
efforts should be concentrated on those boys who begin their
criminal careers early in life.

E. Transition Probabilities in Criminal Careers

Whether juvenile delinquency leads to adult crime is part of a more general question about the probability of one conviction being followed by another. On the basis of the 1962 English *Criminal Statistics*, Little (1965) calculated that, for males under age 21, the probability of a first conviction was 16 percent; the probability of a second conviction following a first was 21 percent; the probability of a third following a second was 47 percent; and the probability of a fourth following a third was 61 percent. The same pattern of steeply rising probabilities is seen in the eleven-year records follow-up of persons convicted in London in 1957 (Home Office 1969). The percentage reconvicted within five years was 36 percent after the first conviction, 57 percent after the second, 61 percent after the third, 71 percent after the fourth, rising to 83 percent after sixteen or more convictions. This percentage decreased with age. For example, 50 percent of first offenders under age 14 were reconvicted within five years, in comparison with 30 percent of first offenders aged 21–29 and only 9 percent of those aged 40 or more. Wolfgang (1974) obtained similar figures in the United States. The probability of a first arrest was 35 percent; of a second arrest following a first was 54 percent; of a third arrest following a second was 65 percent; the figure was between 70 percent and 80 percent for subsequent arrests.

Any theory of criminal careers must explain these kinds of figures. One possibility is that some aspect of official processing makes people more likely to commit crimes, or to be prosecuted for them, in the future. Another is that a "selective weeding" process is operating, identifying a progressively more criminal group after each arrest or conviction. One methodological problem is that these probabilities should be calculated by reference to the time spent in the community at risk. However, establishing the time spent incarcerated by any offender is seldom easy. It is probably easier to determine in a prospective longitudinal survey than in a retrospective search of records.

F. Specialization in Criminal Careers

Do most offenders specialize in particular kinds of offenses? The Cambridge Study found little evidence of specialization in criminal careers, at least to age 21. The vast majority of youths convicted of violence or vandalism or drug offenses also had convictions for dishonesty (West and Farrington 1977).[3] Our results are not unusual. Another English study (McClintock 1963) reported that nearly half of those first convicted for a violent offense had previous convictions for nonviolent offenses, and the same was true for 80 percent of those sustaining a second conviction for violence. In a study of convictions for violence in London and Scotland, Walker, Hammond, and Steer (1967) concluded that most were an occupational risk of a career of nonviolent crime. But in a smaller survey Peterson, Pittman, and O'Neal (1962) found that males aged 40 or more, arrested in St. Louis in 1958, tended to specialize in offenses against property or against the person.

Mott (1973), in her survey of juvenile drug offenders in the London courts, found that only 2 percent of their previous offenses involved drugs. In retrospective searches of records covering more than twenty years, Soothill and Pope (1973) found that very few arsonists had previous or subsequent convictions for arson. Most had previous or subsequent convictions for crimes of dishonesty. The same was true of rapists (Soothill, Jack, and Gibbens 1976), incest offenders (Gibbens, Soothill, and Way 1978), and other serious sex offenders (Soothill and Gibbens 1978). In similar Danish research, Christiansen et al. (1965) found that sex offenders were more likely to have been convicted of previous or subsequent property offenses than previous or subsequent sex offenses.

The most sophisticated investigations of offense specialization were carried out in Philadelphia (Wolfgang, Figlio, and Sellin 1972; Thornberry and Figlio 1978). They showed that the probability of committing the same type of crime twice in a row

---

[3] We were unable to reach any conclusion about sex offenders. Too few appeared in our sample.

did not change with the number of previous offenses, and that the probability of committing any type of crime did not depend on the type of crime committed on the last occasion. These results suggest that there is little point in attempting to derive simple typologies of offenders on the basis of their patterns of offending.

G. Use of Official Records in Studying Criminal Careers

How reliable are official records? Longitudinal research including self-report studies provides a measure. A major problem with the studies discussed above is that they are based on official records. Several problems of retrospective surveys based on official records are discussed in Section II. Suffice it to say that reliance solely on official records raises serious difficulties. To investigate the prevalence of different kinds of crimes at different ages, and the natural history of delinquency, we need longitudinal surveys which include self-reported delinquency measures taken at regular intervals (e.g., every year from age 10 to age 20). Annual interviews may be too infrequent in studying offenses which are committed very often, but more frequent interviews may be more difficult to arrange in practice and may be more susceptible to conscious efforts by subjects to mislead or to repeat earlier statements.

Self-reported delinquency was measured in the Cambridge Study at ages 14, 16, 18, and 21, but these measures were not all comparable. At ages 14 and 16, the boys were asked to admit an offense if they had committed it at any time up to the interview. It was hardly surprising, therefore, that more offenses were admitted at age 16, but it was not possible to say whether the rate or type of offending per year was different at age 16 from age 14. The measures at ages 18 and 21 were more comparable to each other, since the boys were asked about offenses committed in the previous three and two years respectively. The rate of offending decreased significantly from age 18 to age 21 (Knight, Osborn, and West 1977). The declining incidence of convictions of males after age 18 could reflect a decrease in offending, or merely changed patterns of offending (e.g., committing less detectable thefts from work rather than more detectable ones from shops), or police policies (e.g., in patrolling areas where adolescents rather than adults were committing offenses). Our results suggest that, whatever else is happening, there is a genuine decrease in offending after age 18, although we have not progressed very far in explaining why this decrease occurs.

Similarly, continuity between juvenile and adult convictions could reflect continuity in offending or continuity in police policies, in selecting certain families or certain areas for special attention. The Cambridge Study found continuity in offending, but also found that convictions were followed by an increase in offending (Farrington 1977; Farrington, Osborn, and West 1978). Versatility or specialization in convictions could reflect offending behavior or police prosecution policies. Judging from the accounts given by our youths, the police were reluctant to charge them with violent behavior, even for assaulting a policeman. Whether a youth is arrested for a crime of dishonesty may depend on whether he reacts violently toward a policeman, but the tendency to charge the youth only with the crime of dishonesty may hide the true extent of specialization in violent behavior. Against the idea of specialization, cross-sectional self-reported delinquency research (e.g., Farrington 1973, Hindelang 1971) shows versatility in offending.

Perhaps the most impressive demonstrations of the versatility of deviant behavior, and of its continuity from childhood to adulthood, can be found in Robins's (1966, 1978a) longitudinal surveys. In her thirty-year follow-up of children referred to a child guidance clinic in St. Louis, she found that the children stole, were truants, ran away from home, were aggressive, enuretic, disciplinary problems in school, pathological liars, and so on. As adults, they tended to be arrested, divorced, placed in mental hospitals, alcoholics, sexually promiscuous, vagrants, bad debtors, poor workers, and so on. She also found that the diagnosis of antisocial personality in adults was never made in the absence of marked antisocial behavior before age 18.

Such results suggest that it may be a mistake to try to study delinquent behavior by reliance on official criminal records in isolation from other kinds of deviance. The Cambridge Study found that those convicted up to age 18 tended to be deviant in many respects. Many were sexually promiscuous, heavy drinkers, heavy smokers, drug users, heavy gamblers, very aggressive, had motoring convictions, and had unstable, low status job histories (West and Farrington 1977). We also found a great deal of continuity in deviant behavior, notably in aggressiveness (Farrington 1978). Other longitudinal surveys (e.g., Kagan and Moss 1962; Lefkowitz et al. 1977; Tuddenham 1959) also indicate that males who are aggressive at one age tend to be aggressive at another. The study of deviant careers may be more fruitful than the study of criminal careers and can best be done in longitudinal studies including interviews and self-reports. Research which relies solely on official criminal records may mislead and in any event will miss the continuities between delinquent acts and other deviant behavior.

H. Predicting the Onset of Convictions

Longitudinal surveys have also been used in attempts to develop methods for predicting the beginning of criminal careers, or the onset of official delinquency among nondelinquents. Toby (1965) distinguished between two methods of prediction, which he called extrapolative and circumstantial. Extrapolative predictions are based on continuities in behavior rather than on any theory about the causes of delinquency. Circumstantial predictions are based on theories about the circumstances which produce delinquency.

The best known circumstantial method of predicting the onset of delinquency was proposed by the Gluecks (1950) on the basis of a retrospective comparison of 500 institutionalized delinquents and 500 nonconvicted youths. The "Glueck Social Prediction Table" suggests that delinquency can be predicted by a combination of five social background factors: discipline of the boy by the father, supervision of the boy by the mother, affection of the father for the boy, affection of the mother for the boy, and the cohesiveness of the family. A number of longitudinal surveys have been carried out to assess the accuracy of this method. The New

York City Youth Board Project (Craig and Glick 1963; Craig and Budd 1967), the Maximum Benefits Project (Hodges and Tait 1963; Tait and Hodges 1971; Trevvett 1965), and the Australian study by Dootjes (1972) indicate that the Glueck Social Prediction Table has some predictive power, but not as much as claimed by the Gluecks. Some problems of these researches have been summarized by Kahn (1965), Venezia (1971), and Weis (1974).

Two longitudinal surveys directed by Hathaway and Monachesi (1957, 1963) show that responses given on the Minnesota Multiphasic Personality Inventory can fairly accurately predict official delinquency and other events such as dropping out of school. This does not necessarily mean that future delinquents differ in personality from future nondelinquents. Because some of the most predictive items are factual statements about getting into trouble in the past, the results may merely reflect continuity in behavior, or continuity in attracting negative reactions.

The longitudinal surveys of Feldhusen, Thurston, and Benning (1973) and of Fitzsimons (1958) show that children rated by teachers as aggressive or disruptive are particularly likely to be convicted later. Surveys based on cumulative school records by Conger and Miller (1966) and Khleif (1964) also show that negative comments by teachers identify children who become official delinquents. A Yugoslavian study, in which 2,615 children were rated by teachers and peers in 1955 and followed up in criminal records to 1962 (Skaberne et al. 1965), also found that children rated as behavior problems in school tended to be convicted later. Similar results were obtained by the Cambridge Study (West and Farrington 1973) and the National Survey of Health and Development (Mulligan et al. 1963).

The Cambridge Study found that a large number of factors measured before age 10 were predictive of future convictions, particularly low family income, large family size, criminal parents, poor parental child-rearing behavior, and low I.Q. These factors were additive, in the sense that the more adversities a boy possessed the more likely he was to be convicted. Similar results were obtained by Robins and Hill (1966) in their follow-up of black men in St. Louis. Educational retardation, low socioeconomic status, and truancy were additive in the prediction of delinquency.

Another important prediction question which can be investigated in longitudinal surveys with interviews is whether particular factors predict delinquent behavior (as measured by self-report) more accurately than convictions. The Cambridge Study found that official and self-reported delinquency were quite closely related; the predictors of one were quite similar to the predictors of the other, although there were some differences. While having criminal parents was highly related to both official and self-reported delinquency, other factors were better predictors of official delinquency (Farrington 1979a). While several factors appear related to the likelihood of being selected for official processing, having criminal parents was also independently related to the likelihood of committing offenses.

I. Predicting Recidivism

Attempts have been made in longitudinal surveys to predict recidivism and to investigate the course of criminal careers after official processing. The Gluecks were pioneers in this kind of research (1930, 1934a, 1934b, 1937, 1940, 1943, 1968). Unfortunately, they are perhaps best known for *Unraveling Juvenile Delinquency* (1950), which was not a longitudinal survey and which appeared to make exaggerated claims about the accuracy with which delinquency can be predicted. In the context of the 1930s and 1940s, the first three of their longitudinal surveys provided detailed, valuable information about the after-careers of persons released from penal institutions or processed by the juvenile courts. Their attempts to interview men and women between 5 and 15 years after release should be commended, even if their results, in showing a high proportion of recidivists, were depressing to many at that time.

The very long term follow-up studies by Soothill and Gibbens (e.g., 1978) show a low specific recidivism rate for arson and sex offenses, and also show that reconvictions can be long delayed. As many as one-quarter of all recidivist sex offenders were not reconvicted until at least ten years after their original offenses. These results suggest that the common follow-up period of two or three years in reconviction studies based on criminal records may be unduly short. There have been many short-term prediction studies, including prisoners or parolees (e.g., Glaser 1962; Gough, Wenk, and Rosynko 1965; Nuttall et al. 1977; Sinclair and Chapman 1973), juvenile court first offenders (e.g., Hutcheson et al. 1966), probationers (e.g., Stott 1964), institutionalized juveniles (e.g., Ganzer and Sarason 1973) and Borstal inmates (e.g., Mannheim and Wilkins 1955). There is a widespread belief that almost all offenders who are going to be reconvicted will be within five years, and mostly within two years (see, e.g., Brody 1976). The research of Soothill and Gibbens shows that this is not always true. Furthermore, Dunlop (1974) found that the recidivism rates of juvenile institutions began to differ only two and a half years after the boys had been released, and were significantly different after five years. Short follow-up periods may be suitable if the effects of treatment are thought to be short-lived, but Dunlop's research suggests that this is not always the case.

One problem with a short follow-up period is the delay which can occur between committing an offense and being convicted. In the Cambridge Study, fourteen of our ninety-four young adult delinquents experienced a delay of more than six months between commission and conviction for at least one offense. Six of these had a delay of more than nine months, and in two cases there was a one-year delay. Most delays resulted from delays in legal processes, often involving a series of remands, rather than in detection. Delays are usually associated with serious offenses which are referred to higher courts, so it is not inconceivable in a two-year reconviction study that some of the more serious offenders will be classified as "reformed" because they are still waiting to appear in the higher courts.

Among the longer term studies of reconviction, special mention might be made of the follow-up over more than twenty years of prisoners serving life sentences in Finland (Anttila and Westling 1965), the ten-year follow-up of young prisoners in Finland by

Virkkunen (1976), the eight-year follow-up of parolees in the United States by Gottfredson and Ballard (1965), and the five-year follow-up of young prisoners in Holland by Buikhuisen and Hoekstra (1974). All were based entirely on records. Virkkunen found that those who were reconvicted were particularly likely to have experienced the death of a father during adolescence, and Buikhuisen and Hoekstra found that those who were reconvicted were less likely to have changed residence after returning to the community. Anttila and Westling showed that their prisoners, most of whom had been convicted of murder, committed only ten new homicides in more than 4,000 man-years of freedom, almost exactly the same rate of homicides as they committed while incarcerated. One problem in comparing their figures, of course, is that those incarcerated and those released were not comparable groups. Only 2 out of 542 succeeded in escaping permanently, and the average time spent in prison was thirteen years. Clearly, any study of prisoners serving life sentences needs to extend over a very long period.

The Cambridge Study has gradually shifted attention from factors which predict the onset of conviction careers to factors which predict their ending. In particular, one series of analyses (Knight and West 1975; Osborn and West 1978) investigated how far it was possible to identify who, among those who were official recidivists before age 19, would be convicted again before age 23. As might have been expected, the most obvious difference between the "persistent" and "temporary" recidivists was that the persistent recidivists had more serious prior conviction records. Persistent recidivists were also more likely to come from large, low-income families, and to have criminal parents. Furthermore, they were rated as more "antisocial" at age 18, in displaying a variety of behaviors such as sexual promiscuity, heavy gambling and smoking, driving after drinking, and aggression. These results show the lasting predictive power of some of the earliest life experiences and the importance of later deviant life styles.

J. Effects of Penal Treatment

Longitudinal surveys are also useful in investigating the effects of particular events or life experiences on the course of development. A central question in criminology concerns the effects of different penal treatments on criminal careers. Unfortunately, the research which has been carried out so far is rather uninformative, because of its concentration on official criminal records. What is needed is a measure of the change in the offending rate between a certain period (e.g., three years) before the penal treatment and the same period after. The change following one penal treatment should then be compared with the change following another, preferably in an experiment in which detected offenders are randomly allocated to the two treatments. What most studies of penal treatments have measured in the past is the occurrence of at least one conviction during a follow-up period. What they should be trying to measure is a decrease in offending, from (say) 1,000 crimes in the three years before conviction to 500 in the three years after. Furthermore, in order to achieve a fair comparison of penal treatments, the whole period after a court disposal should be counted, regardless of whether the offender is in the community. Were this done, prison sentences might prove to be more effective in reducing offending by convicted persons (at least against members of the public) than noninstitutional sentences. In order to find no difference, there would have to be a dramatic increase in offending after release from prison to compensate for the dramatic decrease which occurs while the offender is incarcerated.

Most comparisons of penal treatment which have had long follow-up periods have compared groups which were not exactly equivalent. A Home Office (1969) follow-up of persons convicted in London in 1957 found that fines were followed by fewer reconvictions within the next five years than any other penal treatment. However, those receiving fines were matched statistically with those receiving other sanctions only by age, type of current offense, and number of previous offenses. There were many uncontrolled differences between these groups, other than the differing sanctions, which might have caused the differing reconviction rates. Similar comments apply to comparisons between probation and other disposals carried out in Australia by Kraus (1974a, 1974b), which had five-year follow-up periods, and to a comparison between open and closed prisons in Finland by Uusitalo (1972), with a ten-year follow-up period.

The only way to ensure that offenders receiving one penal treatment are comparable to those receiving another is to randomly allocate offenders to the two treatments. However, most random allocation experiments have had only short follow-up periods.[4] The Community Treatment Program (Palmer 1971) had a five-year follow-up period, but the criterion of effectiveness used in it (favorable or unfavorable discharge) reflected the discretionary decision-making behavior of adults rather than the offending behavior of the youth, as Lerman (1975) has shown.[5]

In some ways the most interesting random allocation project is the Provo Experiment (Empey and Erickson 1972), because it included measures of offending in the four years before treatment and in the four years after, for control and experimental groups. However, the measure of offending was based on official records, and the "treatment" was so complex and diffuse that it would have been impossible to know which aspect of it had been effective if the experimental group had proved to be significantly less delinquent subsequently than the control group. As in most studies of penal treatments using random allocation, the experimental and control groups did not have significantly different official histories after the treatment.

The Cambridge Study attempted to investigate the impact of penal processing by studying self-reported delinquency before and after convictions (Farrington 1977; Farrington, Osborn, and West 1978). This research was unusual in that a convicted group was compared with an unconvicted group. In most treatment experiments, one variety of a treatment has been compared with another variety of the same treatment, rather than with a quite different treatment or no treatment. This is probably one of the reasons for the preponderance of negative results. For example,

[4] E.g., Berg et al. (1978); Cornish and Clarke (1975); Empey and Lubeck (1971); Folkard, Smith, and Smith (1976); Fowles (1978); Jesness (1971b); Kassebaum, Ward, and Wilner (1971); Reimer and Warren (1957); Rose and Hamilton (1970); Shaw (1974); Venezia (1972).

[5] Berntsen and Christiansen (1965) and Jesness (1971a) also carried out random allocation experiments with follow-up periods of at least five years.

Kassebaum, Ward, and Wilner (1971) compared small and large group counseling and no counseling within a prison. That all the subjects were in the same California prison was probably overwhelming in comparison with any differential effects of the different treatments.

One disadvantage of the Cambridge Study's investigation is that it was a quasi-experiment rather than a random allocation experiment. Youths who were first convicted between ages 14 and 18 were matched on self-reported delinquency at age 14 with youths not convicted up to age 18, and a similar analysis was carried out between ages 18 and 21. Although results obtained in quasi-experiments are less conclusive than those obtained in genuine experiments, random allocation is often impossible and the quasi-experiment is the next best method. Criminologists should try to carry out more quasi-experimental analyses, paying careful attention to Campbell and Stanley (1966). The Cambridge Study's analyses showed that, both between ages 14 and 18 and between ages 18 and 21, youths who were convicted became more delinquent than those who were not.

K. Effects of Events on Development

Few criminological researchers have taken advantage of the potentialities of longitudinal surveys in investigating the effects of discrete events on the course of development. The Cambridge Study carried out a number of quasi-experimental analyses besides that just mentioned. Farrington (1972) investigated the effects on delinquency rates of going to different schools. As might have been expected, boys going to high delinquency rate secondary schools at age 11 were more likely to be convicted than those going to low delinquency rate schools. However, the differing prevalence of convictions between the schools could be largely explained by their differing intakes. Generally speaking, the high delinquency secondary schools received boys who had been troublesome in their primary schools, while the low delinquency schools received boys who had been well behaved. The same result was obtained when truancy rates were studied (Farrington 1979b).

The Cambridge Study also investigated the effects of early marriage on delinquency (Knight, Osborn, and West 1977). Marriage has often been invoked as the reason for the observed decrease in convictions after age 18, and indeed as the most effective treatment for delinquency. The Cambridge Study found that both official and self-reported delinquency decreased between ages 18 and 21. Men who married during this period were compared with those who stayed single, to see if the married group decreased more. The groups did not differ in official or self-reported delinquency at age 21, even after attempts were made to match them up to the date of the marriage. It was also possible to repeat this analysis with the boys' fathers, to see if those who married at an early age decreased their convictions during the following three years. Once again, no effect of marriage could be detected. However, current work in progress, based on men who married at a later age, suggests that marriage may lead to a reduction in convictions.

Longitudinal studies should make more use of opportunities to test the effects of nonpenal events on future delinquency.

L. Testing Biological Theories of Etiology

Several cohort studies have been carried out in the Scandinavian countries to investigate biological theories, and especially the importance of hereditary factors in relation to crime. Christiansen (1968, 1974) followed up all twin pairs born in Denmark in 1881–1910, where both twins survived at least until age 15, the age of criminal responsibility in Denmark. He found that, when one twin had been convicted, the other was much more likely to have also been convicted if they were identical twins than if they were fraternal twins. This result suggests a hereditary component in criminal behavior. However, Dalgard and Kringlen (1976) followed up all male twins born in Norway in 1921–30 and tried to interview pairs containing at least one convicted. They found that, while identical twins were more similar in convictions than fraternal twins, the similarity depended on their subjective feeling of closeness and mutual identity. Fraternal twins who felt similar to each other were just as similar in their conviction records as identical twins. Dalgard and Kringlen concluded that similarity in heredity was less important in relation to crime than similarity in environmental treatment. This research shows the advantages of combining records and interviews in testing biological theories.

Hutchings and Mednick (1974, 1975) followed up all males born in Copenhagen in 1927–41 and adopted by someone outside the biological family. They compared the conviction records of the adoptees with the conviction records of their biological and adoptive fathers and found close relationships in both cases. Since there was generally little direct contact between the son and his biological father, these results suggested that both hereditary and environmental factors influenced conviction records.

In another study which demonstrates the richness of the Danish records for longitudinal research, Witkin et al. (1976) followed up all males born in Copenhagen between 1944 and 1947. The Danish national register provided their current addresses at age 26, and the draft boards, to which all men were required to report by age 26, provided information about their adult heights. The major aim was to investigate the relationship between convictions and XXY and XYY chromosome abnormalities, both of which are known to be more prevalent among tall men. More than 4,500 males with heights exceeding 6 feet were identified, and attempts were made to visit every one of these to take blood samples and buccal smears to determine chromosomal constitution. This determination was made successfully in 91 percent of cases, although only sixteen XXY and twelve XYY males were found. The XYY males were particularly likely to have been convicted.

M. Transmission of Criminality between Generations

Longitudinal research is useful in investigating transmission of criminality from one generation to the next. Ideally, such a study should begin with one generation and follow the next generation of their children from birth onward. One of the few projects which has investigated two successive generations from birth is the National Survey of Health and Development (Wadsworth 1979). Efforts have been made to collect comparable information about both generations, but little information about the transmission of delinquency has yet emerged. More relevant is the follow-up of black men and their children carried out in St. Louis by Robins, West, and Herjanic (1975). The men were originally identified in elementary school records, and attempts were made to interview them between ages 30 and 36. Information about their wives and children was obtained during these interviews, and the children were then followed up in records. As might have been expected, it was found that convicted parents tended to have convicted children. Furthermore, a comparison between the juvenile records of parents and children showed similar rates and types of offenses.

Other researchers have also compared the criminal records of parents and children (e.g., Kirkegaard-Sorensen and Mednick 1975; Mednick and Hutchings 1978). However, very few have supplemented these record searches with interviews. The Cambridge Study (Farrington, Gundry, and West 1975) found, as others have, that convicted fathers and mothers tended to have convicted children. Indeed, the concentration of convictions in some families was remarkable, with 5 percent of the families accounting for half of the convictions. This result is reminiscent of Wolfgang's (1974) demonstration in his Philadelphia cohort that 6 percent of the boys committed 52 percent of the offenses.

In investigating why convicted fathers had convicted sons, we found no evidence that the convicted fathers directly encouraged their sons to commit crimes or taught them criminal techniques. The major difference between convicted and unconvicted fathers was that the convicted fathers exercised poor supervision over their sons. There was some evidence that the sons of criminal fathers were more likely to be convicted, over and above their increased likelihood of committing delinquent acts (as measured by self-reports). It may be that, when the police catch a youth committing an offense, and know that he comes from a family containing other convicted persons, they are more likely to prosecute and secure a conviction than in other cases. This factor, and the poor supervision, were the major links we could find in the chain between convicted fathers and convicted sons.

The most common use of longitudinal information, especially that derived from official records, is to study the development of criminal careers. Few researchers have attempted to fit their data to explicit mathematical models of criminal careers, as developed by such people as Blumstein and Larson (1971) or Carr-Hill and Payne (1971). Longitudinal data has also been used in predicting delinquency and recidivism, and in evaluating the effects of penal treatments, but few researchers have attempted to develop explicit causal models (e.g., after Blalock 1964) or to use techniques like path analysis, as did Lefkowitz et al. (1977). Robins and Wish (1977) carried out one of the most thoughtful causal analyses with nonexperimental data. Few researchers have attempted explicitly quasi-experimental analyses after Campbell and Stanley (1966). Few have attempted cohort analysis, as described by Glenn (1977), although some have collected data which might be susceptible to this (e.g., Langner, Gersten, and Eisenberg 1977). Generally, an increase in methodological sophistication is needed in order to realize fully the potentialities of longitudinal data.

II. Methodological Problems

This section reviews some of the methodological problems associated with longitudinal research, notably the relative advantages of longitudinal and cross-sectional designs, of prospective and retrospective research, and of official records versus interviews. It also discusses sample size, practical problems such as obtaining long-term funding and keeping track of subjects, and some ethical issues.

A. Longitudinal versus Cross-Sectional Research

Many methods can profitably be employed in criminological research. The longitudinal method is especially appropriate for certain research issues. This section discusses a few major differences between longitudinal and cross-sectional research. The comparative advantages and disadvantages of longitudinal and cross-sectional research can best be illustrated by reference to a specific problem. In using a cross-sectional method to investigate changes in attitudes which occur during the course of imprisonment, comparisons might be made between prisoners who were just starting their sentences and groups who had served one, three, or five years. In studying this problem longitudinally, one group of prisoners who seemed likely to serve at least five years could be followed up and tested just after starting their sentences and after serving one, three, and five years.

A major problem with the cross-sectional method is to establish that any observed differences between the groups were not due to selection effects, or to differences which were present before imprisonment. In controlling for selection effects, it would be necessary to obtain four groups of prisoners who were exactly equivalent at the start of their sentences. This would be very difficult. The longitudinal method avoids this problem by following one group, so that each prisoner acts as his own control. It is possible to use more sensitive matched pair or one sample statistics with the longitudinal method. A related problem is mortality, or loss of subjects, which could lead to the group tested at five years being substantially different in composition from that tested immediately after sentence. This could be controlled in the longitudinal method by restricting the analysis to prisoners who were tested at all four stages. The extent to which this group was representative of the original sample could be investigated, and it would be possible to adjust the results so that they were applicable to the original sample.

One problem which arises in the longitudinal but not in the cross-sectional method is the testing effect, or the effect of being interviewed once on the responses given in a second test. It would be possible to control for this or estimate the magnitude of its effects by testing only a subsample of the original group on each occasion. Few criminological researchers have tried to control for testing effects in the past. In the National Survey of Health and Development (Douglas 1970), children seen regularly in the survey were compared with those born in the same week but only contacted once. There proved to be little difference between these groups in public examination results at age 16. This suggested that frequent contacts had little effect, at least on this measure. Problems of changes in measuring instruments are also likely to be more important in longitudinal research.

The validity and reliability of the measures are equally a problem in both kinds of research. It is possible to discriminate changes from random fluctuations if measurements are taken at three or more times (Heise 1969), but statistical regression to the mean needs to be investigated in longitudinal research. It is necessary to control for maturation or aging in both kinds of research. In a longitudinal study, it might be necessary to have a control group of nonprisoners matched at least on age at the beginning of the research. This would also control for the effects of living during a particular time period.

It is impossible to separate maturation and period effects in one longitudinal project. In the Cambridge Study, the proportion of boys who admitted that they had taken illegal drugs increased from 0.5 percent at age 14 (in 1967) to 6.3 percent at age 16 (in 1969) and 31.4 percent at age 18 (in 1971). This increase could have been caused by increasing age or by changes occurring during the period 1967–71. The period effects were probably more important. Gold and Reimer (1975) found that admitted drug use by American boys aged 13–16 increased by 10 times between 1967 and 1972. In order to separate maturation and period effects, it would be necessary to study more than one cohort. One advantage of longitudinal research is that it is usually easier to solve the problem of causal order, although this depends on the frequency of data collection.

For many topics, a combination of cross-sectional and longitudinal research would often be ideal. However, cross-sectional research is much more common. Most studies of the effects of incarceration in penal institutions are cross-sectional (e.g., Banister et al. 1973; Bauer 1976; Hautaluoma and Scott 1973). The only longitudinal survey of the effects of incarceration which I have found involves only two measurements and a total period of only nineteen months (Bolton et al. 1976). Although, as the foregoing discussion indicates, both longitudinal and cross-sectional research have their advantages, it seems clear that more longitudinal research is needed in criminology.

B. Prospective versus Retrospective Research

Although prospective research presents practical difficulties, its advantage, at least when combined with frequent data collection, is that events can be recorded soon after they happen, before they can be distorted by retrospective reinterpretation in the light of later occurrences. Wadsworth (1979) has reviewed a number of noncriminological studies which indicate the importance of retrospective bias. Consciously or unconsciously, people distort past events in order to make sense of the present state of affairs. In his foreword to Wadsworth's book (1979), Douglas states that they "did not set out to test specific hypotheses since existing theories of development relied largely or exclusively only on remembered information which was known to be faulty and biased."

More research is needed to establish the precise nature and extent of retrospective bias in criminological investigations, so that workers can make an informed decision about when a prospective design is necessary. The nearest approach to this research is probably the "reverse record check" used in victim surveys (e.g., Sparks, Genn, and Dodd 1977). A prospective design is likely to be uneconomic if the phenomenon of interest is very rare, such as convictions for rape in England. Retrospective bias is likely to be more of a problem with more subjective, less factual information.

C. Official Records versus Interviews

Longitudinal research on crime and delinquency has usually employed data from official records, notably police, school, medical, and institutional case histories. Occasionally there is direct contact between the subjects, or their families, and the researchers, or persons assisting the researchers, by means of interviews, tests, or other kinds of measurements. Investigators who make direct contact with families almost invariably supplement this with searches of records.

Records of relatively objective events, such as court appearances, can be very useful in checking and supplementing information collected in interviews. In a check on the validity of interviews carried out in the Cambridge Study, West and Farrington (1977) found that only 6 out of 101 delinquents failed to admit any court appearances which had been located in records, and conversely that only 7 out of 288 nondelinquents claimed to have made court appearances which could not be found in records. These results increased our confidence in the interview data.

The advantage of official records is that they are immediately and cheaply available. They can cover a lengthy period, and the information is often recorded contemporaneously with events, before later outcomes of interest (such as convictions or reconvictions) are known. This minimizes the problem of retrospective bias, although this bias may operate when the coding or extraction of data from records is done after outcomes are known. The information in records is often fuller than can be obtained in a typical social survey interview lasting one hour, but voluminous information can create problems for the researcher, in deciding what details to extract and in the time which it can take to read through a lengthy case history to discover the answers to a small number of questions.

One of the most widely recognized disadvantages of criminal records is that they form a rather biased and underrepresentative sample of the true number of criminal or delinquent acts which have been committed. Self-report surveys indicate that somewhere between 3 and 15 percent of all offenses result in a police contact, depending on the people reporting, the offenses, and the definition of police contact.[6] Victim surveys indicate that recorded crimes form the tip of a very large iceberg (e.g., Ennis 1970 in the United States; Sparks, Genn, and Dodd 1977 in Great Britain). However, self-report surveys show that those who have been arrested or convicted tend to have committed the most delinquent acts, even before these people were officially processed. This suggests that criminal records can be used more validly to identify the most delinquent minority than to estimate the prevalence of delinquency.

[6] See, e.g., Elliott and Voss (1974), Erickson and Empey (1963), and Gold (1970) in the United States; West and Farrington (1977) in Great Britain; Elmhorn (1965) in Denmark.

Depending on the researcher's aims, that records are collected for the use of administrators rather than for researchers may be a disadvantage (see, e.g., Belson and Hood 1968). Records may be more useful in studying the administration of justice than criminal behavior.

A major problem, at least for researchers based outside agencies or institutions, is often to get access to the records in the first place. Academic researchers rarely protest publicly about the difficulties they encounter in obtaining access, perhaps because they are afraid of jeopardizing their future prospects of cooperation from official agencies. Nevertheless, these difficulties can be pressing and very real. It may sometimes be quicker and easier to carry out interviews than to get access to official records.

There are many other problems. It is common to locate a record at one time but not at another. This is caused partly by a deliberate policy to destroy certain kinds of records after certain periods of time, but it also reflects inconsistent information given by the subjects (e.g., the use of aliases), inconsistency in reporting by police or courts, the concurrent use of records by other agencies, and human errors and inefficiency in record keeping and searching (see Steer 1973). This means that estimates in retrospective research of the prevalence of convictions may be too low.

Criminal records are often misleading. Facts are often classified in criminal records into legal rather than behavioral categories. The crucial legal distinction in English law between indictable and non-indictable offenses, which has its counterparts in other countries, may make little sense when the actual behavior is considered (Edwards 1974). The same may be true of the distinction between an offense and no offense. An act may, depending on the circumstances and the identity of the policeman who reported it, be classified as an indictable assault occasioning actual bodily harm, as a non-indictable common assault, or as a noncriminal fight between two youths. The legal classifications often have an element of arbitrariness in them, but they can have very real effects. In an experimental study, Shea (1974) showed that different legal labels given to the same act could affect sentencing decisions.

Just as the same act may lead to different legal classifications, the same legal classification may include widely differing acts. Robberies may range from armed bank robberies carried out by gangs of masked men to thefts of small amounts of money perpetrated by one youth on another. The widespread practice of plea bargaining adds a further complication, since defendants may plead guilty to something which they have not done in order to avoid being charged with something which they have done. Two other problems with criminal records are that changes in the law or in recording practices may make it difficult to compare records at one time with those at another, and that it is difficult to know whether persons who have stopped being convicted have died, emigrated, become hospitalized, reformed, or simply become more adept at avoiding convictions.

Moving from criminal records to institutional case histories, one major problem is that they are frequently unreliable. They are often based on uncorroborated information given by interviewees whose self-interest may dispose them to conceal incriminating or inconvenient facts. A false, unchecked statement once recorded may be read and repeated by subsequent interviewers without checking, and may have unfortunate consequences for the interviewee. Case histories, typically written in an unstructured, narrative style, contain a wealth of subjective impressions which are difficult to check. Coverage of topics is often unsystematic. Records may indicate that a boy is or is not living with his (presumably) natural father, or that he is living with a substitute father, or that no (natural or substitute) father is present in the house, or the record may not mention a father. Without an interview to clarify the family situation, the recorded information may be difficult to make sense of and code. Sometimes, absence of information in the record means that the family situation is normal, since interviewers compiling a case history may note only unusual or adverse features, but it is not always possible to be sure about this. Cases with incomplete information are not usually a random sample of all cases. In their classic prediction research derived from borstal case records, Mannheim and Wilkins (1955) based their analysis only on those case histories containing no missing data. This reduced their sample from 720 to 385. Furthermore, the 335 excluded had a much higher reconviction rate (68.7 percent) than the 385 included (42.5 percent).

D. Interviews

Longitudinal researchers should, when possible, supplement information in records by interviewing their subjects. Only in this way can an investigator be sure that he has systematically covered all the topics in which he is interested. Of course, interviews have problems too, and it is desirable to have trained, quality controlled interviewers, to check for interviewer bias, and to check the validity of statements made by interviewees as far as possible. Some longitudinal researchers have employed their own interviewers, while others have used persons outside the research team, such as health visitors or teachers (e.g., Douglas 1964; Miller et al. 1974). It is easier to control and check the quality of interviews if they are carried out by members of the research team. Quality control was probably not a great problem in the two projects mentioned above, because they had health visitors collecting information on medical topics and teachers reporting on educational questions. In both cases, their interviewers should have been competent and experienced in the particular things they were asked to do.

Quality control is likely to loom larger as a problem when commercial market research agencies are employed to conduct interviews in a longitudinal survey. Unless researchers maintain close and frequent contact with the agency, they cannot be sure how much effort is being expended on the tedious, time-consuming, often unrewarding process of tracking down the specified target sample. Furthermore, it is difficult to anticipate in advance all the anomalous cases which may be encountered during interviews. On the basis of pilot work carried out with youths who were not members of the sample of the Cambridge Study, we prepared what we thought was a very extensive coding manual to accompany the instructions for interviewing youths at age 18. However, as the research progressed, we found that it was constantly necessary to discuss unusual cases with the interviewers and amplify earlier coding decisions. That each interview was tape-recorded and transcribed verbatim made that possible, but it was a time-consuming process. Without frequent contact with the interviewers, we might have found ourselves in the unhappy situation of seeking the answers to awkward questions and trying to deal with anomalous cases at the late stage of writing up the report.

Both interviewers and records are indirect methods of collecting information. It would be preferable to obtain direct measures of behavior. In the Cambridge Study, we deliberately gave the youths an opportunity to smoke and gamble for money during the interviews at age 18, so that we could compare their observed behavior with their self-reports. More direct behavioral measures are needed in criminology. A longitudinal survey of prisoners could include such measures. Institutional case records often include haphazard observations of behavior, so it would not be too great a step to replace them with systematic ones.

E. Sample Size

Many compromises must be made in planning a longitudinal survey; sample size is an important example. With fewer than 100 subjects, it is possible to study each one in detail, and to compile individual case histories. It may be difficult, however, to know to what extent the results obtained can be generalized. In a project designed to investigate crime and delinquency, the incidence of convictions among a fairly representative sample is unlikely to exceed about one-quarter among males, and much less among females. This means that, in a study of 100 males, comparisons between convicted and unconvicted persons are likely to be comparisons between 25 and 75, dangerously small samples for the use of statistical techniques, or even for simple comparisons of percentages. Focusing on self-reported rather than official delinquency makes a small sample more feasible, but it is usually desirable to employ both self-reports and official records.

At the other extreme, nationally representative samples of many thousands provide excellent bases for generalizations and statistical analyses, but with such numbers it is difficult to collect anything other than easily available objective information. For example, it is possible to verify in such a sample that convicted persons disproportionately come from large families, but it would be astronomically expensive to interview the parents and children to try to ascertain how subtle aspects of the family environment changed as the number of children increased, and hence to try to explain *why* large families were associated with convictions. We studied about 400 boys in the Cambridge Study as the smallest sample which was thought suitable for statistical analyses and the largest about which we felt it was feasible to compile detailed case histories.

F. Practical Problems: Funding, Staffing, and Others

Prospective longitudinal researches involving interviews have many methodological advantages, but they also present many practical difficulties. Such research often requires a heavy commitment of resources over a long period, and one of the greatest problems is to obtain a long-term guarantee of funding. Most long-term surveys have not had such a guarantee, and long-range planning has suffered. The National Survey of Health and Development was originally planned to assess the availability and effectiveness of the antenatal and maternity services in Great Britain (Douglas 1964). Only when the children were aged 2 was it decided to convert this survey into a longitudinal study of health and development. No one then, or at the times of subsequent extensions, envisaged that it would continue to the present day. The National Child Development Study (Davie, Butler, and Goldstein 1972) did not collect any data between 1958, when the children were born, and 1965, because of funding difficulties. The Cambridge Study has never been sure of funding for more than two or three years ahead, and this is a common pattern.

Long-term planning is necessary in order to get the fullest possible benefits from longitudinal research, but it is very difficult to arrange in practice. Funding agencies are deterred by the high total cost of a long-term survey, but they should perhaps concentrate on the cost per year and consider whether one longitudinal survey is more useful and informative than, say, three cross-sectional ones. Regrettably, however, uncontrollable events can intervene to spoil the design of a long-term project and waste considerable investment of money and effort. The Cambridge-Somerville Study (Powers and Witmer 1951) was originally planned to provide treatment for ten years, but was disrupted by World War II; average treatment lasted for five years. In the Philadelphia cohort study by Wolfgang, Figlio, and Sellin (1972), many of the records were destroyed in a fire. A near calamity for the Cambridge Study occurred when a journalist managed to secure data about the performance of boys in London schools. A garbled newspaper account appeared, providing material for a highly publicized but quite unfounded political squabble. The study nearly came to a premature end.

A second serious problem inhibiting long-term projects is staffing. A stable research team is desirable for continuity and for maintaining the cooperation of subjects. Yet staff are often on annually renewable research grants and senior staff may, quite reasonably, feel that they must move on or lose their places on the academic career ladder. These problems are largely caused by the lack of a career in research outside the government service, and by the generally haphazard way in which research in universities is organized. A related concern is that top quality research workers may be unprepared to restrict their professional work to collection of similar kinds of data on the same individuals. There may be some professional advantages for a researcher to be involved in other, short-term projects concurrently with a long-term one.

One person should have overall responsibility for a project from start to finish. Wadsworth (1979) notes: "were it not for the enthusiasm and persistence of the National Survey's Director, Dr. J. W. B. Douglas, it would have perished many years ago." A similar comment could be made about Dr. D. J. West, the director of the Cambridge Study. Changes in staff may produce changes in the direction of the research or even abandonment of early data. Early data are important in many longitudinal analyses, making pilot work essential before data collection is begun; pilot work, however, lengthens an already lengthy research project. Research workers in a long-term project are often under some pressure to get started quickly.

There are other problems. With time, changes in instrumentation, methodology, and theory may reduce the value of the earliest data.

Many of the most frequently voiced criticisms of past longitudinal surveys have been collected by Wall and Williams (1970). Longitudinal surveys are sometimes said to amass data with no clear idea how it is to be used, and their hypotheses are said to be vague or not stated (e.g., Moore 1959). Surveys are said to start with a mixed bag of variables, to add to them as time goes on, and to accumulate so much information that frequent analysis is impossible and much of the material is discarded. The magnitude of the task of concurrent analyses precludes a systematic reevaluation of such studies in the light of interim findings. Typically, publications are long delayed.

Longitudinal surveys have not often been designed to test one particular theory, although there is no reason in principle why they could not do so. The Cambridge Study tried to measure many factors which might prove important in relation to delinquency. Rather than try to test one theory, we tried to test a wide variety of different hypotheses about delinquency. The advantage of measuring a large number of factors was that it was possible to assess their relative importance in relation to delinquency, and also to investigate how they interacted, or whether one factor was important independently of another. One theory is useful to guide researchers, but it can also blind them to unexpected findings, or to results produced artifactually by the overlap between one factor and another.

G. Attrition

One major practical problem for longitudinal research is attrition, or loss of subjects, for a variety of reasons, including death, emigration, unknown addresses, and refusals. Cooperation from official agencies in tracking down elusive subjects is especially necessary in a longitudinal survey with a noncaptive sample, but it is often not forthcoming. Locating subjects seems to be especially a problem in the United States. The high rate of mobility of young urban males confounded Wolfgang's staff. Wolfgang (1974) was able to interview only 567 of his target sample of 974 (58 percent), despite the fact that no subject who was approached refused to be interviewed. Many could not be located, despite three years of diligent searching, using the Selective Service address file, motor vehicle registrations, post office assistance, the social service exchange, and other agencies. Several other American researchers have discussed problems of locating subjects in longitudinal surveys (e.g., Crider, Willits, and Bealer 1971; Eckland 1968; McAllister, Goe, and Butler 1973; Skeels and Skodak 1965).

Locating addresses does not seem to be a great problem in the Scandinavian countries, because of their national registration systems. It is a considerable problem in England, where the Department of Health and Social Security has the current addresses of all employed persons but will not disclose them to researchers. The Cambridge Study was fortunate in that, at age 18, we located the addresses of all but one youth (he was on the run from the police). It was greatly to our advantage that we had tried to interview each youth every two years. More than three-quarters of the youths were still living at the same address as at age 16. The remainder were traced by inquiring at old addresses, or with the help of the local housing department, probation officers, relatives, employers, the post office, marriage certificates, and telephone directories. However, discovering addresses and making contact with the youths cost a great deal of time and money.

Of the original sample of 411 8-year-olds, we were able to interview 389 at age 18 (95 percent). Of the missing twenty-two, six had gone abroad, one had died, one could not be traced, ten refused to be interviewed, and in the other four cases the parent refused on behalf of the youth. At age 21, the aim was to interview only the convicted delinquents and a random sample of the remainder, rather than the whole sample; 218 of the target group of 241 were interviewed (90 percent). Tracing and interviewing youths are likely to become more difficult after age 21, because many will get married and leave home. Once contact was made with a youth, in most cases he readily agreed to be interviewed. Those who were relatively uncooperative (16 percent) included a significantly high proportion who had been convicted. This harks back to our earlier result showing that parental uncooperativeness toward the researchers when the boys were aged 8 was significantly related to their later official delinquency. The subjects most interesting to criminological researchers are often the most elusive and resistant.

The major problem with attrition is that those who are lost are not a random sample of all subjects. One advantage of a longitudinal survey is that some characteristics of the missing subjects are known, because discovered in earlier interviews, and the maximum error resulting from attrition can be estimated. Robins (1963) found that refusers tended to have dropped out of high school, to be in routine white collar occupations, and to have foreign-born parents. Douglas (1970) reported that the missing families in his survey included a high proportion with unhappily married parents and backward children. Striking an optimum balance is not easy. Attrition of subjects in a longitudinal survey should be kept as low as possible, but it is difficult to know how much time and effort should be devoted to securing the final few especially elusive ones.

H. Ethical Problems

The ethical problems raised in longitudinal surveys are not different in kind from those encountered with other research techniques, but they may be different in degree. There are problems in following people up for long periods without their informed consent, and problems surrounding the release of confidential information by official agencies. Random allocation experiments raise ethical problems, because of their apparent conflict with ideals of justice and equality of treatment. Prediction research would face ethical problems if any attempt was made to draw practical implications from it for the identification of potential delinquents and the application of preventive treatment.

These kinds of ethical issues are difficult because they necessarily involve subjective and idiosyncratic judgments. Most official statements about ethics by professional bodies suggest that the costs of research, especially in terms of the harm suffered by subjects, should be carefully weighed against its benefits, especially the advancement of knowledge. Ethical decisions should be informed by empirical research on the reactions of potential subjects, such as that carried out by Wilson and Donnerstein (1976). It seems to me that most of the research discussed in this paper caused no harm to the subjects, and had a negligible impact on their lives. The invasions of privacy which the subjects have suffered pale into insignificance in comparison with murder, rape, mugging, or incarceration in degrading conditions for many years. Longitudinal research may increase our knowledge about crime and delinquency and ultimately lead to a decrease in both crime and social reaction to it. In my estimation, these social benefits would greatly outweigh the small ethical costs of the existing research.

III. Conclusions and Proposals

Longitudinal research is especially suitable for investigating the course of development, the natural history and prevalence of a phenomenon at different ages, continuities and discontinuities between earlier and later ages, how phenomena emerge, the relationship between earlier and later events, the effects of particular events or life experiences on the course of development, and transmission from one generation to the next. Most existing longitudinal surveys of crime and delinquency have relied on official statistics, with all their known disadvantages and defects. What is required is more prospective longitudinal research involving frequent, direct contacts between the researchers and the subjects.

It is not difficult to suggest projects which would greatly increase our knowledge about crime and delinquency. One of the most urgently needed is a study of the natural history of delinquency from age 10 to age 20. This could be achieved by following up a cohort of perhaps 1,000 working-class boys living in an urban area, preferably obtaining comparable measures of self-reported delinquency once a year. I suggest urban working-class boys partly because they are thought to be the most delinquent group and because they have been the subjects of most criminological research and theorizing in the past. Other groups, such as girls, those living in rural areas, middle-class children, and white collar criminals, could be studied later. The suggested survey should give us much-needed information about the prevalence of different types of delinquency at different ages, and should relate it to such events as getting convicted, getting married, moving from one school to another, the death of a parent, leaving home, and so on. It would be best if this longitudinal survey could be combined with some overlapping cross-sectional surveys of boys aged 10–20, done at least at the beginning and at the end of the long-term project, to give some chance of separating out effects due to aging and period effects caused by such things as social changes and changes in legislation during the course of the ten years.

Another valuable longitudinal survey would follow up a sample of perhaps 1,000 males apprehended by the police for the first time, to investigate their subsequent history and experiences in traveling through various stages of the criminal justice system. Changes in their attitudes and delinquent behavior could be related to their experiences with the criminal justice system and to the social consequences of official processing.

A follow-up of a sample of perhaps 200 prisoners serving very long or life sentences, from the point at which they were sentenced, would also be worthwhile. This could be designed to investigate changes occurring as a consequence of imprisonment, and could include observational measures. As mentioned earlier, it would be necessary to try to control for factors such as aging by having a control group of nonprisoners, although there would undoubtedly be problems in getting comparable groups.

Another valuable project would be a random allocation experiment comparing institutional and noninstitutional sentences, in which two groups were followed up for long periods and interviewed frequently. In order to reduce some of the ethical objections, it might be advisable to take a sample who would normally receive the institutional sentence and randomly allocate half of them to the noninstitutional sentence. It would be important to specify the details of the sentences as precisely as possible, and to measure offending before and after the sentence was pronounced. Few past random allocation experiments on sentencing have included interviews with the sentenced persons.

These are only very brief descriptions of possible projects, of course. The actual projects would have to be very carefully planned and might have much more complex research designs than the skeletons outlined here.

Long-term projects need long-term funding and long-term cooperation from official agencies in tracking down the subjects and in releasing needed records. It may be harder to carry out long-term projects in the United States than in Great Britain or the Scandinavian countries, because of the high mobility of Americans and the lack of a comprehensive national system of records. American federal agencies should take the initiative in sponsoring prospective longitudinal surveys. The obstacles facing an individual academic researcher are very great. Only government departments can provide the assurance of long-term funding, long-term access to information, and an attractive career line.

In my estimation, the benefits of longitudinal research, in terms of increased knowledge about crime and delinquency, would be worth the expense and difficulty. We cannot meaningfully formulate and test criminological theories or models until we have basic information about the natural history of crime and delinquency, and about the progression of detected offenders through the criminal justice system. Our knowledge about these matters is rudimentary and is largely based on retrospective searches of criminal records. Prospective longitudinal surveys including interviews should lead to a significant increase in this knowledge.

APPENDIX

Selection of Major Longitudinal Surveys in Tables 1 and 2

Surveys were included in tables 1 and 2 if they contained significant information about crime and delinquency. The major focus of the research of Lefkowitz et al. (1977) was aggression, but it was included because measures of aggression were related to records of arrests. The survey of Miller et al. (1974) was especially concerned with health and education but was included because it provided detailed information about the prevalence of delinquency. Many psychiatric studies were excluded because of their marginal relevance to crime and delinquency, for example a twenty-year follow-up of 90 children treated at a Pennsylvania hospital for aggressive behavior disorders (Morris, Escoll, and Wexler 1956), a six-year follow-up of 187 adolescents treated at a London hospital for neurotic and conduct disorders (Warren 1965), and a follow-up of 136 New York children from infancy to adolescence (Thomas and Chess 1976). Many such studies have been reviewed by Robins (1978b), or can be found in the volumes entitled *Life History Research in Psychopathology*, edited by M. Roff, D. F. Ricks, and others.

The National Child Development Study (Davie, Butler, and Goldstein 1972) was excluded because the information about crime and delinquency which has been published so far is minimal. This is a study of all 17,418 children born in England, Scotland, and Wales in one week of March 1958. The parents were contacted at the births of the children, and the children have been tested at ages 7, 11, and 16. The only published information about delinquency is contained in Fogelman's summary (1976) of the results obtained at age 16. Of the parents, 6 percent said that their child had never been taken to court; 9 percent of the teachers said that the child had been in trouble with the police. However, these responses were not checked against official criminal records, and there was no attempt to compare delinquent and nondelinquent children, as was done in the similar National Survey of Health and Development (Wadsworth 1979).

Other classic longitudinal surveys were also excluded. Terman and Oden (1959) followed up 1,528 children in California schools who had an I.Q. of at least 135 and were aged 7–14 in 1921. During the next thirty-five years, three major field studies were carried out, together with several mail follow-ups. The incidence of crime and delinquency in this sample was very low. Only one male had been in prison, only six boys had been before the juvenile court, and only two girls had been in trouble with the police, for vagrancy. Other long-term surveys have been conducted in California. Macfarlane, Allen, and Honzik (1954) followed up a representative sample of 126 children born in Berkeley in 1928–29, from birth to age 14. This research was part of the Berkeley Guidance Study, and the subjects were followed into their thirties (Livson and Peskin 1967; Smelzer 1963). The children in another California survey, the Oakland Growth Study, were also followed into their thirties and forties (Block 1971; Elder 1974; Tuddenham 1959).

Among classic British studies, the Scottish Mental Survey (MacPherson 1958; Maxwell 1969b), one of the most impressive, studied a representative sample of 1,200 children, born in Scotland in 1936, from age 11 to age 27. Annual questionnaires were completed by volunteer home visitors, usually teachers. Maxwell (1969a) was able to compare this cohort with a parallel one of 1,000 Scottish children born in 1921, tested in 1932, followed up to 1939, and traced in 1968. Another interesting longitudinal survey was carried out by Himmelweit and Swift (1969), who initially contacted more than 600 boys aged 13–14 in nine London schools in 1952 and tried to interview them again at age 25. Among the data collected were court appearances during the intervening period (Bebbington 1970). Other classic surveys have started at birth and not continued long enough for crime and delinquency to be measured. For example, a third British national sample, of children born in one week of April 1970, is now being followed up by N. Butler and others from the University of Bristol. The National Survey of Health and Development stands alone in following a cohort from birth to maturity and in providing a great deal of information about crime and delinquency.

Some classic surveys had too few subjects to study crime and delinquency feasibly, at least by making statistical comparisons based on official records. Peck (1958) and Peck and Havighurst (1960) reported an intensive survey in a midwestern community of 34 children from age 10 to age 18, in which the children, their parents, and their friends were interviewed each year. Kagan and Moss (1962) followed up 89 Ohio children from birth to age 20, observing the behavior of the child and his mother at home, giving psychological tests to both, and interviewing both, all at regular intervals.

The sample numbers in tables 1 and 2 refer to the initial sample, which is usually greater than the number interviewed at any given age. Some longitudinal surveys were excluded because the initial sample size was not specified. For example, Short and Moland (1976) reinterviewed 52 former black gang members in 1971–72, at an average age of 30, who had first been studied 12–15 years earlier by Short and Strodtbeck (1965). Cross-sectional surveys in which an interview was supplemented by a retrospective search of records are not included in table 2. As an example of such an excluded study, Jessor et al. (1968) interviewed 221 adults aged 20–65 in Colorado in 1962, and also searched for them in court records for the previous ten years. Only a fine line distinguishes surveys in which teacher or peer ratings are followed by a search of records (e.g., Roff 1975; Stott and Wilson 1977) from those based entirely on records.

Finally, in the interest of clarification, it might be mentioned that the two surveys carried out by Hathaway and Monachesi (1957, 1963) included both boys and girls, but their long-term follow-ups on delinquency were concerned only with the boys. The numbers in table 1 refer to the boys only.

REFERENCES

Anttila, Inkeri, and A. Westling. 1965. "A Study in the Pardoning of, and Recidivism among, Criminals Sentenced to Life Imprisonment." In *Scandinavian Studies in Criminology*, vol. 1, ed. K. O. Christiansen. London: Tavistock.

Ball, J. C., A. Ross, and A. Simpson. 1964. "Incidence and Estimated Prevalence of Recorded Delinquency in a Metropolitan Area," *American Sociological Review* 29:90–93.

Banister, Peter A., F. Smith, K. Heskin, and N. Bolton. 1973. "Psychological Correlates of Long-Term Imprisonment," *British Journal of Criminology* 13:312–30.

Bauer, G. E. 1976. "Personality Deviancy and Prison Incarceration," *Journal of Clinical Psychology* 32:279–83.

Bebbington, A. C. 1970. "The Effect of Non-Response in the Sample Survey with an Example," *Human Relations* 23:169–80.

Belson, William A., and R. Hood. 1968. "The Research Potential of the Case Records of Approved School Boys." London School of Economics, Survey Research Center. Unpublished paper.

Berg, Ian, M. Consterdine, R. Hullin, R. McGuire, and S. Tyrer. 1978. "The Effect of Two Randomly Allocated Court Procedures on Truancy," *British Journal of Criminology* 18:232–44.

Berntsen, K., and K. O. Christiansen. 1965. "A Resocialization Experiment with Short-Term Offenders." In *Scandinavian Studies in Criminology*, vol. 1, ed. K. O. Christiansen. London: Tavistock.

Blalock, Hubert M. 1964. *Causal Inferences in Nonexperimental Research*. Chapel Hill: University of North Carolina Press.

Block, S. 1971. *Lives through Time*. Berkeley, Calif.: Bancroft.

Blumstein, Alfred, and R. C. Larson. 1971. "Problems in Modeling and Measuring Recidivism," *Journal of Research in Crime and Delinquency* 8:124–32.

Bolton, Neil, F. Smith, K. Heskin, and P. Banister. 1976. "Psychological Correlates of Long-Term Imprisonment," *British Journal of Criminology* 16:38–47.

Brody, Stephen R. 1976. *The Effectiveness of Sentencing*. London: H.M. Stationery Office.

Buikhuisen, Wouter, and H. A. Hoekstra. 1974. "Factors Related to Recidivism," *British Journal of Criminology* 14:63–69.

Campbell, Donald T., and J. C. Stanley. 1966. *Experimental and Quasi-experimental Designs for Research*. Chicago: Rand-McNally.

Carr-Hill, Roy A., and C. D. Payne. 1971. "Crime: Accident or Disease: An Exploration Using Probability Models for the Generation of Macro-Criminological Data," *Journal of Research in Crime and Delinquency* 8:133–55.

Chaitin, Mildred R., and H. W. Dunham. 1966. "The Juvenile Court in Its Relationship to Adult Criminality: A Replicated Study," *Social Forces* 45:114–19.

Christensen, R. 1967. "Projected Percentage of U.S. Population with Criminal Arrest and Conviction Records." In President's Commission on Law Enforcement and Administration of Justice, *Task Force Report: Science and Technology*. Washington, D.C.: U.S. Government Printing Office.

Christiansen, Karl O. 1964. "Delinquent Generations in Denmark," *British Journal of Criminology* 4:259–64.

———. 1968. "Threshold of Tolerance in Various Population Groups Illustrated by Results from Danish Criminological Twin Study." In *The Mentally Abnormal Offender*, ed. A. V. S. DeReuck and R. Porter. Boston: Little Brown.

———. 1974. "Seriousness of Criminality and Concordance among Danish Twins." In *Crime, Criminology and Public Policy*, ed. R. Hood. New York: Free Press.

Christiansen, K. O., and S. G. Jensen. 1972. "Crime in Denmark—a Statistical History," *Journal of Criminal Law, Criminology and Police Science* 63:82–92.

Christiansen, K. O., M. Elers-Nielsen, L. LeMaire, and G. Sturup. 1965. "Recidivism among Sexual Offenders." In *Scandinavian Studies in Criminology*, vol. 1, ed. K. O. Christiansen. London: Tavistock.

Conger, John J., and W. C. Miller. 1966. *Personality, Social Class, and Delinquency*. New York: Wiley.

Cornish, Derek B., and R. V. G. Clarke. 1975. *Residential Treatment and Its Effects on Delinquency*. London: H.M. Stationery Office.

Craig, Maude M., and L. A. Budd. 1967. "The Juvenile Offender: Recidivism and Companions," *Crime and Delinquency* 13:344–51.

Craig, Maude M., and S. J. Glick. 1963. "Ten Years' Experience with the Glueck Social Prediction Table," *Crime and Delinquency* 9:249–61.

Crider, D. M., F. K. Willits, and R. C. Bealer. 1971. "Tracking Respondents in Longitudinal Surveys," *Public Opinion Quarterly* 35:613–20.

Dalgard, O. S., and E. Kringlen. 1976. "A Norwegian Twin Study of Criminality," *British Journal of Criminology* 16:213–32.

Davie, Ronald, N. Butler, and H. Goldstein. 1972. *From Birth to Seven*. London: Longmans.

Dootjes, I. 1972. "Predicting Juvenile Delinquency," *Australian and New Zealand Journal of Criminology* 5:157–71.

Douglas, James W. B. 1964. *The Home and the School*. London: MacGibbon & Kee.

———. 1970. "Discussion." In *Psychiatric Epidemiology*, ed. E. H. Hare and J. K. Wing. London: Oxford University Press.

Douglas, James W. B., and J. M. Blomfield. 1956. "The Reliability of Longitudinal Surveys," *Milbank Memorial Fund Quarterly* 34:227–52.

Douglas, James W. B., J. M. Ross, and H. R. Simpson. 1968. *All Our Future*. London: Peter Davies.

Douglas, James W. B., J. Ross, W. Hammond, and D. Mulligan. 1966. "Delinquency and Social Class," *Britiss Journal of Criminology* 6:294–302.

Dunlop, Anne B. 1974. *The Approved School Experience*. London: H.M. Stationery Office.

Eckland, Bruce K. 1968. "Retrieving Mobile Cases in Longitudinal Surveys," *Public Opinion Quarterly* 32:51–64.

Edwards, B. 1974. *Sources of Social Statistics*. London: Heinemann.

Elder, G. H. 1974. *Children of the Great Depression*. Chicago: University of Chicago Press.

Elliott, Delbert S., and H. L. Voss. 1974. *Delinquency and Dropout*. Lexington, Mass.: Lexington Books.

Elmhorn, Kirsten. 1965. "Study in Self-Reported Delinquency among School Children in Stockholm." In *Scandinavian Studies in Criminology*, vol. 1, ed. K. O. Christiansen. London: Tavistock.

Empey, LaMar T., and M. L. Erickson. 1972. *The Provo Experiment*. Lexington, Mass.: Lexington Books.

Empey, LaMar T., and S. G. Lubeck. 1971. *The Silverlake Experiment*. Chicago: Aldine.

Ennis, P. H. 1970. "Crime, Victims and the Police." In *Law and Order, Police Encounters*, ed. M. Lipsky. Chicago: Aldine.

Erickson, Maynard L., and L. T. Empey. 1963. "Court Records, Undetected Delinquency, and Decision-Making," *Journal of Criminal Law, Criminology and Police Science* 54:456–69.

Eron, Leonard D., L. O. Walder, and M. M. Lefkowitz. 1971. *Learning of Aggression in Children*. Boston: Little, Brown.

Farrington, David P. 1972. "Delinquency Begins at Home," *New Society* 21:495–97.

———. 1973. "Self-Reports of Deviant Behavior: Predictive and Stable?" *Journal of Criminal Law and Criminology* 64:99–110.

———. 1977. "The Effects of Public Labelling," *British Journal of Criminology* 17:112–25.

———. 1978. "The Family Backgrounds of Aggressive Youths." In *Aggression and Anti-social Behavior in Childhood and Adolescence*, ed. L. Hersov, M. Berger and D. Shaffer. Oxford: Pergamon.

———. 1979a. "Environmental Stress, Delinquent Behavior, and Convictions." In *Stress and Anxiety*, vol. 6, ed. I. G. Sarason and C. D. Spielberger. Washington, D.C.: Hemisphere.

———. 1979b. "Truancy, Delinquency, the Home and the School." In

Truancy: Problems of School Attendance and Refusal, ed. I. Berg and L. Hersov. London: Wiley.

Farrington, David P., G. Gundry, and D. J. West. 1975. "The Familial Transmission of Criminality," *Medicine, Science and the Law* 15: 177–86.

Farrington, David P., S. G. Osborn, and D. J. West. 1978. "The Persistence of Labelling Effects," *British Journal of Criminology* 18:277–84.

Farrington, David P., and D. J. West. 1979. "The Cambridge Study in Delinquent Development." In *An Empirical Basis for Primary Prevention: Prospective Longitudinal Research in Europe*, ed. S. A. Mednick and A. E. Baert. New York: Oxford University Press.

Feldhusen, John F., F. M. Aversano, and J. R. Thurston. 1976. "Prediction of Youth Contacts with Law Enforcement Agencies," *Criminal Justice and Behavior* 3:235–53.

Feldhusen, John F., J. R. Thurston, and J. J. Benning. 1973. "A Longitudinal Study of Delinquency and Other Aspects of Children's Behaviour," *International Journal of Criminology and Penology* 1:341–51.

Fitzsimons, M. J. 1958. "The Predictive Value of Teachers' Referrals." In *Orthopsychiatry and the School*, ed. M. Krugman. New York: American Orthopsychiatric Association.

Fogelman, Ken, ed. 1976. *Britain's 16-Year-Olds*. London: National Children's Bureau.

Folkard, M. Stephen, D. E. Smith, and D. D. Smith. 1976. *IMPACT*. Vol. 2, *The Results of the Experiment*. London: H.M. Stationery Office.

Fowles, A. J. 1978. *Prison Welfare*. London: H.M. Stationery Office.

Ganzer, V. J., and I. G. Sarason. 1973. "Variables Associated with Recidivism among Juvenile Delinquents," *Journal of Consulting and Clinical Psychology* 40:1–5.

Gersten, J. C., T. Langner, J. Eisenberg, O. Simcha-Fagan, and E. McCarthy. 1976. "Stability and Change in Types of Behavioral Disturbance of Children and Adolescents," *Journal of Abnormal Child Psychology* 4:111–27.

Gibbens, Trevor C. N., K. L. Soothill, and C. K. Way. 1978. "Sibling and Parent-Child Incest Offenders," *British Journal of Criminology* 18: 40–52.

Glaser, Daniel. 1962. "Prediction Tables as Accounting Devices for Judges and Parole Boards," *Crime and Delinquency* 8:239–58.

Glenn, N. D. 1977. *Cohort Analysis*. Beverly Hills, Calif.: Sage.

Glueck, Sheldon, and E. T. Glueck. 1930. *Five Hundred Criminal Careers*. New York: Knopf.

———. 1934a. *Five Hundred Delinquent Women*. New York: Knopf.

———. 1934b. *One Thousand Juvenile Delinquents*. Cambridge, Mass.: Harvard University Press.

————. 1937. *Later Criminal Careers*. New York: Commonwealth Fund.

————. 1940. *Juvenile Delinquents Grown Up*. New York: Commonwealth Fund.

————. 1943. *Criminal Careers in Retrospect*. New York: Commonwealth Fund.

————. 1950. *Unraveling Juvenile Delinquency*. New York: Commonwealth Fund.

————. 1968. *Delinquents and Nondelinquents in Perspective*. Cambridge, Mass.: Harvard University Press.

Gold, Martin. 1970. *Delinquent Behavior in an American City*. Belmont, Calif.: Brooks/Cole.

Gold, Martin, and D. J. Reimer. 1975. "Changing Patterns of Delinquent Behavior among Americans 13 through 16 Years Old: 1967–72," *Crime and Delinquency Literature*, pp. 483–517.

Gottfredson, Donald M., and K. B. Ballard. 1965. "The Validity of Two Parole Prediction Scales: An Eight Year Follow Up Study." Davis, Calif.: Institute for the Study of Crime and Delinquency, National Council on Crime and Delinquency. Unpublished paper.

Gough, Harrison G., E. A. Wenk, and V. V. Rosynko. 1965. "Parole Outcome as Predicted from the CPI, the MMPI, and a Base Expectancy Table," *Journal of Abnormal Psychology* 70:432–41.

Hammond, W. H., and E. Chayen. 1963. *Persistent Criminals*. London: H.M. Stationery Office.

Hathaway, Starke R., and E. D. Monachesi. 1957. "The Personalities of Pre-Delinquent Boys," *Journal of Criminal Law, Criminology and Police Science* 48:149–63.

————. 1963. *Adolescent Personality and Behavior*. Minneapolis: University of Minnesota Press.

Hathaway, Starke R., E. D. Monachesi, and L. A. Young. 1960. "Delinquency Rates and Personality," *Journal of Criminal Law, Criminology and Police Science* 50:433–40.

Hathaway, Starke R., P. C. Reynolds, and E. D. Monachesi. 1969. "Follow-Up of the Later Careers and Lives of 1,000 Boys Who Dropped Out of High School," *Journal of Consulting and Clinical Psychology* 33:370–80.

Hautaluoma, J. E., and W. A. Scott. 1973. "Values and Sociometric Choices of Incarcerated Juveniles," *Journal of Social Psychology* 91: 229–37.

Havighurst, R. J., P. Bowman, G. Liddle, C. Matthews, and J. Pierce. 1962. *Growing Up in River City*. New York: Wiley.

Heise, David R. 1969. "Separating Reliability and Stability in Test-Retest Correlation," *American Sociological Review* 34:93–101.

Himmelweit, Hilde T., and B. Swift. 1969. "A Model for the Understanding of School as a Socializing Agent." In *Trends and Issues in Developmental Psychology*, ed. P. H. Mussen, J. Langer, and M. Covington. New York: Holt, Rinehart & Winston.

Hindelang, Michael J. 1971. "Age, Sex, and the Versatility of Delinquent Involvements," *Social Problems* 18:522–35.

Hodges, Emory F., and C. D. Tait. 1963. "A Follow-Up Study of Potential Delinquents," *American Journal of Psychiatry* 120:449–53.

Home Office. 1969. *The Sentence of the Court*. 2d ed. London: H.M. Stationery Office.

———. 1978. *Criminal Statistics, 1977*. London: H.M. Stationery Office.

Hutcheson, Barry R., L. Baler, W. Floyd, and D. Otterstein. 1966. "A Prognostic (Predictive) Classification of Juvenile Court First Offenders Based on a Follow Up Study," *British Journal of Criminology* 6:354–63.

Hutchings, Barry. 1974. "Genetic Factors in Criminality." In *Determinants and Origins of Aggressive Behavior*, ed. J. DeWit and W. W. Hartup. The Hague: Mouton.

Hutchings, Barry, and S. A. Mednick. 1974. "Biological and Adoptive Fathers of Male Criminal Adoptees." In *Major Issues on Juvenile Delinquency*. Copenhagen: World Health Organization.

———. 1975. "Registered Criminality in the Adoptive and Biological Parents of Registered Male Criminal Adoptees." In *Genetic Research in Psychiatry*, ed. R. R. Fieve, D. Rosenthal, and H. Brill. Baltimore: Johns Hopkins University Press.

Janson, Carl-Gunnar. 1977. *Project Metropolitan, Research Report No. 7*. Stockholm: Stockholm University, Department of Sociology.

Jasinski, Jersy. 1966. "Delinquent Generations in Poland," *British Journal of Criminology* 6:170–82.

Jesness, Carl F. 1971a. "Comparative Effectiveness of Two Institutional Treatment Programs for Delinquents," *Child Care Quarterly* 1:119–30.

———. 1971b. "The Preston Typology Study," *Journal of Research in Crime and Delinquency* 8:38–52.

Jessor, Richard, T. Graves, R. Hanson, and S. Jessor. 1968. *Society, Personality, and Deviant Behavior*. New York: Holt, Rinehart & Winston.

Kagan, Jerome, and H. A. Moss. 1962. *Birth to Maturity*. New York: Wiley.

Kahn, A. J. 1965. "The Case of the Premature Claims: Public Policy and Delinquency Prevention," *Crime and Delinquency* 11:217–28.

Kassebaum, Gene, D. Ward, and D. Wilner. 1971. *Prison Treatment and Parole Survival*. New York: Wiley.

Khleif, B. B. 1964. "Teachers as Predictors of Juvenile Delinquency and Psychiatric Disturbance," *Social Problems* 11:270–82.

Kirkegaard-Sorensen, L., and S. A. Mednick. 1975. "Registered Criminality in Families with Children at High Risk for Schizophrenia," *Journal of Abnormal Psychology* 84:197–204.

Knight, Barry J., S. G. Osborn, and D. J. West. 1977. "Early Marriage and Criminal Tendency in Males," *British Journal of Criminology* 17:348–60.

Knight, Barry J., and D. J. West. 1975. "Temporary and Continuing Delinquency," *British Journal of Criminology* 15:43–50.

Kraus, J. 1974a. "A Comparison of Corrective Effects of Probation and Detention on Male Juvenile Offenders," *British Journal of Criminology* 14:49–62.

———. 1974b. "The Deterrent Effect of Fines and Probation on Male Juvenile Offenders," *Australian and New Zealand Journal of Criminology* 7:231–40.

Langner, Thomas S., J. C. Gersten, and J. G. Eisenberg. 1977. "The Epidemiology of Mental Disorder in Children: Implications for Community Psychiatry." In *New Trends of Psychiatry in the Community*, ed. G. Serban. Cambridge, Mass.: Ballinger.

Lefkowitz, Monroe M., L. Eron, L. Walder, and L. Huesmann. 1977. *Growing Up to be Violent*. New York: Pergamon.

Lerman, Paul. 1975. *Community Treatment and Social Control*. Chicago: University of Chicago Press.

Little, Alan. 1965. "The 'Prevalence' of Recorded Delinquency and Recidivism in England and Wales," *American Sociological Review* 30:260–63.

Livson, N., and H. Peskin. 1967. "Prediction of Adult Psychological Health in a Longitudinal Study," *Journal of Abnormal Psychology* 72:509–18.

McAllister, R. J., S. J. Goe, and E. W. Butler. 1973. "Tracking Respondents in Longitudinal Surveys: Some Preliminary Considerations," *Public Opinion Quarterly* 37:413–16.

McClintock, Frederick H. 1963. *Crimes of Violence*. London: Macmillan.

McClintock, Frederick H., and N. H. Avison. 1968. *Crime in England and Wales*. London: Heinemann.

McCord, Joan. 1978a. "A Longitudinal View of the Relationship between Paternal Absence and Crime." Paper presented at the 1978 Annual Meeting of the American Society of Criminology.

———. 1978b. "A Thirty-Year Follow-Up of Treatment Effects," *American Psychologist* 33:284–89.

McCord, Joan, and W. McCord. 1959. "A Follow-Up Report on the

Cambridge-Somerville Youth Study," *Annals of the American Academy of Political and Social Sciences* 322:89–96.

McCord, William, J. McCord, and I. K. Zola. 1959. *Origins of Crime.* New York: Columbia University Press.

Macfarlane, Jean W., L. Allen, and M. P. Honzik. 1954. *A Developmental Study of the Behavior Problems of Normal Children between 21 Months and 14 Years.* Berkeley: University of California Press.

McKay, Henry. 1967. "Report on the Criminal Careers of Male Delinquents in Chicago." In President's Commission on Law Enforcement and Administration of Justice, *Task Force Report: Juvenile Delinquency and Youth Crime.* Washington, D.C.: U.S. Government Printing Office.

McKissack, I. J. 1967. "The Peak Age for Property Crimes," *British Journal of Criminology* 7:184–94.

———. 1973. "The Peak Age for Property Crimes: Further Data," *British Journal of Criminology* 13:253–61.

MacPherson, J. S. 1958. *Eleven-Year-Olds Grow Up.* London: University of London Press.

Mannheim, Hermann, and L. T. Wilkins. 1955. *Prediction Methods in Relation to Borstal Training.* London: H.M. Stationery Office.

Matza, David. 1964. *Delinquency and Drift.* New York: Wiley.

Maxwell, J. 1969a. "Intelligence, Education and Fertility," *Journal of Biosocial Science* 1:247–71.

———. 1969b. *Sixteen Years On.* London: University of London Press.

Mednick, Sarnoff, and B. Hutchings. 1978. "Genetic and Psychophysiological Factors in Asocial Behavior." In *Psychopathic Behavior: Approaches to Research*, ed. R. D. Hare and D. Schalling. New York: Wiley.

Miller, F. J. W., W. Z. Billewicz, and A. M. Thomson. 1972. "Growth from Birth to Adult Life of 442 Newcastle upon Tyne Children," *British Journal of Preventive and Social Medicine* 26:224–30.

Miller, F. J. W., S. Court, W. Walton, and E. Knox. 1960. *Growing Up in Newcastle upon Tyne.* London: Oxford University Press.

Miller, F. J. W., S. Court, E. Knox, and S. Brandon. 1974. *The School Years in Newcastle upon Tyne.* London: Oxford University Press.

Monahan, T. P. 1960. "On the Incidence of Delinquency," *Social Forces* 39:66–72.

Moore, T. W. 1959. "Studying the Growth of Personality," *Vita Humana* 2:65–87.

Morris, H. H., P. J. Escoll, and R. Wexler. 1956. "Aggressive Behavior Disorders of Childhood: A Follow-Up Study," *American Journal of Psychiatry* 112:991–97.

Mott, Joy. 1973. "London Juvenile Drug Offenders," *British Journal of Criminology* 13:209–17.

Mulligan, Glenn, J. Douglas, W. Hammond, and J. Tizard. 1963. "Delinquency and Symptoms of Maladjustment," *Proceedings of the Royal Society of Medicine* 56:1083–86.

Nuttall, Chris P., E. Barnard, A. Fowles, A. Frost, W. Hammond, P. Mayhew, K. Pease, R. Tarling, and M. Weatheritt. 1977. *Parole in England and Wales*. London: H.M. Stationery Office.

Osborn, Steve G., and D. J. West. 1978. "The Effectiveness of Various Predictors of Criminal Careers," *Journal of Adolescence* 1:101–17.

Palmer, Ted B. 1971. "California's Community Treatment Program for Delinquent Adolescents," *Journal of Research in Crime and Delinquency* 8:74–92.

Peck, R. F. 1958. "Family Patterns Correlated with Adolescent Personality Structure," *Journal of Abnormal and Social Psychology* 57:347–50.

Peck, R. F., and R. J. Havighurst. 1960. *The Psychology of Character Development*. New York: Wiley.

Peterson, R. A., D. J. Pittman, and P. O'Neal. 1962. "Stabilities of Deviance: A Study of Assaultive and Non-Assaultive Offenders," *Journal of Criminal Law, Criminology and Police Science* 53:44–48.

Polk, Kenneth. 1975. "Schools and the Delinquency Experience," *Criminal Justice and Behavior* 2:315–38.

Polk, Kenneth, D. Frease, and F. L. Richmond. 1974. "Social Class, School Experience, and Delinquency," *Criminology* 12:84–96.

Powers, Edwin, and H. Witmer. 1951. *An Experiment in the Prevention of Delinquency*. New York: Columbia University Press.

Reimer, E., and M. Warren. 1957. "Special Intensive Parole Unit," *NPPA Journal* 3:222–29.

Robins, Lee N. 1963. "The Reluctant Respondent," *Public Opinion Quarterly* 27:276–86.

———. 1966. *Deviant Children Grown Up*. Baltimore: Williams & Wilkins.

———. 1978a. "Aetiological Implications in Studies of Childhood Histories Relating to Antisocial Personality." In *Psychopathic Behavior: Approaches to Research*, ed. R. D. Hare and D. Schalling. New York: Wiley.

———. 1978b. "Longitudinal Methods in the Study of Normal and Pathological Development." In *Psychiatric der Gegenwart*, vol. 1, *Grundlagen und Methoden der Psychiatrie* (2d ed.), ed. K. P. Kisker et al. Heidelberg: Springer-Verlag.

Robins, Lee N., and S. Y. Hill. 1966. "Assessing the Contributions of

Family Structure, Class and Peer Groups to Juvenile Delinquency," *Journal of Criminal Law, Criminology and Police Science* 57:325–34.

Robins, Lee N., P. A. West, and B. L. Herjanic. 1975. "Arrests and Delinquency in Two Generations: A Study of Black Urban Families and Their Children," *Journal of Child Psychology and Psychiatry* 16: 125–40.

Robins, Lee N., and E. Wish. 1977. "Childhood Deviance as a Developmental Process: A Study of 223 Urban Black Men from Birth to 18," *Social Forces* 56:448–73.

Roff, Merrill. 1975. "Juvenile Delinquency in Girls: A Study of a Recent Sample." In *Life History Research in Psychopathology*, vol. 4, ed. R. D. Wirt, G. Winokur, M. Roff, and D. F. Ricks. Minneapolis: University of Minnesota Press.

Rose, Gerald N. G. 1968. "The Artificial Delinquent Generation," *Journal of Criminal Law, Criminology and Police Science* 59:370–85.

Rose, Gordon, and R. A. Hamilton. 1970. "Effects of a Juvenile Liaison Scheme," *British Journal of Criminology* 10:2–20.

Savitz, Leonard. 1970. "Delinquency and Migration." In *The Sociology of Crime and Delinquency* (2d ed.), ed. M. E. Wolfgang, L. Savitz, and N. Johnson. New York: Wiley.

Sellin, Thorstin. 1958. "Recidivism and Maturation," *NPPA Journal* 4:241–50.

Shannon, Lyle W. 1978. "Predicting Adult Criminal Careers from Juvenile Careers." Paper presented at the 1978 Annual Meeting of the American Society of Criminology.

Shaw, Margaret. 1974. *Social Work in Prison*. London: H.M. Stationery Office.

Shea, Michael A. 1974. "A Study of the Effect of Prosecutor's Choice of Charge on Magistrates' Sentencing Behavior," *British Journal of Criminology* 14:269–72.

Short, James F., and J. Moland. 1976. "Politics and Youth Gangs: A Follow-up Study," *Sociological Quarterly* 17:162–79.

Short, James F., and F. L. Strodtbeck. 1965. *Group Process and Gang Delinquency*. Chicago: University of Chicago Press.

Sinclair, Ian, and B. Chapman. 1973. "A Typological and Dimensional Study of a Sample of Prisoners," *British Journal of Criminology* 13: 341–53.

Skaberne, B., M. Blejec, V. Skalar, and K. Vodopivec. 1965. "Criminal Prevention and Elementary School Children," *Revija za Kriminalistiko in Kriminologijo* 16:8–14.

Skeels, H. M., and M. Skodak. 1965. "Techniques for a High-Yield Follow-up Study in the Field," *Public Health Reports* 80:249–57.

Slater, S. W., J. H. Darwin, and W. L. Richie. 1966. "Delinquent Generations in New Zealand," *Journal of Research in Crime and Delinquency* 3:140–46.

Smelzer, W. T. 1963. "Adolescent and Adult Occupational Choice as a Function of Family Socioeconomic History," *Sociometry* 26:393–409.

Soothill, Keith L., and T. C. N. Gibbens. 1978. "Recidivism of Sexual Offenders: A Re-appraisal," *British Journal of Criminology* 18:267–76.

Soothill, Keith L., A. Jack, and T. C. N. Gibbens. 1976. "Rape—a 22-Year Cohort Study," *Medicine, Science and the Law* 16:62–69.

Soothill, K. L., and P. J. Pope. 1973. "Arson: A Twenty-Year Cohort Study," *Medicine, Science and the Law* 13:127–38.

Sparks, Richard, H. G. Genn, and D. J. Dodd. 1977. *Surveying Victims.* London: Wiley.

Steer, David. 1973. "The Elusive Conviction," *British Journal of Criminology* 13:373–83.

Stott, Denis H. 1964. "Prediction of Success or Failure on Probation: A Follow-up Study," *International Journal of Social Psychiatry* 10:27–29.

Stott, Denis H., and D. M. Wilson. 1977. "The Adult Criminal as Juvenile," *British Journal of Criminology* 17:47–57.

Tait, C. Downing, and E. F. Hodges. 1971. "Follow-up Study of Predicted Delinquents," *Crime and Delinquency* 17:202–12.

Taylor, Roy S. 1960. "The Habitual Criminal," *British Journal of Criminology* 1:21–36.

Terman, L. M., and M. H. Oden. 1959. *The Gifted Group at Mid-Life.* Stanford: Stanford University Press.

Thomas, Alexander, and S. Chess. 1976. "Evolution of Behavior Disorders into Adolescence," *American Journal of Psychiatry* 133:539–42.

Thornberry, Terence, and R. M. Figlio. 1978. "Juvenile and Adult Offense Careers in the Philadelphia Birth Cohort of 1945." Paper presented at the 1978 Annual Meeting of the American Sociology of Criminology.

Thurston, John R., J. J. Benning, and J. F. Feldhusen. 1971. "Problems of Prediction of Delinquency and Related Conditions over a Seven-Year Period," *Criminology* 9:154–65.

Toby, Jackson. 1965. "An Evaluation of Early Identification and Intensive Treatment Programs for Predelinquents," *Social Problems* 13:160–75.

Trevvett, N. B. 1965. "Identifying Delinquency-Prone Children," *Crime and Delinquency* 11:186–91.

Tuddenham, R. D. 1959. "The Constancy of Personality Ratings over Two Decades," *Genetic Psychology Monographs* 60:3–29.

Uusitalo, P. 1972. "Recidivism after Release from Closed and Open Penal Institutions," *British Journal of Criminology* 12:211–29.

Venezia, Peter S. 1971. "Delinquency Prevention: A Critique and a Suggestion," *Journal of Research in Crime and Delinquency* 8:108–17.

———. 1972. "Unofficial Probation: An Evaluation of Its Effectiveness," *Journal of Research in Crime and Delinquency* 9:149–70.

Virkkunen, M. 1976. "Parental Deprivation and Recidivism in Juvenile Delinquents," *British Journal of Criminology* 16:378–84.

Wadsworth, Michael E. J. 1975. "Delinquency in a National Sample of Children," *British Journal of Criminology* 15:167–74.

———. 1978. "Delinquency Prediction and Its Uses: The Experience of a Twenty-One Year Follow-up Study," *International Journal of Mental Health* (in press).

———. 1979. *Roots of Delinquency: Infancy, Adolescence and Crime.* London: Martin Robertson (in press).

Walker, Nigel. 1971. *Crimes, Courts and Figures.* Harmondsworth: Penguin.

Walker, Nigel, W. Hammond, and D. Steer. 1967. "Repeated Violence," *Criminal Law Review* 1967:465–72.

Wall, W. D., and H. L. Williams. 1970. *Longitudinal Studies and the Social Sciences.* London: Heinemann.

Walters, A. A. 1963. "Delinquent Generations?" *British Journal of Criminology* 3:391–95.

Warren, W. 1965. "A Study of Adolescent Psychiatric Inpatients and the Outcome Six or More Years Later," *Journal of Child Psychology and Psychiatry* 6:141–60.

Weis, Kurt. 1974. "The Glueck Social Prediction Table—an Unfulfilled Promise," *Journal of Criminal Law and Criminology* 65:397–404.

West, Donald J. 1963. *The Habitual Prisoner.* London: Macmillan.

———. 1969. *Present Conduct and Future Delinquency.* London: Heinemann.

West, Donald J., and D. P. Farrington. 1973. *Who Becomes Delinquent?* London: Heinemann.

———. 1977. *The Delinquent Way of Life.* London: Heinemann.

Wilkins, Leslie. 1960. *Delinquent Generations.* London: H.M. Stationery Office.

Wilson, D. W., and E. Donnerstein. 1976. "Legal and Ethical Aspects of Non-Reactive Social Psychological Research," *American Psychologist* 31:765–73.

Wirt, R. D., and P. F. Briggs. 1959. "Personality and Environmental Factors in the Development of Delinquency," *Psychological Monographs* 73(15), whole no. 485.

Witkin, H. A., et al. 1976. "Criminality in XYY and XXY Men," *Science* 193:547–55.

Wolf, Preben. 1965. "A Contribution to the Topology of Crime in Denmark." In *Scandinavian Studies in Criminology*, vol. 1, ed. K. O. Christiansen. London: Tavistock.

Wolfgang, Marvin. 1973. "Crime in a Birth Cohort," *Proceedings of the American Philosophical Society* 117:404–11.

———. 1974. "Crime in a Birth Cohort." In *Crime, Criminology and Public Policy*, ed. R. Hood. London: Heinemann.

Wolfgang, Marvin, R. M. Figlio, and T. Sellin. 1972. *Delinquency in a Birth Cohort*. Chicago: University of Chicago Press.